The Roman Imperial Succession

The Roman Imperial Succession

John D Grainger

Pen & Sword
MILITARY

First published in Great Britain in 2020 by
Pen & Sword Military
An imprint of
Pen & Sword Books Ltd
Yorkshire – Philadelphia

Copyright © John D Grainger 2020

ISBN 978 1 52676 604 5

The right of John D Grainger to be identified as Author of this work
has been asserted by him in accordance with the Copyright, Designs
and Patents Act 1988.

A CIP catalogue record for this book is
available from the British Library.

Printed and bound in the UK by TJ International Ltd,
Padstow, Cornwall.

MIX
Paper from
responsible sources
FSC® C013056

Pen & Sword Books Limited incorporates the imprints of Atlas,
Archaeology, Aviation, Discovery, Family History, Fiction, History,
Maritime, Military, Military Classics, Politics, Select, Transport,
True Crime, Air World, Frontline Publishing, Leo Cooper, Remember
When, Seaforth Publishing, The Praetorian Press, Wharncliffe
Local History, Wharncliffe Transport, Wharncliffe True Crime
and White Owl.

For a complete list of Pen & Sword titles please contact

PEN & SWORD BOOKS LIMITED
47 Church Street, Barnsley, South Yorkshire, S70 2AS, England
E-mail: enquiries@pen-and-sword.co.uk
Website: www.pen-and-sword.co.uk

Or

PEN AND SWORD BOOKS
1950 Lawrence Rd, Havertown, PA 19083, USA
E-mail: Uspen-and-sword@casematepublishers.com
Website: www.penandswordbooks.com

Contents

List of Illustrations

Unless otherwise stated, all images were sourced from Wikimedia Commons, with grateful thanks.

List of Genealogical Tables

The aim of these charts is to bring out the relationships of the emperors to each other, for one of the main contentions of this study is that heredity was a mainspring of the succession process. Certain conventions are used: names in capitals are emperors; dotted lines indicate adoptions.

List of Tables (Emperors)

Introduction

This book is an investigation of the processes by which a man could become a Roman emperor. I considered, briefly, entitling the book 'How to become an Emperor', before, if a little reluctantly, concluding that it would be as off-putting as it is enticing, but it would certainly have shown well enough the gist of my intention.

There are about eighty men who have been 'recognized' as emperors. The number is only approximate because there has never been a clear definition of the process of recognition that would separate the 'legitimate' emperors from the 'usurpers'. It is, in fact, a matter of personal opinion in the marginal cases, though it is also the case that most historians believe that they can discern those who have achieved some sort of acceptance. Yet there has been, so far as I can find, no survey or study of what happened so that one particular man could be entered on the list, whereas others were not.[1] There are those who are generally dismissed as 'usurpers' or 'pretenders' and are usually listed separately, or perhaps are distinguished by being named in italics, or they might be omitted altogether. Yet many of the most notable emperors, including even Augustus, the four emperors of AD 68–69, Nerva, Septimius Severus, many of the third-century emperors, Constantine, perhaps Theodosius, and some of the fifth-century men were originally usurpers in that they rebelled against the ruling emperor and then forced themselves into power.

Classifying men as usurpers is a subjective judgement, or perhaps one made with the use of hindsight: no one really counts Augustus or Constantine as usurpers, yet they were both men who fought their way to the imperial office from the position of outsiders, using force to impose themselves. Their acceptance is presumably because they were clearly very successful emperors, and those reigns were long in years. In that case, why classify anyone as a 'usurper'? Some of the men classed as usurpers ruled huge parts of the Empire for several years – Pescennius Niger, Clodius Albinus, Magnentius, Magnus Maximus – before succumbing to attacks by an 'official' or 'legitimate' ruler. Also how does one classify the rulers of the 'Gallic Empire' of the third century? These 'usurpers' were clearly accepted by their subjects as legitimate rulers, and even in some cases, briefly, also by their own 'official' competitors, and the Gallic regime lasted for a decade and a half, longer than most emperors. Then there is a curious set of emperors in the West in the third quarter of the fifth century, imposed often by one outsider 'barbarian' or another; why are some accepted as emperors whereas others are not?

These are not really questions that can be answered other than subjectively, so it seems to me best to ignore them, and so to ignore the supposed distinction between usurpers and legitimate rulers. (Latin, in fact, does not have a word for 'usurper', which suggests that it is a modern European notion, based on the practice of a legitimizing coronation, which is imposed on the ancient situation.) So I shall avoid as much as possible the concept of usurper, and consider any man who achieved any sort of acceptance as an emperor to be an emperor, though we will also need to distinguish those who were quickly eliminated from those who did them down; perhaps some sort of minimum time in power, and a clear geographical range of authority might work, but that would only open up another area of fruitless and endless controversy. In fact, of course, the list of usurpers would be much the same as a list of failures, but it is not really a modern historian's task to award such labels and it will be most straightforward to regard all of them as emperors, however long they ruled and whatever the geographical extent of their power. This will, in turn, allow an unbiased consideration of their careers without labelling them in a derogatory way from the start.

The first essential in considering the success or failure of an emperor in establishing his rule is to discover what actually took place at the time he was made emperor, that is, at his accession. The actual process of proclamation and acceptance is one of the keys to understanding; another is to locate the groups of Roman subjects who do the proclaiming and accepting. In many cases these groups are revealed to be relatively small in number and restricted in composition, and were formed overwhelmingly of the powerful and wealthy; in only a very few accessions do any of the ordinary people of the Empire have any influence. The choice of emperor, therefore, is one that was made by a relatively small set of wealthy and powerful men: the Senate, the army, the provincial governors, and sometimes the bureaucracy do have a say, however, and when there are disputes between them over an accession one can see fairly clearly the accession process in action. It is the support of some or all of these sets of people that ensured a man reached and stayed on the imperial throne.

As with anything else in the Roman imperial system, it is necessary first of all to consider the motives and methods and practices of the first emperor,

Augustus. His claim to authority was based on his inheritance from his uncle, Julius Caesar, and it was his wish to be the father of a dynasty. At the same time he co-opted the Senate into accepting his rule, while his achievement of power is based essentially on his control of a successful army. His various expedients and improvisations in pursuit of his domestic policies set the pattern for the various accession processes of later emperors, a pattern of methods which, in some cases, was still visibly active in the fifth century. That is, the long-time essential keys to becoming emperor were the army, the Senate, and dynastic inheritance.

Beyond the seizure of power by Augustus, whose long reign convinced most in the Roman Empire that an imperial system was here to stay, his constitutional contortions did not need to be repeated. As a result there was also, for the next five centuries, an emperor already in office when the next one was contemplating his own accession. So the preferences of the ruling emperor had to be considered, and the *accession* of an emperor was very often also a *succession*; one of the major influences on the choice of a new emperor was always the wishes of his predecessor. This was not, however, always paramount, and again it is in cases where there were disputes that a brighter light is shone on the process. Despite the disputes and the obvious power of the army and the Senate, it is clear that heredity was always a major influence on the choices made; yet this was a process that could produce emperors of the very worst sort.

This has helped to determine the organization of this book. Every now and again the choice of emperor became the occasion for a major imperial crisis. A change of ruler is always a problem; even in law-abiding Western democracies, the police, and even the armed forces, are on alert at an election or an inauguration or a coronation. In Rome, where no clearly accepted succession process existed, the occasion was always fraught with danger. At times it was more than a problem, but was a crisis that might develop into anything from a quiet and acceptable *coup d'état* to a lengthy civil war. These occasions are distinguished here as 'crises', in each of which a new pattern of the selection process was established and then became the norm for the next historical period. Each 'crisis' is, therefore, followed by a consideration of its 'consequences'.

The Empire itself was regarded by many as an illegitimate political entity, at least during the first century or so of its existence. Apart from incorrigible rebels like the Jews, or other unwillingly conquered or conscripted subjects, a category that could be applied to almost everyone outside Italy, many of the Roman nobility were convinced that the imperial regime was one that had no right to exist. It was the view of this group that the emperor had seized the power that rightly belonged to 'the Senate and People of Rome'. These were, above all, the senators, whose power was leashed and diminished by the existence of an emperor, and they were eventually reconciled by time, by suppression, by co-optation, by weary recognition, and by the sheer continuance of the imperial regime. How far Augustus' sleight-of-hand 'restoration of the Republic' convinced them is not clear, but was probably very limited. (There were also senators who did not object so much to the imperial regime as to the fact that they themselves were not the emperor; a source of some instability in all reigns. No imperial reign was free of such instability, and all because of Augustus and his methods.) Even so, the influence and anti-imperial argument by the dissidents remained everlasting and sapped the right of any man to be regarded as the ruler of the world. Not even the eventual support of subservient Christianity, co-opted into power by its sworn enemy, could help in this.

This perceived imperial illegitimacy is one of the explanations for the continuing savagery and violence of the succession process. Many emperors swept the board clean of their possible successors, especially those who were members of their own families, since any obvious successor was thereby a threat. Once hoisted on the imperial petard, many emperors had to wield the sword to stay aloft, and many did not last very long. This, of course, was ironic: emperors always looked to found a dynasty, yet their murderousness operated to deny their families the chance to survive and succeed. This again is a pattern initiated by the first emperors. The majority of emperors died violently: seven out of the first twelve.

This is a study of historical process, in which I hope to discern any changes over time – that is what history is, after all – but also to note when change did not take place. It follows that the chronological approach is the only one that makes sense. I end at the expiry of the last emperor of the West, with a few remarks on the system as it continued in the Eastern Empire. For it is the absence of an emperor – puppet or ruler – which is correctly taken to mark the end of the Empire itself, in 476 in the West, and 1453 (a date that stretches the definition of the 'Roman Empire' to breaking-point) in the East. So one of the results of this study will be to illuminate another aspect of the 'fall' of the Empire. At least the succeeding 'Roman' Empires – Russian Tsardom, the Ottoman regime of the 'Sultan-i-Rum' (Sultanate of Rum) – do not need to be included, though their histories have many parallels with that of the original.

Part I

Augustus Defines the System

Chapter One

Augustus

Roman society in the Republic was always hereditary: sons followed fathers as property-owners and as politicians; men who were elected to political office thereby made their family a political force; to be the son of a patrician, the oldest class of nobility, meant that election to office was easier and could be achieved at a younger age than for plebeians. Noble Roman families were so desperate to ensure that they continued in existence that adoption even of an adult male was not infrequently resorted to. For noble Roman families heredity was their claim to power and wealth, as if by right.

At the same time, the Roman Republic was organized politically in such a way as to deny that heredity was the all-important criterion for office and power, though that is what nobles tended to assume. It provided for election to the offices of governing authority at all levels, and the non-nobles had a large part in the electoral process. It was always possible for 'new men' to elbow their way into the ranks of the active politicians by displaying wealth and ability, and by using the links of patronage. It was normal practice to split the authority of offices between two or more magistrates: two consuls, two *aediles*, several *praetors*, and *quaestors*. Their conduct was overseen by the institution of the Senate, of which they became members on election to one of these offices and, less importantly, by several *comitia*, assemblies of citizens whose spheres of authority overlapped. This complex system was, so the theory had it, instituted to prevent authority in the Republic from becoming concentrated in the hands of a single man such as a king, and had emerged because the last king had developed into a tyrant. This elaborate system of division and balance eventually failed, and in the last century of the Republic the policies or ambitions of several men who commanded armies loyal more to them than the state strained the system to breaking-point, as well as the difficulties the Republic faced in controlling a large overseas empire. The Senate proved to be incapable of adapting to the strains of controlling such men. The result was intermittent one-man dictatorships – an almost extinct Republican emergency office that was revived and greatly extended – culminating in Julius Caesar's assumption of a perpetual dictatorship, followed by a series of civil wars lasting nearly twenty years. Finally there was Octavian, the winner in the civil wars, who became Augustus, the sole ruler who the system had been developed to avoid. He was a bloodthirsty competitor for power; as Augustus he claimed to be repairing the damage to the Republic.

The imperial system was, therefore, not one that could easily be accommodated to the Republic out of which it grew. The dictators of the first century BC came to their sole power by subverting, overthrowing and battering down the practices of that constitution, using brute force where words or threats did not work. So the first emperor, Octavian/Augustus, who had achieved his sole power by those very same methods, had to work very hard for a very long time to achieve acceptance as emperor by his senatorial peers. His personal advantages – youth, political ingenuity and affability – were complemented by a vigorous resort to ruthlessness whenever he felt it necessary, and his longevity meant that he outlived all his enemies.

Octavian owed his position first of all to his inheritance: he was the grand-nephew and the nearest male relative of Julius Caesar, and he thus became C. Julius Caesar by his adoption.[1] Julius Caesar's own position was, however, only in a minimal part the result of heredity, and Octavian's own origin and descent were fairly obscure. Caesar's father, though noble and patrician, was of no particular distinction, and Caesar himself was wont to emphasize his supposed descent from the goddess Venus rather than his immediate parentage, and his amorous behaviour was supposed to confirm that descent, but he had achieved a dominating political position at Rome by his own brutal, cunning and devious efforts and heredity played only a small part in it.

Octavian was the son of C. Octavius, who had only reached the rank of praetor before dying relatively young. He had married the niece of Julius Caesar well before the dictator achieved great eminence, and only became dynastically important because Caesar himself had no children. Octavius the son, while still a student, gained his career boost of massive proportions by retrospective adoption by Caesar as his son. This was done in the dead man's will, presumably for the want of any closer relative. He also inherited Caesar's wealth, his status as a patrician (by his adoption), and his political prestige and, after Caesar's divination, the right to call himself the son of a god, a collection of attributes that gave him instant prestige and authority even as a teenager.

Above all, he developed the same driving ambition as his adoptive father. What he made of this was his own work, from his early ferocious bloodletting and his political thrusting and timing to victory in several civil wars, despite having minimal military and naval command abilities. His prime ability was in politics, and he was able to retain the devotion of a group of men whose own abilities made up for his deficiencies. In the process his rivals fell away or died or were destroyed, and by 31 BC he was alone on the same pinnacle reached by Caesar, and had achieved it by not dissimilar ruthless methods. Caesar had kept his pre-eminent position for no more than a year or so before being murdered at the age of 56; Octavian kept his for life, a long life, and he died a natural death at the age of 76.

Having gained sole power and imposed this in Rome, Octavian was given the quasi-divine title/name of Augustus. He then spent the next four decades or more alternately seeking ways to maintain and perpetuate his power, and stamping about the Empire organizing it and seeing to the conquest of new territories. His lack of military ability was neutralized by the abilities of his colleagues, above all the able and faithful M. Vipsanius Agrippa and his stepson Ti. Claudius Nero (the future Emperor Tiberius), whose joint and successive achievements in Augustus' name gave him the reputation of being the greatest conqueror in Roman history in terms of territory acquired. Augustus might not have been much of a commander in the field, but as an organizer of victory and an employer of talent he was a master.

He had to operate to a large degree within Roman traditional methods. This was a matter of public relations, but also in order to disguise the changes he was making and to operate within public expectations; it was also his own personal preference. So he held the traditional Roman office of consul, eschewing Caesar's dictatorship for life; though he was consul repeatedly, a less than traditional practice which bred resentment in those denied the office by his occupation of it. He carefully avoided even the implicit offer of a royal crown. He spent some time experimenting with various combinations of offices and powers before finally settling on a choice selection which he held in effective perpetuity; they were usually awarded for terms of years, but were always renewed. *Tribunicia potestatis*, the power (not the office) of tribune, allowed him to legislate through control of the citizens' assembly, and incidentally had the advantage of conferring sacrosanctity: the power of a Roman commander to control the legions (*Imperator*, which became in effect his name), and the authority of a proconsul to govern the provinces and to appoint deputies (legates) to go out to govern these for him. Above all, it was the *auctoritas* that came from the accumulation of these posts and his long-lived power that secured his position. He held many more consulships (eventually thirteen) than any other Roman could aspire to, and had been given repeated salutations as *Imperator* by the troops of which he was the sole (if usually absent) commander.

In the background all the time, however, was the army. It was more Augustus' army than Rome's, and he appointed its commanders – legates again – and the troops fought in his name as much as in that of the 'Senate and People in Rome' which was blazoned on their standards. Always behind him loomed that army; his power was ultimately based on it, as was that of every emperor who came after him.

The ten or fifteen years after achieving sole power by the victory at the Battle of Actium in 31 BC were spent in devising ways of ensuring that the power he had gained remained his and remained acceptable to most Romans. He first tried the old idea of holding successive consulships, being consul every year from 31 to 23 BC, which was annoying to Roman nobles who expected to hold the office by right of birth. With a dozen of these offices behind him, however, he had accumulated sufficient *auctoritas* that he could stand back and let other nobles in, but he also used his prestige to control access to the office and to the other offices as well. He therefore gradually reached the position where he reckoned that the tribunician power (*tribunicia potestatis*) and the authority of the governor of provinces (*proconsular imperium*), modified so as to remain to him when within the city, were all the offices that were really needed, plus the religious authority of chief priest (*pontifex maximus*) and near divinity as the son of a god, all backed up by control of the army of course.

This set of offices and powers was by no means the sort of thing that would have been acceptable to any Roman before him. However, he had won a civil war, he commanded the whole army, he had gained that immense *auctoritas*, and above all he had brought peace of a sort to the city and to the Empire. By working within the old offices and their powers he made his unprecedented position broadly acceptable, but he always faced enemies and his actual power was always somewhat limited.

It is a mark of the limits of the emperor's power at this stage in imperial history that Augustus felt he had to bow to the wishes of the Roman aristocracy. His political support among them was a good deal less than it was among the ordinary people of Rome, who could be relied on to demand that he, not the Senate, take action in any emergency. Nevertheless, the particular offices he held proved to be sufficient, and by giving up continuous consulships he allowed more of those who expected to be consul by right to take up the office. At the same time, in a subtle way, by his not being consul he devalued the office which, of course, was no longer the head of the state as it had been in the past.

In theory these various offices and powers were given him by the laws of the Roman people, which had to be recommended by the Senate to the popular assemblies, the *comitia*. The latter, however, had been effectively hobbled by Augustus' time, so that their ratification of senatorial measures had become a formality. (They lingered on through the first century AD, the last sign of their existence coming at the time of Nerva's accession in AD 96.) In effect, therefore, the Senate had become the primary legislative body of the Empire, which should have enhanced the authority of the members, but the emperor's powers included the right to issue legal decisions, which amounted to the right to legislate – this was part of his tribunician power – and in effect it was a matter of bureaucratic decrees. What the Senate had gained, the emperor removed.

The tribunician power was cloaked in a religious aura which provided the personal protection of sacrosanctity. This aura was reinforced by the new name awarded him by the Senate, after consultation, of course. 'Augustus' was a word that implied a priestliness, a contact with the gods, and sacrosanctity. It gave him a further element of *auctoritas*, one far above any other Roman, aristocrat or citizen had or could have, though this was personal to him alone. The power of the proconsular *imperium* gave him authority to appoint governors in the provinces he ruled (which was most of them), as well as command of the armies in those provinces; this task, of course, was delegated to the governors, or to the legionary commanders, all of whom were his legates and chosen and appointed by him.

This proconsular power had to be tweaked somewhat, just like many other powers he took, since a proconsul was not, under the Republic's rules, permitted to enter the city while still commanding troops. Augustus' effective control of the Senate was sufficient to gain him a special dispensation, another break with the Republican system. This was the clearest indication, if anyone cared to look, that the position he had reached was wholly anomalous to anything in the Republican system. It had been fundamental to that system that political discourse in the city should be conducted unarmed, and that offices of power should be duplicated to prevent the use of power by one man. Augustus' whole position was summed up in the title he affected, *princeps*, an adaptation of a Republican term, but it was the adaptation that was significant; 'First Man' would be a fair translation.

As a result, and in a sense as a *quid pro quo* for this concession, he was now able to relinquish into other hands the elective offices he had monopolized, though they largely ceased to be subject to election for he retained the right of nomination. So he no longer shut out others from the great offices of state: consul, tribune, priesthoods, praetor, even occasionally *imperator*. His personal prestige could now permit this: the 'Augustus' title, thirteen consulships, repeated salutations as *imperator*; no one could approach this record.

It was this set of positions and powers and offices which amounted to the power that adhered to this and future emperors. Each man who became or aspired to that post acquired or claimed these powers. The award of at least some of them, above all the tribunician power, became the way in which an emperor designated his successor. Also by controlling the elections to other offices – from *quaestor* up to consul – the emperors were able to define the composition of the Senate, which was the only source of legitimate power that could compete with him.

Above all, despite several periods of illness and any number of plots against him, Augustus lived on. He died almost the oldest man ever to be emperor, as well as the first. By the time he died in AD 14, aged 76, no one could remember the old Republic; even the oldest man alive could not recall anything before Augustus, except the civil wars, the memory of which all agreed was exceptionally hideous. Augustus outlived both his contemporaries and most of the next generation as well. So the system he constructed became the norm; a return to the scramble of the Republican politics was impossible since no one knew how to do it.[2]

It was in organizing his own heredity that Augustus met his greatest problem and one that repeatedly defeated him. From the time when he cleared his last political hurdle, the destruction of the competing power of M. Antonius at Actium, in order to pursue his programme of the 'restoration of the Republic', the first emperor searched for a successor. The record shows that, above all, he wished it to be one of his own blood. (In this, as ever, he showed himself a true heir of Julius Caesar, both in the ambition and in his inability to provide such an heir.) His frequent illnesses made the necessity for a choice clear, at least to him, but all too often the chosen one inconveniently died, while he himself recovered and lived on.

Augustus' basic problem was that first, he had no son, and second, that his wish for a successor conflicted with the desire of the Roman aristocracy not to see a dynasty of rulers establish itself. Augustus eventually succeeded here also, but not in any way he had wished, nor in the person hoped for. His methods established a process of organizing the succession that was devious and very adaptable, though these very qualities meant that the process was often unclear. In the absence of a son, he had to rely for dynastic continuity on his only daughter, Julia, born of his second marriage with Scribonia. Julia's marital experience was therefore dictated by her father for his own political requirements. It was not an experience she enjoyed.

He also had a sister, Octavia, the second string to his bow, and her marriages were similarly arranged for Augustus' political ends; she had been married to M. Antonius during the decade-long Cold War between the two men in the 30s BC. She then returned to her brother's court with two daughters by Anthony; she had been married earlier to C. Claudius Marcellus and had two daughters and a son by that marriage as well. These became more of Augustus' marriage pawns. Augustus' own third marriage, to Livia, was childless, but she had two sons, Ti. Claudius Nero and Nero Claudius Drusus by her own first marriage. All these people were thus the unfortunate instruments of Augustus' search for a successor, and thoroughly unhappy he managed to make them in the process. (See Genealogical Tables I and II.)

I   The Julio-Claudian Dynasty.

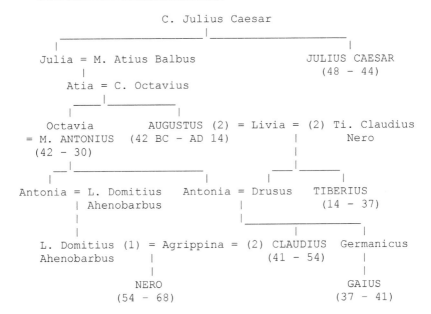

The strong insistence Augustus displayed on inheritance within his family is curious in that both he and his great-uncle, Julius Caesar, were essentially self-made men; similarly the opposition by the Roman nobility to the establishment of an imperial dynasty was paradoxical, since the foundation of Roman society was hereditary succession in noble families. However, Caesar had made his own way, to be sure with an insistence upon his own pride and dignity, but he had little inheritable prestige from his ancestors; Augustus' father had reached the praetorship, but before him there was essentially no one who counted. Neither man had sons, and only a single daughter each. Yet both were determined to be dynastic founders, so proving themselves to be true members of Rome's nobility. The prevailing sense of hereditary rights among the Roman aristocracy therefore affected them as well, so that if they could not look back over a long and distinguished line of forebears, they could show a determination that there would be an even more distinguished line to follow them. Instead of being the final twigs on their family trees, or lone plants, they would be the roots.

One of Augustus' problems in this area was that, despite the hereditary imperatives within which he operated, because his political settlement involved the political sleight of hand that he called the 'restoration of the Republic', he was unable to designate someone openly as his political successor. After all, the imperial regime did not yet exist, and the fiction was that he was simply the 'first man' of the state. The further fiction was that what he had to do was to designate a single person as heir to his personal possessions. Having done so, he then had to provide the chosen one with a particularly notable political career so that the successor would follow him as the most obvious next 'first man'. This would include, at the least, one or preferably several consulships, experience in the governorship of one or more provinces, command of an army for a time, preferably successfully, and a long and detailed experience in the intrigue-ridden and dangerous world of Roman politics, and the chosen one had also to survive all this.

This career could be speeded up by the application of the *auctoritas* of Augustus, but it could not be evaded, and all these jobs should preferably be completed before the final award of the *tribunicia potestatis* and, what went with it, the authority of the proconsul. These distinctions would thus be the final indication that the chosen one was the chosen political successor. Because of his determination to respect the republican system, if that is not too misleading a formulation, Augustus had to do this by means of the traditional methods, by working with and through the Senate. It was all

II <u>Augustus' Search for a Successor.</u>

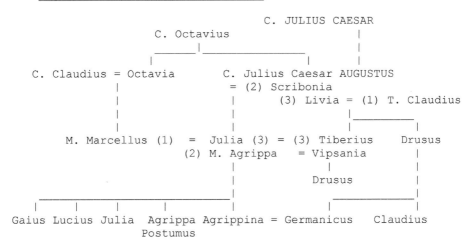

a daunting task that would take years to accomplish and, as it turned out, Augustus had to go through it all four times. His actual successors gradually pared away at these requirements.

The process of training a successor necessarily took several years, for the various offices were annual affairs and could not be held simultaneously. Because he had no son, it was the husbands of his daughter and sister and the children they produced – his grandsons and nephews and his stepchildren – who were the people assumed to be his heirs, and for a time there was plenty of choice. (See Genealogical Table II.)

Octavia's first husband, C. Claudius Marcellus, was from a highly-distinguished Republican lineage; their son Marcus, familiarly referred to simply as Marcellus, was Augustus' first choice. He was born in 42 BC, so was 15 years old in 27 when Augustus began his search for a successor. Marcellus was promoted rapidly with an early induction as a priest, and he was *curule aedile* (a magistrate) at the age of 16. These rapid promotions, combined with his marriage to Augustus' daughter Julia in 25, were clear signs of his selection. It might be, however, that Marcellus was seen only as a son-in-law and as the father of Julia's children in the future and not actually intended to be the next emperor. Nonetheless he was clearly singled out. He was given the status of praetor without having had to go through the tedium of holding the office, and the right to stand for election as consul ten years before the legal age; since he was a patrician, this meant he would be able to do so at the age of 22 in 20 BC.

Success in the election was, of course, guaranteed. At the same time Livia's eldest son Tiberius Claudius Nero, and so Augustus' stepson, was elected *quaestor* (one rank down from *aedile*) and given the right to stand for consul five years early. He had been born in the same year as Marcellus, so he could not stand until 15 BC. Since the only previous case of an early election had been that of Augustus himself, who became consul at 19, the implications were clear: Marcellus was going to be trained as Augustus' successor, while Tiberius' prize of advancement was generally assumed to be the result of pressure from Livia. In fact, Tiberius worked his way through several offices, conscientiously performing his duties. As for Marcellus, before he could reach his promised consulship, he died, in 22 BC. He had not even done his procreative duty, for he and Julia had no children.

Julia was now quickly married off to Augustus' strong 'right arm', M. Vipsanius Agrippa, the man to whom in many ways Augustus owed his military successes. Julia was 17 and Agrippa was about the same age as her father. He was of undistinguished birth, but he had great abilities both as a military commander and an administrator: he was a friend of Augustus' from their student days, and he was undeviatingly loyal to Augustus and always willing to undertake the most difficult tasks uncomplainingly. He was despised for all this by many of the less successful but more highly-born Roman nobles. He had already been married to Marcella, Marcellus' sister, with whom he had a daughter, Vipsania. Now Agrippa was ordered to divorce Marcella and marry Julia, who thereupon did her dynastic duty by producing five grandchildren for Augustus. The first two were boys, Gaius and Lucius, and it was on them that Augustus now fixed his dynastic plan, but in case he died – this must be the reason – he brought Agrippa into the scheme as well. He was already the biological father of the boys, and was wholly trustworthy in any task Augustus gave him. The two boys were adopted by Augustus as his own sons, and Agrippa was given the same powers as Augustus himself – tribunician and proconsular authority – limited to five years, but renewable. (He had already held the consulship three times, more than any other contemporary except Augustus himself.)[3]

The plan, evidently, was for Agrippa to fill in as temporary *princeps* if Augustus died, until the boys, or a survivor of them, became old enough to rule. Meanwhile Agrippa was kept busy trouble-shooting in different parts of the Empire, and the two boys could be trained, and fast-tracked to the necessary offices when adult, under Augustus' personal supervision. In the background, as a second string, were Tiberius and Drusus, Augustus' stepsons. The former now had praetorian rank, and Drusus had also been awarded the right to stand for election five years early. Augustus therefore could feel that he had lots of strings to his bow, but all this planning and scheming came to a crisis in 13–12 BC. Tiberius was serving as consul at the age of 29, three years early, when in that winter Agrippa, commanding once too often in a winter campaign, died on his way back to Rome. (For Agrippa as the progenitor of emperors, see Genealogical Table III.)

```
III   M. Agrippa as an Imperial Ancestor.

       Marcella (2)   =  M. Vipsanius = (3) Julia
                |                      |
     TIBERIUS = Vipsania            Agrippina = Germanicus
               |                        _____|_____
               |                       |                       |
         Drusus       CLAUDIUS = Agrippina = Domitius    GAIUS
                                            |
                                          NERO
```

By the time of Agrippa's appointment as joint *princeps* in 18 BC it had become clear how the choice of a successor was to be managed. The choice was Augustus' to make, though the actual selection had to be partially disguised so as to soothe Republican and senatorial feelings. If the chosen one was adult, the powers of tribune and proconsul would be awarded by the Senate at the 'request' of Augustus, though in effect, of course, the Senate had no choice. If the chosen man was sub-adult he would be promoted quickly through the offices of state, skipping those that were the most tedious; again, this had to be done by arrangement with the Senate at the formal request of Augustus. By reducing to 22 the age at which the nominee could be consul, he would gather the necessary prestige to face the Senate and in the meantime he could be taken or sent on military and diplomatic missions to introduce him to the provincial power-men, the provinces themselves, and above all to the army. A quick and victorious campaign with the chosen one in nominal command would be a bonus.

This process could scarcely take less than ten years. If the nominee was adult he would have gone through some of the earlier stages in the normal sequence, though accelerated, but even so, these several elements could still take several years. If the candidate was a child, his selection would still mean he would only be available to succeed to full power in his 20s.

Because Augustus felt that he had to cooperate with and through the Senate, the Senate's approval was necessary for the choice of successor, at least in theory. Yet, despite all this planning, no one could know what would really happen when Augustus died. The Senate would need to give some sort of collective decision on a successor, or a successor regime, which in part explains the Senate's involvement from the start. If the Senate was not presented with a clear successor the whole of Augustus' work could well fall apart, and he was concerned, not surprisingly, that his work should endure.

The death of Agrippa in 13 BC did not, in the event, derail Augustus' plans too much. Gaius and Lucius had by this time survived the dangerous first five years of life. They had also been joined by two sisters, Julia and Agrippina, and by another brother, Agrippa Postumus. For the next decade Augustus fixed his hopes and plans on the two elder boys, who were now, because of his adoption, called Gaius and Lucius Caesar. In addition, his Claudian stepsons, Tiberius and Lucius, were now adult and had benefited from their advancement, and both grew into very capable generals and administrators. Tiberius was consul in 13 BC and Drusus in 9 BC, both some years in advance of the legal age, by senatorial dispensation.

Indeed, Tiberius appeared to take Agrippa's place in many ways. He had campaigned successfully in Pannonia, one of Agrippa's areas, and he and Drusus campaigned successfully in Germany. After Agrippa's death, Augustus made Tiberius marry Julia; to do this Tiberius had to divorce his wife, who was Agrippa's own daughter Vipsania. So Tiberius was married to his stepsister, who was also the mother of his ex-wife. He very much resented having to break with Vipsania and did not at all like being married to Julia. They had a child, which was Augustus' aim, but it died in infancy and they then lived apart. Augustus' schemes paid little attention to his victim's feelings or their preferences.

The marriage-and-divorce policy of the first emperor is another sign that he was dynastically-minded, in contradiction to his claimed achievement of 'restoring' the Republic. It was not merely a matter of trying to ensure that his bloodline continued, though he clearly regarded his daughter as a sort of brood mare whose main purpose was to produce children. He was also concerned to select marriage partners for Julia from a fairly restricted range of men. Marcellus and Julia were first cousins, Tiberius and Julia were step-related, Tiberius' brother married Antonia, a daughter of Octavia, and so they were also in the same step-relationship, Tiberius' first wife Vipsania was the granddaughter of Octavia, and so they were also in the same step-relationship, Tiberius' first wife Vipsania was the granddaughter of Octavia. This was dynastically important for Augustus, clearly, but genetically it was likely to be dangerous if pursued into another generation. (These intermarriages are reminiscent of the similar dynastic system practised by the Ptolemies in Egypt, as if Cleopatra's influence permeated and hovered over the life of her greatest enemy.)

On the other hand, other members of the imperial family married out: Octavia's eldest daughter Marcella (*maior)* married L. Domitius Ahenobarbus; Julia's eldest daughter (also Julia) married L. Aemilius Paullus; and, of course, Octavia had been married to M. Antonius and to C. Claudius Marcellus. This was genetically safer, but Augustus' purpose, paralleling his work to define the succession – for he was in control of these marriages as well – was to link these important Republican families with that of the *princeps*, so providing it with the good ancestral Republican aura that Augustus himself did not have, and bringing aristocratic support to the newly-imperial family.

Eventually Tiberius became weary of Augustus' manipulations. His brother Drusus died in 9 BC, while he was consul and campaigning in Germany. Tiberius spent the years after Drusus' death campaigning there, which he reduced to some order, and when he returned to Rome in 6 BC he decided he had done enough – or had had enough – and announced that he would retire to Rhodes. Augustus attempted to recruit him to his schemes by awarding him the tribunician power for five years in the pattern of Agrippa's career, but Tiberius was less biddable than Agrippa. He went to Rhodes anyway, where he stayed for the next eight years. After his tribunician power expired in 1 BC, he became very vulnerable.

Augustus, perforce, now concentrated his plans on his two elder grandsons, his adopted sons. The elder, Gaius, was made *princeps iuventutis* in 5 BC, the year after Tiberius' withdrawal, and Augustus took up his twelfth consulship at the same time to do the boy honour. Therefore, if anyone had any doubts, they were now set at rest: Gaius, with his title echoing Augustus' own, was clearly destined to be the next emperor. His brother Lucius had the same distinction awarded him in 2 BC, when Augustus held his thirteenth consulship. The emperor was awarded, or rather finally accepted, a new title, *pater patriae*, at the same time.

For a few years this scheme worked. Gaius became consul in AD 1, aged only 20 – just about the age Augustus had been when he forced himself into that office at the head of an army – and was then employed with some modest success in the East. Lucius was sent to Spain in AD 2 for the same purpose, to gain experience of government and a province. Yet in only two years, the whole scheme then collapsed. Lucius died on his way to Spain; Gaius actually commanded in the East, but was wounded in a siege; he died in Lycia from the wound in AD 4. The elaborate plan had failed. For the third time, Augustus' choice as successor had died.

The two boys had a younger brother, Agrippa Postumus, but he was not considered suitable material, being regarded as akin to a wild animal, or at least so it was said; though unlike his brothers he was healthy and tough. He was exiled to an island, Planasia, off the Etrurian coast, where he was kept under guard. As a result the government's propaganda about him could not be checked by direct investigation, if anyone had the temerity to try.

When Gaius died, Augustus was faced by the necessity of making yet another new choice of heir. By this time the emperor was in his mid-60s, in a time when the average length of a man's life was half that, though it was certainly higher for the better-fed and better-doctored upper-class men. However, Augustus could not seriously expect to live another ten years (although he did), during which period another child could grow to adulthood and be groomed for the succession. There were some male plebeian relations still available: his grandson Agrippa Postumus, and Germanicus and Claudius, two sons of Drusus. They were Augustus' grandnephews, but Claudius suffered a disability and was not regarded as suitable imperial material any more than Agrippa Postumus; Germanicus, aged 16, might be a suitable candidate, but hardly in advance of his uncle Tiberius. Tiberius himself returned to Rome in AD 2.

Augustus was, therefore, compelled to select the mature, experienced and competent Tiberius as his successor in place of the series of immature children he had so far favoured. A complexity of adoptions was designed, together with a determined display of reluctance by Tiberius which compelled Augustus to argue publicly for his scheme and so be pinned down to it. Tiberius adopted Germanicus as his son, and Germanicus therefore joined Tiberius' own son as one of the next generation of successors. Augustus then adopted Tiberius and Agrippa Postumus as his own sons. Agrippa was only an adolescent at this point, and regarded as unsuitable successor material; there could be no implication that Tiberius was to be coequal with him. To make it all quite clear, Tiberius was given tribunician and proconsular authority for ten years, a period during which it was no doubt assumed that Augustus would die, and during which the younger generation – Agrippa Postumus, Germanicus and Drusus – would mature. This was not what Augustus really wanted, but it was only what he could get in the light of the failure of his own line. As a consolation, the eldest of the younger set, Germanicus, was betrothed to the daughter of Julia and Agrippa, Agrippina. If they survived and had children, Augustus' line would survive after all through them. (For the design, see Genealogical Table IV.)[4]

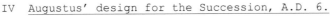

```
IV  Augustus' design for the Succession, A.D. 6.

                          AUGUSTUS
                             | .
          .  .  .  .  .  .  .|. .  .  .  .  .  .  .
          .                  |                  .
     TIBERIUS (1)           Julia       (Agrippa Postumus)
        | .                  |
        |. . . . .           |
        |          .         |
      Drusus        .        |          () - excluded as
     ___|_____    .        |                unsuitable
     |         | .           |
 (Claudius) Germanicus = Agrippina
              (2)          |
                    (3) GAIUS
```

The historian Tacitus claimed that Tiberius' selection was due to the influence of Livia over her husband; 'his mother's secret machinations', he called it. No doubt her influence really was exerted in favour of her only surviving son, but with or without her influence, it is difficult to see who else Augustus could have chosen if he had wished his life's work, by contrast with his descent by blood, to continue. It was not possible to go to someone outside his extended family, since that would only annoy all the others who felt that they had an equal 'right' to be chosen; Tiberius was the only member of his family who was both capable and adult and, for that matter, able to assert a degree of independence, which should have been one of the criteria Augustus was looking for all along.

For here was the rub. The thoroughgoing ambiguity of Augustus' political system that is summed up in the term 'principate', which moderns tend to apply to it, was basic to his problem and his choices. Principate means, of course, rule by one man, the *princeps*, but this was a system of rule based on influence and authority rather than direct control. Augustus' accumulation of honours and offices was such that his influence was a hugely powerful force, but his system had always been a fairly delicate balance between one man's *auctoritas* and the continuing Republican system of elections and the work of the Senate and even the popular Assemblies. Augustus could use his personal power to ensure, mostly, that the elective offices were held by men who would not make trouble, a preference that rapidly translated into choosing men he felt were due for rewards and favours. He could take power as censor and thereby purge the Senate of men he disliked, men who were inadequate, personally or in wealth, or men who opposed him too vigorously and too intelligently, a purge he carried out three times. At the end of all this there can have been few senators left who were willing to stand up to him. However, the forms were generally observed, and the Senate, above all, continued to be active and respected.

If this carefully-constructed and managed system was to continue after Augustus it had to be run by someone who had experienced it. It was far too delicate for an outsider – Agrippa Postumus, for example, exiled on his island – to be expected to do so. It depended too much on the dispensing of favours, the knowledge of individuals and their families and ambitions, and the interaction of the fairly limited set of men, and some women, that comprised the senatorial class. These were the men who held the old Republican offices, who governed provinces, who commanded legions, who conducted wars, who operated the judicial system; in short, those who sat in the Senate. An outsider could not work such a system without the intimate knowledge of the people involved and how the system worked, which could only be gained by existing within it for years. This is why Augustus had been at such pains to train up his various young descendants over a period of thirty years. The investment in time and emotion in the series of failures would have crushed many men.

It was considered by some that there were alternatives to a successor who would take over Augustus' place in the system. Tacitus pithily noted these alternatives were 'freedom' or civil war.[5] Freedom meant a return to the old Republic, of which no one then living had any experience. Civil war was either feared or desired; those who desired it were surely thinking in terms of assuming Augustus' place as victors (just as he had assumed Caesar's place as the victor after his own civil wars).

Those wishing that such possible alternatives might come about were deemed by Tacitus to be few, though he cannot have known any number and the secret wishes of most men remained secret. He does say that most people, when it was known that Augustus was dying, discussed his possible successors. Therefore, if this is the case, one may say that Augustus had achieved success in one part of his work: the system he had developed had been accepted by the great majority of the political class in Rome, and the question now was not how to dismantle the system or change or replace it, but who would operate it and with what success. Yet until an actual succession had taken place it could not be seen as a permanent system. So Augustus would never know whether his system survived, or whether his family became a ruling dynasty.

The years and deaths and incapacities had eventually reduced the potential candidates to five: one of them, Agrippa Postumus, was ruled out as untrained, even untrainable, but he was Augustus' adopted son and he had to be considered; Tiberius was full of years and competence, had the authority of two consulships and the tribunician and proconsular powers; Tiberius' own son Drusus and his nephews Claudius and Germanicus were all three deemed too young, though Drusus and Germanicus had commanded armies by the time Augustus died and Germanicus was singled out as Tiberius' adopted son. Judging them to be too young was, of course, a judgement also on Augustus' selection methods. However, promoting these boys ahead of their adoptive-father-cum-uncle would defeat Augustus' hereditary predilections and it was something that Tiberius, now in a very powerful position, would scarcely permit. When it came down to a choice, in the last year or so of Augustus' life, there was in effect no choice left: it had to be Tiberius.

Tiberius' qualifications for the succession were the offices he had held, together with Augustus' final acquiescence. After all Augustus' experimentation, it was the list of offices and achievements of Tiberius that became the required set awarded to future emperors, and it was the absence of the training Tiberius had had which became the problem for Augustus' posterity and thus for the fate of his system. After all, if a potential successor received the proper training, why should he wait for the emperor to die? A trained successor was an immediate danger. It thus became impossible to train one.

The imperial office did get into the hands of outsiders – by which is meant those without the training for the job by going through the rigours of the system itself – and this development was in fact inevitable, but it turned out that the proper training, by occupying and running the several magistracies, commanding armies and governing provinces, simply could not be combined with selection as an heir. The chosen heir had to be selected young, which meant he would be too young to go through the offices; if an adult was chosen he would have gone through them already and would be an outsider to the family. Adults could not be chosen, since they would not be of the family unless they married into it like Agrippa or, indeed, like Tiberius. So future emperors would inevitably be inexperienced; in terms of the way the system worked, they would be outsiders, and would be faced with having to operate the system in ignorance of its construction and capabilities. That is, the system of a 'restored Republic', as designed by Augustus, could not continue; in the face of a quasi-hereditary system of succession, it would have to change into an autocracy.

Tiberius had been consul twice, having worked his way through the preliminary offices from *quaestor* onwards. He had commanded armies, of from one to ten legions, in campaigns in the Balkans and in Germany and in the East; indeed, it was under his command-in-chief that Germany had first been conquered, and it had been under him that it had been held after the disaster contrived by P. Quinctilius Varus in AD 9, and Varus was another of those closely connected to the *princeps*. In all this Tiberius was way ahead of any other Roman, none of whom had more than one consulship to his name, and only Tiberius' own son Drusus and his own nephew and adopted son Germanicus had commanded armies of similar size and importance with real success. The seal was put on his position in AD 13, when his tribunician power and proconsular authority expired: they were renewed for another ten years, and he was also given power to conduct the census as well. In all respects except years and prestige, he was now Augustus' equal in authority.[6]

Augustus died a year later. He did so slowly, making it possible for people to become accustomed to his approaching death, and for Tiberius to be summoned to the death scene (from Illyricum, where he was intending to campaign), so as to be able to take over full control without serious disruption. He was the man who gave the watchword to the Guard, thereby establishing his right to command it, and as soon as Augustus was dead the body was taken to Rome (from Nola in Campania, where he died), by Tiberius and his mother Livia, Augustus' widow. Tacitus implies that the announcement of the death was delayed so that Tiberius could take control; if so it made good sense, but it was probably not necessary.[7]

This was the first time that one *princeps* had succeeded another. There seems to have been a certain hesitation all round as to how to proceed. Ignoring Tacitus' cynical interpretation of everyone's actions, what occurred was actually quite straightforward. The coffin containing Augustus' body was taken ceremoniously from Nola to Rome with Tiberius walking behind it all the way, and then there was about a week for the cremation and the funeral to take place. Only then did the Senate meet, summoned by Tiberius in his capacity as a holder of the tribunician power, to discuss the future. The new *princeps*, who clearly had the authority of that office by virtue of the grant of powers the year before, received oaths of allegiance from the magistrates in order of seniority. First the consuls (one of whom was a Pompeius, the other a relative of Tiberius by marriage), then the Guard Commander and the Prefect of the Corn Supply, and followed, though Tacitus does not mention this, by the other magistrates – *praetors*, *aediles*, tribunes and *quaestors* – then 'the Senate, army, and public', presumably all senators, all army officers present, and those of the public who wished to do so.[8]

In fact, as Tacitus makes clear, Tiberius was already *princeps* when all this was taking place. He had received all the requisite powers the year before, and he was provided with his own guard at that time, so for the past year he had in fact been joint *princeps* along with Augustus. The ceremony at Rome – the funeral, the Senate meeting, the oaths of allegiance – was thus largely a formality, but it was a necessary formality, since it is a requirement of any process of succession that it should take place in public. In Republican Rome, the consuls took up their posts in public by a familiar ceremony, visible to spectators, as did other magistrates. A secret succession is automatically a questionable one; a public succession – that is, one which is visible to and observed by many people, whether or not they took an oath of allegiance – was indispensable.

There was also another action that may well be necessary at a succession: the killing of any serious competitor. So Agrippa Postumus was murdered by his guardian, on orders given by one of Tiberius 'confidants', whatever that may mean. Augustus had interviewed Agrippa personally at his island exile not all that long before, and it seems likely that he had left contingent orders for the killing to be done as soon as he himself died. That this was a necessary precaution to avoid serious trouble is shown by the fact that there was at least one plot to 'rescue' Agrippa from his island and take him to the army in Germany, no doubt so as to proclaim him emperor,[9] and there were at least two cases of 'false Agrippas' attempting to cause trouble in the next two decades. Agrippa's death was yet one more to add to the long list of Augustus' victims: he may have claimed to restore the Republic, but he had done so by a series of fictions and over the bodies of many thousands of Romans and provincials; that his last victim was his own grandson was all too typical of his ferocity.

In Rome, the succession was accomplished with due solemnity and formality, and in the provinces the news of the change occasioned no real surprise. The army was different. A concentration of three legions in

Pannonia staged a riot that developed into a mutiny, replete with demands for better pay and conditions of service, and the beatings and murders of unpopular officers. The mutiny was quelled only by concessions agreed on the spot by Tiberius' son Drusus. This was a disturbance in part due to the fears of the soldiers that the change of emperor might worsen their conditions; it was not the component of a succession crisis.[10]

The army in Germany was a good deal larger than that in Pannonia. It was under the overall command of Germanicus, now Tiberius' adopted son. Part of the army, the four legions at Ubii (the later Cologne), also mutinied. The same sort of grievances were aired and demands put forward as in Pannonia, and this time some of the men apparently wanted to make Germanicus emperor, though this idea did not get very far. The same sort of timely concessions on pay, length of service and so on brought these disturbances to an end fairly quickly. As in Pannonia, it was the prospect of an improvement in their lives that the soldiers grasped at.[11] It would need someone with a taste of political intrigue to bring such a force to the point of proclaiming an alternative emperor. The slave who concocted the plot to bring Agrippa Postumus to the army in Germany had that very idea. So, obviously, had Augustus.

That the army as a whole accepted the change was due, one would say, to a fairly obvious set of conditions: Augustus was very old, and his death had surely been expected for years; Tiberius was well-known in the army and the Empire, and well-known to be Augustus' choice as heir; and he had been invested in advance with the necessary powers. There were alternatives to Tiberius, as the German army clearly appreciated, as did the slave who wanted to proclaim Agrippa Postumus. The actual succession all went smoothly because of good advance preparation. It would not always be so, and the army had already shown that it knew it had the power to make an emperor, disregarding formal qualifications. Augustus' fiction might work in Rome where the senators could appreciate its subtlety and its necessity, but it was seen to be transparent and vulnerable elsewhere.

Part II

The Augustan Process

The First Julio-Claudians

Julius Caesar (Dictator 48–44 BC).

Augustus (30 BC–AD 14). (*Adobe Stock*)

Tiberius (14–37). (*Adobe Stock*)

The Later Julio-Claudians

Gaius (Caligula, 37–41).

Claudius (41–54).

Nero (54–68).

Chapter Two

The First Imperial Family

Augustus established the pattern and the process for the selection of an imperial successor all too clearly: he was to be selected by the ruling *princeps*, and this was his responsibility and his alone, though no doubt intrigue and influence went on that was designed to inform or distort his choice. That choice, as was shown in Augustus' long search, which he had had to repeat several times over during his reign of more than forty years, was restricted to members of his own extended family. The signal that he had made his choice was the adoption of the chosen successor as his son. If the successor so chosen was still too young, a guardian-*princeps*, an Agrippa-figure might also be chosen.

It was intended that the successor would have gained extensive experience of political administration and military command during the reign of his adoptive father, a process of political education that could scarcely last less than a decade, given the complications and personal nature of the Roman system and the size of the Empire, though the deaths of three of Augustus' chosen men on their travels was a sign that it might be better to keep them in Rome. This process of education and induction could only be completed after the reigning emperor died, when the Senate must signify its acceptance of the new emperor by a sequence of actions, including the award of the necessary tribunician and proconsular powers if they had not already been awarded, the offering of oaths of allegiance by the current magistrates, the administrative officers, the senators, any army commanders and officers who were present, and any members of the public who were present and wished to do so.

There were therefore three sets of people who had to be involved in the selection and installation of a new Roman emperor: the imperial family, in particular the reigning emperor; the Senate, whose task and formal power it was to invest the chosen man with the imperial powers, a role which at least theoretically carried with it the power to refuse to do so; and the people, whose role was largely passive but who had to be involved, even if only as spectators, in order that the succession was seen to be public and publicly acceptable. In addition, the presence of the Guard and the army mutinies on the death of Augustus were signs that the soldiers, whose units were organizationally descended from Julius Caesar's own troops, would need to be involved as well in some way.

The ceremonial installation of Tiberius in the Senate was not strictly necessary, since he already had all the powers needed for assuming sole power, but it was required to convince the public that the thing had been done properly. Tiberius himself had hesitated, or delayed, in assuming full control, supposedly in the hope that the Senate might be induced to take a share in the burden; more probably it was to compel the Senate to insist publicly that he take on more of the powers. Like his insistence on Augustus' public announcement of Tiberius' own status as heir, this forced the Senate into a public declaration it could not revoke.[1]

There was thus a disjunction in the various elements involved in a succession, or at least there should be. The choice of the man and the award of the powers should properly precede the installation ceremony, and should have been publicized. This would ensure a smooth takeover of authority and eliminate possible confusion. Above all, the chosen successor needed to be publicly identified before his predecessor died; if he was not and the choice remained open, there was no obvious procedure for finding a new emperor other than a discussion in the Senate, and probably a vote there.

At a distance from Rome the oath-taking was repeated in all the army camps, and in all the cities and the administrative centres of the Empire. Here was clearly a danger point if the successor was not clearly signalled in advance; the procedure of oath-taking might be pre-empted by an ambitious interloper. Augustus had also, posthumously, added one more element to the process: potential alternative successors could be killed out of hand. It was clearly going to be more convenient to eliminate challengers and potential challengers before the emperor's death; the potential for killing was considerable. The potential for disruption by the untimely death of an emperor was even greater; this was the inevitable penalty of monarchic rule.

The will of the deceased emperor would be found and read, if there was one. Augustus had been very careful to specify that all the soldiers, the citizens, and the senators should be rewarded. Of these groups, the riots by the German and the Pannonian legions had shown that it was the army that had to be attended to most carefully. Tiberius, an experienced commander, had first ensured that the Praetorian Guard at Rome was his, and only then had he attended to the Senate and the citizens. The Guard was clearly vital since it was the only body of professional troops in Italy. The armies on the frontiers had been eventually quieted by attention paid to the grievances of the soldiers and by the gift of money from Augustus' personal fortune, in accordance with his will.

Mortality ensured that, as soon as an emperor began to reign, the question of his successor became insistent. Augustus' long quest was partly responsible, but the main reason was that life was short and emperors were very vulnerable. Tiberius was already over the age of 50 at his accession; that he would live to reign for another twenty-three years was unexpected. These men lived in public, they met all sorts of people and they had many enemies. Tiberius survived a plot as early as in his first year.[2]

For Tiberius there were two ready-made heirs, his own son Drusus and his nephew and adopted son Germanicus, both of whom were adult and had shown their loyalty to him in facing down the mutinous soldiers, and both were capably employed in conquering Germans. Furthermore, both men by now had sons of their own. Drusus was married to the former wife of Gaius Caesar, Livilla, the daughter of Tiberius' brother, and they had a daughter, Livia Julia, and twin sons; all three of them were still children. Germanicus was married to Agrippina, the daughter of Agrippa and Julia, and so a granddaughter of Augustus, a fact that she never let anyone forget; she was therefore a sister of Gaius and Lucius Caesar, and of Agrippa Postumus, all now dead. (Had she been male, she would in all probability have been emperor, or already murdered.) She and Germanicus had six children: three boys – Nero Caesar, Lucius Caesar and Gaius, this last called Caligula by the soldiers from his being exhibited to them in small versions of the soldiers' boots – and three daughters: Agrippina, Drusilla and Julia Livilla. The two eldest children of the two families, Nero Caesar and Livia Julia, were soon married to each other. (Note that the intermarriages within the family were continuing.)

There was thus a considerable bank of blood relatives on which Tiberius could draw in organizing the succession, spread over three generations (and there was also the disregarded Claudius, Germanicus' younger brother.) However, as Tiberius lived on into his 60s and then into his 70s, he faced the same problem that had plagued Augustus. The initial long list of possible heirs that existed in AD 14 was gradually reduced in size over his reign until there remained only two.

The process of reducing that list was, as with Augustus' list, a chapter of accidents, illnesses and intrigues. Germanicus died on an Eastern tour in AD 19, leaving his vengeful widow Agrippina and their six children, who thus now became much more likely possibilities for the succession, not least in the view of Agrippina. Until his death, Germanicus had been the most likely choice. He had been consul for the second time, along with Tiberius, in AD 18, whereas Drusus had only one consulship to his name. Also Germanicus was on a major political and diplomatic journey through the East (just as Tiberius and Gaius Caesar had been in the past) when he died. Rumours of murder, of course, circulated.

Tiberius had been using Drusus as his commander in Germany (a task Germanicus had already undertaken with some success) and he triumphed in AD 20 after the conclusion of the war in Illyricum. Next year, if not before, he was clearly marked out as Tiberius' new heir. He was consul in 21, along with his father Drusus, for the second time, Tiberius for the fourth, and was now nominated as the chosen successor. Tacitus' summary of Tiberius' letter of recommendation to the Senate is a concise statement of the qualities required for the future emperor: he had had 'eight years' probation, including the repression of mutineers, completion of wars, a triumph, and two consulships', so that he 'knew the work he was to share', and in addition he was married with three children and had reached the age at which Tiberius had assumed similar responsibilities.[3]

So, in the year after his consulship Drusus was invested by the Senate with the tribunician power. The proconsular power is not mentioned and was probably omitted; it could be awarded when needed, or perhaps it was now subsumed in his position as recognized heir. Then, next year, in 23, he died; it was later alleged that he had been murdered on the orders of L. Aelius Sejanus, the emperor's confidant and Commander of the Guard, by means of a slow-acting poison. However, accusations against Sejanus after his death are hardly firm evidence, and a slow-acting poison's symptoms may be the same as those of any number of diseases. Drusus had certainly been Sejanus' enemy and competitor, and had complained that Tiberius heeded the confidant more than the heir; the very fact that Drusus uttered these sentiments aloud suggests that discretion was not his major virtue; he was also said to be all too fond of wine. His death was hardly unusual; it was just another case of a prince who died while still young.

The series of appointments and adoptions arranged originally by Augustus in AD 4 after the death of C. Caesar and the return of Tiberius to favour had clearly been an attempt to organize a succession for the next two or three generations. (See Genealogical Table IV.) Indeed, Tiberius' position

V   The Succession to Tiberius.

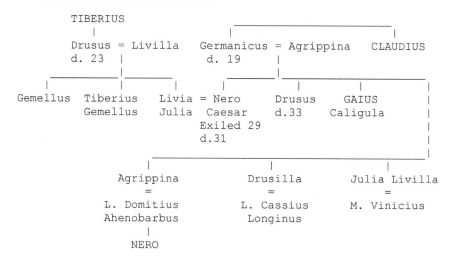

was rather like that intended for Agrippa, as 'emperor-regent' until the next generation, specifically Germanicus, was mature enough to take over. It is certainly the sort of long-range scheme that Augustus was capable of devising, though by then it should have been obvious that chance intervened all too readily. If he had so devised it, the plan was now in ruins.

Tiberius now faced the same problem as Augustus had repeatedly encountered. (For Tiberius' possible selections, see Genealogical Table V.) Germanicus had been adopted, and then Drusus had been specifically nominated, but their deaths had followed soon after their nominations. Even before Drusus' nomination, Tiberius had been looking, as Augustus had been, to the next generation. In 20 Nero Caesar, Germanicus' eldest son, was promised a five-year advancement in the age at which he could stand for office, and his younger brother Drusus Caesar was now linked with him in this. After Germanicus' death Drusus had acted as their protector, so that while he lived, the outline of the succession was reasonably clear to all; on his death, however, the presumptive heirs were still only children, and so were too young to be considered as successors. Germanicus' eldest son was 14 in AD 23, so an adult protector would clearly be needed if Tiberius died, and he was 65 in that year.

It is possible that Tiberius saw his Guard Commander, Sejanus, in the Agrippa-role of emperor-regent and protector of the heir for a time. Sejanus had spotted a means to power by using the Guard, which he concentrated into a single fortified barracks overlooking Rome, and he gained Tiberius' trust as few others ever did. Sejanus' power certainly expanded in the later 20s, and he set his sights on greater things. He was widely disliked in the Senate, of which he was not a member until Tiberius awarded him a consulship, and he had to operate mainly through his imperial contact.

Whether he really contributed to the successive removals of the potential heirs is not always clear, but suspicions existed and grew. Of the possible heirs after Drusus' death, the sons of Germanicus and Agrippina were now the eldest, but Drusus' son was also clearly available. The steady elimination of these children until only one was left could easily be blamed on the powerful and unpopular Sejanus, even if it was not true. One of the twin sons of Drusus died in the year after his father, but his twin Tiberius Gemellus was still alive when the old emperor died in 37. The two eldest sons of Germanicus were removed, first Nero Caesar into exile in 29, where he died a year or so later. Nero Caesar had been seen by all as the likely heir, and Tiberius had indicated as much in a letter to the Senate in 25 when he indicated to Sejanus that he might be his choice as regent.[4] However, Nero had become involved in a plot against Sejanus and this led to the boy's exile. He might also have died a natural death, even if he had not been in exile.

Sejanus himself fell from power in dramatic fashion two years later. Tiberius sent his new Guard Commander to the Senate to read out a list of Sejanus' misdeeds, on the day when Sejanus himself was expected to be given new powers; he and the Senate were taken by surprise, but while the first was dismayed, the senators were jubilant. Then in 33 Drusus Caesar was condemned to death by starvation. In all this only Drusus Caesar was actually killed, perhaps because Tiberius came to the conclusion that he was unacceptable as his heir. He had the curses that the starving man shouted as he died read out to the Senate, presumably believing this would convince the senators that he really was an unsuitable candidate. In fact, they read more like the uncomprehending rage of an innocent man wrongly condemned.

The series of deaths seems to replicate hideously those under Augustus. Sejanus was held responsible for the removal of Nero Caesar and the disgrace of Drusus Caesar, but it was only when he began a similar denigratory campaign against their younger brother, Gaius Caligula, aged 17 in 31, that Tiberius decided to remove him. The emperor was then left with only two possible candidates for the succession: Gaius and his cousin Tiberius Gemellus. Yet at the same time that this 'dynastic catastrophe', as it has been called, was taking place[5] in the form of the long line of royal family deaths that stretched from AD 19 (Germanicus) to 33 (Drusus Caesar), the emperor was also acting to preserve and increase the number of political heirs. He took Gaius and Ti. Gemellus to live with him on Capri, which removed them from the intrigues, backbiting and plots of Rome, and may thereby have preserved their lives. However, it also prevented them from developing their political, military and administrative skills which they could only develop by living and working in the city and with the army.

Tiberius had clearly modified the requirements in an heir that he had listed when recommending his own son to the Senate ten years before. Now there could be no question of an extensive training in Roman politics or in military affairs; the city was too dangerous. After the deaths of the children of Germanicus he had decided that keeping his heirs alive was now the priority, and that only he could do it. In contrast to Augustus, who had faced the same problem, he now had no Tiberius- or Agrippa-figure to rely on; he had to do the job himself.

The womenfolk of the imperial family were, however, also attended to, their marriages being clearly arranged for dynastic purposes. The elder Agrippina, Germanicus' widow, died in 30, still angry, just as her two eldest sons were being brought down by Sejanus. All three of her daughters were then still alive, and as they reached the appropriate age, the emperor chose husbands for them. The eldest, another Agrippina (usually called Agrippina II) was married in 29, the year her brother Nero was exiled, to a representative of the high Republican nobility, Cn. Domitius Ahenobarbus. He was also a grandson of Octavia and M. Antonius, so this was a marriage within the extended imperial family and between people of equal rank. The other girls, Drusilla and Julia Livilla, were both married in 33, but this time their husbands were of much less distinguished origin. Drusilla was married to L. Cassius Longinus, consul in 30, a noble family perhaps, but as a descendant of the assassin of 44 BC, hardly a competitor for the supreme power; in addition, he was plebeian, and was the younger of two brothers and the lesser of the two in reputation. Julia Livilla was married to M. Vinicius, of a family only fairly recently consular, the son of one of Augustus' generals, an orator but of no particular distinction or descent. There was also the sister of Ti. Gemellus, Julia, Tiberius' own granddaughter, who was the widow of the deceased Nero Drusus. She was now remarried, this time to a man of even less note than Longinus or Vinicius, C. Rubellius Blandus; he was elderly (he had been consul as far back as AD 15) and the grandson of an *eques* (knight).[6]

These marriage choices were no doubt quite deliberately made by Tiberius with the intention of removing these women, who had to operate politically through their husbands, from political affairs. It did not wholly work, for the proximity to imperial affairs that their husbands had achieved by these marriages stimulated ambitious thoughts in at least one of them. So the intended reduction in the women's interest in the succession was entirely denied by the increase in their husbands' interest; the women may well also have felt insulted by their apparent demotion. For the present, however, the undistinguished husbands largely removed the women from consideration as political players, and any children would not be adult for many years. This policy thus did succeed in concentrating the emperor's succession intentions on the two cousins, indeed specifically on Gaius.

Tiberius was fully aware that once he was dead and Gaius was emperor, the life of Ti. Gemellus was effectively forfeit. He was destined for the same fate as Agrippa Postumus and for the same reason. The old emperor is recorded as weeping as he clutched the boy to him, and crying to Gaius, 'You will kill him.'[7] This was not a personal instruction, but a statement of the political necessity that Gaius would be under. Tiberius himself had largely escaped blame for the killing of Agrippa Postumus by scattering that blame over Augustus, the centurion who did the deed, and the 'confidant', though he did not prevent the starving to death of Drusus Caesar for exactly the same reason as was given for Agrippa's killing: his unsuitability to be emperor. He could not afford, however, to kill either Gaius – who he clearly favoured as his heir – or Ti. Gemellus, in case one of them died before him. So many princes had died in untimely fashion that it was clearly necessary to have at least one spare one available.

Gaius had therefore emerged as the emperor's choice for his successor in the same way that Tiberius had for Augustus; he was the only candidate still alive and adult when the old emperor died. The difference was that Tiberius had by that time had long experience of all the intricacies of the Roman political system, whereas Gaius had effectively had none, apart from the experience of living in the closed world of the court of a world-weary paranoid recluse secluded on the island of Capri. To be sure, it took a certain skill to survive this experience; he is thought to have had a hand in the downfall of Sejanus, though since he was no more than 18 at the time this would seem to be excessively precocious of him. Yet the experience of years in Capri was not the sort that would help in manipulating the Senate, the magistrates, the governors or to command the army, for which charm, courage and an outgoing political intelligence were much more useful. Within the group around Tiberius he was clearly the heir, and was recognized as such, and as the old emperor's strength faded, the allegiance of those present with him shifted towards the obvious successor. Tiberius did not actually designate Gaius specifically, nor did he arrange for him to be awarded the necessary imperial powers, but then he did not need to. Ti. Gemellus was the only alternative and he was still too young, younger even than Gaius. When Tiberius finally died, possibly assisted into death by the Guard Commander Q. Naevius Sertorius Macro (another beneficiary of Sejanus' fall), Gaius automatically became *princeps* without question.[8]

Gaius therefore became emperor at Tiberius' death-bed, not by the nomination of Tiberius, though his preference was clearly known, but by the collective decision of the courtiers present in the death chamber, led by Macro the Guard Commander. The Senate and the army were presented with a *fait accompli*, and, while the soldiers, at least the legions in Germany, had fond memories of 'Caligula', the Senate was surely less than happy about the situation and any apprehensions the senators had were, of course, fully justified.

So the new *princeps* took power without having been awarded the institutional offices that were required to operate the political system, without being nominated by the preceding emperor, and without any training for the office. Tiberius had already had those offices – tribunician and proconsular powers, now simply described as the 'imperial powers' – when Augustus died, and he had also gone through a long and careful programme of public acceptance, resolutions and votes in the Senate, public oath-taking, and so on. This time matters were organized very differently.

The Guard Commander, Macro, did the organizing, and he had clearly thought out the problems beforehand. Once again, as with Augustus, the emperor had co-operated by reaching a great age and then dying slowly, so that such arrangements could be made. Macro had contacted certain senators and discussed the matter with them well in advance. This included one of the consuls of the year, a distinguished legal expert, Cn. Acerronius Proculus, who worked quickly to pre-empt any possible opposition, particularly in the Senate.[9]

In the event the Senate as a whole was more than pleased to be rid of Tiberius. He had shown his contempt for senatorial servility too often. Senators co-operated fully in the process designed by Macro and Proculus. On the night following Tiberius' death, Macro sent letters to the provincial governors reporting the death, and reporting the accession of Gaius, who was provided with the title *imperator*,[10] by which he was saluted by the soldiers at Misenum as soon as the death took place. This was no longer simply a title awarded either by the soldiers of a victorious Roman army or by the Senate in recognition of a victory, but had become an alternative title to *princeps*, indicating the word it eventually became in later languages: 'Emperor'. Language was shifting to accommodate the realities.

Note that Macro did all this once Tiberius' death was certain, and without consulting anyone other than, presumably, Gaius himself. Yet it is particularly significant that his letters to provincial governors and army commanders were accepted by their recipients, and that the news they contained was acted on at once. We know of two widely-separated reactions to the news. In Jerusalem, the governor of Syria immediately took oaths of allegiance to the new ruler as soon as he received Macro's letter; in Spain, the governor of Lusitania did the same.[11] Neither of them, and presumably no other governor or commander, waited for the official word from the Senate.

The Senate, however, also acted quickly. Two days after Tiberius' death, on 18 March 37, it was convened and immediately annulled Tiberius' will. This was clearly done by prearrangement – the lawyer Proculus who was consul at the time was obviously involved – and was done because Tiberius had made Gaius and Ti. Gemellus joint heirs to his estate, perhaps in an attempt to preserve Gemellus' life, though given his youth it was certain that Gaius would be in charge. (The problem had not arisen with Augustus' will because he had left the largest part of his estate to Tiberius, and the rest to his wife Livia, Tiberius' mother, whence it was eventually to go to Tiberius; later imperial wills were so regularly annulled that emperors stopped making them.) The annulment of the will, however, also involved the cancellation of his bequests to other individuals; Gaius solved the problem by giving the bequests as personal gifts and adding a bonus on top.

By doing this, the Senate in theory had also annulled Gaius' position as *princeps/imperator*. In fact, the Senate had not had any say in the succession. Macro's letters had bypassed the Senate on the way to the army and the provinces, and the fact that it was the Guard Commander who was orchestrating the succession meant that the section of the Guard that was stationed with the emperor in Campania and at Misenum, the naval base, took the oath of allegiance as soon as Macro could administer it; the Senate was thus not involved.

What is more, any possible objections in the Senate were also pre-empted by the popular reaction. Gaius repeated the slow journey from Campania to Rome that Tiberius had made, walking behind Tiberius' coffin dressed in mourning, but this time the public reaction was joyful and Gaius was greeted with cheers and acclamations along the whole route. This public acceptance tended to pre-empt any discussion or objections the Senate might have indulged in. So when Gaius reached Rome on 28 March and met the Senate, the whole set of powers and titles that Augustus had spent decades sorting through to achieve the correct and judicious balance of powers was granted to Gaius in a single act.[12]

This set of events was similar to those that had occurred when Tiberius succeeded Augustus – indeed, the funeral procession was deliberately copied – but the individual elements came in a significantly different order. Tiberius did not need a grant by the Senate, which for Gaius came last. However, Tiberius had made sure that his very first act after Augustus died had been to give the watchword to the Guard, which ensured that he was in command, and this in effect was what had happened when Macro ensured that the Guard at Misenum hailed Gaius as *imperator*, and told the generals and governors of the succession. Tiberius and Gaius, therefore, both had a keen appreciation of the immediate realities of power: the Guard first, then the Senate. The popular acclamations were a bonus but not essential, though they had proved useful in persuading the Senate, to which a certain deference was shown in the voting, rather than the assumption, of the final legal imperial powers. The order of events therefore had been acceptance by the Guard, then by the people, and then the imperial powers were voted by the Senate.

Gaius was accepted, but it was because of his proximity to the dying emperor that he had been nominated, and his elevation had turned on Macro's control of the Guard more than his acceptance by the Senate. This sequence, much clearer in Gaius' accession than in Tiberius', makes it certain that it was still control of the army that was the vital element. Macro had, in fact, carried through a skilful *coup d'état*. It was possible to do so because neither Augustus nor Tiberius had legislated for a clear succession procedure. This was Augustus' fault. He had refrained from establishing an imperial regime by law, preferring a 'restoration of the Republic', and this meant that the position of emperor remained legally anomalous. It followed that no clear legal procedure for the succession could exist, only precedents whose elements could be juggled as circumstances dictated. The army, the Senate, the family, the dead emperor all had their say, and important men such as Macro could therefore seize on the moment of confusion at the death of an emperor to impose their own choice. One wonders if the Senate, given a free choice, would actually have chosen Gaius – one rather hopes not – but the point is that they did not get the opportunity to choose.

Having thus cleverly achieved power, Gaius then proceeded to make himself so generally disliked that plots to kill him swirled around the court almost from his arrival in Rome. One of the elements in the conspiratorial atmosphere must have been a feeling that Gaius' accession was less than legitimate. He might have received the necessary powers, been the apparent choice of the previous emperor, and been accepted by the various acclamations, but he had no government experience of any kind before becoming emperor (at the age of 25) and he was almost wholly unknown, except by name, to most of the senatorial class. While Tiberius had gone out of his way in the early years of his reign to respect the Senate and in his later years had at least made a show of keeping the senators informed about events, Gaius had no real conception of the importance of this attitude. The sequence of events at his accession, where the Senate's role came last, will have confirmed that ignorance. He did make early gestures of respect towards the Senate, but this attentiveness did not last. So, to a sense that he had somehow become their ruler in part illegitimately was added the spectacle of a man who disdained the Senate, and who believed that he was an autocrat. In this belief he was, of course, quite correct, but in Rome at that time to act as an autocrat was politically inept.

His murder, after a reign of less than four years, was therefore not at all unwelcome. He had alienated the soldiers by ludicrous and insulting behaviour during the supposed preparation for the invasion of Britain, where he abandoned the expedition and instead ordered the army to pick up seashells; he was so careless as to repeatedly insult in public a member of his own Guard, Cassius Chaerea. Chaerea, increasingly annoyed at the emperor's insults, sensed the atmosphere of disgust and contempt that had developed and of which Gaius was apparently unaware; who would dare tell him? After discussing it with others of the Guard, he killed the emperor in a public corridor at the games.[13] This was not, therefore, quite so spontaneous an act as it might have seemed, nor was it merely an act of pique at being insulted. Behind Chaerea were not only some of his fellow Guardsmen, but others more highly-placed. He was actually the instrument of a full-blown conspiracy aimed at the emperor's assassination.[14]

The conspiracy also involved a number of senators including C. Cassius Longinus, the brother-in-law of Gaius' sister Drusilla, and M. Annius Vinicianus, a nephew of M. Vinicius, who was married to Gaius' sister Julia

Livilla. Both marriages had been arranged by Tiberius but, far from the wives sliding out of the political limelight because of their less than prominent husbands as had probably been intended, the husbands and their families had their political interests and ambitions sharpened and enhanced. Several other men were on the fringes of the plot, or had heard of it, and it is possible that Gaius' uncle and nearest relative Claudius had also heard something. There were so many plots and rumours of plots in the year before the actual assassination that every senator would have known that something was going on, whether or not it was the truth. It seems likely that, even if Chaerea had failed to take action, or had failed in his plot, another plot would have succeeded. In fact, Chaerea only wounded the emperor; several other men immediately joined in, and he died from multiple wounds.

Gaius' death was quickly followed by that of his wife and infant daughter, murdered by Guardsmen so that no focus of loyalty to him should survive, which is an interesting commentary on the force of heredity in Roman politics. Gaius' German Guard, loyal even after death, hunted for the perpetrators for a time and killed some of them. The men soon calmed down when they saw the obvious confusion and distress of many of the people as they heard the news of the emperor's death; he had not been unpopular with everyone, only among the powerful.

The main perpetrators had been Guardsmen, abetted by some senators, but as soon as the deed was done, this political alliance ended. The Guards searched the palace and found Claudius in hiding.[15] This is portrayed at times as a fortuitous event, even a joke. Claudius had long been assumed to be so physically and mentally disabled as not to be considered as a successor, but it is more likely that he was the deliberate choice of the Guard, possibly in advance of the assassination, who would now want a new emperor to be of the imperial family, and a man who would be beholden to them, and so in their hands, as Macro had clearly intended Gaius to be.

The Senate met and debated what to do. There were the usual hopes among a few that the Republic could be revived, but this notion had no real support. Instead the debate centred, reasonably enough, on who should be the next emperor. It was apparently known that the Guard had control of Claudius, so he was one candidate. Two tribunes were sent to suggest that Claudius should pay heed to the Senate's wishes rather than those of the Guardsmen, and to invite him to attend their meeting; he was, of course, a senator himself. Claudius sent a carefully neutral and diplomatic reply, saying that he was forcibly detained and could not attend the Senate. This may be thought to be a refusal to trust himself to the Senate out of fear, but it was certainly not a proclamation of himself as emperor. He and the Guard were theoretically leaving the decision to the Senate.

This all happened on the day of the murder. After a night to think things over, another meeting of the Senate took place, with probably no more than 100 senators present, though whether the missing men had fled or had not appeared because of fear or were simply not near enough to Rome to attend cannot be known. The meeting discussed the possible successors. The notion of a return to the Republic had now vanished. Apart from Claudius, already declared as a candidate, three others either put themselves forward or were suggested as possible emperors. All three were connected with the imperial family: M. Vinicius, the husband of Julia Livilla and so the dead man's brother-in-law; Vinicius' nephew, L. Annius Vinicianus; and D. Valerius Asiaticus, who was married to a sister of Gaius' former wife Lollia Paullina, who had connections to several old noble families. All three of these men had probably been involved in the assassination plot. (For the connections of the candidates see Genealogical Table VI.)

VI   The Candidates after Gaius' Death.

(a)   *The Royal Family.*

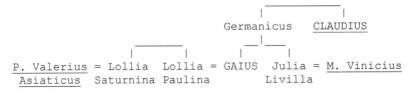

(b)   *The Vinician Connection.*

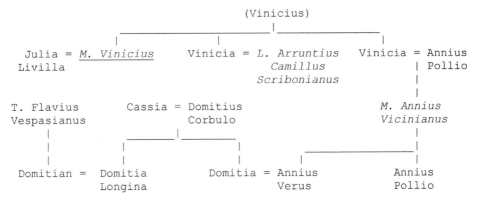

Candidates/Claimants are Underlined; plotters are in Italics.

It was, however, difficult to take any of these men, apart from Claudius, seriously as possible emperors. Claudius' close family relationship to Gaius and Tiberius guaranteed him serious consideration. Asiaticus came from Narbonensian Gaul, the first from his province to become consul (in 35), but to the senators this was a clear bar to his candidacy; Vinicius, though a consul (in 30), was of small account and had been chosen by Tiberius as a husband for Julia Livilla for that very reason; his nephew Vinicianus may well not have been a fully declared candidate at all but may just have been Vinicius' promoter (and heir). The absence of other candidates – there were surely senators who were fully capable of running the Empire, but who were simply not considered – shows that it was considered necessary that some sort of relationship with the imperial family was required for a man to be thought emperor material; *capax imperii*, as Tacitus put it. In that case, Claudius clearly had the edge. Asiaticus had another claim, however, for he had confronted a crowd outside the Senate House the day before. The crowd had been angry at the death of Gaius, who had retained a good deal of popular appeal. Asiaticus had successfully calmed them down, even though he had been asked if he was involved in the plot and had replied, ambiguously, that he wished he had been. In the Senate many may have seen him as a popular candidate with the implicit threat of a crowd storming the Senate in his favour.

Claudius was in the strongest position because he was much more clearly of the imperial family and because, after a night in the barracks of the Guard, he had made a good agreement with the Guardsmen. He was also careful to send respectful but firm messages to the Senate, promising good government if the Senate had accepted him but vengeance if not; the Guard would be quite capable of murdering the rump of senators who were still meeting. Only one-sixth of the 600 members were attending the meeting, so the Senate's warning to Claudius the night before not to conduct a coup rang hollow; this was exactly what the Senate itself seemed to be doing.

In the end the Senate accepted him, and face was saved all round by his going in solemn procession, protected by the Guard, to the Senate House, where he was welcomed and invested with the imperial powers. At least the Senate could be sure that they had an emperor who was fully familiar with their proceedings and with the imperial system. Claudius had repeatedly asked Tiberius to be allowed to stand for office, but was always put off; then Gaius had made him consul with him in 37, and he was clearly an active politician, already well-known in Roman political circles, who cannot have taken too seriously the stories of his disability and unsuitability.[16]

Gaius had thus to a certain degree cleared the way for Claudius to succeed him. While he had not indicated any one man as a designated successor, not surprisingly since he was still in his 20s, he had removed at least two possible competitors. Ti. Gemellus, as was to be expected, did not survive the first year of Gaius' rule, being killed around the end of 37, even though Gaius had formally adopted him with the implication that he was next in line.[17] The second husband of Drusilla, Gaius' sister, M. Aemilius Lepidus, was at one point, while the emperor was ill, in some way designated his heir. When Gaius recovered, Lepidus was a marked man; a designated successor had a vested interest in compassing an emperor's death and he was killed in 39 as part of Gaius' reply to a fairly widespread conspiracy designed to remove him.[18] As a result only Claudius of the bloodlines of Augustus and Tiberius survived. If a hereditary succession was expected, he was the only possible heir to Gaius.

The succession system that Augustus had organized, which had worked with Tiberius and had been put under enormous strain by the accession of Gaius, had almost broken down under the impact of Gaius' assassination. The system in part depended on the successor being publicly known and acknowledged by the ruler before the latter's death. Gaius had at least been publicly assumed to be Tiberius' heir, and had lived with him at Capri for six years, even if a formal designation had not been made. However, Gaius' gestures towards nominating a successor, Ti. Gemellus and M. Lepidus, were both swiftly retracted. In the event, between them, the Guard and the Senate reached the conclusion that Claudius, Gaius' nearest and almost only male relative, was the proper successor. The negotiations between them lasted only a day and a night, and, despite the assassins having had no candidate available before the murder, the crisis was effectively over within two days.[19] So it could be claimed that, if one was an optimist, even in such an extreme case, the Augustan system had survived and had operated properly.

Of course, it had not. Neither Gaius nor Claudius had been properly trained for the office; both had been candidates of a faction within the Praetorian Guard; both had been foisted on the Senate, the rest of the army, and the Empire without consultation beyond the few Guardsmen at Misenum and in the barracks at Rome. The Senate, supposedly the real fount of power to whom Tiberius and Augustus had regularly expressed respect, had been sidelined in both cases. If the accession of Gaius had been in a disguised *coup d'état*, that of Claudius was a visible one. The one aspect of the Augustan scheme that had survived was that both men were members of the imperial family, and there seems to have been no question that candidates not from the family were universally excluded.

The accession of the new emperor did not, therefore, mean that Augustus' scheme, now threadbare, would continue to survive much longer. Claudius was a man in his 50s whose disability made him ridiculous to some and an easy target for others. Vinicius, the other plausible candidate of 41, did not give up but apparently realized that he needed a figurehead of greater aristocratic stature than himself, such as his brother-in-law L. Arruntius Camillus Scribonianus (see Genealogical Table VI), who was now governor of Dalmatia. In 42 Scribonianus sent a message to the new emperor, ordering him to cease to rule and to lay down his offices. This quixotic opening of an intended coup presupposes two things: that Scribonianus believed that his command of the two legions in his province outweighed Claudius' control of the Guard – and certainly his troops outnumbered the Guard, probably by at least two to one – and that the rest of the army would stand aside in the crisis: and, second, that he believed he had senatorial support. (It also indicated Scribonianus' political naivety, of course.) It emerged that the trigger for the rising was a message sent to Scribonianus by L. Annius Vinicianus in Rome.[20]

Scribonianus certainly had wide senatorial connections, and M. Vinicius had been deeply implicated in the successful plot against Gaius the year before. Vinicianus had also either suggested his uncle as a candidate for emperor against Claudius' candidature, or had suggested himself (or perhaps both). Between them these men clearly felt that their support in the Senate, combined with Scribonianus' forces, would ensure success against Claudius and the Guard. It failed because they were wrong on both counts: Scribonianus' two legions, except for a few officers, came out for Claudius, thus removing the ground on which he stood, and the Senate as a whole was hostile. After all, it was only a year since the Senate had deliberated and had accepted Claudius after a reasonable discussion, in which Vinicius and Vinicianus had been considered and rejected; there was no reason why the Senate as a whole should have changed its mind in the interval.

Scribonianus was an Arruntius by adoption only; his biological father was L. Furius Camillus. He was married to Vinicia, the sister of M. Vinicius and the aunt of Vinicianus. A comment attributed to Augustus, that his father L. Arruntius was a man capable of being emperor (*capax imperii*), may well have been the source of Scribonianus' ambition. Vinicius' marriage to Julia Livilla, and so his own association with the imperial family, fairly distant though it was, was presumably what made him put himself forward as an alternative to Claudius in 41. So if Vinicius had failed, maybe Scribonianus, with a descent a good deal older and more noble than either Vinicius or Claudius, might succeed.

The connections of the plotters suggest very strongly that it was high personal pride combined with their distant imperial connections that drove these men into their plots; quite probably it was the consciousness of his noble descent that was one of the main elements in Scribonianus' attempted coup. It would not be the last time that such an attitude resulted in such an action. Also perhaps there was a perception that if a disabled character like Claudius could be made emperor, so could they. Scribonianus did have some support from the intransigent Republicans, but a revival of the Republic by this time was impossible, and Scribonianus aimed to be emperor, not to dismantle the imperial system.

Given such presuppositions, the *pronunciamento* of Scribonianus was by no means as hopeless as it now seems. He had the connections, the origins, the command of an army and the personal ambition which are all factors that were required; as a provincial governor he had the administrative and perhaps the military experience that both Gaius and Claudius lacked. If his legions had supported him he could have been a convincing candidate, but of course, it was a failure of his troops to go along with him – that is, that they were loyal to the Julio-Claudian dynasty and to the decisions of the Senate – which was the crucial matter. The disguised primacy of the army in the imperial succession was confirmed.

Claudius thus survived this challenge without difficulty, but he was the only member of the imperial family available and he was an elderly man. He had already been married three times. His son had died in an accident, and a daughter was also deceased; his other daughter Antonia was old enough to be married soon after he became emperor; and Claudius' current wife, Messalina, gave birth to a son three weeks after the accession. He was named Tiberius Claudius Caesar Germanicus, later also called Britannicus. They also had a daughter, Octavia. Later, after Messalina's disgrace, he married Agrippina (II), the former wife of L. Domitius Ahenobarbus and the daughter of his brother Germanicus; hence she was Claudius' own niece. By then he was almost 60, but his new wife had a son of her own, L. Domitius Ahenobarbus, the later Emperor Nero. As a result, when Claudius died in 54, there were two male children in line to succeed (as when Tiberius died); of the two imperial daughters, Antonia was married to Cn. Pompeius Magnus who was killed in 47, and then to Faustus Cornelius Sulla Felix, though she apparently had no children by either husband; Octavia was married to her stepbrother Nero. Two male children: it was eerily reminiscent of the succession of Gaius.

In addition, there were more distant imperial family branches which, as Vinicius had shown, had to be taken into account. There was Rubellius Plautus, who was the son of Julia, Tiberius' granddaughter. She had been married to Rubellius Blandus who, like Vinicius, had been assumed to be of no account, but as the imperial line thinned, any imperial descent became important. Then there was M. Junius Silanus and his two brothers, grandsons of another Julia, Augustus' granddaughter. Also there was the family of M. Licinius Crassus Frugi, one of whose sons was the Pompeius Magnus who married Antonia in 41; he had three brothers. The family counted descent from the triumvir Pompeius and had great, even arrogant, family pride, though this only made them normal among the Roman nobility. However, to consider these men, Rubellius, the Crassi, the Junii, as part of the imperial family was only to emphasize the shortage of direct male heirs. The dynasty essentially depended, when Claudius died in 54, on his son Britannicus, aged 14, and his stepson Nero, aged 16.

Once again, as in 37, the succession was clear, though, also as in 37, there could have been competition from others. The two adolescent boys had equal claims. Nero was the older, a descendant of Augustus and of Octavia, and who had already given evidence of competence and intelligence; Britannicus was the biological son of the late emperor, descended in both parents from Octavia, but younger than Nero. This was not decisive since Nero was also Claudius' son by adoption, and so the senior of the two by age. The decisive factor, in fact, was that Nero's mother Agrippina was wholly determined that her son should rule, and it was she who organized the succession.

As Claudius died, Agrippina prevented Britannicus and his sisters from gaining access to their father, but contacted the Guard Commander, Sex. Afranius Burrus, who was clearly fully aware of what was going on and what was required. Burrus escorted Nero to the battalion of the Guard that was on duty, had him saluted as emperor, and then took him to the barracks. Nero made a short speech, promising rewards, and was acclaimed. He then went on to the Senate, where he was voted the imperial powers.[21]

The whole process might have been organized in advance, but it is clear that the pattern was that of Claudius' accession rather than that of Tiberius or Gaius, and not only because Claudius, like Gaius, died at Rome. The prominence of the Guard is emphasized because the accession was, once again, in the nature of a *coup d'état*. Claudius' will was suppressed (just as Tiberius' had been), and Britannicus was deliberately kept in ignorance of what was going on. It is probable that Claudius intended the two boys to succeed jointly; it is certain that Agrippina was just as determined to see that Nero succeeded alone. In the event, the decisive factor was that Agrippina was alive and Claudius was dead.

Nero and his mother Agrippina were determined to rule. A preliminary move was the marriage of Nero with Octavia, his stepsister. Britannicus did not survive more than a year; he was too close to the throne, had as good an hereditary claim to it as Nero, and the court was, for the time being, under the control of Agrippina. Her earlier career had demonstrated a steely decisiveness that had brought her only son to the supreme position, and it will have been clear to her from the first that Britannicus could well be the ideal figurehead for an intriguing person of her own type. Some of the Guardsmen who first proclaimed Nero emperor are said to have asked where Britannicus was. So Britannicus inevitably went the way of Agrippa Postumus and Ti. Gemellus and Gaius' infant daughter. By then the dynasty depended solely on Nero, and he and Octavia had no children.

This situation simultaneously weakened and strengthened Nero's own position. The lack of an heir rendered plots and intrigues with the aim of assassinating him pointless, unless a non-imperial man was chosen, but no obvious candidate existed, or, while Nero lived, was likely to survive. The absence of any heir made Nero's own person rather more valuable; if he died one possible result would be a civil war. The end of the Republic was in no-one's actual memory now, but it was a well-worn historical topic of fear and horror. All aristocratic families had suffered in the civil war, and its horrors were fully understood. Yet for a dynasty to depend on a single life was clearly overall a source of weakness and might encourage the more distant family members to fancy their chances. The obvious parallel, for those with historical inclinations, was the situation among the Macedonians when Alexander the Great died: thirty years of civil warfare and the destruction of his Empire followed.

For a time this situation held its balance. During the 'five good years' the emperor's imperial duties were essentially carried out by his mother; then, when he had contrived her death, by his former tutor and the chief of the Guard, Seneca and Burrus, in co-operation with the Senate. Nero's assumption of sole power was indicated by the death or exile (or both) of

Seneca and Burrus, and by his divorce of Octavia, closely followed by her murder. He married Poppaea, whose earlier husband, L. Salvius Otho, was despatched to govern Lusitania, as far from Rome as he could be sent. The imperial marriage produced a daughter. Yet, like every other emperor, Nero's paranoia grew: threats, real and imagined, and possible competitors, real or imagined, were progressively eliminated. Poppaea was murdered while pregnant; their daughter died. All distant branches of the extended imperial family were affected: L. Junius Silanus, M. Licinius Crassus Frugi, Rubellius Plautus, C. Cassius Longinus, all of them died. M. Annius Vinicianus, son of the Vinicianus who plotted against Gaius and had been interested in the throne in 41, made another attempt and died. In the end there were no family members, near or distant, left. When Nero died, so did the dynasty.

It turned out that a distant threat was the most dangerous. An ancient sprig of the Republican nobility, the governor of Hispania Tarraconensis, P. Sulpicius Galba, mounted a challenge that was less easy to scotch than the conspiracies that were hatched or imagined at Rome. By that time it was no longer possible for Nero to select an heir. He could only do so from a member of the imperial family, and there were none left. Then Galba showed that this was not actually as important as it had seemed. The Senate, the real source of the opposition to him, was quite prepared to see the Julio-Claudian dynasty founded by Augustus eliminated.

This was the final failure of the system of organizing the succession set up by Augustus. The basic problem was that it was always capricious. Any emperor could, and should, nominate a successor, but there was no guarantee that the man chosen would reach the higher position for which he was intended; indeed, his very selection marked him for death. Of those selected, or assumed to be selected, to be the heirs of the five emperors of the Julio-Claudian family, three actually succeeded – Tiberius, Gaius and Nero – but perhaps ten or more did not (counting Agrippa Postumus and Ti. Gemellus as potentials). In this calculation Nero's murderous paranoia was actually one of the least of the dangers; Augustus himself had been more lethal, though sometimes inadvertently. For, once a man had been chosen, he became immediately vulnerable. Plots and conspiracies seem to have been more or less continuous from the time of Augustus' assumption of sole power to the death of Nero, but the dynastic failure was due mainly to the wear and tear of travel and work. The number of these men who died away from Rome, in carrying out the work of the emperor who could not leave the city, or could not go out to command an army, is instructive. They worked hard at times in dangerous places, and they fell ill, were wounded, became worn out and died.

In this, the normal mortality to be expected was assisted by the practice of intermarriage within the imperial family. It is a feature of the dynastic problem that so many of the emperors had so few children and this must in part be due to the insistence, begun by Augustus, on intermarriage, which perpetuated a degree of sterility evident all through the family, several of whose branches died out in the century of his dynasty's reign. On top of this sterility, the murderousness of the emperors who apprehended and imagined plots against them greatly thinned the range of possible candidates.

The participation of the Senate in the process of succession and selection had turned out to be less important than that of the Guard, though Augustus, and at first Tiberius, had not intended that the Guard should be involved at all. The Guard's importance increased with the imperial paranoia, and it did not take much to intimidate the Senate; a couple of judicial murders, perhaps a disappearance or two, a threat of a purge, were quite sufficient, especially if a senator could not know if he was next. After Gaius' murder only a sixth of the senators turned up for the crisis debate on the succession. A fuller attendance would have been much more impressive and may well have intimidated, or at least impressed, even the Guard; it might also have led to a different result. Senatorial initiatives were stifled, including any that pushed for the selection of a successor or even suggested one, for this would be a move tantamount to betrayal, since any man nominated by anyone other than the emperor was immediately suspect.

At the same time the participation of the Senate in the inauguration of the new emperor was obviously vital. Tiberius had no need of the Senate's approval for his assumption of the imperial office, having the requisite powers already, but he nevertheless sought and received it. This made it clear that this was a part of the process which was essential. Macro might bypass the Senate in announcing Gaius' succession, but Gaius still had to go to the Senate to have those powers voted to him and, indeed, Macro's early evasion of the Senate in announcing Gaius' succession to the Empire was a backhanded tribute to its importance. Claudius required the approval of the Senate to become emperor; the Guard's military muscle was not sufficient, and the situation was resolved by negotiation. The same was the case with Nero; the Guard acclaimed him, but it was the Senate that proclaimed him and voted him the necessary powers, and it was the Senate's disapproval that eventually finished Nero off.

What Augustus had constructed was an autocracy that was effectively unbridled, though this was probably not his actual intention. Instead it seems clear he had been aiming at a partnership with the Senate, and that had also been Tiberius' early intention, though he had become impatient with its servility towards him and its long-windedness. However, the actual power of the emperor proved to be without real restraints. The only restraint on an emperor's actions was the Guard, which was scarcely concerned with legality or even with controlling an emperor's madness or impulsiveness. Emperors could voluntarily exercise restraint, but some, such as Gaius and Nero, simply refused to do so, perhaps not even recognizing what it was. So, as with all autocracies, this meant that the only way of dealing with an emperor who refused all restraint was by assassination. In such a system it was opposition from within the imperial family that is the most potent, for the members of that family were the only ones who had the right to claim the throne, or indeed, had easy access to his person. Augustus had created, by his insistence on founding a dynasty, a toxic political system that regularly killed off those closest to the political fire. Had he been properly determined in making the Senate his partner in government, any dynastic succession would not have been considered; the Senate would then have chosen his successor, though whether they could ever have come to a peaceful choice is impossible to say. The potentialities, the lack of restraint and the sources of opposition were fully revealed by the career of Gaius, whose peculiar genius it was to appreciate fully what Augustus had produced.

Since the main danger to an emperor came from within his extended family, it followed that it was the members of that family who above all felt the full weight of his power. As a result the family, as a collective unit, in effect committed suicide, being the most obvious victim of Augustus' work. The end result was a narrowing-down of the pool of potential rulers, first to one life, and finally into extinction. When eventually Nero lost his nerve and committed his assisted suicide, succession within the dynasty ceased to exist, but the system as Augustus had created it was left for the later emperors to live or die with.

Augustus' system of finding a successor had been fatally flawed, since, without a legal and accepted system – a law, in fact – the only way of organizing a succession was by violence, implied or explicit, and by *coups d'état*. Only one imperial succession had actually worked as Augustus intended; the others were manipulated by the Guard or by courtiers and later ratified by the Senate, and two of the successions (at least) also involved the murder of the incumbent emperor. When the last of the emperors died without an heir of his family, the violence implied in the successions of Gaius, Claudius and Nero broke out. The civil war that followed was another of Augustus' legacies to his Empire.

(NB: It is normal to refer to this set of emperors, from Julius Caesar to Nero, as the 'Julio-Claudian dynasty'; in fact, this group does not constitute anything like a real dynasty but a set of five families, linked usually by marriage, but also by adoption: the Julii, the Claudii, the Domitii, the Pompeii and the Antonii. The irregularity of the several successions is demonstrated by the failure of any emperor to be succeeded by his biological son. On the other hand, discarding the term 'dynasty' seems impractical, for an accurate replacement can scarcely be found.)

Chapter Three

The Crisis of 68–69

T he sequence of successions from AD 14 to 54 was not as formal and dynastic as can be portrayed; instead, as suggested in the last chapter, they were more like a sequence of *coups d'état*. Augustus won his position as a result of his victory in the civil war; Tiberius had virtually forced himself into the position of successor to Augustus when the chosen boys Gaius and Lucius Caesar died; in 37 Gaius Caligula became emperor by Macro's deviousness, by whom his accession was announced to the armies and the Guard long before any senatorial decision could be made, almost as though the two men feared rejection by the Senate; Claudius was the Guard's candidate, and there always remained a suspicion that, as the main beneficiary of Gaius' murder, he had something to do with it; Nero became emperor, so rumour had it, because Agrippina murdered her husband and then persuaded the Guard to proclaim her son.

These seizures of power, even if they took place within the extended family descended from Julius Caesar, Augustus, M. Agrippa and Livia's Claudian first husband, testified to the methods by which the founders of the imperial regime achieved their pre-eminence. From the point of view of a Republican Roman, the rule of Augustus (and Julius) and his whole family was a blight, an abomination and wholly illegitimate. There were men in the Senate all through the century of Augustus' and his family's rule who said so, and there were others who continued to say so for yet another generation. They were always in a minority, and a decreasing minority, but the emperors were very liable to strike them down simply for their political opinions and their criticisms, probably because they could not combat these opinions by argument, thereby proving the accuracy of the critics' words. The majority, both of senators and citizens, did not voice such opinions, but instead got on with contributing to the administration of the Empire.

It was these last, the pragmatists, who were the senatorial supporters of the imperial system, reckoning that any attempt to return to some sort of Republican system for ruling a huge empire was only asking for another civil war, such as that which had brought the original Republic to an end.

It is such men who had put up with Tiberius' morose absences, and then with Gaius' jokes, Claudius' disabilities and Nero's artistic temperament for the past three decades, and had still kept the Empire operating as senators, governors and officials. Yet even these men cannot have been seriously surprised that the death of Nero in 68 brought on a new civil war.

There had been a number of attempts, even during the century of Julio-Claudian rule, to install an emperor who was not of the imperial family. These are worth contemplating, for they will give some notion of what such men felt was needed to make their attempt successful. Most of what we know about them comes from the details of the plots as recorded by the Roman historians. They were generally hatched in Rome, and obviously designed to kill the current emperor as a first step. Most of these are only poorly known and their precise aims are often obscure; the record, after all, was written by those who suppressed the plots, but three are known in some detail.

The one successful plot in the city, that which resulted in the killing of Gaius, was, of course, carried out by Guardsmen and some others, in part at the instigation of some senators. Neither group seems to have planned anything beyond accomplishing the murder. In particular none seems to have considered it necessary to have an alternative imperial candidate ready, no doubt assuming that this was a problem for someone else. The Senate would probably be the responsible authority in most people's minds, particularly in those of the senators involved in the conspiracy; some senators were certainly involved. The hunt for and discovery of Claudius in the palace was evidently done by other Guardsmen, men who were not the murderers. (How far Claudius himself was involved in the plot is unknown; it is difficult to believe he knew nothing of it.) The senators involved in the plot were so unprepared that at least two of them put themselves forward to the Senate as putative alternative emperors in competition with Claudius and each other. This cannot be said to have been an intelligently-plotted conspiracy, though it does shed light on general attitudes towards the Senate in the matter of the succession.

The plots in Rome necessarily involved Guardsmen because they were the emperor's last line of defence and his personal protection, and senators because they had the political authority to inaugurate a new emperor. In all probability the killing of Gaius was successful precisely because the plotters included elements of both groups. Guards or senators alone were unlikely to succeed without support. Macro's coup at Misenum was successful partly because Tiberius died outside Rome, and partly because everyone was relieved that he was gone. The real test of how a plotter went about his business lies in those who worked outside the city where neither the Guard nor the Senate had direct power or presence.

Apart from the attempted *putsch* by Scribonianus and Vinicius in 42, discussed in the last chapter, two other attempts to replace an emperor are known in enough detail to be worth examining. One is the plot in Rome known as the Conspiracy of Piso in 65. Its full details escape us, though it is known that it was fairly widespread; Nero was beginning to threaten an ever larger number of senators, or so they thought, and this propelled several of them into supporting or participating in the plot. It included at least three senators and some members of the Guard, including one of the Guard Prefects. This was a similar cast of characters as in the plot against Gaius, but this time the plotters had a candidate for the throne ready and willing to take part. This was C. Calpurnius Piso, whose family had always been very conscious of the higher noble status they enjoyed compared with that of the Augustan imperial family; in that sense it resembled the attitude of Scribonianus.

As a plot this was clearly as important as that against Gaius in that the plotters were numerous and diverse. In that they had a candidate ready to be installed, it was a good deal more serious and better prepared. It failed because of delays, loose tongues, internal divisions and the fatal hesitation of Piso himself. Once revealed, it was not very difficult for the emperor to discover what and who was involved and to hand out punishments accordingly.[1]

This was always likely to be the result of any conspiracy organized within the city of Rome itself, where the government was at its most alert and effective and, by this time, after a century of conspiracies, both the Guard and the Senate were obviously the most likely sources of any plot. The numbers of plots uncovered between 30 BC and the suicide of Nero are not known, but they must run into several dozen. Of these, only one, that against Gaius, succeeded. To organize a plot outside Rome, therefore, was to do so away from the close unwinking gaze of the government and its informers, and it could also be done at a more leisurely pace and with a much greater degree of secrecy and security. Yet, as the two of which we have some detail demonstrate, these plots still required the same array of participants as those that developed in the city. Outside Rome, the military participants were not Guardsmen but the army which was guarding the frontiers or holding down provinces, composed of soldiers who were paid their wages in the emperor's name and in his coins, and where the Senate had to be represented by men of senatorial standing rather than senators operating in the Senate.

The curious attempt by L. Arruntius Camillus Scribonianus to replace the new Emperor Claudius in 42 has been discussed in the last chapter. Scribonianus believed that the army in his province would obey him, and he also believed that he had senatorial support. It is assumed that he aimed to be emperor himself. The plot therefore had the three necessary elements for success: military and senatorial supporters, secrecy and a candidate. Its failure was due to the narrowness of Scribonianus' support, which amounted to no more than a few officers and a few senators. That is, the conspiracy had not been prepared with any thoroughness, and as soon as his intentions became known, some of his soldiers killed him. He had apparently relied on the officers, whereas the soldiers had been expected simply to obey orders. This fits well with Scribonianus' apparent sense of social superiority, and suggests that he did not understand the nature of the Augustan system in which the army was the emperor's and was not simply a group of soldiers under the command of provincial governors. Later plotters took due note, and among them were surely those who promoted Piso as their figurehead in 65.

One of those involved in another conspiracy but who escaped for the moment was Annius Vinicianus, the son of the Annius Vinicianus who had been involved in Scribonianus' attempted *putsch*, and the grandnephew of M. Vinicius who had been involved in Gaius' death and the debate over his successor. Little is known of this latest escapade by the family beyond its labelling as the *coniuratio Viniciana* by Suetonius.[2] However, Vinicianus was married to Domitia Longina, the daughter of Nero's great general, Domitius Corbulo, and this connection was one of the factors that brought Corbulo's downfall and forced suicide. Domitia Longina was later married to Domitian, the son of the Emperor Vespasian; many of Corbulo's legates in the East, where he had commanded a large army for a decade in complete loyalty, willingly joined in Vespasian's *putsch* later. One conspiracy's suppression led on to the next, and then to another.

The other extra-urban rising against Nero where a reasonable quantity of detail is known was that by Ser. Sulpicius Galba in 68. Galba was another man with long Republican antecedents, an exalted sense of his own birth, importance and worth, command of an army, and the governorship of a major province. His army was actually smaller than Scribonianus' and even more distant from Rome, but this appears to have worked to his advantage by compelling him to make adequate advance preparations. As governor of Hispania Tarraconensis Galba controlled a large and potentially turbulent province. He had command of a single legion, VI *Victrix*, plus a number of auxiliary regiments, but he also had support among those he ruled, something which, it seems, Scribonianus did not consider necessary. Galba's style was as an old-fashioned Republican martinet, which appealed to those who appreciated his strict enforcement of laws and rules. He even found some popularity among his soldiers, who do not usually appreciate a martinet, and this suggests that much of his reputation was propaganda. Further, in spite of having been governor of Tarraconensis for eight years, he was well remembered at Rome, where he had been a prominent senator and official since Tiberius' reign, and where his early career had been sponsored by Augustus' wife, Livia. He had been notably successful as governor in Germany and Africa, and had been closely associated with the emperors Tiberius, Gaius and Claudius. He had been appointed to Tarraconensis by Nero as a way of getting him away from Rome, for his antique style scarcely appealed to the essentially frivolous emperor; this might have been seen as a compliment by some, certainly as a comment on Nero's own style. He had survived all four emperors, even though his name had been floated as a possible emperor when news reached Germany of Gaius' death; he had refused the suggestion firmly and convincingly enough to block any further moves there and to earn Claudius' gratitude.

So Galba, when he rose against Nero, knew that he would have at least some support, or at least sympathy, in Rome. He must also have been goaded beyond endurance by Nero's conduct. He could count on his own legion, officers and men, and on the backing of his provincial subjects, both of which groups he had carefully sounded out. He also carefully consulted with his neighbouring governors. The governor of Aquitania had already contacted him when the unsuccessful revolt led by C. Julius Vindex broke out in Gaul, asking for his help; the governor of Lusitania, M. Salvius Otho, who had a personal grudge against Nero as the previous husband of the murdered Poppaea, joined him with alacrity; the governor of Gallia Narbonensis, T. Vinius Rufinus, joined him; and so did the *quaestor* of Baetica, A. Caecina Alienus, though the actual governor there was less than enthusiastic. Galba therefore could count on all Spain and much of Gaul, though only his own province had a worthwhile armed force. He immediately began recruiting a second legion, which became the VII *Galbiana*. It would be raw and probably undermanned, but it would be a useful reinforcement for his other legion, and could remain in Spain as a replacement garrison.

All this argues a lengthy period of reflection, planning and preparation, with plenty of time taken up by negotiation with his allies and discussion with his officers, who clearly did not make the mistake of Scribonianus' officers in assuming that the men would automatically follow the governor and their officers. It also demonstrates the utility of conducting such a conspiracy away from Rome. Galba's control of the roads and the official machinery of provincial government must have been one of the main means by which he kept all this secret from Nero's government in Rome.

The signal for Galba's revolt came when his own Guard saluted him as 'General of the Senate and People of Rome' instead of the customary 'General of Caesar', a salutation that was undoubtedly prearranged; soldiers do not do such things spontaneously. He then collected the available men in the region who were of senatorial rank – again his knowledge of the existence of such men, where they were and what their attitude would be argues much research and preparation – and formed them into a mini- or mock-Senate, and then publicized his pretensions in the usual way by issuing his own coins, an imperial prerogative. The slogans they bore included 'Liberty Restored' and 'Gallia and Hispania Agreed'. He had statues made of himself in the usual dignified pose, and sent letters in all directions announcing his rebellion – which is what it was at first – and in effect asking for more support.

This was a considerably more sophisticated and imaginative rising than that of Scribonianus, and it suggests that lessons had been learned from that failure and from events in Rome, including Piso's failed conspiracy. Galba clearly understood that it was necessary to display considerable political support before attempting to deal with the emperor himself, and his collection of senators, his military display (he took to wearing a military cloak on all occasions), and his busy recruitment of a new legion from the Spanish provincials were all useful propaganda elements. Having thus indicated essential support in the three governmental areas that previous emperors had also identified as vital at such moments – the army, the governors and the Senate – he could stand forth as a credible alternative to Nero. His letters to other political supporters would have asked either for support or for neutrality. A governor or any commander who did nothing in this crisis in effect supported him. Galba's personal reputation for probity, dignity and frugality also contrasted vividly with that of an emperor who claimed to be an artist, then neglected his work for frivolities and spent money like water on extravagances.[3]

Galba's actions, following the revolt of Vindex in Gaul, finally broke the mystique protecting Nero. The soldiers who beat Vindex suggested that their commander Verginius Rufus should make himself emperor in place of Nero; Rufus had won a battle, Nero had never come near an army. Galba's soldiers supported his bid; the troops in Dalmatia supported the candidacy of Verginius later, but Rufus bluntly and consistently refused his soldiers' offers. In Africa the governor L. Clodius Macer gathered support from the legion in Africa, recruited more soldiers and was able to count on the same sort of local support that Galba had gathered in Spain; this looks like a deliberate copying of Galba's methods.

Nero made some of the right moves to defeat the threat from Galba and others. He recruited troops from the fleet into a new legion, and concentrated forces in northern Italy, a move which had he followed through would obviously have kept Galba out of Italy. However, much of the army was concentrated in the Eastern provinces, where Vespasian commanded against the Jewish revolt, and that army was largely officered by men who fiercely resented Nero's order to their earlier commander Domitius Corbulo to commit suicide. Whether Nero understood this or not, that army was potentially as disloyal as the German, Spanish and African armies and, of course, Nero had no military experience to speak of. He held the loyalty of several good generals, but his will to continue failed when it became clear that the Senate, hitherto quite docile, even servile, before an emperor, turned against him. He even failed to commit suicide and had to be killed by a slave.

Galba's success in reaching the imperial office was therefore primarily the result of Nero's failure to resist him, rather than his own accomplishments and attractiveness. The news of the emperor's death when it reached him was greeted with disbelief at first and then joy and relief when it was confirmed.[4] Galba then faced his competitors. Clodius Macer in Africa had been elevated by his own army. At Rome the Commander of the Guard, Nymphidius Sabinus, attempted to rule through his office until it proved impossible. In Germany Verginius Rufus appeared to support Nero, and might seize the moment of Nero's death to proclaim himself after all; the governor of the Germania Inferior was murdered by two of his own officers when he showed signs of the same ambition.

Galba, however, had been the first in the field, had the requisite distinguished lineage (Verginius Rufus had been a 'new man'), and by convoking his provincial Senate he had signalled that he would listen to advice and would co-operate with the Senate at Rome. In Rome it was only the Guard's threatening presence that kept the Senate from declaring for Galba, and when Nymphidius Sabinus heard that Nero had fled, he brought the Guard round to Galba's side. Thereupon the Senate also announced for Galba, thus cancelling its earlier branding of him as a public enemy.[5]

The essential difference between the risings of Scribonianus and Clodius Macer on the one hand and that of Galba on the other was therefore Galba's advance planning. He had clearly thought through the problem beforehand in some detail, and had evidently been doing so for some time. The rebellion of Vindex in Gaul, in the name of liberty from Nero's increasingly unpleasant, neglectful and repellent behaviour, was seized on as a pretext by Galba, but there was also a larger background. Galba clearly knew of the decay of Nero's capacities and reputation, no doubt through regular correspondence with his friends in Rome. He had also taken note of the failures of Scribonianus and Piso, and his own conspiracy took elements from each of these, and added in his own capabilities and reputation, so much more convincing than either of these. He used that reputation as a man of ancient dignity and made it a deliberate contrast with the evasive nonsense of Nero. He made sure that the armed force at his disposal was adequate and loyal to him; he guarded his back by his alliances with neighbouring governors, which would have reassured his Spanish provincial subjects that they were not about to be invaded from the south and west. This was a contrast with the rising of Macer in Africa, whose failure was said to be the result of his own unpleasant behaviour in office. Yet perhaps Galba's brightest idea was the local Senate. After all, it had been only a senatorial rump of about 100 men that had acted for the whole in inaugurating Claudius; Galba could find that number of senators and senators-equivalent in the Spanish region to provide him with the semblance of support from that group in society, and it suggested a new imperial respect for the Senate in Rome.

Galba's success thus emphasized above all the role of the Senate. He had only one legion at his back (the newly-recruited VII *Galbiana* would have been pretty useless in battle for some time). The other armies held themselves aloof. The armies in Germania Superior and Germania Inferior adopted neutral stances; that under Verginius Rufus in the Upper Province pledged its loyalty, rather pointedly, to the Senate; the murder of Fonteius Capito in Germania Inferior by his officers was indeed designed to prevent him from claiming the throne, but it scarcely indicated support for any other candidate, not even Nero. The army in the East was locked into the Jewish War and the siege of Jerusalem and could not possibly disengage and intervene.

The legions in Syria and Anatolia had to keep a wary eye on Parthia, whose king might be tempted to take advantage of Roman disturbances. Galba would appear to have had suspicions of the Eastern commander, Vespasian, if the story of him sending assassins to the East is really true. (He certainly arranged the death of Clodius Macer in Africa.) In Rome it was the Senate's accolade to Galba that was decisive. There, it was the failure of the Guard to support Nero that allowed the Senate to do this, but it was the Senate's decision that conferred legitimacy on the approaching rebel. As Tacitus commented, emperors could be made outside Rome, but it was the Roman Senate's voice that carried most weight.

It is necessary to emphasize this because it is not infrequently said or implied that the decisive voice in choosing emperors was the army's. There is no doubt that the army, or rather the army's senior officers, had influence in the decisions if they could make themselves heard, but in most cases they were only one voice against the many in the Senate. The role of the Guard in the elevation of Gaius, Claudius and Nero was not as decisive as it might seem. In all cases it was the Senate that the Guard had looked to for a decision once the soldiers, or rather their officers, had made their choices. Claudius was clearly no more than a candidate when he was in the barracks of the Guard, and the Senate continued its debate regardless; the proclamation of Gaius was in effect the work of Macro, not the Guard as a whole, and the Senate did not need any persuading for Gaius had clearly been Tiberius' chosen successor; in the case of Nero, the voice of the Guard was secured first, but not decisively, for the Guard then passed the matter to the Senate for a final decision. It is clear that in the only case where there was uncertainty, in 41, the Senate was able to debate in relative tranquility, and the absence of most senators was not necessarily due to fear of the Guard.

This conclusion is important because of what occurred in the crisis of 68–69. Galba's rebellion was carefully crafted to exercise pressure first of all on the Senate, and secondly on Nero personally. In constitutional practice, as it had evolved since the time of Augustus, the decisive voice on the succession was that of the Senate, though the soldiers had their weapons. They had not yet used them against the senators in a succession crisis. Guardsmen had been involved in the death of Gaius, so the time might well come when the Senate was directly threatened, but in 68 it was the failure of the Guard to act in support of Nero that left the Senate free to proclaim Galba, and so it was still clearly up to the Senate to make the decisive move. In essence this was the same situation as in 41 and 54.

The decisiveness of the Senate's role had been confirmed by the accession of Galba, even if he began as a usurping rebel, and this only confirmed what had been clear since the death of Augustus and even before. It had been Tiberius' action in going to the Senate and there receiving oaths of allegiance from senators, army men and so on that had been the moment when his sole rule had become clear and accepted. Certainly he already possessed the requisite powers, granted by that same Senate and renewed the year before, but without a public acknowledgement of this position, by the Senate openly displaying public acceptance of him, that position would obviously have been in doubt.

Gaius had had to do the same, and had been granted those powers by the Senate; Macro might have largely pre-empted the Senate's decision, but Gaius met the Senate and there the 'imperial powers' were voted to him; only then was his new position fully legal and accepted. If the Senate had refused Gaius the requisite powers, other letters would have gone out countermanding those of Macro. Claudius' accession had made it even clearer: he had the support of the Guard, but that was not sufficient; the Senate's investiture was vital. The installation of Nero, who had already been granted certain powers three years earlier, was similar. Now Galba's rising was successful because, and only because, the Senate said so. Galba had not, in fact, claimed the title of Caesar or emperor until invited to do so by the Senate. In every change of emperor from AD 14 to AD 68, the role of the Senate was the one that was decisive.

As soon as Galba became emperor, formally and legally, in the summer of 68, the problem of the succession to him arose. Galba had no living children and he was 72 years old. The question was therefore immediately urgent, but it was not until January of 69, Galba having been in Rome for three or four months, that he made his choice of successor. Several candidates had been suggested, or had suggested themselves. They included M. Salvius Otho, one of Galba's first supporters, a candidate at least in his own mind; Cn. Cornelius Dolabella, who was Galba's grandnephew and a scion of an old family even more distinguished than Galba's own; and the man he eventually chose, L. Calpurnius Piso Licinianus.

Piso was a curious choice. He was the younger son of a man who had been executed by Claudius; his brother had been the titular head of the conspiracy of 65. He was 30 years old, had been in exile since his childhood (because of his father's crime), and had no experience of government, little even of Rome itself, and none of the army. In this he was no worse qualified than Gaius or Claudius or Nero, but that was hardly a recommendation to be emperor, though it may have been so in Galba's eyes. Galba's choice was apparently dictated by respect for aristocratic descent, the supposed high character that this implied and maybe pity for the family's misfortunes, though these had actually been largely self-inflicted. Galba surely assumed that he would live long enough to ensure Piso's political and military education, but it looked far too like a return to a Gaius or Nero figure for comfort and it was a disastrous choice for both men.[6] Galba may have been a master conspirator and a well-liked and successful governor, but he was an unpopular emperor and a poor judge of a successor.

There followed a year that was a disaster also for Rome, for its Empire, and for its emperors: the civil wars of 69. Otho had Galba and Piso killed and was proclaimed emperor, but was defeated by L. Vitellius, the governor of Germania Superior, and committed suicide; Vitellius was a throwback to a Neronian type in personality and greed, and was defeated by Vespasian's army from the East and was killed; Vespasian arrived as the next emperor. Soldiers and civilians died in their thousands, cities were sacked and barbarians invaded the Empire; revolts took place or were encouraged; the prime shrine of the whole Empire, the temple of Jupiter Capitolinus in Rome, was burned, and all because a properly constituted and installed emperor had made a bad choice of his successor.[7]

For Galba's choice of Piso was certainly the trigger for the whole process, though it is, of course, simplistic to blame the whole crisis on that one decision. The basic dispute in 69 was over who was to be emperor. Galba's decisions made in Rome had already annoyed or alienated many elements of the army, much of the Guard, many senators and a good proportion of the citizens. He had proved to be as brutal and un-legal in his decisions as Nero or Claudius or Gaius, as unwise in his choice of advisers as Nero and as vindictive as Gaius; all the marks of a man who was out of his depth. The rebellion of Vitellius had, certainly, begun before he announced the choice of Piso as his successor, but it was Otho's disappointment at that choice that was the direct cause of Galba's own murder, and later of Otho's defeat at Vitellius' hands. Galba, in facing Vitellius, would have had much more support than Otho, for Vitellius as emperor was no more than a joke. Otho could not but be seen as an unfaithful and ungrateful murderer, and only ever had a tenuous and temporary grip on power and no legitimacy for the post of emperor.

The three brief emperors of 68–69 – omitting Vespasian for the moment – provide clear cases of the limitations of military power in installing an emperor. Galba had used very little of such power in his rebellion, and it was the Senate that was finally responsible for his success and his installation as emperor. However, his choice of Piso as his successor was unpopular and misguided. Choosing Otho would have been as bad. His choice was apparently based on the Piso family's long opposition to the Julio-Claudians and paid no heed to personal ability or the needs of the Empire. Just as Galba himself assumed that his ancestry fitted him to be emperor, so he imagined a similar ancestry in Piso was sufficient. Such an attitude alienated too many men who should have been his supporters. As a result, within five days of his announcement of Piso's selection, both Galba and Piso were murdered in public in the city. That is, it proved to be very easy for Otho to persuade the Guard (which had been disappointed in the donative it had expected) to carry out the murders. It is a mark of Galba's collapse into deep unpopularity so quickly that this could take place and that no one protested.[8]

Otho went through the motions required for accession. He was, like Claudius, with the Guard at the time of the murders and went from their barracks to the Senate. There he was recommended to the popular Assembly to be consul, and motions were passed to give him the imperial powers.[9] He already faced competition from the governor and army in Germania Inferior (which had already made restless movements the year before), where L. Vitellius was acclaimed.

Vitellius was an even less suitable candidate for emperor than Otho, but he could not make his candidature good until he could meet the Senate; that is, for some time he was in the same position as Galba on his march from Spain. He only met the Senate after defeating Otho's forces in northern Italy, and after Otho himself had committed suicide. Like Galba, Vitellius took no actual powers or titles until he was awarded them by the Senate.[10] His justification – rather late in the day – was revenge for Galba (his acclamation had been on 1 January; Galba was murdered on the 15th, so this was certainly a late invention). He was thus claiming to condemn Otho as a non-emperor, but insisting that his own new position was legitimate, though he had claimed the throne while Galba was alive and in power and before he had heard of his death. This was a rewriting of history of the type that is not unknown in other totalitarian states.

So both Otho and Vitellius required senatorial approval to make their role technically legal, just as had Galba. Otho had the support of some of the Guard, whose bloodied swords metaphorically stood with him in the Senate; the threat was real, if not actually visible, and the Senate really had no choice but to pass the necessary measures to invest Otho with the tribunician and proconsular powers and give him the titles of Caesar and Augustus, which were now no longer names alone, but this was essentially the same situation as with the accession of Claudius. Vitellius was hailed as emperor by a deputation of senators when they met him in north Italy, but he was only granted the powers and titles of Augustus when in Rome at a regular meeting of the Senate. Again the Senate had no choice, with Rome occupied by Vitellius' army, but the forms were gone through.

Vitellius lost his meagre early popular acceptance very quickly, and his forces were beaten by those fighting for Vespasian. Vespasian, commander of a large army in Judaea, had been slow and careful in laying out his claims. His procedure had been much closer to that of Galba, who he claimed to have intended to support, than to those of either Otho or Vitellius. Otho had used the Guard, Vitellius his provincial army; neither seriously looked for more extensive support, presumably believing that by occupying Rome and intimidating the Senate they could achieve rule, but Galba and Otho had both quickly seen that this was not enough. Vespasian, more cautious and geographically distant from Italy, canvassed a wider support among the troops and their commanders outside his province, in Egypt, in Syria, in Africa and on the Danube, before he made his move and he gained the explicit support of governors in several provinces. Galba had convened a sort of local Senate; the supporting governors and legionary legates – all technically senators – were Vespasian's equivalent of Galba's local Senate. The ordinary soldiers, whose enthusiasm for Vespasian and Titus was clear, were substituted for the Roman people in Assembly. Yet Vespasian might claim the throne, and might date his assumption of power from July 69, but only when Vitellius was dead was he formally awarded, in his absence, the imperial powers. Once again, the precedent was that of Galba, and once again, the Senate was asserting its right to make an emperor.[11] Vespasian's dating of his assumption of rule, however, meant that he was claiming that Galba had been the last legitimate emperor before him, and that neither Otho nor Vitellius were true emperors; in an objective view, this could hardly be gainsaid.

In other words, it had not been enough for Vitellius and Vespasian to win battles and occupy Rome to be emperors, just as it had not been enough for Otho to command the loyalty of the Guard and to get the soldiers to murder Galba. These military forces may have been necessary for each man to make his play for the throne, but it was only the Senate that conferred on them the powers that gave them the right to give imperial orders and to be obeyed. It did not matter that the emperors dated their rule from the days of their proclamation – Vitellius from 1 January, Vespasian from 1 July – for it was only the Senate's award that legitimized them. Indeed, the successive messages of the three emperors, Galba, Otho and Vitellius, to Vespasian had led him to recognize the legitimate authority of all three before he was persuaded to make his own throw. He was, therefore, no matter what he claimed later, a rebel until the death of Vitellius, and only then did the Senate confer the imperial powers on him.

The Brief Emperors of AD 68–69

Galba (October 68–January 69).

Otho (January–April 69).

Vitellius (April–December 69).
(© *Marie-Lan Nguyen / Wikimedia Commons*)

The Flavian Dynasty

Vespasian (69–79).

Domitian (81–96).

Titus (79–81).

Chapter Four

The Consequence of Civil War: The Flavian Dynasty

Vespasian was the first emperor since Tiberius who reached the throne and had adult sons (and Tiberius' sons died before him). Further, his eldest son Titus was a vigorous, healthy and accomplished man. The younger son, Domitian, was still a teenager when Vespasian became emperor, and had survived successfully in Rome during the crisis, even avoiding the assassins who were looking for him. In addition, both sons were loyal to their father, though Domitian was very jealous of his older brother. Vespasian's own brother, who had been the City Prefect, had been killed in the civil war. When it became clear that Vespasian's armies had prevailed and Vitellius had been hunted down and killed, the Senate swiftly marked its relief and appreciation by voting the imperial powers to the survivor, and by making Vespasian and Titus joint consuls *ordinarii* for the next year (AD 70).[1]

The succession had been a major problem for all the emperors of the years of crisis. Nero had no successor of his family; Galba's attempt to solve the problem had brought the death of both himself and his chosen man; Otho, unmarried and with no children but still in his 30s, had apparently never addressed the issue, but then he had been under attack from Vitellius from the moment he seized power and hardly had time to consider the matter; Vitellius had made a display of his son, but he was only 6 years old, so this was a reprise of the early years of both Claudius and Nero, and the prospect of another teenager inheriting the Empire was scarcely enticing after Nero. (The boy was killed by one of Vespasian's generals when he took control of Rome; Vitellius' daughter survived and was protected by Vespasian. Such were politics at Rome.)

The awards of honours to Titus and Domitian, Vespasian's sons, brought a new and important development in the succession issue. Titus, who had been left in command of the Roman army besieging Jerusalem while his father travelled towards Italy, was awarded the consulship at the age of 30 (and therefore below the legal age), to be held along with his father (consul for the second time); Domitian, aged 18, was designated *praetor* for the coming year, but with an *imperium* equivalent to that of a consul. Both were also awarded the titles of Caesar and *princeps iuventutis*.[2] The elected *praetor*, Sex. Julius Frontinus, vacated his post so that Domitian could take it; it was a shrewd move by Frontinus and brought him office and profit for the next thirty years.

The two sons, therefore, by these honours and offices, were clearly marked out from the first as Vespasian's successors, though this was not yet a formal, senatorially-approved designation. It seems that this was done by the Senate's own decision before Vespasian reached Rome, and was awarded as recognition of Vespasian's status as emperor, but only as honours to his sons, not an official mark of the right of succession. Yet their succession could hardly be doubted. Of the family, only Domitian was in the city during the crisis, and he had already been addressed as 'Caesar' by the leaders of the Flavian group in Rome in recognition of his father's new status. The Senate may well have pre-empted any decision on this by Vespasian himself, but it was certainly in line with the requirements of the moment, and was a further indication of senatorial authority in the matter, following on from the activity of the Senate since before Nero's death. By publicly appointing Titus and Domitian as Vespasian's heirs to the throne, the Senate was also pointing out the folly of any other attempts at rebellion. Titus was one of the great soldiers of the age, and would certainly fight for his inheritance. For the present Vespasian and Titus were well separated geographically, so removing either of them would only precipitate a further war, and both men had proved their command abilities and their popularity, and had gained the recognition of the Senate.

These measures were a clear indication by the Senate that it was the Senate itself that made such decisions. Yet it was also, at the same time, an abdication from the decision-making. As ever, the Senate could legislate and ratify; it could not initiate. It may well have been that the prospect of an experienced general with adult sons in place of three temporary emperors with only a single child to follow them was something of a relief to the senators after the violence of the year.

It was clearly expected that Vespasian would establish his family as the ruling dynasty and that he could do this rather more effectively than anyone had done so far, at least since Tiberius. The deliberate reminiscences of Augustus' reign (and even Nero's) in the awards of powers and honours were a further sign of this. A darker side was the elimination of potential rivals that was taking place even as the Senate was meeting. The son of Vitellius was one victim, but Piso's brother Crassus Scribonianus and the son-in-law of the governor of Africa who had aimed at the throne, M. Clodius Macer, were also both killed; Cn. Cornelius Dolabella, Galba's grandnephew, had already been killed by Vitellius. These were all men who might have felt they had a claim to the imperial powers by virtue of their relationship to an emperor or an earlier claimant. In removing these competitors, Vespasian's reign took up where Nero's and Galba's had left off, though Vespasian carefully left it to his lieutenants to do the killings. All this meant that it was quickly obvious that the new regime had the same concerns as the old. It was the nature of the autocracy government to remove in the most drastic way any claimant, usurper or rebel; not to do so would be to recognize that these others' claims to supreme power had some validity.

Vespasian was 61 years old when he reached Rome, a decade younger than Galba at the same stage of his career. Having reached such an age and being hale, he could expect to live some years more, though perhaps not many. By making Titus his commander against Jerusalem and *consul ordinarius* for 70, Vespasian indicated clearly his choice of successor, and next year the Senate awarded Titus the tribunician and proconsular powers alongside his father.[3]

Yet the Senate quibbled over the award. Vespasian requested that Titus be awarded the requisite powers; some senators, notably Helvidius Priscus, objected and apparently wished that the Senate itself make the selection of successor. The spectacle of a hereditary system – a return to the Julio-Claudians – apparently was not appealing. There were, as a result of the recent crisis and the civil war, several precedents besides the hereditary one: Galba had been, at least technically, chosen by the Senate, and had indicated that a successor should be chosen there also, though in the event he was pushed to nominate Piso without that consultation. Nero's absence of an heir had indicated that the Senate would probably need to make a decision on the matter anyway, and there was a precedent in the choice of Claudius in 41. Between them, however, Vespasian and Titus had the political and military weight to overcome senatorial hesitancy. Vespasian certainly allowed a debate, but made it clear that what he wished for would have to be agreed. In the end the Senate did agree.[4]

For the next eight years the two men and Domitian accumulated consulships at a rate unprecedented since Augustus. When he died in 79, Vespasian had been consul nine times (he missed only two years while emperor), Titus for seven and Domitian six. By this time it was normal for ordinary consuls to resign partway through the year, and for two more to take up the office afterwards as suffect consuls. Vespasian began by serving for six months, but gradually reduced this; later it was normal for there to be six or seven consuls in the year, sometimes more, and if an emperor took the office of ordinary consul he would normally resign after only a fortnight. Other men could therefore accumulate more than one period of office, but it had clearly become an honour rather than a source of power. Even so, the larger the number of consulships a man held, the grander his prestige; hence Vespasian's accumulation, and hence his sons' as well.

This was a practice Vespasian resorted to partly in order to build up his personal prestige and that of his sons. Not since Augustus had the emperor collected so many consulships. The later Julio-Claudians had not bothered overmuch about this, having the prestige of the dynastic membership to bolster their pride; nor did later emperors bother much, usually being content with three or four consulships only. That Vespasian, already emperor and therefore with the prestige that went with that office, must have had a further motive is evident. He may have lacked family prestige – his father was said to have been a muleteer – but as emperor he controlled the consular nominations. By occupying the post so often he was shutting out other senators, and by nominating those who did serve he was ensuring that only his own supporters achieved the prestige of a consulship. It was all, in other words, a matter of security as well as prestige. Titus and Domitian continued to exercise such control, though Domitian eventually did so with some display of contempt.

Since both sons were still alive when Vespasian died (in 79, at the age of 69) the succession problem was solved for the foreseeable future. He was succeeded by Titus, who already possessed most of the necessary powers. There is no description of any ceremony when he achieved sole rule, but there must have been at least the administration of an oath of allegiance to the senators and other officials. It was so routine that one historian, Suetonius, passes over it in silence, and another, Cassius Dio, in a sentence. He assumed the titles and offices of Augustus, *pontifex maximus* and *pater patriae*, all of which do imply senatorial votes, even if only formal ones.

By all accounts Titus did not get on well with his brother, who was described as involving himself in conspiracies and stirring up the troops. It is noticeable also that Domitian was not awarded any of the imperial powers while Titus was alive, though they did share the consulship in 80, Domitian's seventh. Titus, of course, was still fairly young, aged 40 when his father died, and he might expect to reign for a decade or two, so it might seem that he need not be in a hurry to share his powers with his brother, and if Domitian was so avid for power that he conspired to seize it, it was perhaps best not to encourage him.

Both of Titus' marriages had ended in divorce, having produced only one daughter, Flavia Julia. Maybe he was intending to marry again with the intention of procreation, yet he did not. His reputation as a profligate before his father's death transmuted into 'the good emperor' during his own sole rule, but he clearly made no detailed provisions for the succession, merely allowing Domitian to be presumed his successor, and referring to him as his 'partner and successor', which was clearly an informal recognition.[5] In the circumstances, of course, Domitian could probably behave as badly as he liked – though the scurrilous account of his plotting and fraternal arguments are somewhat doubtful – but Titus could not afford to execute him, since this would have exposed him to yet more, and more dangerous, conspiracies.

VII   The Flavians.

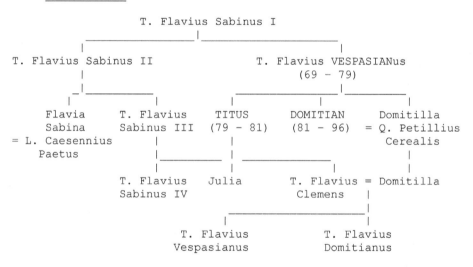

So when Titus died in 81, unexpectedly, at the age of 42, Domitian was the obvious successor, though he did not possess the imperial powers. He moved quickly to secure control, even before Titus was actually dead (or so it is said), thereby demonstrating an acute appreciation of the needs of the succession: square the Guard first, then accept recognition by the Senate. He was awarded the imperial powers, possibly at the meeting of the Senate at which eulogies for Titus were pronounced, most likely the day after the imperial death.[6] There would seem to have been no dispute about his accession, but then he had already held seven consulships and was clearly his brother's heir, even if somewhat unofficially. Yet the day's delay may have been the Senate's way of demonstrating that it was the senators who decided.

The old question of the succession, dormant for ten years, now arose once more. Domitian had a daughter, and Titus had a daughter, but his only son had died in infancy and it seems that no other children were likely. The continuation of the dynasty depended now on Domitian's choice of successor. He found himself in the same situation as Augustus, Tiberius, and Nero, not to mention Galba and Otho. If he chose an adult he picked out a man who became a danger to him; if he chose a child the chosen one had to be trained over a long period of years. All the time the emperor would be getting older and was vulnerable to plots, and the plots would obviously multiply and become steadily more serious.

Domitian did have a reasonably extensive collection of relatives in his extended family. His uncle, T. Flavius Sabinus, who was killed in 69, had left a son and a daughter, each of whom had two sons. (For the details of the family see Genealogical Table VII.) The sons of Sabinus' eldest son, also Sabinus (distinguished as 'III') were within the succession group (Sabinus IV and Clemens), and the elder was married to Titus' daughter Flavia Julia. Here again was the intermarriage within the ruling dynasty, as with Augustus' family. (Titus and Sabinus III were first cousins, being the sons of brothers; they had also married sisters, so Sabinus IV and his wife were both first and second cousins.) This man, T. Flavius Sabinus IV, was the successor presumptive from the time Domitian himself succeeded. He gave himself airs, reputedly dressing his servant in imperial white. He had been Domitian's colleague as consul in 82 (replacing the dead Titus, who had earlier been intended for that office). He was then executed soon after; the stories about this event imply that Sabinus IV had presumed too much.[7] Domitian was, quite rightly, constantly suspicious of plots, and his presumed successor was a natural source of or vehicle for such plots. He did not designate an adult as his successor again.

Sabinus IV's younger brother T. Flavius Clemens had seven children, at least two of whom were boys, an unusual display of fertility both in this family and indeed in any imperial family. Their mother was Domitian's niece, the daughter of his deceased sister. (The marriage was once again between first cousins.) The dynasty was, in the marriages of Sabinus and Clemens, behaving typically dynastically, indulging in both intermarriages and family executions. The two boys, sons of Clemens, were singled out as Domitian's heirs by about 90, but Clemens was kept out of political office until 95, when he became consul at last, along with the emperor himself. It would seem that Domitian was considering a similar situation to that of Augustus and Agrippa, for the two boys were now renamed T. Flavius Domitianus and T. Flavius Vespasianus. Their father was clearly not intended to be emperor, but he would become regent if the boys were still under age when Domitian died. However, service as consul may have ignited ambition in Clemens; Domitian had him executed soon after he ceased to be consul. The boys remained his designated successors.[8]

No imperial ambitions are imputed to any of Domitian's other relations, and after the fates of Sabinus IV and Clemens this is hardly surprising. Sabinus III's sister Flavia Sabina was married to L. Caesennius Paetus and they had two sons; both boys survived and prospered under all these emperors. Titus' and Domitian's sister Flavia Domitilla was married to C. Petillius Cerealis, who had two sons by an earlier marriage; one died young and the father and the surviving son both became consuls, but no more. Even more distantly related were the Arrecini and the Iulii Lupi families and their own more distant connections. One of these was apparently threatened with execution at about the time of Clemens' execution, though it seems not to have happened; otherwise the families were essentially undisturbed. They were clearly not generally suspected of imperial ambitions, and after the execution of Sabinus IV in 82 or 83 it is not surprising that these attitudes prevailed.

Domitian clearly had difficulty in personally contemplating his own mortality, which is what was required when an emperor selected a successor. As an experienced conspirator himself, he was apparently adept at detecting plots by others, and perhaps hyper-alert to any threat of a plot within the family; even in his bedchamber he kept a dagger under his pillow. His various attempts at selecting a successor, however, do show that he was operating within the same framework, constitutionally speaking, as his predecessors all the way back to Augustus. The senatorial disquiet at the prospect of hereditary succession, apparent in 70–71, had not necessarily gone away, though it was clearly inadvisable to raise the issue with Domitian on the throne. To do so would imply that the emperor's choice was wrong or bad, or that he had not made one and should. In fact, of course, by executing those who had been singled out and then by choosing children, Domitian was deliberately evading the issue, and by doing this he was leaving himself increasingly vulnerable. Yet the issue was clearly one he regarded as a family matter. The upheavals in 68–69 had not displaced the assumption that the imperial succession was to be hereditary.

The civil wars of 68–69 had not seriously changed the constitution of the Empire, in so far as it had one, or the methods by which an emperor designated his successor. The only real change brought about by that period of violence was that the method by which an emperor could be removed had become much clearer. This was the lesson of Galba and Vespasian, who in turn had learned their lesson from the earlier failed plots. To remove an emperor in safety, it was necessary to do two things above all: assassinate the incumbent and have a successor ready, willing and waiting.

This was what occurred in 96, when Domitian, despite the dagger under his pillow (it had been disabled in advance) and a guard on his door (suborned in advance) fell victim to a group of ancient senators, perhaps the least likely set of plotters he could have imagined.

Chapter Five

The Crisis of 96–97

The murder of Domitian in September 96 was part of a conspiracy whose organization and execution was a clear improvement on all the previous plots against ruling emperors. Lessons had already been learned from the previous cases of Scribonianus, Piso, Galba and others, and the whole affair against Domitian went off most competently. A member of the Palace administration suborned a servant of the emperor's to do the actual killing; contact was made with a disaffected group of senators and with one of the prefects of the Guard. A strategically-placed door was locked to prevent the emperor's loyal servants from interfering in the murder, and the knife the emperor kept handy in his bedroom for such events was disabled. Also, as a grace note to the achievement, when the murder had been successfully committed, the murderer himself, one of the palace servants, was killed by a Guardsman who had also been suborned by the official, so preventing the truth from being broadcast and hiding the names of the plotters. Finally the chosen successor was already in the Palace, waiting for the good word.

Needless to say, several of the plan's details went wrong. Domitian almost succeeded in fighting off his attacker; the chosen successor, M. Cocceius Nerva, was frightened almost out of his wits as he waited, fearing that the killing might fail. Above all, the one element of power in the state that had not been squared beforehand, the army on the frontier, proved to be very unhappy over the whole affair. The army had not been involved – apart from some of the Guard – for the very good reason that Domitian was well-liked by the officers and men. So it turned out that, by killing Domitian and installing Nerva as the new emperor, the conspirators had only created an even bigger crisis. Also there was a witness, a boy who attended to the family shrine in the emperor's bedroom and who had hidden under the imperial bed as the killing took place; he was able to relate what had happened later, which is why we know the details. So the plot worked, but the unexpected also happened.[1]

The killing took place on the evening of 18 September 96 in the Palace in Rome. By the morning of the next day the Senate had been summoned to meet by the consul Ti. Catius Caesius Fronto, and Nerva was invested in the by now time-honoured way with the tribunician and proconsular powers. (He dated his reign from the 18th, the day of Domitian's death, but the Senate's inauguration was actually the next day; the implication of such dating, of course, was that the Senate's approval was not necessary, an interpretation Nerva would probably have contested while he was still only a senator.)

To men who were not involved in the plot, the installation of Nerva himself as emperor may have come as a considerable surprise, but a moment's consideration would have convinced them that he was a likely candidate, given that Domitian was dead and that his own chosen successors (the two boys he had adopted) were not to be considered. Nerva had been twice consul already, he had been the intimate of every emperor since Nero – who had awarded him triumphal insignia for his part in exposing the Piso conspiracy – and he had been one of the first to be made consul (*ordinarius*) with Vespasian after the latter's victory; he had also been a member of Domitian's *consilium*, the near formal group of advisers the emperor gathered around him. Nerva's age – he was in his 60s – and experience made him exactly the sort of emperor the Senate would always choose if it was given the chance, a man likely to reign for only a short time, and one without personal heirs; the Senate would, in theory, have the opportunity of making another choice soon.[2]

This *coup d'état* may well have been well-organized, but even in hardened Roman political mouths, a bad taste was surely left. If anyone had been particularly favoured by the Flavian dynasty it was Nerva, both by the father and by the sons. Both of his consulships had been awarded in moments of political difficulty – in 70 as Vespasian struggled to establish himself as emperor and in 91 in the aftermath of an exceptionally serious conspiracy against Domitian – and these emperors had clearly relied on Nerva as a source of stability at difficult moments. His betrayal of Domitian and the memory of his work with the Flavian emperors must have sickened quite a few men.

Not only that, but it had been the emperor's plan to go off to Germany to conduct a major war with the aim of conquering the German tribes of the Marcomanni and the Quadi in the Bohemian area. An army of no fewer than ten legions had been gathered in Pannonia for the purpose, and a whole web of diplomatic contacts throughout Germany from the Rhine frontier to the Vistula had been woven. Domitian's death prevented this plan from being carried out, a plan that looks very much as though, had it succeeded, would have significantly altered the balance of power on the northern frontier, allowing much of Germany to be absorbed, and resuming the processes of imperial expansion for the first time since the reign of Augustus. It follows from the situation that Nerva's main problem as emperor was the army, and that force on the northern frontier was hardly pleased, having made all the preparations and found that no orders came. Nerva began this relationship badly by apparently not directly informing that army of Domitian's death and his own accession.

Nerva was also an old man, 63 at his accession, and in poor health; he was unmarried, had no children, nor did he have, so far as can be seen, any close relatives. His only in-laws were either unsuitable as candidates for the succession or vehemently refused to be considered. His father had been married to the sister of a man who had married Rubellia, a granddaughter of Tiberius and the sister of Rubellius Plautus, who was one of Gaius' victims; their grandson was alive but, since he eventually reached the consulship in 131, he was still only an infant. Nerva himself had a sister who was married to L. Salvius Otho Titianus, the brother of the deceased brief emperor Otho. This was a reminder of Nero's days, as was Nerva's own early career. Nerva's nephew, L. Salvius Otho Cocceianus, had been consul in 82 and was possibly of an age and experience suitable for a potential emperor, but the Otho connection immediately condemned him. Nevertheless, it is a sign of the widespread connections within the Roman aristocracy that Nerva was related, in however distant a way, to two previous emperors.

So, in addition to his age and poor health, the new emperor had no obvious successor. The various disabilities ruled out Nerva's few relatives, but it is likely that they were not disabilities in the eyes of the senators who chose him as their candidate. To them, the point of removing the young and healthy Domitian, who had several younger relatives, and putting in his place an old man without relatives, was precisely that he had no heirs to be his successors. The coup against Domitian was a senatorial coup. The fact that the army in the north was unable to intervene, at least immediately, was a bonus for the conspirators, but it is likely that that was all. The Senate was reclaiming the right to choose the emperor which had been taken from it by Augustus and by Vespasian in their emphasis on hereditary succession. The historian Tacitus (who became consul by Nerva's choice the next year) pointed out in his history of the events of 68–69 that it had been shown in that crisis that 'an emperor could be made elsewhere than in Rome'; the coup of 96 by a group of senators implied that this judgement would need to be reversed and that emperors really had to be made in Rome. Nerva's lack of heirs meant that the Senate would have to choose one for him, and since he was sickly they would be able to do so fairly soon. No doubt several of the conspirators would have had the possibility of an early succession choice in the forefront of their minds.

Nerva had to take the lead in the choice, of course, and, given his age, it was one of his more important and urgent tasks. His age was in this sense an advantage, for it could be supposed that he would not live very long – and apart from his age he was not in good health – so whoever he chose would probably become emperor within a fairly short time. This might persuade whoever was chosen to wait for his demise rather than carrying out his own coup, but it could only intensify the competition. From the time of his accession, the issue of who was to follow him once again arose, but his age meant that all interested parties – above all, the Senate and the army in the north – could wait, and in the meantime, develop their plans.

Since the new emperor had no relatives considered suitable as candidates, the pool of possible successors automatically widened to include many other senators. Every emperor had been a senator before his accession, except for the youngsters Gaius and Nero, and Nerva's main qualification for the post had been that he was old. He never displayed much capability as emperor, and he was completely unfamiliar with either the army or the provinces.[3] He had, so far as can be seen at this distance, never travelled more than 100 miles from the city of Rome, and he had never, so far as we know, performed any military duties. Any experience and knowledge he had of the Empire came therefore only from his activity as a senator or as the adviser to emperors in the privacy of the royal council. This was a man of the politics of the court and the Senate; his ability to rule the Empire was clearly minimal.

The senators from whom he would need to choose a successor were men who were a generation younger than he was but who were also adult and mature; they should therefore preferably complement Nerva's deficiencies. The pool of possible candidates included senior senators who had held the office of consul, especially those who had held the post more than once, the generals in command of the major armies, and the governors of the major provinces, in so far as all these were distinct. Generally a consul would have been either an army commander or a governor before becoming consul, and would go on to other posts afterwards. However, Nerva's own life showed that this sequence and experience was not necessarily always the case, as did those of Gaius, Claudius and Nero, and, for that matter, Domitian. Nerva was an insider, a Roman politician; that is, a politician operating within the hothouse politics of the city and the royal court, and the danger was that he would choose a man in his own image, one of his fellow senators who had as little experience of the rest of the Empire as Nerva himself.

These requisites would have produced a shortlist of perhaps a round dozen or so men. There were three men besides himself who had held two consulships. In 97 one of them, M. Verginius Rufus, held his third, by the gift of Nerva, and another man, Cn. Arrius Antoninus, his second. Verginius was an interesting case, for he now became by far the most distinguished consular alive, apart from Nerva himself, but he was also notable for having once refused to allow himself to be proclaimed emperor, in 68 at the time of Galba's insurrection. He was also notable for having been on Otho's side in the Battle of Cremona in 69 and a month later he had emerged on Vitellius' side, and he was a consul later in 69 on Vitellius' nomination. Yet he had safely survived the Flavian emperors as well as the emperors of the crisis year. He was, however, a man of Nerva's age and generation, and so his age tended to rule him out. Of the generals, the commanders of the major armies who were also the provincial governors in Syria, in Britain, on the Rhine and on the Danube, were also obvious candidates.

Then there were the perennials. Ser. Cornelius Dolabella had been consul in 86; he was the son of the Dolabella who was Galba's nephew and had been one of the casualties in the civil war of 69. There was C. Calpurnius Piso Licinianus, consul in 87, and the nephew of Galba's chosen and murdered heir. Both of these men clearly felt that their ancestry alone was sufficient to make them candidates, and their connections with Galba, the martyred emperor – another ideal emperor for senators – only enhanced their self-esteem. They had the same attitude as the several near-nonentities to whom Tiberius had married off his female relatives in that their ability, or rather lack of it, was of no account in the imperial competition; birth alone in their view was the criterion to adopt. Dolabella had the sense to stay out of affairs, if he was still alive, but Piso Licinianus, true to his ancestry, concocted a plot.

He did so in such a staggeringly incompetent fashion as to make it quite clear why every emperor who knew him automatically crossed him off the list of candidates. He chatted to his gossiping friends about forming a conspiracy, so that all the details became well-known to Nerva beforehand; he spoke to some of the Guard, making promises of great rewards, a detail that also reached Nerva. He had obviously made some of the right moves, the sort of things everyone knew had to be done in a plot, but he had done it all so publicly that his case was closed before he made his first open move. He was also plotting against one of the masters of the genre: Nerva had not only conspired his way to the throne, but he had earned triumphal insignia from Nero for his part in exposing the plot of Piso – the new plotter's grand-uncle – in 65. This, of course, made the Piso of 96 an automatic target for Nerva's investigators even before the plot had been hatched. So here was another failure of Piso's imagination. In the end Nerva, weary of waiting, pre-empted any actual move. He called Piso and his friends into the imperial box at the games, gave him a sword and invited him to get on with it. He backed down, of course, and was exiled to Tarentum.[4]

The army could not be dealt with in such a straightforward and easy fashion, and in fact Nerva had virtually no control over any of the generals. The campaign in the north involved a huge army that was gathered together from several provinces, which brought together the legionary commanders and provincial governors of all these areas, all of whom had been given their posts by Domitian, whose war it also was. These men then selected their own candidate for emperor, who they proposed to Nerva as his successor. This was M. Ulpius Traianys, governor of Germania Inferior and a former long-time commander of the VII *Gemina* legion in northern Spain. He was also a provincial, from southern Spain.

If Nerva was a link with Nero's time, Trajan was a Flavian. His father had been a legionary commander in Judaea under Vespasian and Titus, was made a patrician by Vespasian and consul in 70, had been governor of several provinces during Vespasian's reign, and he had married a sister of Titus' former wife. Trajan himself had been consul in 91, the year after Nerva's second consulship. He and his family hailed from Italica in Spain, but both father and son, being senators and Roman politicians, were well domiciled at Rome.[5] Nevertheless, as a provincial by origin he would have been automatically excluded from consideration by any group of the power set except the army.

Trajan was by no means the most obvious man to be the army's candidate. The commander-in-chief of the expeditionary force was the governor of Pannonia, Cn. Pinarius Cicatricula Pompeius Longinus, and he might have been the obvious choice. He was Trajan's almost exact contemporary, and had been consul the year before Trajan, but he was not a patrician. The other generals were plebeian and only first-generation nobles. Trajan therefore seems to have owed his selection by the generals to his birth, his father's achievements and his patrician rank rather more than to his military ability, which in truth was only modest. That is, it would seem that the criteria of the generals were much the same as those favoured by the senators. Their pool of candidates was as restricted as that of the Senate.

Trajan was already known, if only briefly and at intervals, to Nerva, and also, no doubt, to many other senators. The two men had been consuls in adjacent years – Nerva in 90 and Trajan in 91 – and Trajan's father had been consul in the year before Nerva's first consulship; Trajan had been in Rome in September 96 at the time of the plot and had probably attended the Senate meeting that awarded the imperial powers to Nerva. His appointment as governor of Germania Superior was one of Nerva's earliest actions, though it was probably something already intended by Domitian.

The message from the north was unlikely to have come as a total surprise to the emperor, and he was not presented with a completely unknown candidate as successor. Nerva had apparently made no move to nominate his own choice of successor by this time, and the proposal from the generals in the north arrived at Rome at some point during 97 at a time when matters in Rome were becoming seriously unsettled, probably as a consequence of Nerva's dithering. The Guard had turned on their prefect, who had participated in the plot against Domitian, and had murdered him, despite the personal appeals of Nerva for him to be spared. The Guardsmen were in fact demanding the punishment of all the participants in the murder of Domitian, one of whom was their own prefect, but this was also an indirect threat to Nerva himself, who had clearly been involved in the plot and was thus also indirectly responsible for Domitian's death. All it had needed at the time was a man to head the riot and there would have been a repetition of the *putsch* against Galba, imperial murder and all.

Similarly, the generals were demanding the appointment as successor to Nerva of a man who had been a Domitianic loyalist, indeed a man whose family owed its very rise to the sponsorship of the Flavian family, and who had been closely associated with both Vespasian and Domitian. Nerva therefore, faced by the enmity of the Guard and by a manifesto from a group of generals who between them commanded no fewer than thirteen legions – half of the whole army of the Empire – had no option but to accept Trajan as his successor. There is no sign that he liked having to do so, but at least he was now relieved of the necessity of making his own choice.[6]

Needless to say, this was not a situation with which everyone was happy. There were two other major armies, in Britain and in Syria, whose sizes gave the governors of those provinces plenty of clout. The British governor was probably P. Metilius Nepos, consul in 91 along with Trajan (though this is not wholly certain); he was also the brother-in-law of Ser. Cornelius Dolabella, which might have made him dangerous except that Dolabella showed no interest in the throne, if he was still alive; it was also the case that the army in Britain, three or four legions strong, was no match for the force of thirteen legions that had been concentrated for the German war under the command of Pompeius Longinus. In Syria the governor was M. Cornelius Nigrinus Curiatius Maternus, another Spaniard, consul in 83 and so perhaps a decade older than Trajan, which put him in his 50s; possibly rather too old to be a candidate but he would not perhaps have agreed. He certainly made a fuss of some sort, but seems to have been bought off with the second consulship that he held late in 97; again, his army was also no match for the great concentration of force in Pannonia.[7]

Once Nerva's agreement had been obtained to Trajan as his successor, all was in place. Nerva publicly announced it in Rome in October 97, without Trajan's presence. The mechanism, as in earlier cases going back as far as Augustus, was for Nerva to adopt Trajan as his son, and to announce that he would be consul *ordinarius* for the next year, along with Nerva himself (holding his fourth consulship). At once the Senate, fully alert no doubt to the situation, awarded the imperial powers to Trajan, who thus became joint emperor just as Titus or Tiberius or Agrippa had been.[8] The precedent was, in particular, that of Augustus and Tiberius in the last decade of Augustus' life: Nerva, like Augustus, stayed in Rome while Trajan, like Tiberius, fought the wars on the frontier. All this swiftly solved Nerva's problem in Rome and stifled any further plots that might have been under contemplation. The Guard was both mollified by their murder of their guilty prefect and deterred from further action by the looming Trajan and his army. There was no point in plotting to kill an aged emperor in Rome when there was another already installed elsewhere, surrounded by several tens of thousands of soldiers who were only too pleased that their man had been 'chosen'. Galba should have thought of this ploy.

This was a succession crisis on a par with that in 68–69 and that in 193–197, more than a century later, though without the violence. In connection with the events of 68 Tacitus had remarked that it was revealed that an emperor could be made elsewhere than in Rome. This, like many of Tacitus' *bons mots*, is memorable but not wholly accurate: Augustus had been made emperor in Greece at the battle of Actium; Tiberius and Gaius had been emperors in Campania before they ever reached Rome. Galba's, Vitellius' and Vespasian's assumptions of the powers of emperor were thus occasions even more distant from Rome than these earlier cases. Location, in fact, had no relevance and never had had. What was still important was senatorial acceptance, and this, of course, was what Tacitus really meant.

The elevation of Trajan was different for another reason: it was the first time that an emperor had been chosen and successfully installed by the army. This army was not the Guard, nor a small section of the army such as Galba's Spanish legion or Vitellius' Rhine Army, but actually a committee of the commanders of about half of the whole imperial military force stationed on the Danube frontier; Longinus' thirteen legions did amount to almost half the imperial army, which counted twenty-five or twenty-six legions. Tacitus' comment would have been more apposite if it had been applied to the situation in 96–97. (Perhaps it was, but we do not have his version of events.) Also, because it was a decision of this cabal of generals, it was a rather more important matter than the confused events of 68–69. For the revelation of 96–97 was that the army was able to impose its imperial candidate not just on the reigning emperor, but on the Senate as well, and from outside Rome, and it was able to do this not by killing a reigning emperor (as with Gaius, Galba, Vitellius or Domitian) but from a distance. The army was revealed, for the first time, as the supreme determining political factor in the state.

The killing of Domitian had been the third case of imperial murder in Rome, Gaius and Galba being the two earlier ones. (Nero, Vitellius and Otho were effectively no longer emperors when they died; Claudius was a doubtful case, as was Tiberius.) It had been a neat and sleek deed, well-prepared and, given the likely glitches always to be expected in such an affair, well executed. Above all, the pre-selection of Nerva was a masterstroke, for it pre-empted any immediate action by the Guard and guaranteed immediate support in the Senate, while the personality of Nerva himself virtually ensured no subsequent blood-letting. In addition, his age showed everyone that the real issue was not him but the person of his successor. In 41 the Guard had been able to put forward Claudius as their candidate because they had him in their power in the barracks. The Senate had not been compelled to accept him, as the debate that then took place showed. If the senators had chosen differently, they may have faced a massacre by the Guard, or the Guard may have been bought off and would then have killed Claudius. In 96 a part of the Senate met early in the morning of the day following the murder and swiftly and without debate installed Nerva as emperor. The attendance at the meeting had been pre-selected, the consul having summoned only those on whom he could count to support the coup, but there were certainly enough in attendance to convince everyone else that this had been a legal and quorate meeting. In 41 100 senators had accepted Claudius; there were probably more than that who accepted Nerva. The Guard had liked Domitian, as their later actions in hunting out and killing the murderers showed, but they did accept Nerva as emperor, if grudgingly, partly because one of their prefects was in on the plot, but also mainly because the Senate had itself accepted and proclaimed him. The sequence of events showed that the Senate's authority was clear and accepted.

The imposition of Trajan as Nerva's successor, however, was a new development. Until 97 every successor had been chosen by his predecessor, except for the cases of Claudius and Nero. The year 69 had produced clearly anomalous cases that could be argued away. In every succession except that of Piso chosen by Galba, the successor had been the previous emperor's nearest male relative, if one stretched the point with Augustus and Tiberius (the latter had, of course, been adopted in the end); again the exception was Galba/Piso. Emphasis had always been on hereditary male succession. It was, of course, as the events of 97 made clear, the Augustus/Tiberius case that provided the most compelling precedent for both the army and the Senate, but even there Augustus had had his hand forced by Tiberius and Livia, and by the repeated failure of his own choice of successors, not by the army.

However, to ascribe to 'the army' the nomination of Trajan as emperor-successor is to attribute a collective will to a force of tens of thousands of men. Clearly this was not the case. The choice was made by a group of senior commanders from among themselves. They did not look outside the small set of governors and legionary legates involved in the war on the Danube, even though there were several men with equal or better qualifications than Trajan in their midst. They clearly felt that any wider trawl through the ranks of senators was unnecessary since they evidently believed they had an acceptable candidate in their own group.

The principle of heredity could no longer operate in the conditions of 97, thanks to the Senate's installation of Nerva. It was still just possible to imagine the candidature of the two adolescent Flavians, Domitianus and Vespasianus, if they were still alive. Their emergence might well have been popular among the Domitian loyalists, of whom there clearly were many, particularly in the Guard and the army. However, the situation in 97 demanded someone who could take over from Nerva at a moment's notice, who could command the army, which was fighting a difficult war in the north, and whose very name would calm the fraught situation in Rome, and this included being accepted by the Senate. The announcement of two adolescent boys as the slain emperor's successors would not be a good move (and would imply that Domitian's death had been wrong, and would open his successor and his clique to recriminations). The announcement of the immediate adoption of Trajan and the immediate award of imperial powers to him was a response to the situation in Rome that was construed as an emergency by the army, by Nerva and by the Senate, and it worked.

However, no matter what reasons or excuses are found for what had happened, the fact remains that the imposition of Trajan was a military *coup d'état*. It was to a degree, of course, disguised. An official letter – 'laurelled' – claiming a victory on the frontier, was sent to Nerva, who thereupon announced that he adopted Trajan as his son. The swift acceptance of Trajan's candidature by both Nerva and the Senate argues that the whole business was a prearranged stunt. Yet the fact was that neither of these had chosen him, and probably he was not even on any list of candidates being considered, officially or unofficially, in Rome. Trajan was imposed on the emperor and the Senate by a military cabal.

Trajan became sole emperor in January 98 when Nerva died suddenly, as was probably always expected.[9] There was no need for Trajan to travel to Rome, for he already had the necessary imperial powers, granted the year before; like Titus and Tiberius he was already in office as joint emperor. The surprise occasionally voiced in modern accounts, and the resentment no doubt felt in Rome itself, at his failure to visit the city for over a year and a half is overdone. Like Tiberius, he did not require the Senate's approval for taking up sole power for it had already been given, and the war in Germany was still on and required his close attention, as it would have Domitian's.

The whole process of the nomination and accession of Trajan marked a decisive change in the method of the succession of emperors. The action of the army and its generals was the source of the nomination of Trajan, and this meant that the Senate had been effectively sidelined. The selection of Nerva, on the other hand, had been a senatorial matter; the killing of Domitian may have been a conspiracy but it is evident that a large number of men were involved: senators, including Nerva himself and at least one of the consuls, one of the Guard Prefects and some of his men, officials and servants in the Palace. This was in effect a representative sample of the

Roman establishment, with the crucial exception only of the generals of the frontier army. Next morning the Senate, under no obvious pressure even if lightly purged, had met in a regularly constituted session and had freely voted to have Nerva as the next emperor. Neither the Guard nor the army had any say in the matter, and had exerted no pressure on the Senate. They had clearly accepted the new emperor simply by not protesting. This was the process of imperial succession that the Senate had always wanted.

The Guard may well have complained that the murderers of Domitian had not been punished. Some of the men did so nearly a year later, but by those very complaints, which they expected Nerva and the Senate to address, they indicated their acceptance of the new regime. Similarly the army, by staying where it was and fighting the war that Domitian had designed but was now waged in Nerva's name – he was hailed as *imperator* after some victory late in 96 – accepted his authority as emperor. Yet the army was scarcely pleased with Nerva as emperor in place of Domitian, particularly since the new emperor had no military experience or authority. When the news arrived of riots in Rome and threats by the Guard, the generals took action.

However, the imposition of Trajan changed the game. Neither the Senate nor the emperor had any choice in the matter, except to accept the army's decision. If Trajan's name had been rejected by either of them, the implication was that the army would take action to insist. In earlier crises the Senate had been menaced, to be sure, but in 41 there had been negotiation and a senatorial decision, and in 69, Otho and Vitellius had been overthrown almost at once. At the end of 69 and in early 70, the Senate debated matters with vigour, even though Vespasian's troops occupied the city. Yet accepting Vespasian was to accept the result of the civil war; the balance between senate and army was then already tilting the army's way. In 97 the army emerged as the main political arbitrator; the Senate could not discuss or debate, it was Trajan or force. The result was that a different succession process emerged for the next century, and emperors had to pay much more attention to the army; hence Trajan's wars, Hadrian's travels and Marcus Aurelius' wars. The one restraint on the army's interference was heredity, and none of the next three emperors, like Nerva, had sons; the Senate could be used in the succession issue, but only to confirm an emperor's previous choice, or that of the army, which was there and knew its power.

The First Antonines

Nerva (96–98).

Trajan (98–117).

Hadrian (117–138).

The Later Antonines

Antoninus Pius (138–161).

Marcus Aurelius (161–180).

Lucius Verus (161–169).

Chapter Six

The Consequences of Trajan:
The Antonine 'Dynasty'

Trajan spent his reign in and out of Rome, fighting wars, collecting glory, and paid no heed to the nomination of a successor. This, given the circumstances of his own nomination, seems reprehensible. Alternatively, it may have been a matter of self-preservation, since an eager heir was dangerous. Rather as with Tiberius' and Titus' successors, this attitude was partly because his successor was generally assumed to be

VIII   The Antonine 'Dynasty': Actual (Genetic) Relationships.

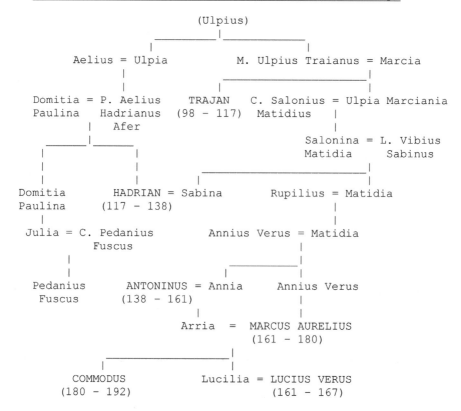

Hadrian, who was his distant cousin and also his nearest male relative. It may also have been in part a recognition of the necessary role of the Senate in the emergence of a successor. (See Genealogical Table VIII.)

Since Trajan became sole emperor, Hadrian had been closely associated with him; he had brought the news of Nerva's death to Trajan at Colonia Agrippina in early 98; he had married Trajan's grand-niece, Sabina (she was thus also his own cousin); he had been pushed through the sequence of magistracies at Rome as swiftly as possible, though without too much acceleration; he became consul in 108, only just under the legal age for patricians. He had been military tribune in three legions and had commanded a legion; he had governed two major frontier provinces: Pannonia and Syria. There could be no serious doubt that Hadrian was intended by Trajan to be his successor, if anyone was, and that he had been well-trained for the role. Yet the preference Hadrian had been given had not been particularly obvious; no formal statement had been made of his selection, nor had he been invested with the necessary imperial powers.[1]

It was thus something like the situation of Domitian during Titus' reign in that he was assumed to be, but not publicly acknowledged as, the emperor's successor. In the event, the situation differed in that Domitian was with Titus when he died, not far from Rome, and so could present himself at the Senate right away. No record actually says this, but Domitian was probably voted the imperial powers the day after Titus' death, so he was presumably present. The absence of comment rather implies that everything went smoothly; in particular we might assume that Suetonius, who did not like Domitian, would have commented if something had been untoward or had gone wrong. There were certainly adverse comments on Hadrian's actions when Trajan died, but these can in part be put down to Trajan's carelessness in dying where and when he did and in not naming Hadrian specifically as his successor. The real cause of the new procedure was Trajan's coup against Nerva in 97, which outlined a new method of succession.

When Trajan died, he was on campaign, or rather he was returning from yet another attempt at conquest. He had suffered a stroke in the spring of 117 while he was at Antioch, and he set out to return to Rome soon after, travelling by sea, intending to celebrate yet another triumph. He was taken seriously ill in August in Cilicia, at the small town of Selinos, dying on the 11th. It is the remoteness and isolation of his death which is at the root of subsequent controversies. He seems to have been unable to communicate, and his wife Pompeia Plotina took over his correspondence. In particular, she wrote to Hadrian, who was now governor of Syria and in command of the Parthian War which was going badly. The day after Trajan died, Hadrian, at Antioch in Syria, had himself proclaimed emperor. He had received a letter, supposedly from Trajan, a couple of days earlier, officially adopting him as Trajan's son. Having administered the oath of allegiance to the troops under his immediate command – that is, the garrison of Syria and the whole of the expeditionary force with which Trajan had been trying to conquer Mesopotamia and so a large proportion of the whole imperial army – Hadrian wrote to the Senate describing what had occurred.[2]

There has always been a whiff of conspiracy about this sequence of events. Any sudden death of a ruler in the ancient world brought rumours and accusations of poisoning and this was no exception. In fact Trajan's earlier stroke and a list of his physical ailments makes it clear that his body was breaking down. Plotina signed the official documents at this time in Trajan's name, and there were rumours linking her with Hadrian in an unlikely amorous affair. The fact that Trajan had named no successor publicly was also the subject of rumour, to the effect that he had already favoured someone other than Hadrian. The one nugget of truth in all this was that it was Plotina who sent the news to Hadrian of Trajan's sudden illness, of his adoption, and his subsequent death. All this may well have been the doing of either Trajan or Plotina, or by Plotina in Trajan's name (the most likely alternative), or both together, possibly planned and arranged well in advance. She was abetted in this coup by the Prefect of the Guard, P. Acilius Attianus, who was also an old colleague of Hadrian's, which produced yet more suspicions.

One of the stories that circulated was that Trajan had not named a successor because he respected the constitutional principle that it was the Senate's prerogative to choose a new emperor. This is an anti-Hadrian interpretation, reflecting the fuss that Helvidius Crispus had made at the time that Vespasian wanted Titus to be named as successor. The Senate had only once ever named a new emperor, Claudius, and even then it had been prompted to do so by the Guard. (Nerva had been presented as already installed.) In fact, the naming of a successor by the reigning emperor was by this time a prerogative of the emperor and had been so for almost a century and a half, ever since Augustus' long search for one. Furthermore, the political and military situation in the East in August 117 was such that it was not possible to wait for the Senate to invest a successor. The Empire was at war, and the largest section of the army was concentrated in Syria and actually under Hadrian's command by delegation from Trajan. It would take several weeks at least for word to get Rome, for the Senate to debate, and for the chosen successor (if it was not to be Hadrian) to get to the army; in the meantime it would be quite possible for new candidates to emerge, with the attendant risk of civil war. In practical terms it was essential that the army be under imperial command and that meant installing Hadrian as emperor there and then.

For it has to be emphasized that the army was the emperor's, not the Senate's, and any attempt by the Senate to interfere in army commands was met by an instant and decisively negative imperial response. Also, since it was the emperor's army, a period without an emperor meant that the army was out of control, for the officers had no commissions that were valid and the soldiers were free of their oaths. To object that Hadrian should have awaited the Senate's decision on the succession is to ignore that basic fact.

Then there was the other 'constitutional practice' involved, dating from Trajan's nomination: the cabal of the senior generals. It was those men who had chosen Trajan, who had thus been imposed on both the Emperor Nerva and the Senate. Hadrian was in a similar situation, for a similar group of high commanders was gathered in Syria where Trajan had gathered nine full legions, together with vexillations of eight more, for the Parthian campaign. This was equivalent to the force collected for the Northern War in 96–98, and it was to these men that Hadrian immediately turned when he knew of Trajan's death or near death. His first act was to administer the oath of allegiance to the army, which implies that he was acceptable to the men on the spot, and in particular to the senior officers, who would take the oath personally in Hadrian's presence and who would then go on to administer the oath to their legionaries. (He also quickly withdrew from the war, with little military complaint; perhaps this was something he promised to do.)

Needless to say, the Senate did not like this procedure. Selective senatorial memories would emphasize the accession of Nerva, when the Senate had been consulted, but not that of Trajan, which was the precedent Hadrian was following. It is from senatorial circles that many of the rumours about Trajan's death and questions about Hadrian's accession emanated, all designed to discredit Hadrian. It was certainly the case that the Senate had been sidelined, even ignored. It was only after having been proclaimed emperor, having been acclaimed as such by the army in the East and having taken the oath of allegiance from the army, that Hadrian had sent word of his accession to the Senate. Like Trajan, he was the army's candidate.

In his letter Hadrian paid lip service to the Senate's authority in the matter, blaming an over-hasty salutation by the soldiers for his assumption of power.[3] However, he did no more than this, and he had already exercised his imperial authority in replacing the governor of Judaea and ordering the evacuation of the areas of the Parthian Empire that were still under Roman occupation. When he set out to march west, he appointed a new governor of Syria to replace himself. All these were imperial decisions, accomplished well before he had any response from the Senate.

The Senate actually responded with extravagant praise for Trajan, who was deified unanimously, something that Hadrian had requested in his letter, but the Senate also added 'many things in his honour which Hadrian had not requested'.[4] Hadrian's withdrawal from the Eastern conquests, and from parts of Dacia that had also been conquered by Trajan, was not popular in Rome, and the great praise the Senate bestowed on Trajan's memory was in some sense a senatorial snub to the new ruler. It was also in a way an insult that he was offered the triumph to which Trajan had been entitled, and which the deceased emperor had been intending to enjoy once he had reached the city. Yet the imperial powers could not be denied to Hadrian, and were perforce awarded in formal terms. It was perhaps in reaction to the Senate's coolness that Hadrian deliberately cultivated his image as a quiet, civilized gentleman, and that he spent so much of his reign on his empire-wide travels.

Hadrian had in fact followed the precedent set by Trajan: first, a late adoption by the reigning emperor, then an acceptance by the army, and only then a reference to the Senate and the voting to him of the imperial powers. The Senate's annoyance was therefore the result of Trajan's dying outside Rome, where the Senate could not take part in the process except retrospectively. There is no sign that if Trajan had died in the city, accession would have been any different. Trajan's accession had been an army coup, an expression of military annoyance at the murder of Domitian, an expression of no confidence in Nerva, but above all a deliberate removal of the Senate – from whose ranks Nerva had emerged – from the decision-making process. In a way the Senate had only itself to blame for having accepted in Nerva such an obviously civilian figurehead, ignoring the fact that the emperor's basis of authority had always been the army, which required to be commanded by a man of some stature and experience in military matters. The rebellions against Nero had also been in favour of better commanders: Galba, Verginius Rufus, Vespasian, even Vitellius.

Despite the involvement of the generals, and hence the army, in the selection of Trajan in 97, it was the ruling emperor who had emerged as the determining element in the succession. The actual moment of appointment came when Nerva announced his adoption of Trajan in Rome just as the letter announcing Trajan's adoption of Hadrian was the moment when the succession in 117 was decided. The Senate had not been involved in Trajan's 'emergence' – Nerva had merely announced Trajan's appointment – though it soon awarded him the necessary imperial powers, nor was it involved in Hadrian's accession. This was the essential result of the crisis of 96–97; the sidelining of the Senate and the powers of imperial succession were now firmly in the hands of the emperor and the army. This was the result of the senatorial coup in 96: the generals were reacting against what appeared to be a reassertion of the Senate's authority.

It may be argued that this had been the case earlier, in particular under the Flavians, but the Flavian succession had in effect been determined by the Senate in 70 when the emperor's sons were fast-tracked along the route of elective offices. This was partly the result of Vespasian's victory in the civil war, but also because, for once, the emperor had adult sons. Now, once more, emperors were childless. Under the Julio-Claudians this gave the Senate the power of appointment as with Gaius and Nero, but above all with Claudius. The childlessness of Nerva and Trajan should have brought the Senate back into the game but it did not; that power instead gravitated back to the emperor, and there it stayed. The return of the Senate to the centre of the selection process in 96 had been so botched – Nerva was as poor a choice as Vitellius, Nero or Gaius, if in different ways – that the power of imperial confirmation had been taken from it. Trajan in many ways was a revival of Domitian, in policy, in age and in capacity.

It may have been the military situation that weighed most heavily with the Senate in deciding its response to Hadrian's coup. Trouble had erupted in Britain, in Mauretania, in Dacia, in Egypt and in Palestine even before Trajan was dead, and the new emperor had to spend much of his first year in power attending to the most dangerous of these problems, along the Danube. It was all in addition to the Parthian War, which Hadrian at once closed down; in all, a clear demonstration of the need for a military commander to take charge, and in the circumstances that could only be Hadrian.

The discontent in the Senate, however, clearly reached Hadrian, and this must be the basic cause of the murders of four extremely prominent men who were killed during Hadrian's first year, before he even reached Rome.

They were A. Cornelius Palma, twice consul, one of Trajan's better generals and conqueror of the Arabian province; L. Publilius Celsus, twice consul; Lucius Quietus, the deposed governor of Judaea who came from Mauretania and may have been involved in the revolt there; and C. Avidius Nigrinus, who was accused of having plotted the murder of Hadrian. The personal and political connections between these four men were no more than tenuous; their real connection is their earlier enmity towards Hadrian, together with the senatorial discontent, which could have provided the political setting and background for a coup. They were all also, sometimes explicitly, seen as possible successors to Trajan during his lifetime and so alternatives to Hadrian, just the sort of men who could have been put forward by factions of the army in any gap between emperors, the gap Hadrian had foreclosed by his instant assumption of power in Syria. A coup in favour of any of them would now, of course, necessarily have required the killing of Hadrian as a first step; this was the lesson of Domitian, Nero and Gaius. If a coup was planned, these distinguished men were exactly the group who needed to be recruited to head it, just as Nerva, twice consul, had headed a high-level group of consulars to remove Domitian. They could then turn to the Senate and exert their accumulated authority towards whoever was to be the new emperor; Avidius Nigrinus may well have been their choice.

These men, if one takes a larger view, were as qualified as either Trajan or Hadrian to be emperor. For one of the results of the coups of 96 and 97 was that the qualifications looked for in a new emperor had become extremely vague. Neither Trajan nor Hadrian had been active senators; both had been too busy as military commanders and provincial governors, so it now seemed that it was an ability to administer a province and to command an army which were the imperial requisites, neither of which abilities had been required of any emperor since Tiberius. Vespasian and Titus had good military reputations but, like Domitian, their military work as emperors was in high command, not active fighting. The four men involved in Hadrian's pre-emptive coup were all well-qualified in both these new requirements and indeed, better qualified than Hadrian. This may be the basic cause of his killing them.

A plot by Nigrinus looks rather surprising – if he was the choice of the plotters – but it was quite possible; it rather seems as though the plot had been discovered, and that Hadrian then took the opportunity to eliminate the other three men, who were certainly personal enemies of his.[5] Their deaths no doubt had as salutary an effect on the attitude of the Senate as had the news of the numerous calamitous uprisings, and this will have been another of Hadrian's purposes.

Hadrian's assumption of power, and above all his disregard of the Senate and of its claimed right of determining the succession, was a direct result of the crisis of 96–97. The Senate itself at that time had deliberately broken with the principles of hereditary succession and selection by the reigning emperor, which had been the main elements in the imperial transfer of power since the time of Augustus. Its acceptance of Nerva as emperor in place of the successors chosen by Domitian was a deliberate violation of the practice of imperial hereditary succession, more than a century old by then. The only break before then had been in 68, when Nero had died without an heir or any close relatives. The hereditary principle, which was deeply engrained in Roman society, had been reinstated by Vespasian and had therefore operated for well over a century when Domitian was murdered, though to describe the succession from Augustus to Nero as hereditary is stretching the meaning of the word. It was only by an intricate set of adoptions that the whole scheme could be described as a dynasty.

In 96, however, Nerva's assumption of power was swiftly ratified by the Senate, which clearly could have chosen someone else in the circumstances, and many of whose members would seem to have had knowledge of the plot to kill Domitian. It is thus reasonable to regard the change in the system as having been accomplished by the Senate quite deliberately, presumably with the intention of senatorial selection becoming the new process. Yet it turned out badly. Nerva was brushed aside; Trajan was imposed on him and on the Senate by the generals, acting in the name of the army, for the good of the Empire of course.

It was this process that now became the model for the succession of Hadrian. He had not needed the validation of a senatorial appointment. Just as with the imposition of Trajan on Nerva, the seizure of power by Hadrian was a military *coup d'état*, the army imposing Hadrian on the Senate. It is not surprising that his first year was spent (as was that of Trajan) in enforcing his military authority. Rebels were crushed wherever they appeared. Plots were exposed and punished. It is therefore no surprise that of the four men murdered on Hadrian's orders (though he denied doing so years later, in his autobiography and on oath), three of them were accomplished generals: Palma, Celsus and Quietus. A military man as a new emperor could not allow more distinguished military men to outshine him, and they were just the sort of men who were capable of heading a coup.

Hadrian therefore owed nothing to the Senate, which meant that he had full control over naming his own successor. This, to be sure, was not a new situation, but he did have an exceptional freedom in the matter, comparable in fact to that exercised by the Senate in 96 if the senators had stopped to think rather than greeting Nerva as one of their own becoming emperor. Further, as with both Nerva and Trajan, he had no children and few close relatives. Indeed, he seems to have cordially disliked or even hated those men who were his relatives. Perhaps because of this he made no attempt to single out any one man until the last two years of his life when he became seriously ill. (He was acting, that is, very like Trajan in this, though in Trajan's case a clear, likely successor did exist in Hadrian himself.)

Hadrian exhibited strong indications of paranoid suspicion all through his reign, beginning with the killings of the four consulars in his first year. He was thus inherently unwilling to name a successor since this might conjure a threat where there had been none before. This did not prevent many men from coveting the throne, but if one voiced an ambition or showed resentment at one of Hadrian's choices when he finally made one, punishment would follow. The man who he had installed as governor in Syria in 117 when he made himself emperor, L. Catilius Severus, was later made City Prefect. He had served Hadrian for two decades, then was dismissed for and accused of having imperial ambitions.[6] Hadrian thus safeguarded himself by pre-empting any coups organized in the dying days, but he had also to ensure a smooth succession when he did die. In this he improved on Trajan; perhaps this was more the result of his long terminal illness, whereas Trajan had died in the end quite quickly.

So Trajan's failure to nominate a successor was an example not worth emulating, but Hadrian made heavy weather of his own process of selection. He began by publicly adopting L. Ceionius Commodus as his son, who thus took the name L. Aelius Caesar, but Commodus was a ludicrous choice: old, in bad health and unlikely to live long enough to succeed; a Nerva-like choice. He was also married to the daughter of Avidius Nigrinus, the supposed plotter of 118; possibly his selection was therefore a gesture of conciliation towards the Senate. It may be that Commodus was chosen to be a stopgap to prevent others being suggested or suggesting themselves, and that Hadrian already wanted Commodus' future son-in-law, Marcus, to be his real successor. In other words, this might be seen as that old idea: the emperor-regent such as Agrippa or Tiberius. It could be that he was chosen so as to deflect plotters, for two emperors were obviously more difficult to kill than one, and it is doubtful if anyone wanted another Nerva situation. Commodus was invested with part of the imperial powers – the tribunician power and the proconsular power, but over the Pannonian provinces only – and sent to the Danube, where there was some trouble. He was also designated as consul for the coming year, 139.[7]

Two men in particular objected to this procedure and Commodus' selection: L. Iulius Servianus, Hadrian's brother-in-law; and Servianus' grandson, Cn. Pedanius Fuscus Salinator. These two were actually Hadrian's nearest male relatives and the latter in particular seems to have assumed that he would have been his successor, though there is no evidence that he did any work to earn it or that Hadrian had ever given any indication that way. In reaction to the choice of Commodus he formed a plot, was denounced and executed. His old grandfather was later forced to commit suicide, protesting his innocence and cursing Hadrian as he died. Despite his age of 90, Servianus was clearly seen as dangerous to the emperor's scheme, and may well have been capable of organizing a coup when the emperor died. Servianus was a highly-distinguished man, having been consul no less than three times, and he had connections throughout the power set in Rome. The deaths of these two men show Hadrian at his most ruthless. He began his reign with consular executions, and he was ending it in the same way.[8]

The deaths of these two men meant that the path of Commodus to the throne was now unimpeded. He was already invested with much of the authority he would need, and now also had some experience with the army and in governing a province. However, he died, suddenly but hardly unexpectedly, on his return to Rome, on 1 January 138, as he was about to become consul.[9]

Hadrian thought about the problem for three weeks. He was now very ill himself. This time he organized the nomination differently, summoning a group of senior senators to his sickbed and naming one of them, T. Aurelius Fulvius Boionius Antoninus, as his choice. It is not clear if Antoninus knew of this in advance, but it is certain that he took his own time over accepting. The nomination meeting took place on 24 January (Hadrian's 62nd birthday), but it was not until a month later, on 25 February, that Antoninus was formally adopted as Hadrian's son, a procedure that by now had become the essential preliminary step to the succession. He was awarded more of the imperial powers than Commodus ever had: tribunician power, the title of *imperator* and full proconsular authority, apparently without the provincial limitation that had been imposed on Commodus. This was no doubt one of the reactions by Hadrian to his own illness.

We do not know what occurred in between the two meetings between Hadrian and Antoninus, but the results have all the hallmarks of an agreement reached between them privately. Antoninus was in effect made joint emperor, on the pattern of Nerva/Trajan, Augustus/Tiberius or Vespasian/Titus. Yet there was also another element. It is recognized that Hadrian actually favoured the succession of Marcus Aurelius, his distant cousin, but the boy was still only 16, too young to rule. So Antoninus was also being installed as emperor-regent for Marcus with the duty of ensuring Marcus' quality upbringing, continued life and political training, and Antoninus' age rather implied that his stewardship would not last very long.[10]

The new heir was 51 years old, only eleven years younger than Hadrian himself. He had been consul as far back as 120, and had a daughter, though two sons and another daughter had fairly recently died. He was the son of a consul and grandson of a double consul, a pedigree that should please the Senate, from whose ranks he had indeed been selected. He had never commanded an army, but had certainly had some administrative experience, having administered part of Italy for a time and been proconsul of Asia for a year. Nevertheless, there was a distinct whiff of the Nerva situation about him. His ancestry was from Narbonensian Gaul, though his family had been domiciled and politically active in Rome for at least three generations; he was as Roman as anyone else. His age was perhaps one of the elements in all this that attracted Hadrian since it was unlikely he would rule for very long. Both Trajan and Hadrian died in their early 60s; Antoninus could expect a reign of perhaps ten years or so. This opened the way for the next generation but one to succeed.

It seems clear that the man Hadrian really wanted to succeed him was Marcus Aurelius, who was the son of Annius Verus and the grandson of M. Annius Verus, three times consul, and the colleague of Antoninus' father in the consulship of 97. This man was also married to a grand-niece of Trajan, so the inheritance was, in this sense, being kept within the family (see Genealogical Table VIII). There was also the young son of Hadrian's former heir, L. Ceionius Commodus, now called Aelius and in future to be known as Lucius Verus. Both these boys were now brought formally into the line of succession by a series of adoptions. (See Genealogical Table IX.)

As part of the adoption process Antoninus, already adopted as Hadrian's son, now adopted both Marcus and Lucius as his sons. His own sons were dead, so he was not excluding them. His daughter was to be betrothed to Lucius, though she was a number of years older than him. Hadrian was, in other words, emulating Augustus and perhaps Vespasian, who were the only previous emperors who had gone about the organization of the succession in such a detailed and farsighted way. Augustus had organized the adoption by Tiberius of Germanicus, while Tiberius himself was Augustus' adopted son, thus determining the succession for the next two generations; and Germanicus himself had sons by that time, one of whom, Gaius, Tiberius had ensured would succeed him. Vespasian had left two adult sons when he died, and did not need to organize the succession quite so obviously. However, Augustus' scheme failed when Germanicus died only five years after Augustus himself; Germanicus' son did eventually succeed, of course, as the Emperor Gaius, but this was hardly a happy precedent. Also Vespasian's succession scheme lasted only a quarter of a century, ending with Domitian, another unpopular if capable ruler. Hadrian might propose a scheme, therefore, but the odds were clearly against it working for more than a couple of decades, or a single generation. Trying to determine the succession in this way meant excluding others who might have legitimate hopes. It might, that is, provoke plots, as it did with both Gaius and Domitian.[11]

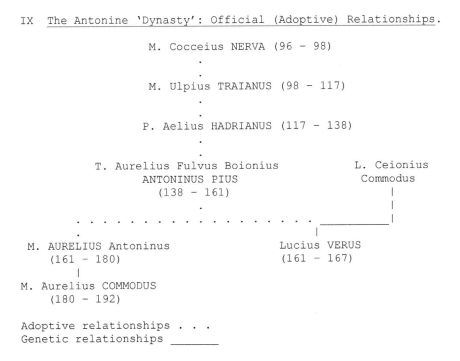

```
IX   The Antonine 'Dynasty': Official (Adoptive) Relationships.

                    M. Cocceius NERVA (96 - 98)
                                  .
                                  .
                    M. Ulpius TRAIANUS (98 - 117)
                                  .
                                  .
                    P. Aelius HADRIANUS (117 - 138)
                                  .
                                  .
           T. Aurelius Fulvus Boionius          L. Ceionius
                  ANTONINUS PIUS                 Commodus
                    (138 - 161)                      |
                         .                           |
     . . . . . . . . . . . . . . . . . .  _____|
         .                        |
   M. AURELIUS Antoninus       Lucius VERUS
      (161 - 180)              (161 - 167)
          |
   M. Aurelius COMMODUS
      (180 - 192)

   Adoptive relationships . . .
   Genetic relationships  _____
```

This foreclosing of future options was not necessarily a popular idea, therefore. It was his reaction to all this that brought down L. Catilius Severus, the City Prefect, and at the same time the long-standing Prefect of the Guard L. Marcius Turbo, another old Hadrianic loyalist, and Ummidius Quadratus, a son-in-law of Marcus' grandfather. None of these men was put to death but merely proscribed or ostracized, so it does not seem that their threat of further action was very serious; perhaps they merely complained.

The surprising thing is not that Hadrian should produce this scheme, but that it more or less worked, surely against the odds. Antoninus succeeded to sole power in July 138, and at once made it clear that his own chosen successor was Marcus. The boy – he was only 16 when Antoninus succeeded – was *quaestor* the following year, at about the normal age or perhaps a little younger. He was now designated consul for 140 when he was 18 (fourteen years ahead), and five years later he held a second consulship, in which year he married Antoninus' daughter Faustina (who was transferred to him from Lucius).

Marcus' marriage was a fertile union, producing children who outlived their father, which made a change. Marcus himself was made the titular joint emperor in 147, being awarded the tribunician and proconsular powers at that time, though his education and training continued for some time yet. This was the timetable that Hadrian (and perhaps Antoninus) had surely envisaged when he arranged the succession and the adoptions. Had Antoninus died at the same age as Trajan and Hadrian, Marcus would have become sole emperor about the time he was granted these imperial powers. His age was then 25, the same age as Gaius when he succeeded Tiberius (and about the age of Domitian when he succeeded), but his education had been much more rigorous, even practical. Above all, he was much more clearly singled out as the future emperor than Gaius had been. Marcus was, in fact, the first man to go through a successful training for the imperial office. No one else, before or after, ever did.

As Antoninus was dying in 161 (having reigned for twenty-three years and reached the age of 74, somewhat surprisingly) he clearly nominated Marcus as his successor (the process done by Trajan and Hadrian), and Marcus next day attended the Senate. He put on a show of reluctance to take up the sole power, thereby giving the Senate – which had no choice – the opportunity of insisting.[12] So Marcus collected the final powers, including the office of *pontifex maximus*, but he also insisted that Lucius Verus, his adoptive brother, be made joint emperor with him. The Senate did as he wished; again, it really had no choice. There were thus two emperors, Marcus being marginally the senior, reminiscent of the joint Augustus/Agrippa, Augustus/Tiberius and Vespasian/Titus combinations, though the most obvious precedent was Nerva/Trajan, for Cassius Dio claims that Lucius Verus was the military half and Marcus the non-military half of the partnership.[13]

Lucius Verus died in the winter of early 169, leaving no surviving children, and Marcus therefore continued as the sole emperor for several years. When he himself died several of his daughters were still alive, but only one son, six other sons having died before him. For the first time in a century an emperor was succeeded by a son of his own body. The boy, Commodus, was only 18, but he had been granted the imperial powers several years before: first the proconsular *imperium*, so that he might join his father in a joint triumph, then consul at the age of 15, and then the tribunician power. This was the same set of powers his father had held, but all about ten years earlier.[14]

Marcus was rather more respectful of the Senate than Trajan and Hadrian had been, following in this the attitude of Antoninus, whose whole adult life had been spent as a senator. He had scrupulously involved the Senate in the progress of his son to the position of joint ruler, but it was very clear that he was doing so for dynastic reasons and the Senate in fact, as usual, had no real choice in the matter, though to be fair there is no sign that there was any dissent over Commodus' promotion.

Marcus' reign is notable for an attempt to supplant the ruling emperor by an armed rebellion, the first since Domitian's reign. Since it failed it is generally reckoned to be a usurpation, but investigation rather suggests that the story is not an attempt like that of the successful Galba or the unsuccessful Scribonianus, though it had elements of both of these. This is the case of Avidius Cassius, the first of a series of superficially similar actions that took place over the next two centuries and more, and as such it deserves a fairly detailed treatment. It is, however, also a rather unusual example, and by no means easy to relate to other cases.

Usurpation in fact is a modern value judgement that should not be made, for it implies that the usurper is in the wrong, or rather that those 'usurpations' that succeeded, and so the 'usurpers' becoming regarded as legitimate emperors, were therefore mounting righteous rebellions. So Galba, condemned as a public enemy by the Senate and so as a heinous rebel, was then welcomed by that very same Senate, when Nero died, as the saviour of the state. Vitellius and Vespasian, who were both counted as legitimate emperors, began in the same way. Classifying unsuccessful rebels as usurpers is therefore pointless: 'unsuccessful emperors' will be the formation used here, or even simply emperor. These men proclaimed themselves as alternatives to the ruling emperors, sought support, minted their own coins and exerted their imperial authority in the territories where they were recognized. They might be proclaimed emperors, at times against their will, by others. In the third century these men can be counted in dozens, and their purposes and types will be considered later (see Chapters 8 and 9). They tended to ignore Rome and to fasten their hopes on part of the army stationed in the provinces; Galba is thus the archetype, also Vitellius and Septimius Severus, but Trajan was as potent an example. This is yet another legacy of the events of 96–98.

M. Avidius Cassius was a successful governor and army commander, in office as governor of Syria from 169, following the conclusion of the war with Parthia that had occupied much of the previous decade. He had also been given a general supervisory role over the 'orient', an area that seems to have included Egypt and parts of Anatolia as well as Syria, Palestine and Arabia. This was a position recalling that of Domitius Corbulo under Nero, and of Agrippa under Augustus. He was also the direct successor in the East of the Emperor Lucius Verus, a factor of unknown potency.

Cassius was therefore the most powerful man in the Empire after the emperor, Marcus Aurelius. He was a comparatively young man, born in Alexandria about 130, the son of a high official of Hadrian's called Heliodorus, whose wife claimed to be descended from the Hellenistic Seleukid dynasty by way of the kings of Kommagene. He was therefore in many ways a local boy in the East, with connections throughout the area for which he was responsible. He had also been brought up in close association with the court of Hadrian and Antoninus Pius, and he was much the same age as Lucius Verus, his predecessor, and of Marcus' wife Faustina.

He had exercised power in the East for a decade, first as the commander of one of the columns that invaded Mesopotamia in 165, then as governor of Syria from 169. It is clear that he had the trust of Marcus Aurelius, who was very busy over much of that time fighting on the Danube frontier. His brief would be to maintain the peace with Parthia, since the Empire could not afford to fight two major enemies at the same time. He had at one point to put down a minor rebellion in Egypt, but otherwise he was a successful governor. We have no details, but the fact that he held the position until 175 is clear evidence of his success and of the emperor's favour.

In 175 he had himself proclaimed as emperor. The trigger is said to have been a report of the death of Marcus, who was known to have been ill, but this is not a sufficient explanation by itself for Cassius' action. The further detail that makes it convincing is that he was asked by Faustina to take up the imperial office in the guise of emperor-regent for her surviving son Commodus, who was only 13 in 175.

This makes some sense of a curious episode. Cassius was well-known to Faustina and the court. He was experienced and capable, as his record showed, and presumably he was therefore trusted. Marcus, in the aftermath, is said to have regretted that; since Cassius had been killed, he had lost the opportunity to exercise clemency. When the news arrived in Syria that Marcus was still alive and well, Cassius was killed by his soldiers and his son Maecianus by other soldiers. His daughter Alexandria was spared.

This scenario is not unfamiliar from the previous two imperial centuries; the model was clearly Plotina and Hadrian. Cassius was solicited to proclaim himself emperor by Faustina, who believed Marcus to be dying, and she clearly envisaged him acting as protector of Commodus. This was a position that Augustus had envisaged for Agrippa, then for Tiberius, and Tiberius for Sejanus; it was the position into which Hadrian had put Antoninus, emperor-guardian for Marcus. (Faustina's anticipation of Marcus' death is reminiscent also of Domitian's action as Titus lay dying.)

Faustina and Cassius were thus working within a recognized process and system. That it became regarded as a rebellion was due to the emperor's unexpected recovery from his illness. Cassius was clearly too quick to respond to the news, though he was accepted as emperor throughout the Eastern provinces; not surprisingly since he had governed them since 169.[15] This is in fact exactly what happened with Hadrian; the only thing missing was senatorial recognition. It was not the Senate that stopped him, but the news reaching the soldiers that Marcus still lived; the soldiers therefore killed Cassius in part to cancel out their earlier acceptance of him as emperor.

The main result of Cassius' action was to accelerate Commodus' progress towards power. He was put through the ceremony of adulthood before Marcus marched off to the East and was simultaneously made *princeps iuventutis*, marking him as heir to Marcus. On Marcus' return Commodus was awarded the several imperial powers, putting him in the position of joint emperor. So when Marcus died in 180, only four years later, Commodus, like his father, only required such offices as *pontifex maximus* to be given him to acquire the full official powers as emperor. The exact process is not noted in any source. Commodus was on the northern frontier for some months after Marcus died; presumably the Senate dutifully voted him the details in his absence. The precedent would be Trajan and Hadrian.

Commodus' youth when he became sole ruler surely raised doubts in some senatorial minds about an emperor, the sole ruler of the whole Roman Empire, taking office at such an age. The precedents – Nero and Gaius – were hardly encouraging. Marcus had been singled out as the heir by that age, but his education and training went on for another ten years or so after that. It seems unlikely that Commodus would submit to a teacher now that he was sole emperor. It also seems that Marcus himself had doubts, for he left in place a ring of administrators chosen by himself for their integrity and ability, who were to operate the administration for the new emperor. However, with Marcus dead Commodus had the powers of appointment and dismissal, and having others to do the hard work was hardly good training. He was, despite his position as joint emperor over the previous half decade, essentially untrained for the post, perhaps deliberately so, for Marcus' long training had maybe been tiresome and stultifying, and he may not have wanted his only surviving son to go through such an experience, and there was nothing either the Senate or Marcus could do about it. Marcus was trapped in the requirements of heredity and with only one surviving son, he had no real choice. This was the real legacy of the *coup d'état* of 97; the Senate had lost all control over the succession and could not interfere in the emperor's wishes. Everyone was stuck with Commodus.

The Emperors of the Crisis of 193

Commodus (180–192).

Pertinax (January–March 193).

Didius Julianus
(March–June 193).

The Contenders of 193 and After

Septimius Severus (193–211).
(*Adobe Stock*)

Pescennius Niger (193–194).

Clodius Albinus (193–197).
(*Sailko via Wikimedia
Commons*)

Chapter Seven

The Crisis of 193

Commodus as emperor was extravagant, irresponsible, intellectually lazy, administratively incompetent and all too willing to have others do his work. (That is, he was exactly the son Marcus Aurelius brought up, having had no training for his job.) Obsessed with the arena in the same way that Nero had been with music and the stage, he is counted as one of the worst of emperors. There seems no doubt he was a neglectful ruler, obsessed with his own pleasures, but this was not necessarily bad for the Empire. If he chose good administrators he could reign without having to rule, entertaining people the while. That he lasted for twelve years as sole ruler was partly due to the vigilance of those who surrounded him, and partly to the fact that he was genuinely popular among the ordinary people in Rome; yet he regularly insulted, humiliated and executed those around him who did the work he should have been doing. Needless to say, he was the object of regular plots against his life throughout his reign, but for ten years (the first plot was in 182), he survived.

In the end the plot that removed him – in the only way possible, by assassination – was concocted by a group of his friends and ministers who finally understood that they were going to be his next victims. He had made no attempt to nominate a successor, no doubt from a well-founded suspicion that this would make him an even more inviting target, but he was only 30 years old when he died, and he might have expected as long a life again. Several plots came and went without result, except for the execution of the plotters. The one that succeeded was organized not just by people with access to the man himself, but in the knowledge that they had a willing and credible replacement emperor available. Many of the earlier plots were fuelled simply by anger or envy, and so they failed.

The final plot was, as with earlier cases, only superficially spontaneous. The Prefect of the Guard, Q. Aemilius Laetus, appointed only in 191, and the Chamberlain of the Palace, Eclectus, appointed at about the same time, came to understand that they were going to be killed on or soon after New Year's Day 193; the later story was also that the new consuls, the first of the year 193 – that is, the *ordinarii* – were to be executed even as they took up their office and that Commodus would then install himself as sole consul. This seems too extravagant even for Commodus, who, whatever else he was, was not a fool. It is, in fact, a classic example of an invented post-crisis story developed to justify to the Senate what had already occurred. (There are similar propaganda stories attached to the murder of Domitian.) Laetus and Eclectus determined to strike first. They would have appreciated the widespread fear and hatred of the emperor among the senatorial class, inspired by Commodus' behaviour. Cassius Dio, a member of that class, has a chilling story of the emperor slaughtering beasts in the arena, and at one point stopping before Dio and his group, hefting his sword and holding up several ostrich heads and grinning at the men.

The plotters enlisted the emperor's mistress, Marcia, as their instrument, and she administered a poison but this did not work. An athlete called Narcissus, the emperor's trainer, was sent in to kill him in the bath. Commodus was a strong, fit man, and a strong, fit man was required to kill him. This attempt succeeded. Even those closest to the emperor had come to tire of his behaviour and to fear for their lives; one cannot imagine what a state Commodus himself had reached by this time. He may well have welcomed death as a release from a life that cannot have been less than a torment.

The official version of his death implies that it was a sudden decision to kill him by a group of imperial servants who felt threatened, but this looks to be a way of removing the senators involved from any blame. A whole series of other stories are told that were intended to display just how unbalanced Commodus had become, including that in which Commodus planned to kill the consuls. The plot, however, was not simply a sudden decision based on the fears of a few palace servants. It was a long-planned, well-conducted, very successful *coup d'état*. The central figure was not the Guard Prefect or any of the Palace servants or officials, but the Prefect of the City, P. Helvius Pertinax, a remarkable figure who had climbed through the military and administrative ranks from being the son of a freedman to twice holding the consul's office. On the way he had commanded legions and governed the major provinces of Syria, Britannia and Africa. He was made Prefect of the City in 189, and so was in command of the Urban Cohorts, a disciplined force of about 1,500 men who acted as a police force in the city.

To have survived so long, to have held so many offices, to be popular with the plebs and respected by the Senate, and to retain a reputation for probity indicates remarkable abilities in Pertinax. Note that he had also survived three years in an official position that brought him into frequent contact with Commodus; note also that Commodus must have appointed him in the first place, suggesting acute judgement in the emperor. For Pertinax was also a loyalist, and had revealed the existence of at least one plot to the emperor. However, Commodus' deteriorating behaviour had apparently finally convinced even Pertinax that for the wellbeing of the Empire, the emperor had to be removed. (Yet it is surely a tribute to Commodus' judgement that Pertinax was so well and consistently employed throughout his reign.)

The evidence that the plot was not a spontaneous killing lies in part in the fact that Pertinax was in place at the time of the murder in order to claim the throne. In this the *coup d'état* had similarities with that of Nerva nearly a century before, but there were differences suggesting that lessons had been learned both from that affair and from the failure of the series of anti-Commodus plots in the previous decade. It had been a failure to understand the correct procedure that doomed the earlier plots to failure.[1]

Pertinax was not actually in the Palace when the killing took place, but then neither was Commodus who disliked the Palace and had moved into a smaller house in the Caelian Hill. Yet Pertinax was certainly available, and he was the first man the conspirators informed when they knew that Commodus was actually dead. He sent a friend to check that this was true (thus avoiding Avidius Cassius' mistake, another lesson learned), then he went to the camp of the Guard, where Laetus was in command, and he made a speech, stating that Commodus was dead – he claimed that it was natural – and that Laetus and Eclectus had proposed him for emperor.

Here was the second difference from the events of 96. Pertinax and his fellow plotters felt that they had to have the Guard's acquiescence before anything else, even though the Guard Prefect was part of the plot. The Senate was still sidelined; the effects of 97 still operated and the Guard took some persuading. Pertinax alluded to 'many disturbing features about the present situation', probably referring to the fact that the Treasury was empty, but to the soldiers this seemed threatening. The Guard had not seen any fighting for a dozen years and had no wish to get involved in warfare, which may have been what the soldiers thought he meant. They required reassurance and needed the sight of a confident man in command, but they saw an old man, not a good orator, referring to 'disturbing features' and seeming to be nervous, as he surely was, but they got the idea that he meant to go to war. As with Nerva's coup, the Guard had been content with the dead emperor and had no wish to change things.[2]

The Guard was temporarily won over and Pertinax at once turned to the less important institution, the Senate. It took some time to open up the Senate House and assemble the senators (it was still night-time), but he was obviously safe with these men. They had been humiliated by Commodus, their colleagues had been murdered, and Cassius Dio's description of his reign makes it clear that most of them hated him. General respect for the senators cannot have been very great, for they had on the whole endured these killings and humiliations without protest, which, of course, would only have brought about more killings. Yet the sequence of events in the House shows that the Senate as a whole was still composed of a formidable group of men. Before voting Pertinax the imperial powers, there was a celebration of Commodus' demise and a discussion as to what to do with his body. Pertinax told the senators he had already ordered it to be buried, and there was some grumbling about this for some voted to punish the dead man's body. In place of revenging themselves on his corpse, however, the Senate voted that his statues should be overthrown.

Then, after these preliminary but surely deeply satisfying measures, symbolically themselves assassinating the dead man, the imperial powers were voted to Pertinax, including, unusually, *pater patriae*, which was normally taken up only after some years. He did, however, refuse the titles of Augusta and Caesar for his wife and son, and indicated that he himself would prefer to use the title *princeps senatus*. This was clearly thought out in advance, and the decision to deny his son the title of Caesar carried with it the clear indication that he did not accept the hereditary principle, and this was in a sense confirmed by his choice of title, which was the old Republican term for the senior senator. The further implication was that Pertinax saw the emperor as no more than the chief member of the Senate, and that in his reign the Senate would have a much more active part in government than for the past century and more. He was intending to reverse the verdict of 97 and perhaps even the victory of Augustus in the civil war that ended the Republic, and to restore governing power to the Senate. It would also seem that the position of successor was now open, and that the choice was to be the Senate's.[3]

No doubt the senators were pleased, but many of the Guard were not. Their original acceptance of him had been reluctant and many were not happy at having an emperor in his 60s, or at the thought that he might take them off to actual war once more. The fact that Pertinax had gone to them first perhaps gave the Guardsmen an inflated sense of their importance in the succession issue; no doubt references were made to their participation in the elevations of Claudius and Nero and in the murders of Galba and his chosen successor.

A further indication that the coup was long prepared and that only the moment of action was spontaneous lies in the series of provincial appointments that had been made in the previous year. The governorships of four of the most well-garrisoned provinces – Moesia Inferior, Dacia, Pannonia Superior and Britannia – had gone to men from Africa, and it seems that at least three other governors – those of Egypt, Asia and Africa – were connected personally and politically with these men. The source of these appointments seems to have been the Guard Prefect Laetus, also an African. The implication is that this was a cabal aiming at securing control of the provinces and the main armies in preparation for seizing power at Rome. Of course, this is only a deduction from our knowledge of these appointments; there is actually no direct evidence of this cabal, and another interpretation may simply be that Laetus was obliging his friends. At the same time it looks very much like a new version of the military cabal that propelled Trajan to the imperial throne in 97.

It is more suggestive still that none of these men made any move when the news of Commodus' murder reached them. It is, of course, not clear what they could or should have done, but in the pattern of 68 or 97, one or more might have put himself forward as a replacement in competition with Pertinax, but none of them did. This is not to say that these men were part of the conspiracy in Rome. Some of them did not believe the news when the couriers arrived and put them in jail until confirmation arrived, assuming it was either a trick by Commodus or a provocation by some plotters. However, their lack of reaction indicates the general antipathy towards Commodus in the provinces and the army as well as in the Senate, and a certain pleasure at his replacement by Pertinax, as well, perhaps, as foreknowledge of the plot in some cases.

So there was no re-run of any of the previous coups. Not only was the exact set of conditions different, as always, but also time and experience had moved on. Lessons from earlier failures dictated that the conspirators had to have a new emperor ready, willing and on the spot when Commodus was killed. This may well have taken the plotters some time to arrange; volunteering to head a plot was not something every senator would do. Yet others could learn from the past as well. The Guardsmen were clearly convinced of their crucial role, and persistently indicated dissatisfaction with the new regime.

X.   Pertinax and his Competitors.

(a)   *The Relatives of Marcus Aurelius.*

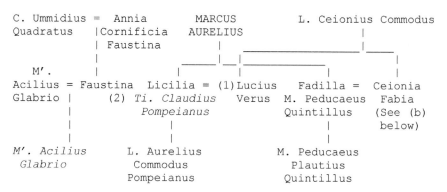

```
C. Ummidius = Annia        MARCUS          L. Ceionius Commodus
Quadratus   |Cornificia   AURELIUS                   |
            | Faustina         |        _____|____
            |              ____|_|_____        |
   M'.      |             |      |           |        |
Acilius = Faustina  Licilia = (1)Lucius   Fadilla = Ceionia
Glabrio |        (2) Ti. Claudius  Verus  M. Peducaeus  Fabia
        |            Pompeianus           Quintillus  (See (b)
        |                |                    |        below)
        |                |                    |
M'. Acilius        L. Aurelius          M. Peducaeus
  Glabrio           Commodus              Plautius
                   Pompeianus            Quintillus
```

(b)   *The Erucius Connection.*

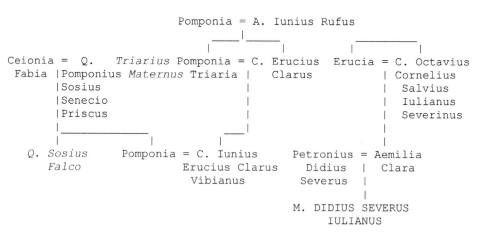

```
                        Pomponia = A. Iunius Rufus
                           ____|____          _____
                          |        |         |          |
Ceionia = Q.    Triarius Pomponia = C. Erucius   Erucia = C. Octavius
Fabia  |Pomponius Maternus Triaria |  Clarus          | Cornelius
       |Sosius                     |                  | Salvius
       |Senecio                    |                  | Iulianus
       |Priscus                    |                  | Severinus
       |_____             |                  |
       |             |         ____|                  |
  Q. Sosius    Pomponia = C. Iunius   Petronius = Aemilia
    Falco          Erucius Clarus      Didius   | Clara
                   Vibianus            Severus  |
                                                |
                                      M. DIDIUS SEVERUS
                                           IULIANUS
```

(c)   *Pertinax' Family.*

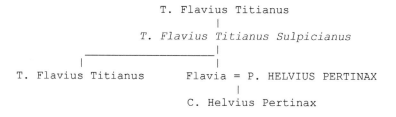

```
                    T. Flavius Titianus
                           |
              T. Flavius Titianus Sulpicianus
         _____|
        |                        |
 T. Flavius Titianus      Flavia = P. HELVIUS PERTINAX
                                 |
                       C. Helvius Pertinax
```

Contenders in 193 in Italics; Victors capitalised.

On 3 January, only two days after Pertinax' elevation, some Guardsmen tried a coup of their own, putting forward one of the new consuls as their candidate, the well-connected senator Triarius Maternus. He simply fled to Pertinax for protection. The other consul, Q. Sosius Falco, was involved in another plot later, also instigated, it seems, by Guardsmen; Falco is alleged to have known nothing about it, but since he was probably a grandson of Hadrian's first choice of successor, L. Ceionius Commodus, a fact that was no doubt public knowledge, it seems unlikely that he was a dupe. (See Genealogical Table X(a).) It is more likely that he was naïvely ambitious and too easily persuaded. These were typically amateurish attempts and rightly failed.

In fact, deeper investigation shows that these men were related in a fairly distant way, but Falco also seems to have been connected with the Antonine royal family. Two other men who appear in the story of the coup of 193 were also involved: Ti. Claudius Pompeianus and M. Acilius Glabrio, both of whom were married to Antonine women. In the course of events during the night of the coup, Pertinax met Pompeianus in the Temple of Concord and urged him to take the post of emperor, but Pompeianus refused; later in the Senate Pertinax is said to have urged the claims of Glabrio, who also refused. It is at that point that Pertinax accepted installation on condition that his family were not given imperial titles, and that he was to be known as *princeps senatus*, not 'Augustus'. Pertinax was thus being installed as a stopgap candidate until someone else was available, perhaps a son of Pompeianus or Glabrio. This would thus open the way for other men – Maternus or Falco, for example – who might be considered candidates because of their connections to the (former) royal family. Of these men, two refused out of prudence, and the others, the new consuls, either refused or were thought unsuitable. (For the conjectural connections of these candidates, see Genealogical Tables X (a) to (c).)

If Pertinax was considered to be a temporary emperor awaiting replacement this explains in part the attitude of the Guard, and the hesitations he showed in his speech at the barracks. However, the longer the temporary emperor lasted, the more the Guard would be unhappy. The antipathy of the Guard towards Pertinax necessarily increased with each of their failures and with the necessary execution of Guardsmen participants, a process that only enraged their comrades. In the end, on 28 March, a group of 200 or 300 of the men went off to the Palace, swords in hand. The Guard Prefect Laetus avoided them by leaving; Pertinax, over-confident, then went to face them personally. He was as unpersuasive as he had been in the camp on the night of the killing of Commodus. One of the guards ignored his words and killed him.[4]

As ever, the killing of the emperor did not solve whatever problem or problems the Guardsmen had. This really may have been a spontaneous killing, though the rapid desertion by Laetus is suspicious and some have supposed that he was implicated in the event. Certainly there was no successor in place or immediately available, suggesting spontaneity. Yet it seemed as if the Guard as a whole now held the decisive card, and for a fairly short time this turned out to be so. (One may recall the Guard's killing of Galba and Piso, and their brief time as Otho's men.) Some of the men wanted to give the throne to T. Flavius Sulpicianus who was Prefect of the City and Pertinax' father-in-law; others put forward M. Didius Severus Iulianus. Both men were well-qualified, having been consuls together late in Marcus' reign and both were previous governors and friends and colleagues of each other and of Pertinax.

It is to the point, perhaps, that none of the former candidates – Pompeianus, Glabrio, Maternus and Falco – were now involved. Their connections with the earlier royal family had been the one thing that linked them, but the murder of Pertinax clearly removed them from consideration. In other words, it was the killing of Pertinax that severed the link between the Antonine family and the imperial throne, not that of Commodus. Note, however, that Sulpicianus was Pertinax' father-in-law, and that Didius Iulianus was also related to the Erucius family and so was of a distant connection to the former royal family, but this method of gaining the throne paid no attention to such a relationship (see Genealogical Tables X (a) and (b)).

Both Sulpicianus and Iulianus were attracted to the idea of being emperor. Their ages, experience and personal qualities made them suitable candidates, but they made the same mistake as Pertinax himself: they thought that the Guard's support would be decisive and sufficient. In a notorious scene, they competed with one another, one inside, the other outside the Guard camp, by offering ever bigger donatives to the soldiers of the Guard; Iulianus won. This is sometimes characterized as a 'sale' of the Empire by the Guard, but it is hardly that; note that the men may have been rich themselves, but what they were doing was bidding with public money for the post.[5]

The Senate was therefore faced by the new imperial candidate leading a mass of Guardsmen to the House, carrying standards and arranged in battle array. The men at least had the sense to stay outside, and Iulianus did at least act in a gentlemanly and senatorial way, stating that he felt he was the best qualified man to fill the empty throne. Yet there could be no doubt, he was being made emperor by the Guard, and the Senate, under threat of violence, had no choice but to submit and vote him the imperial powers. The alternative, clearly, would have been a senatorial massacre, something it is doubtful that the Guard would have balked at. However, Iulianus, if he was at all sensitive to the senatorial atmosphere, was surely fully aware that he had little or no support beyond the men of the Guard.

The penalty for the unpreparedness and naïveté of the Guard and the gullibility of Iulianus came in only two months. The governor of Pannonia Superior, L. Septimius Severus, marched on Rome. He had three legions under his command, and had prepared the way by making contact with his neighbours; his brother governed Moesia Inferior (two legions in the garrison), and the governor of Pannonia Inferior was later highly favoured by him (three legions), all three from Africa. These three commands accounted for eight legions. With support or acquiescence from these men and perhaps from the German and Dacian armies (seven legions), his back was covered and he could safely leave his province. He was proclaimed *imperator* by one of his legions and, after a conventional show of reluctance – which had been conspicuously missing in Iulianus – he announced that he was marching to avenge Pertinax, and even added the dead man's name to his own.[6]

Iulianus had no chance of survival now, particularly since Septimius' forces marched exceptionally quickly. The plebs in Rome had already rioted against him. The provincial armies in Britannia, Hispania and Africa came out for Septimius, though it took the promise of recognition as Septimius' successor to bring over D. Clodius Albinus, the governor in Britannia; he had ambitions for the throne himself, but was content for the moment with the promise, thus demonstrating a political naïveté not far short of that of Iulianus, which would bode ill for him. More decisively, in Syria the governor C. Pescennius Niger had himself proclaimed emperor and since he controlled, either by himself or through associates, sixteen legions, he had good support, but his distance from Italy meant that he was effectively neutral in the decisive arena. The Senate, now that it had a countervailing armed support, proved capable of defying Iulianus. Emissaries and assassins sent by Iulianus to intercept Septimius alike failed, and even the fickle Guard mostly deserted him. When Septimius sent an order to the Guard to arrest the murderers of Pertinax, their obedience signalled to Iulianus that even this prop was being knocked away; he was killed in the empty Palace by a soldier.[7]

This marked the nadir of the influence of the Guard. It had never been a decisive instrument in the succession, except in the negative sense that it was capable of killing ruling emperors. In making emperors, which is a very different process, the Guard had been entirely and repeatedly unsuccessful. In theory the Guard claimed to have been instrumental in elevating Claudius, but as we have seen, it was in fact the Senate that had a decisive voice; it had been to the Guard that Agrippina had turned in 54 when she wanted Nero to be the sole emperor, but he was the obvious candidate anyway. Nerva's pleas to the Guard had been disregarded in 97, and this is probably the crucial moment when both Nerva and Trajan recognized that a successor from the army was necessary in order to retain or regain control in the city, for in a physical contest, the Guard's swords would easily prevail over the Senate's oratory but the army would prevail over the Guard. Now the Guard had murdered one emperor and then proclaimed and just as quickly deserted another, both of whom had relied on the Guard for support. So at no point, except in 193 in the elimination of Pertinax and Iulianus, had the Guard been more than transiently politically important, and this last cowardly, dishonourable and violent display sealed the Guard's fate.

Iulianus was not deserted only by the Guard but also by the Senate, which could at least plead that its acceptance of him had been at the swords' points. Even before he was killed, the Senate had refused to give Iulianus advice on what to do, a clear enough statement in itself, and had then met, summoned by one of the consuls in office, Silius Messalla. A sequence of votes accomplished the required changes. Iulianus was condemned to death as a public enemy (but then so had Septimius a little earlier), the throne was declared vacant, Septimius was proclaimed emperor and Pertinax was deified. A deputation of 100 senators set out to meet and intercept Septimius, whom they found at Interamna, 80 kilometres from the city.[8] (The number of senators in the deputation is the same as that which met to choose Claudius; one wonders if this was a coincidence.)

It was clear, from the events of the previous six months, that it would not be possible to keep control of Rome if the present Guard remained there. The army could beat the Guard, but the present necessary situation of the emperor was on the frontier. The Guard's place was around the emperor, but the Guard had become wholly untrustworthy; Septimius could not go to the city while it was the main armed force there. The news of Niger's self-proclamation as the rival emperor meant that Septimius would need to march east as soon as possible. The Guard was clearly out of the control of its prefects, and was quite likely to produce another emperor if left in Rome or turn on Septimius if he took it with him or fall to the bribes of another senator as soon as he left.

So this was the first matter requiring attention. The Guard was summoned to meet the new emperor, and ordered to wear parade dress but without weapons. On the spot, Septimius discharged all the men and banished them at least 100 (Roman) miles from the city. It seems likely that he would also have recovered the donatives they had recently been promised. Money was power; it would not do to dismiss the Guard and leave them holding enough money to finance a grasp at power by someone else.[9]

The Guard being thus disposed of, Septimius entered Rome, carefully changing to civilian dress at the city boundary, though he was still escorted by his armed soldiers, reasonably enough, since an imperial Guard no longer existed. He first went to sacrifice on the Capitol, then to the Palace. By these two visits he enlisted the gods and the imperial administration on his side. He was also doing exactly the same as any other emperor returning to the city. Finally, next day, he went to the Senate House. There, once again guarded by his own armed soldiers, he made a speech in justification of his conduct and proposed a motion by which no senator should be executed by the emperor unless it was by the wish of the Senate itself. No doubt the more cynical senators voted for this in the full knowledge that it would be impossible to make the emperor obey, but it was in the spirit of Pertinax' assumption of the title *princeps senatus*, and it implied that Septimius would be much more attentive to the Senate than Commodus had been.

On the other hand, his appearance in the Senate guarded by his own soldiers and a near riot of the donative-demanding troops outside surely conveyed a clear and chilling message to the senators. Septimius was being as intimidating and threatening as any emperor before him, perhaps more than any of those emperors, and certainly more so than any since Trajan or Hadrian. The presence of the armed guards in the actual chamber while he made his speech effectively cancelled out any good impression produced by his theoretical renunciation of the right of senatorial execution.

Presumably it was at this meeting that Septimius was awarded the imperial powers by a vote of the Senate. He had deliberately refrained from taking the full set earlier, though he had assumed proconsular power (which as governor he already had for his province), and had taken the titles of *imperator* and

Augustus. Part of his army demonstrated outside the Senate during the meeting, demanding a donative, and he managed to pacify the soldiers and also to reduce their demands. This, whether intended or not – the whole demonstration and pacification might have been staged – was a clear signal to the Senate that his base of support was the army, not just the fickle Guard; as if, with the new Guard around him and his soldiers filling the city, they could ever forget. It seems likely that the Senate was fairly satisfied with the new man anyway, and would scarcely need a reminder. They were at least rid of Commodus and Iulianus, and of the old Guard.[10]

From the point of view of the study of how one emperor was succeeded by another, the whole sequence of events from the death of Commodus in December 192 to the arrival of Septimius at the Senate House in June 193 should be taken as a whole. In that half-year at least ten men were proposed or installed as emperor, some with success for a time, though only one of them gained a long-term hold on the position. The question therefore is to decide why it was that L. Septimius Severus succeeded where Pertinax, Iulianus, Sulpicianus, Albinus, Niger, Falco, Maternus, Pompeianus and Glabrio all failed.

It is first necessary to be clear that all these men did fail. It may be that Pertinax and Iulianus are normally listed among the legitimate occupiers of the imperial throne, while the others are relegated to the ranks of pretenders, usurpers, rebels or refusers. A tenure of eighty-seven days (Pertinax) or sixty-six days (Iulianus), followed by their murders, is only a brief success. Falco's and Triarius' immediate refusal of the post, and Pompeianus' and Glabrio's refusal even to be considered, eliminates them even as candidates. Niger and Albinus held their initial positions for a time – one and four years respectively – and were obeyed in their provinces as emperors, just as those who operated at Rome were obeyed. These therefore succeeded, like Pertinax and Iulianus, only briefly. The author of the *Historia Augusta* included both Niger and Albinus in the sequence of emperors, albeit writing largely fictitious biographies of them, for in their areas of command they did exercise the imperial powers during their brief reigns. (He had done the same with Avidius Cassius and earlier with the brief Aelius Caesar.) These four, though not usurpers, may therefore be counted as unsuccessful emperors.

Pertinax and Iulianus had gone through the requisite process of acclamation, proclamation and the senatorial voting of the imperial powers, and had the uncertain support of the Guard for a time, but Septimius, Niger and Albinus were only acclaimed by their armies. Niger held a great meeting of soldiers and civilians in Antioch at which he was acclaimed as *imperator*, and Augustus a distorted facsimile of what occurred in Rome but very similar to the process of acclamation of Galba in Spain while Nero still lived. Albinus seems not to have gone so far, but by failing either to support or oppose Septimius he was able to accept Septimius' offer of the title of Caesar and the position of successor. Septimius had also taken the titles of *imperator* and Augustus, based on the support of his troops and his neighbouring governors. His success therefore was due not just to military support, but to the one thing he, Pertinax and Iulianus were all able to do, which was to gain, willingly or not, the Senate's vote of the imperial powers. His rivals failed to do this. Septimius, in fact, was copying Trajan by being the candidate of a group of generals and governors, but so were his rivals. His control of Rome and the vote of the imperial powers in the Senate gave him a greater degree of legitimacy than the rivals, yet this was only the first stage.

Septimius' eventual success was thus due to his command of an army that could defeat those of Niger and Albinus, and his acceptance and support from the Senate. That said, he began with the command of only three legions, scarcely enough to prevail if seriously opposed; three legions comprised only one-tenth of the whole Roman army, and if that was all he had he would not have won through. He also proved himself to be a more agile politician and a better general than any of the competitors – the rapid march on Rome and the gentle treatment of the Senate were clever moves – and so it was these qualities that brought him to the throne.

In the bigger picture, however, it was his army that was his instrument of power. The Senate, even though it had participated in the events of 193, was even more sidelined than before. The humiliation heaped upon the senators by Commodus not been erased by Pertinax' evident respect for them, or by Septimius' words. Instead, in sequence, the Guard, then Iulianus and his bribe, and then Septimius' army had demonstrated where power now really lay. It would be a considerable time before the Senate regained the respect that was a necessary foundation for its power.

Septimius was acceptable as emperor because he had the widest imperial support: several governors of garrisoned provinces, a substantial army and a large part of the Senate, even if the latter had to be intimidated first. None of the others commanded such wide support, and those looking to the Guard were the least successful. Septimius' disbandment of the Guard was thus in a sense superfluous, for the Guard always failed in proclaiming a new emperor, except that in so doing he was safeguarding his own life. The Guard was the least important player in the imperial succession game. Now that it had been disbanded so easily, its place was taken by the Senate as the player with the least serious influence.

Septimius' success was therefore a more violent repetition of the similar success of Trajan a century earlier. Trajan had revealed the Senate's essential unimportance in the matter of the succession when confronted with military power. Septimius merely emphasized this, in his own rather more brutal fashion, and Niger and Albinus were, of course, intending to do the same if they could. The Senate had managed to recover considerable prestige since Trajan's coup only because emperors formally consulted and publicly deferred to it, but in the matter of the succession no emperor had paid much heed to senatorial wishes and, so far as can be seen, the Senate as a body had never proffered collective advice to an emperor on the issue. However, senators were, when a dynasty failed, still always the preferred candidates, but then only those men with command experience were ever candidates; it was their status as soldiers, not as senators, that commanded respect.

The Family of Severus

Julia Domna, wife of Septimius.

Caracalla (211–217). (*Marie-Lan Nguyen/Wikimedia Commons*)

Geta (211–212).

The Berlin Tondo.

The Later Severans

Macrinus (217–218).

Elagabalus (218–222).

Alexander Severus (222–235).

Chapter Eight

The Consequences of Septimius

T
he success of Septimius Severus in holding the loyalty of the
governors along the European frontier and in securing acceptance
by the Senate left Pescennius Niger out on a limb. There were
men who would have supported him if he had a chance of success, but after
Septimius' meeting with the Senate in June 193, the result had to be either
submission by Niger or a battle between the rival armies. As a biography
of Niger in the collection known as the Augustan History remarks, he was
rendered a pretender – the term used is *tyrannos* – by Septimius' victories.
However, that also means that until defeated he was a Roman emperor in
his part of the Empire. He did, of course, lose and so became, after a year of
power, an 'unsuccessful emperor'.[1]

D. Clodius Albinus had accepted the title of Caesar and the position of
heir to Septimius Severus because he was ambitious to be emperor, but did
not have enough armed strength and was too far from Rome to accomplish
that ambition immediately; equally he could not emulate Galba's ploy of
convening a local Senate since Britannia housed very few men of senatorial
rank. He was therefore in the same situation as every other pretender to
the throne that had been briefly occupied by M. Didius Iulianus. He had
the power of the three legions of Britannia behind him, but his distance
from Rome precluded him from gaining any senatorial investiture. The only
difference between Albinus and Niger is that he lasted a little longer, and
that was only because Niger posed the greater danger to Septimius and so
had to be tackled first and quickly. In 195, with Niger removed, Albinus
finally appreciated his isolation when Septimius raised his own eldest son,
Bassianus, to the rank of Caesar and retroactively adopted himself into
the family of Marcus Aurelius. He was now the son of the deified Marcus
and, of all things, the brother of the deified Commodus;[2] Pertinax in effect
disappears from the account. Albinus' reply was to have himself proclaimed
emperor, and he gained the support of some Western governors and army
units, but not the main legionary forces in the Rhineland. He was eventually

defeated in battle at Lugdunum in 197 and committed suicide to avoid capture.[3]

Septimius' successor would therefore be his son, now officially named Marcus Aurelius Antoninus, known familiarly as Caracalla. By 197 he was being called, perhaps unofficially but entirely accurately, 'emperor designate'. By the next year, Septimius named him as joint emperor with the title of Augustus. Caracalla was 9 years old at this point. Septimius' second son, Geta, now became Caesar; he was two years younger. Septimius was taking Marcus Aurelius as his model in all this, but investing his sons at an even younger age. Caracalla was made consul in 201, and both boys were consuls in 205. There could be no doubt of Septimius' succession intentions; it seemed that the dynasty would follow the pattern of Marcus and, even more, of the Flavians.[4]

XI   The Severans.

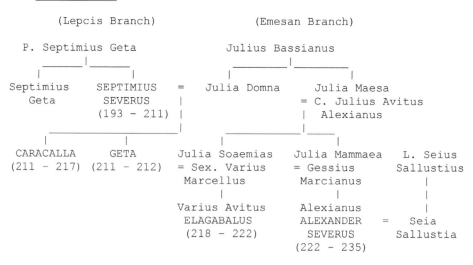

```
         (Lepcis Branch)                      (Emesan Branch)


    P. Septimius Geta                     Julius Bassianus
    _____|_____                     _____|_____
   |                 |                    |                   |
Septimius       SEPTIMIUS      =    Julia Domna         Julia Maesa
  Geta           SEVERUS       |                        = C. Julius Avitus
               (193 - 211)     |                        |  Alexianus
    _____|                        |____
   |                 |              |                    |        |
CARACALLA         GETA        Julia Soaemias      Julia Mammaea    L. Seius
(211 - 217)    (211 - 212)    = Sex. Varius       = Gessius        Sallustius
                               Marcellus           Marcianus       |
                                  |                    |           |
                              Varius Avitus        Alexianus        |
                              ELAGABALUS           ALEXANDER    =   Seia
                              (218 - 222)           SEVERUS        Sallustia
                                                   (222 - 235)
```

The promotion of Caracalla and Geta took place in Syria, in celebration of Septimius' successful conclusion of the Parthian War that had followed on from his defeat of Niger. It therefore involved only the army and not the Senate. It is not clear when, or even if, Caracalla was ever invested with the imperial powers by a vote of the Senate, but it cannot have been until after he returned to Rome in 202 with his father, by which time he was already being called Augustus. The brothers detested each other, so it was not possible for Septimius to nominate only one of them as his heir. If he did so, he would sign the death warrant for the other. (That is, the Gaius/

Ti. Gemellus situation, and that of Claudius' son Britannicus next to Nero, was recurring. One's appreciation of Vespasian grows; his two sons may have quarrelled and intrigued, but they stood by each other at the end.)

Septimius Severus was only able to solve this problem by making his sons joint heirs. He died on campaign at York in 211, almost as far as he could get from Rome and still be in the Empire. The succession, ignoring the hatred between the two brothers, went smoothly enough, but Septimius had nominated the army as the guardian of his sons.[5] There was, indeed, nothing to do but announce Septimius' death and the accession to power of his sons as joint emperors, for both were already Augusti. The two did manage to return to Rome together and there conduct Septimius' obsequies, but soon afterwards Caracalla contrived Geta's murder. Again, this was technically no more than the reduction of the number of emperors from two to one, and all Caracalla needed to have done was announce Geta's death. However, he had a problem, and his behaviour following his brother's murder is revealing. Septimius' designation of the two as joint rulers and the nomination of the army as their guardians was presumably done to guard the emperors from each other. It had not worked.

Caracalla rushed to the camp of the Guard to give his (mendacious) explanation of events, claiming to have survived a plot by his brother, who had then been killed. This was a likely enough event in the circumstances, but his own plot was clearly more advanced. It was in fact a group of Guard centurions who had done the actual killing and Caracalla at once rewarded them. The Guard as a whole would seem to have accepted the story, no doubt with a cynical nod and a wink.[6]

However, the Guard was not the army. Septimius' treatment of the Guard in 193 had led him to take precautions to prevent its successor – for a force of imperial Guardsmen in Rome and with the Emperor was clearly essential – from behaving as it had done under Pertinax and Iulianus; he had stationed a legion of regular soldiers, the II *Parthica* legion, near Rome at Alba. Caracalla had a much more difficult task of persuasion with this legion than he had with the Guard. From the Guard barracks he went to Alba, where he was treated very coolly. The legion clearly took its role as a guardian of both emperors more seriously than did the Guard, but there was nothing the soldiers could now do. By promising the soldiers a large donative and that their conditions of service would be unaffected, Caracalla was eventually able to stifle their misgivings and to persuade them to accept him as sole ruler.[7]

It was much the same at the Senate, his next stop, where his lies and excuses were not well received, though they had to be accepted. The Senate would have known of his visits to the Guard and the legion, and it was clear that the senators had no real choice but to accept Caracalla's explanation. They could not bring Geta back, the soldiers had done nothing to fulfil their guardianship role, and the Senate had no physical or armed resources. In the circumstances the cool reception of Caracalla's speech amounted to a virtual display of opposition.[8]

The order in which Caracalla made his explanations reveals his clear political understanding of the distribution of power in Rome. He had little difficulty in gaining the Guard's acquiescence, and this gave him the crucial initial support. He had much more difficulty with the legion and the Senate. Had he visited these groups in a different order he would have faced far greater problems. Without the Guard or the army behind him, the Senate might well have denounced him and this could have tipped the balance with the legion. (He had armed guards with him actually in the Senate House, just like his father twenty years before.) If they had both condemned him, it is unlikely that the Guard would have stood by him. It was a new permutation of the elements of power compared with Nerva and Trajan in 96–97.

Caracalla was always insecure on the throne. He murdered several possible competitors: the father-in-law of Pertinax, T. Flavius Sulpicianus, who had been Iulianus' rival in the imperial auction in 193; Pertinax' son; several of the descendants of Marcus Aurelius; and some of his own relations. These were all killed presumably because they were seen by Caracalla (and so by his enemies) as potential figureheads or leaders of conspiracies to remove him. The odd thing is that they had clearly survived his father's reign, even though Septimius had been more murderous than most emperors. It is a mark of Caracalla's uneasiness and vulnerability that he should have killed these people now.

Needless to say, plots followed him anyway, and his behaviour was so erratic, bombastic and murderous that it was the men closest to him who were often his targets and so in the end became his killers. The Commodus situation was thus returning (and the Gaius and Domitian situations). Caracalla began a military campaign against Parthia and while in Mesopotamia the Guard Prefect M. Opellius Macrinus organized a group of officers as a conspiracy. A soldier called Martialis who hated Caracalla sufficiently to become his killer was persuaded to act. Most of the soldiers in fact were his strong supporters, for he had raised their pay just as his father had done, but Martialis hated him for some personal reason. When he found Caracalla alone, relieving himself, Martialis killed him; then, having thoughtlessly kept his grip on the bloodstained dagger, he was himself killed by the emperor's personal guards. This severed the link between the plotters and the murder (shades of Domitian's killing). Macrinus then successfully dissembled his part in the murder and distanced himself from the plot; then he allowed himself to be proclaimed emperor by the soldiers.[9]

Macrinus did not last long. The troops he had to lead were devoted to the Severus family, no doubt because of Septimius' and Caracalla's generosity to them. The Senate was affronted by the fact that Macrinus was an *eques*, a bureaucrat and a Numidian – three unpopular elements – and that he stayed in the East rather heading at once to Rome. He had inherited a war with Parthia from Caracalla, and he could hardly leave the front to attend to the Senate's grumblings. This did not impress the senators any more than the same situation had with Hadrian exactly a century before. Nor did Macrinus' absence from Rome please the plebs, who began rioting at his continued absence. Caracalla had had a certain popularity among them, and though his death is unlikely to have affected them very much, the absence of the emperor reduced the donative the Romans were likely to receive, or at least delayed it, and this may have been the mainspring of the riots.

Macrinus made his son Diadumenianus his Caesar (which by now had become the title for the emperor's heir), and he took the imperial powers to himself without waiting for the Senate to award them. This, in fact, may not have been the first time this had happened. It was hardly news to anyone, though, that the army was a decisive element in the disposition of imperial power. This was partly the result of Septimius' actions in 193, when he took all the imperial powers except the tribunician before reaching Rome, and also of Trajan's nomination by the army commanders a century before. Now Macrinus simply took all the powers without waiting for a Senate vote, which would in fact have been a pure formality, or so it was by this time assumed.

The Senate did not like to be so obviously ignored, but it did in the end respond positively to Macrinus' accession, largely no doubt because it was so pleased to be rid of Caracalla. Diadumenianus was made *princeps iuventutis* and Caesar by a senatorial vote, and enrolled as a patrician; these actions imply that his father's assumption of the imperial powers had been ratified. Diadumenianus was therefore also clearly identified as Macrinus' successor.[10]

Having lost power to Macrinus, however, the Septimius family now regained it in much the same way as Septimius himself had originally acquired it. Septimius' sister-in-law, Iulia Maesa, who had been ordered back to her birthplace of Emesa by Macrinus, now promoted her grandson Varius Avitus as the heir to the family fortunes. She claimed, from a physical likeness between the boy and Caracalla, that he was really Caracalla's son. She successfully played on the affections that the army professed for the family. Macrinus was unnerved by this and fled from the battle that resulted; he had been a Palace bureaucrat, never a soldier, despite his post as Guard Prefect. His army, which had been winning the battle, naturally at once surrendered to and joined the Severans. Both Macrinus and Diadumenianus were captured and killed. This was, in effect, another *coup d'état* within the army.[11]

One of Macrinus' major weaknesses, politically, had been the very reluctant support he received from the Senate. The newly-restored Severan regime, which controlled the army in the East as soon as Macrinus was dead, showed the same tendency to ignore senatorial prerogatives. Varius Avitus became the Emperor Elagabalus at the age of 14, assuming to himself the several titles and powers of the office while still at Antioch – and also, as it happened, while still a public enemy, according to an earlier vote of the Senate – but then so had Galba been, and others who began their imperial career as rebels. It is probable that the Senate, as soon as it was clear that Macrinus was dead and Elagabalus was in control of the army in the East, acquiesced in the usurpation and carried through the necessary votes, but it remained the fact that Elagabalus had seized power in a coup and by violence, and the Senate had had no say in the matter.[12]

(This sequence – Caracalla-Macrinus-Elagabalus – is a perfect example of the difficulty and pointlessness of classifying emperors as usurpers. Caracalla had usurped his brother's position, Macrinus conspired to overthrow and kill Caracalla, Elegabalus took Macrinus' position; all three were usurpers before becoming 'legitimate' emperors; all three are recognized as such in ancient and modern lists.)

The plotting was all done, of course, on the new emperor's behalf by his backers, notably his grandmother. He was taken to Rome on a slow journey, and there he preoccupied himself with installing his own Emesan god in the temple of Jupiter, building a huge new temple, and attempting to make other religious changes. In so doing he annoyed just about all sections of Roman opinion, though this preoccupation did keep him away from everyday political affairs, so the Empire could be run by his ministers. Elagabalus was not wholly devoid of political sense, as his successive marriages to women of high political importance showed (but to be married four times during his teenage years was to invite both contempt and ridicule). As he reached the age of 18 he was still preoccupied with his religious practices, but at that age he would soon be able to free himself of his ministers. The prospect was unpleasant to all. He adopted, at the urging of Iulia Maesa and his ministers, his cousin Alexianus as his heir, who then became Marcus Aurelius Antoninus Caesar; he was five years younger than the emperor. This was done in the regular way, before the Senate.[13] (For the relationships, see Genealogical Table IX.)

During Elagabalus' reign, inevitably, several men made attempts to seize power, though as with other unsuccessful attempts to assassinate emperors, they generally failed because of poor preparation, apparently imagining that all that needed to be done was to kill the emperor and everything would then be all right, a common delusion among assassins. These men are in some cases only names, though some seem to have been relatively serious threats. Many more of these evanescent claimants to power appeared during the later third century in many parts of the Empire, for a whole variety of reasons. Later, in Chapter 11, those who appeared between 238 and 284 will be considered as a set; here it is possible to look at the small group who cropped up in the reigns of Elagabalus and his cousin as an indication both of the problems of the insecure dynasty and the problems of studying the men themselves.

An example of the difficulties in studying these people is a man called Seleucus. His origin and identity are not known, but attempts have been made to identify him as a Roman senator, though it is much more likely that he was neither a senator nor Roman; the name is, of course, Greek, though some later Roman senators also had this name. His actions and pretensions, even whether he really was aiming to be emperor, are wholly unknown. He is referred to as *tyrannos* by the only source, the unreliable *Historia Augusta*, and *tyrannos* is the label often given to men who aimed at imperial power but failed, Pescennius Niger for example. In addition, the name Seleucus suggests he was probably a man from Syria. It is all very indefinite and it is not at all clear that Seleucus was much of a threat to Elagabalus. However, his probable Syrian origins are a link with another man. Taurinus was certainly connected with Syria in some way, though little more than that is known about him. Again he was described as a *tyrannos*. (For these men, see Table I.)

The Syrian connection links to Elagabalus himself and to the wider Severan family, which was half-Syrian and half-African in Caracalla's generation. To go further would be to wander even further from the realms of uncertainty into those of pure guesswork, but it seems clear that Syria was a very distracted region between 215 and 222. There are two other possible cases in Elagabalus' reign: 'Gellius Maximus', who may be the commander of the legion IV *Scythica* stationed at Seleukeia Zeugma, the main crossing-point over the Euphrates; and 'Verus', who was also located in Syria. Even less is known of the latter and he may well be merely fictitious.[14]

Table I: Unsuccessful Emperors, 220–238

Date	Emperor	Challenger	Region
218	Elagabalus*		
		Seleucus, Taurinus	Syria
		Gellius Maximus, Verus	Syria
222	Alexander Severus	Sallustius	Rome
		Uranius Antoninus	Syria
235	Maximinus Thrax*	Quartinus	Germany
		Magnus	Germany
238	Gordian I/II*		

(* These emperors began as challengers.)

These four are thus little more than names now, which rather suggests that they were never much of a threat. Syria had in the previous generation been the scene of Pescennius Niger's imperial attempt (and of that of Avidius Cassius before him), of the successful coup by the bureaucrat Macrinus, who had risen from near poverty to the throne, and another by one child who was pushed on by his mother and grandmother to become the Emperor Elagabalus and another who became Alexander Severus. It may have looked an easy process, and such doings may well be imitated. Syria had been fought over twice in the last reigns and now Elagabalus had taken much of the army away with him to the west. Seleucus and Taurinus and the others (if they existed) may have fancied their chances. It would not have escaped anyone's notice that it was first necessary to gain control of a military force, and that the Syrian garrison was now much reduced, but Elagabalus had begun with not much more than a legion.

In 222, it became clear to the ministers that Elagabalus, now 18 years old, was seriously thinking of getting rid of them. What followed has all the characteristics of a well-executed plot. A Guard riot in favour of his cousin Alexianus brought Elagabalus and his mother to the Guard's camp for protection. Iulia Maesa then produced Alexianus, who had been rumoured to be on the list to be killed, proving he was still alive. The plot seems to have been directed at killing Elagabalus, but his mother was also killed. Alexianus was made emperor, taking the throne name Marcus Aurelius Alexander Severus. That same day, at least according to the *Historia Augusta*, the Senate awarded him the titles of Augustus and *pater patriae* (though he was only 13), and the tribunician and proconsular powers.[15] The speed with which the thing was done is the most obvious clue to its having been a well-prepared conspiracy, though it tends to seem spontaneous in the *Historia* account. The participation of Iulia Maesa is another indication. When Elagabalus became adult she would lose her power, and by replacing him with another child she could continue in control; her death in these events suggests the participation of Alexander's own mother, Iulia Soemias, who may have gone along with the original plot and then turned on Iulia Maesa to take her place as supervisor of the young emperor. The Guard was easily persuaded, it seems, and the Senate's instant response shows that at least some senators knew what was going on.

In this sequence the process of succession was, in a sense, returning to its previous system: the emperor nominates a successor, dies, and then the designated successor is invested with the requisite powers by the Senate. The problem was that the emperor's death had been caused by murder by the Guard, and it was in fact a coup by the Guard; the initial riot was no doubt a ruse to get the emperor into the camp. The Guard had never liked Elagabalus. The Senate felt the same and was clearly prepared to accept and applaud the Guard's action. The new emperor was even younger than the dead one. He could not possibly rule, and would need to be guided by ministers and his mother, Iulia Mammaea (his grandmother, Iulia Maesa, died soon after Alexander succeeded). It would be almost a decade before Alexander would be able to assume full control.

The mess into which the central government had descended since the death of Caracalla would seem to have convinced the Senate, which included the distinguished lawyer Ulpian for a time, that it was necessary for the Senate to directly participate in the government. Macrinus had been reliant particularly on the *equites* and the freedmen of the bureaucracy, and on his brief control of the army in the field in the East. This seems to have been continued during the regime of Elagabalus, who, of course, took over control of that same army. The Senate was anxious to return to a position of influence, having been largely excluded ever since Septimius' time. With the elimination of Elagabalus, most of the central government offices of state went to senators, and often to men who had entered the Senate over a decade before in Septimius' reign; many of these were awarded second consulships.

Such a policy might have provoked the Guard, which had, so it thought, put Alexander on the throne. This may be a partial explanation for an attempted coup early in Alexander's time. There were others, but the best-recorded case – which is not saying much – is that of Alexander's father-in-law, who was probably called L. Seius Sallustius. He was made Caesar on the marriage of his daughter to the emperor, and so by implication was now heir to his son-in-law, though perhaps it was intended only as an honorary title or perhaps just a surname. He became dissatisfied, apparently as a result of the treatment of his daughter, through whom he no doubt expected to exercise influence, if not more; in fact, it was Iulia Mammaea, the emperor's mother, who ruled in the Palace. Sallustius went to the Guard with his complaints, but they apparently did not react. He was arrested and executed, and his daughter was banished to Africa.[16] This happened only a short time after the elevation of Alexander himself, and the Guard could scarcely have become dissatisfied with the new emperor quite so quickly. It all showed a misunderstanding of Roman politics to assume that the Guard could have put him on the throne by itself.

There was also, possibly, another rising in Syria in Alexander's time, by a man who is referred to twice by Zosimus under his two names of 'Uranius' and 'Antoninus', as though he was two men. It is also possible that he had become confused with another Uranius Antoninus, whose rising in the next generation is better attested. This first case may thus simply be a mistake. If it did happen, it was another Syrian problem, for these men were Emesans from the home town of Elagabalus and the Severan women. The date is generally thought to be about 230 or 231, but it must be said it is not certain that anything actually happened.[17]

Alexander Severus survived as emperor for thirteen years. Two of our sources for his reign claim that he had a council of senators to help run the state, though they contradict each other as to numbers and composition with Herodian putting the number at sixteen and the *Historia Augusta* at a highly unlikely seventy.[18] It does, however, seem a reasonable notion that the council existed, given the deliberate and extensive honouring of old senators that also took place. (The *Historia* has a long passage on the reign as a golden age of senatorial influence, which may be exaggerated but not perhaps invented.) It was clearly time that some sort of a grip was taken on events in Rome where, by report, at one point the Guard fought through the streets with the

citizens for several days and lost. In fact, it is likely that the success of the
Guard in foisting their candidate on the Senate was resisted by the Romans
in the same way that they had been annoyed at the installation of Iulianus
thirty years before and Macrinus after Caracalla's murder. No doubt the
Guardsmen also became particularly obnoxious after their success. Yet the
existence of a committee of senators formed to assist in the government of
the Empire under Alexander Severus fits with the reassertion of the Senate
in the crisis of 193, its suppression under the Severans – no doubt resented
by the senators – and the need for a measure of stability under Alexander,
whose mother would have had little control over the government; it also fits
with events in the next crisis.

Alexander Severus, despite his distinguished names, was not an emperor
that the army could respect. In the end, still dominated by his mother, he
was murdered in the legionary camp at Moguntiacum in 235. The murders
(his mother was killed as well) were provoked by the news of a revolt by the
officer in charge of recruits, C. Iulius Severus Maximinus. The revolt was
well-prepared in a military sense, and a substantial force lay to hand for the
rebels to use. At the morning parade a group of officers and men greeted
their commander as emperor and put a purple cloak around his shoulders.
He resisted feebly – the usual purely formal gesture of reluctance – but then
publicly accepted the position in the knowledge that he had the support
of the officers and most of the men. Next day he marched his men against
the garrison in the camp of the emperor, some of whom he had already
suborned. The emperor and his mother were swiftly killed, probably by their
own soldiers.[19]

The new Emperor Maximinus was a professional soldier, allegedly
Thracian, but from his full citizen name he came from a family that had
been citizens for nearly a century.[20] Like Macrinus he was an *eques*, and
so immediately unwelcome to the Senate, but unlike Macrinus, who was a
skilful administrator but had no military ability, he had considerable military
experience and ability, but was neither a politician nor an administrator.
The basis of his support was narrow, exclusively military support that he
bought with generous donatives. He paid little heed to the Senate or the
city, and does not seem ever to have visited Rome while he was emperor.
He also increased taxation and attempted to tax the senators, neither policy
conducive to his popularity, not least in the Senate.

He was acclaimed by the army he commanded – Alexander's, earlier –
and, as with Macrinus and Elagabalus, he assumed the imperial powers and

titles by virtue of army support, perhaps without fully understanding what they meant. The Senate fell into line and voted him those powers later (on 25 March, according to an inscription) but reluctantly. His coup meant that the Senate had lost much of the influence it felt it had gained (or regained) in Alexander's reign, and plots against him began immediately.

The two plots of which we know some details were both headed by senators. One involved a senator called Quartinus (possibly Titus Quartinus, but his full name is not known). He persuaded a regiment of Osrhoenian archers to support his bid, or perhaps he was persuaded by them. They dressed him in purple and obeyed him for no more than eight days. Their commander changed his mind after a week and killed him. The commander in turn was executed by Maximinus, despite giving himself up; he had, after all, instigated the original coup.[21]

Quartinus' attempt looks to be merely opportunist. Note, however, that the Osrhoenians were a Syrian regiment, which links this plot with those in that region in the previous reign, and even with Edessa, the capital of Osrhoene, and the supposed scene of other episodes of trouble under Alexander Severus. It is hardly likely that this was merely a coincidence. Edessa's dynasty, the Abgarids, had been pushed around in the previous thirty years as a result of being trapped between the two hostile empires of Parthia and Rome; discontent, and perhaps dynastic loyalty to the local dynasty, is very likely. Possibly the troops were also annoyed that Maximinus was concentrating on the German enemy, not those in the East.

The leader of the other plot is identified simply as 'Magnus', though, since he is said to be both a patrician and a consular, he was very probably C. Petronius Magnus. The plot involved some of Maximinus' soldiers. When the emperor crossed the bridge into Germany, they were to cut the bridge and leave him stranded on the other side. The plot, as described by Herodian, was pretty amateurish. It was discovered before the expedition could set out, and executions followed. The involvement of a man of Petronius' history suggests, as with Quartinus, a senatorial involvement.[22]

These plots are notable for their ineptness which, of course, only makes them typical. Only in one case, that of Quartinus, was the purple robe actually assumed, so far as can be seen, and then only for eight days and perhaps only among the men of the Osrhoenian regiment. Magnus apparently simply wanted to get rid of Maximinus; there is no sign that a replacement emperor was present or even available, so to amateurishness in intention is to be added an unpreparedness for success. No wonder the attempt failed. Attempts to tamper with military loyalty were almost bound to fail where an emperor such as Maximinus was the target. He was very popular with the soldiers and such an attempt would enrage him, for he could not but be aware that this position rested solely on the soldiers' support. The *Historia* exaggerates by reporting that he executed 4,000 men for involvement in Magnus' plot; the numbers are way too high but the sentiment that produced the exaggeration is exactly right.

Two points emerged from these pathetic rebellions in the 220s and 230s: one is that plots may be either hatched close to the emperor with the aim of killing him, though both Magnus and Quartinus were keen to get someone else to do the deed; or they could be local and distant from the court. These latter cases, in this period, were Syrian and they were surely prompted by local problems and issues in Syria and the notion that only the emperor could solve whatever problems agitated the rebels. The consideration of later cases will confirm these two types and add others.

The lesson of the previous forty years, since 193 if anybody cared to note it, was that it was necessary for an emperor to have a wide base of support, both in the Senate and the army; the people of Rome and the Guard were also useful, but hardly essential or sufficient. The support of the Senate or the army separately was good only for a short reign. Unfortunately the lesson taken from Septimius' success was that the army's support was enough. He had even pretended to believe it himself, if his final advice to his sons to reward the soldiers and despise everyone else is reported accurately. Septimius may have believed this at the end of his life, but in 193, when he reached Rome, he had resorted immediately to the Senate for confirmation of his position. Yet Caracalla, Macrinus and Maximinus, whose reign was to last for only three years, had assumed that the army was the one essential; the two later Severi, by contrast, relied first on the army or the Guard but then rapidly secured senatorial recognition. Despite a considerable weakening in senatorial influence, the active support of the Senate was still necessary. It also suggested, from the fates of Caracalla, Macrinus, Alexander and later Maximinus, that to rely solely on the army was suicidal and a guarantee of a short reign. The army was very liable to shift its allegiance to another soldier in the most dramatic way.

In the period from the death of Septimius in 211 to the accession of Maximinus in 235, six emperors came to power. Only one succession, Alexander's, took place in Rome; the rest all occurred in the provinces: Caracalla and Geta at York, Macrinus in Syria and Maximinus on the German frontier. As far as we can see all of these men assumed the several imperial powers as of right on their accession, as a consequence of their acclamation. Caracalla and Geta already had them, of course, but Macrinus, Elagabalus and Maximinus simply took them and were apparently indifferent as to whether the Senate voted for confirmation or not.

Alexander took office in the regular 'constitutional' way, by a vote of the Senate. He also had the support of the Guard, which had just killed his cousin, and he gained that of the army, for a time. This was clearly satisfying to the senators, and the wider basis of his support, including the committee of senators, is one of the reasons for his rather longer than average reign for the time. (It is also presumably largely due to the political sense of his mother, Iulia Mammaea.)

The period as a whole, in terms of selecting and installing emperors, is therefore one of a contest between the Senate and these other power agencies, in particular the army. The Guard was usually of little account except, as ever, destructively. The Roman mob was merely helpful in rioting. It was the Senate and the army that counted, and despite the prominence and importance accorded the army by Septimius' methods, the reign of Alexander and perhaps that of Elagabalus, shows a clear recovery of the Senate's influence. The existence of a council of senators under Alexander marks this change, and indicates a helpful spirit of innovation among the senators.

None of these emperors survived long enough to be succeeded by a son or by another nominee, though both Macrinus and Maximinus had adult sons who they promoted as their successors, actions guaranteeing their sons' deaths when they themselves were overthrown; Elagabalus was also succeeded by his nearest male relative, though inadvertently. In all these cases, be it noted, the designated successors resorted to the Senate for their nominations to be confirmed, the title Caesar being awarded by a vote in the House. Conciliation of the Senate was thus a priority of most emperors; even of those whose early support had solely been the army.

The contest had gone the army's way, thanks to Septimius' favours, and the accessions of Caracalla, Macrinus and Elagabalus seemed to confirm the army's seniority. The Senate regained much ground by the process of the accession of Alexander. (The extravagant words of the *Historia Augusta* on this surely reflect some reality.) Alexander's debt to the Guard was soon cancelled by the defeat suffered by the Guard in the fighting with the Romans the year after he succeeded, but then the Guard was never as influential as it thought it was. During Alexander's reign the Senate returned to the centre of power with a vengeance, occupying the senior offices, advising the emperor in a permanent committee, which looks as though it may well have been that the emperor's *consilium*, until then a fairly informal body, had been established on a more permanent basis and so had become responsible as much to the Senate as to the emperor.

The killing of Alexander and elevation of Maximinus as the army's candidate was therefore a setback for senatorial power and influence, all the more galling for the hopes senators would have had of a return to power, and all the more serious in that Maximinus deliberately ignored not just the Senate but Rome itself. The two plots against him that were led by senators are thus not at all surprising, and they would seem to be a result of the Senate's rude rejection by Maximinus. What was unusual is what the Senate did next.

Part III

The Senate's Revival

The Contestants of the Crisis of 238

Maximinus Thrax (235–238).

Balbinus (238). (*Adobe Stock*)

Pupienus (238).

Gordian II (238).

Senatorial Emperors

Gordian III (238–244).

Decius (249–251).

Philip the Arab (244–249).
(*Rabax63 via Wikimedia Commons*)

Chapter Nine

The Crisis of 238

The position of the Senate in the reign of Maximinus Thrax was of an institution in a classic pre-revolutionary situation. After a lengthy period of declining influence and under increasing menace from the imperial power (Severus to Elagabalus), there came a period of relief and a return to the Senate's 'rightful' scale of influence (during the reign of Alexander Severus), but this was then followed by a sudden, even brutal, return to a period of minimal influence and authority when even the person of the emperor was absent and he displayed only negligent contempt for it (reign of Maximinus Thrax), nor did he hesitate to execute senators or to threaten their position by aiming to impose taxation on them. This must be the moment of least senatorial influence since the murders of senators in the civil wars that ended the Republic. Revolutionary theory now points to the dashing of mounting or reviving hopes as the likeliest moment for a revolution to break out. It is perhaps too much to consider the Roman Senate as a revolutionary instrument, but it is nevertheless certain that in 238 the Senate instigated a series of measures that resulted in its revival as an effective organ of government for the next generation.[1]

The anger of the Senate at the Emperor Maximinus' seizure of power, his failure to attend to the senators' opinions and perhaps his failure to come to Rome for the award of the imperial powers was further fuelled by the ruthless way in which taxes were imposed and collected to pay the expenses involved in his campaigns. The collection fell heavily on those most able to pay; that is, merchants, landowners and the wealthy, of whom the senators themselves were a part. The injustice – senators were traditionally exempt from ordinary taxation – was widely felt among those whose wealth was therefore reduced.[2] Maximinus' policies thus marked a clear division between the two groupings in the state: the army and the senators, personifying the rich. The author hesitates to use the term 'parties', for they were scarcely well-organized or coherent. This separation is, nevertheless, the key to understanding the process of the selection and accession of emperors in the next half-century.

The resentment of the Senate was displayed very clearly in its reaction to the news from Africa that a man, a senator more than 80 years old, had been proclaimed emperor. He was M. Antonius Gordianus Sempronius Romanus, the governor of the province of Africa. A tax revolt had begun in Thysdrus (now El Djem), a prosperous town some distance south of Carthage, during which the procurator of the province was killed by a group of young men from local wealthy families. This could well have been a local reaction to the increased taxation of Maximinus' government, though tax riots were hardly unusual. Having done this, the mobs of young men went to a house in the town where Governor Gordian was staying and persuaded him, without much difficulty or resistance on his part, to declare himself Augustus. He then set off to Carthage, where he was accepted as emperor.[3]

The place and the man are, to say the least, surprising. The province of Africa was senatorial. The governor was always appointed from the Senate and was a post to which senators arrived by rank and which they could expect to reach if they lived long enough. The province had no troops stationed within it other than a proconsular guard and the urban militia, though there was a legion next door in Numidia. Bearing in mind the method and the tradition of usurpations in the Roman Empire, it seemed to make no sense to launch such an attempt without getting armed backing first. Also the fact that Gordian was 80 and had had a fairly undistinguished career, though Herodian claims he had held many provincial commands, meant that the man himself was a most unlikely imperial candidate. However, the two other senatorial plotters of this reign, Petronius Magnus and T. Quartinus, were of no particular distinction either. In one way Gordian's emergence as a challenger to Maximinus is of the same type as these two. Indeed, by staging his rising in a province with no armed forces, it might be said that it was an alternative to them; if their plots had failed because the army objected, try a plot where there is no army to oppose the attempt.

Yet there are also elements in all of this suggesting that the matter was not nearly as spontaneous as it is made to seem. It is more than curious that the tax revolt and the killing of the procurator should take place just at the time when the governor was also in the town, presumably with his official guard, and so a long way from the main provincial centre at Carthage. The procurator and the governor had rather conflicting offices and are unlikely to have been seen as colleagues. Apart from the governor's own guard, which would have been with him, the procurator also had an armed guard, which was trounced by the clubs and fists of the young assassins and their followers. These 'followers' were in fact the clients and tenants of the organizers, who had been summoned to the town for the occasion. So the defeat of the procurator's guard left the governor's guard – which had not assisted in putting down the riot – in sole armed control of the province. Gordian's resistance to his proclamation as Augustus is emphasized by the historian Herodian, but it was in fact little more than a gesture, of no greater moment than that of Maximinus three years before; a token resistance was part of the process of seizing power and was expected; it did not do to appear too eager to take power. This coup, in other words, looks to have been planned at this local level; the procurator had no doubt been identified as the main obstacle to the coup, quite apart from being detested for his tax-collecting activities. He was therefore removed first, and Gordian's presence in the town, and therefore his availability to head the coup, was deliberate.

Gordian's first action after having the purple robe put round his shoulders – it just happened to be handy, of course – was to send letters to several of his senatorial colleagues in Rome, supposedly asking for their support, and he activated the network of his friends and relations. The necessary manifesto was sent, setting out the reasons for his action – a condemnation of Maximinus and a promise of a restoration of good government and the righting of wrongs – and emphasizing that he had the unanimous support of his province. He appointed his son Gordian II as his fellow emperor and despatched his *quaestor* to Rome, no doubt with oral messages. Other men were also sent to the city; among them, it is said, P. Licinius Valerianus, who was a member of the governor's staff and who fifteen years later became emperor himself. The messages included an instruction to see to the death of the 'commander of the forces in Rome', who Herodian calls Vitalianus,[4] that is, the Praetorian Prefect P. Aelius Vitalianus. The main body of the Guard was with Maximinus on the frontier, but the prefect was in charge in Rome during his 'continued' absence. The City Prefect, named as Sabinus, was also a Maximinus loyalist; his removal would also be a priority.

All this – the local events, the instant messages to Rome, the plans to remove Maximinus' key people in the city – looks to be rather too well thought out and organized to be quite as spontaneous as the account in Herodian suggests. (In the same way, the apparent spontaneity of the coup that removed Elagabalus and installed Alexander is belied by the speed and sequence of the subsequent events.) At Rome, indeed, coinage in the name of the Gordians was issued very quickly, and it seems that the dies might already have been prepared.[5] This would imply that any senators, and the major part of the administration at Rome, had already been suborned, and that the revolt at Thysdrus had also been organized well in advance.

Consider further the sheer unlikeliness of the events in Africa. The governor was a man 80 years old or thereabouts, he had no military experience so far as we can see, and he had at his command no serious military forces; indeed, he was to be overwhelmed and suppressed in only three weeks. He was challenging a competent and experienced soldier who had the loyalty and support of the greater part of the Roman army. This is a sequence of events so unlikely to lead to success that it is necessary to investigate further. A senator would scarcely put himself in harm's way so readily, with the probable consequence of a humiliating death for himself and his family and the confiscation of his property, if he was not both driven by strong emotions and, much more important, assured of wider support. The lack of distinction of Gordian in his previous career suggests a man content to obey any emperor who came along, and a man of little ambition; it would take a convincing conspiracy for such a man to take the actions attributed to him.

Several items combine to suggest that the coup was pre-planned on a much wider scale than Africa. The suggestion that the coin dies at Rome were produced in advance has been noted. Perhaps still more convincing is the fact that the Senate was always deeply impressed by age and by accumulated experience. A senator aged 80 merited respect from his fellows because of his age and descent (note the emperors Nerva and later Tacitus, both of them senatorial and aged emperors; the *Augustan History* claims that Gordian was descended from the Republican Scipios and from Marcus Aurelius[6]). If Gordian was prepared to take the lead, this could well have been the catalyst that brought the conspirators from expressions of discontent into the active phase of a plot. Supporting this is the fact that Gordian had an adult son, probably in his 40s. Like his father he had gone through the traditional sequence of elected offices – *quaestor, aedile, praetor* and consul – or so the unreliable *Historia Augusta* claims, though this is quite likely.[7] His age would mean the elder Gordian as emperor would probably leave much of his work to his son, who was already acting as his legate in Africa, and that the son would inevitably succeed to the throne fairly soon.

There were also other prominent men with him, including at least one of consular rank, M. Licinius Valerianus: Gordian was able to use these men as his messengers to the Senate, where their rank would ensure them immediate attention. There was also still another generation of the family, Gordian I's grandson, the son of his daughter. A series of Gordians placed on the throne and reigning for the foreseeable future and put there by the influence of the Senate would have been a most attractive notion to the senators who were especially resentful at the greedy, upstart and neglectful Maximinus, the Thracian; one can almost hear the contempt in the senatorial voices at such a description. (See Genealogical Table XII.)

XII   The Gordians.

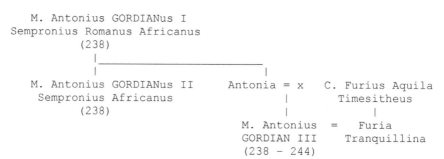

```
        M. Antonius GORDIANus I
     Sempronius Romanus Africanus
             (238)
              |
              |_____
              |                          |
    M. Antonius GORDIANus II     Antonia = x   C. Furius Aquila
       Sempronius Africanus         |             Timesitheus
             (238)                  |                |
                            M. Antonius  =   Furia
                            GORDIAN III     Tranquillina
                            (238 - 244)
```

So the plot in Africa was probably well-prepared, with the equal probability that the groundwork had been done in Rome in advance. The eruption at Thysdrus seems to have taken place early in 238, between January and March. Gordian I had become proconsul of Africa only during 237, so this was good going: the whole plot laid out and detonated within perhaps six months. The senatorial plots of Quartinus and Magnus had failed in the previous year or so, which will have indicated just what was likely to go wrong. It was clearly necessary to plan carefully and in detail, as well as, of course, secretly. Above all, it was necessary to have an emperor-candidate ready to assume power from the beginning. It was also necessary to keep clear of the army, which was generally loyal to Maximinus. Further, the conspiracy needed to be accomplished quickly to avoid leaks and betrayals. It is possible that the killing of the procurator was merely the accident that sparked the conspiracy into action. (If so, this argues all the more for detailed existing planning.) All those involved were assisted, of course, by the continued absence of the emperor from Rome and by his failure as a result to develop a group of senatorial supporters there, so one of the elements most causing resentment was one of those most helpful to the plotters.

The messages from Africa to Rome would have taken only about a week, perhaps less, to reach their recipients in the city. The messengers are described as killing the 'commander of the forces', Vitalianus; whether they did so or not – the *Augustan History* says he was killed at the Senate's command – the news they brought certainly stimulated an immediate riot in the city. A meeting of the Senate was convened at which Maximinus was declared deposed. The two Gordians were then voted in as joint Augusti. The procedure was to vote that Maximinus' authority as a magistrate was abrogated (that is, his tribunician and proconsular powers were withdrawn), and he was then declared a public enemy. The legal authority as emperors, the imperial powers, were then granted to the two Gordians, father and son.[8]

Here was a distinctive touch bringing reminiscences of the election of pairs of magistrates in the long-defunct Republic or, perhaps more relevantly, of the joint rule of Marcus Aurelius and Lucius Verus; Gordian I had been born in the reign of Antoninus Pius and could presumably recall the joint rule of Marcus and Lucius in his childhood. Other instances also abounded, of Augustus and Tiberius, of Vespasian and Titus, of Nerva and Trajan, even of Septimius with Caracalla and Geta. (Maximinus had also associated his son with him as joint emperor.) The difference here was that the two Gordians were appointed simultaneously and so had equal authority, subject only to the deference that the younger man would naturally exercise towards his father. Yet both were Augusti, *imperatores*, and had tribunician and proconsular powers, and they were both nominated as consuls for the next year. It would no doubt be expected that Gordian II would reign alone fairly soon, so perhaps the nearest parallel was with Nerva, appointed by a vote of the Senate, and his adopted son Trajan, the legendary 'best of emperors'. After two and a half centuries of imperial rule, not only was an emperor found to be necessary but there were plenty of precedents for almost any combination of rulers.

The other difference was in regard to the army. Neither the Gordians in Africa nor the Senate in Italy had much in the way of armed forces at their disposal. They certainly had nothing that would face the army, battle-hardened and loyal, commanded by Maximinus. At the time Maximinus was at Sirmium in Pannonia and about to launch an attack north over the Danube (shades of Domitian's plan at his death).

This deliberate ignoring of the army seems on the surface to be paradoxical and even suicidal, but it may well be that the plot was actually predicated on avoiding any early contact with the army on the assumption – the hope, perhaps? – that the authority of the united Senate would prevail over that of the upstart military *eques* who had made himself emperor, that 'Thracian'. After all, the two senatorial attempts to suborn Maximinus' army had scarcely lasted a week. So, if opposition from the army seemed certain, then gaining time to make the troops have second thoughts, to impress them with the Senate's resolve and authority, to summon help from other provinces, to rouse public opinion, to spread the word, and to remind the soldiers of Maximinus' unpopularity outside the army was all to the good.

It seems that Maximinus was taken aback by what had happened. He heard the news in the camp at Sirmium and took two days to think through his response. Then, as he was bound to, he turned his army around and marched on Italy.⁹ The Senate, in a move that certainly once again looks pre-planned, now set up a committee of senior members, twenty in number, who took charge of affairs.¹⁰ This was a reminiscence of the committee that had existed to advise Alexander Severus only a few years earlier, which had been peremptorily disbanded by Maximinus three years before, and no doubt quite a few of the members of the earlier committee were on the new one. (The membership, other than the names of four men, is not known.) Preparations were made to defend Italy, and these preparations were apparently begun even before it was known that Maximinus was on his way.

The Senate sent out letters to the provincial governors, detailing the changes. No doubt Maximinus sent out letters of his own, refuting the Senate's doings, but the Senate had a few days' start and controlled the communications from Rome to the provinces, while Maximinus' letters had to travel from the frontier. The result for all those so addressed in the provinces was most uncomfortable, especially since events in Italy and Africa moved so quickly. The decisions in all the provinces can be roughly estimated by a few comments in written sources, from coin issues, and from changes made to inscriptions. Since the Gordians were originally from Anatolia, it is not surprising to see the whole of that land cleaving to them without apparent hesitation. Egypt and Greece did so as well, as did, though by the evidence of only a single inscription, Syria-Palestine, but in the West and North it was Maximinus who prevailed. Spain, Numidia, Gaul and Britain, as well as Pannonia where Maximinus and his army were, all remained loyal. In Germany, however, at least some troops joined the Senate's side and marched to Italy to resist Maximinus. The decisions in these latter areas were important since these provinces held all the armies that were capable of reaching Italy easily. It is noticeable that the provinces supporting the Gordians tended to be, like Africa, senatorial; that is, without legionary garrisons. In Moesia Inferior the governor declared for the Gordians, but one of his legions disobeyed him and had to be defeated in battle. The decision in each province technically lay with the governor, but governors of provinces containing elements of the army were clearly constrained by that fact, and it would seem that they supported Maximinus largely because their troops did.¹¹

This division of the Empire, East against West, military against senatorial, was obviously dangerous for the Senate and its emperors, and threatened widespread civil war. For the emperors in Africa indeed, the danger turned out to be immediate and fatal. They were attacked by the troops of the III *Augusta* legion, commanded by the governor of Numidia, Capellianus. He was a personal enemy of the elder Gordian, if not both of them, and who was therefore, if for no other reason, a Maximinus loyalist. (This is perhaps the basic reason they did not try to bring him to their side or tamper with the loyalty to him of his legion.) Capellianus moved quickly, defeated and killed the younger Gordian in a battle; the elder one then committed suicide as a less unpleasant alternative to falling into Capellianus' hands.[12]

The explanation for Capellianus' actions – personal enmity – is difficult to accept as his sole motivation. He had to move out of his province to attack the Gordians, not a practice encouraged by emperors of any sort. On the other hand, there was just about enough time for an order to do so to go from Maximinus in Sirmium to Capellianus in Numidia; if the winds in the Adriatic were favourable, a ship could have reached Numidia in perhaps a week or so and Capellianus' task, against the virtually unarmed emperors, would have been relatively straightforward. This might also help to explain the relatively slow response of Maximinus and his army, for if the Gordians were eliminated, it was reasonable to assume from previous experience (Alexander Severus, Quartinus and Magnus) that the revolt would rapidly collapse.

The reign of the two Gordians lasted only about three weeks; like their enemy Maximinus, they never reigned in Rome. They are counted as official emperors because of the votes in the Senate, and the brevity and geographical limitations of their rule means that they ought to be counted as 'unsuccessful emperors', or, like Maximus and Quartinus, as 'usurpers'. For Maximinus was still in charge of much of the rest of the Empire and of almost all the army. The Senate, which had nailed its colours to the mast very publicly, was now faced by the need to replace its emperors quickly. The news of the deaths of the Gordians presumably did not arrive as too much of a surprise. The enmity of Capellianus, a senator, towards the Gordians was probably well-known, and messages about his attack would have gone to Rome, probably asking for armed help, very quickly, possibly even before he attacked. So when the news of their deaths arrived, the Senate would have had some advance warning that measures to replace them were going to be needed.

At any rate, action was taken at once. Two members of the Committee of Twenty, M. Clodius Pupienus Maximus and D. Caelius Calvinus Balbinus, were elected to replace the Gordians.[13] Again, it was to be a joint reign, suggesting that the double investiture of the two Gordians had been a deliberate choice, and that this had been a decision of the Senate in the first place. The election of Pupienus and Balbinus is more evidence that the whole scheme was fully understood in advance, and that a large part of the Senate (perhaps the members of the Committee of Twenty, who might thus have been the original conspirators) was involved from the beginning. It cannot have been planned precisely in the way it happened, of course, but the general principles – the deliberate ignoring of the absence of military support, doubling the emperorship and the predominant role of the Senate – were clearly fully worked out, no doubt in private debates, before the event. The absence of the emperor from Rome for the last three years no doubt facilitated the conspiracy. His apparent contempt for the Senate also perhaps led him to underestimate its capacity for intrigue and planning.

Of course, the senators were relying on luck and for a time Fortuna smiled on them. Maximinus allowed himself to be distracted into besieging the city of Aquileia, perhaps hoping, or assuming, that the deaths of the Gordians would end the whole affair. This delay annoyed his troops, notably the men of the II *Parthica* legion, whose families were in the camp at Alba, near Rome. Maximinus had also taken a considerable time on his march, presumably on the other assumption that the mere threat of his army invading Italy would cause the opposition to crumble. However, by the time he reached northern Italy the Senate and its emperors had displayed unwonted activity, and had gathered considerable forces to oppose him. The people of Aquileia proved to be supportive of them as well, and were under the command of two consular senators, Rutilius Pudens Crispinus and Tullius Menophilus, both probably members of the Twenty, who had been sent there by the Senate. Maximinus' siege of the city was resisted vigorously. After a fairly short time his forces began to go hungry and to suffer from disease.[14]

The Senate's two emperors had by this time succeeded in gathering support from other armies. Pupienus was at Ravenna, the headquarters of the Adriatic fleet, which therefore presumably supported the Senate (and could bring supplies and troops into Aquileia), and he was about to receive reinforcements from the army in Germany, the very army that had put Maximinus on the throne in the first place. The source of these troops is not clear, for the German army generally seems to have been loyal to

Maximinus; Pupienus had been governor in one of the provinces there and so the troops may have joined him for that reason; there may also have been some resentment at the killing of Alexander Severus.

Pupienus was in charge of the defence of Italy, while Balbinus, considerably the older of the two emperors, remained in Rome, where a pitched battle developed between the plebs and those of the praetorians who were present, which ended in destruction in the city but the defeat of the Guard.[15] At Aquileia, equally, the citizen militia managed to hold off the professionals of Maximinus' army. All this surely came as something of a shock to the soldiers, whose self-image was of defenders of the prestige and the people of the Empire. To find that they were hated by those very people was surely an unpleasant surprise. They had already been discouraged by the fact that the inhabitants of Emona, which lay on their route from Sirmium, had evacuated their city rather than receive the army. Herodian says the army was annoyed at the consequent lack of food, but it must have been even more unpleasant to find that their own people, in a loyal province, feared the Roman army even more than their barbarian enemies, and the local hostility also contributed to the shortage of supplies.

No doubt the moving spirits in Aquileia were those who detested Maximinus' tax policies; that is, the merchants and the landowners. The knowledge that the Senate was conducting the war against them – two of the Twenty were in command in Aquileia, one of the emperors was at Ravenna, another of the Twenty was recruiting troops in Milan, and the senior emperor was in control of Rome – would have led some of the men in Maximinus' army to question their purposes in besieging an Italian city rather than fighting barbarians. The news of the defeat of the Guard by the citizens in Rome meant that the threat to their families felt by the men of II *Parthica* was now all the greater, and the news of fighting at Rome would have surely bothered the rest of the soldiers as well. The longer the fighting in the north of Italy went on, the more politically isolated Maximinus became.

It cannot have been unknown to the soldiers that Maximinus was disliked by the Senate: the attempts by Quartinus and Magnus were not secret, nor that of the Gordians, and now the two emperors whom the Senate had publicly elected and was supporting made that clear enough. The soldiers had a sense of decorum in political matters, and to find the emperor at odds with the Senate was a distortion of what the soldiers felt was right. All through the third century, the soldiers displayed this attachment to correct constitutional practice, and Maximinus was one of its first victims. In the end, the soldiers of II *Parthica* and the detachment of the praetorians who were on duty at the emperor's quarters turned on him, killed both him and his son, and then the men of their council as well, which was no doubt a group of senior officers.[16]

The soldiers were doing the same as had been done to the previous supporters of assassinated emperors. Maximinus' son had been made Caesar, so he had to be killed to ensure that Maximinus' regime ended; their advisers and ministers had to go too, as had those who had governed for Caracalla, Macrinus, Elagabalus and Alexander. However, this practice was exactly what the reassertion of senatorial authority was intended to stop, and it is a clear sign that the troops did not yet comprehend what the change meant; nor did they ever, in fact.

At Rome popular pressure compelled the Senate to make Gordian I's grandson Caesar. This was a further sign that matters were not really under full senatorial control.[17] There is no doubt that the senators, given the exercise of their free will, would not have made a 13-year-old boy the heir of Balbinus and Pupienus. Pupienus had a son who he may have wished to succeed him, though Balbinus seems to have had no direct descendants. The election by the Senate of the two emperors suggests that the intention was to maintain that doubling, but not to permit direct succession within a family without election. No doubt it was also expected that a further change would be accomplished, perhaps by adding a second Caesar to continue the doubling commenced by the first two Gordians. The two–Augusti-and-a-Caesar pattern prefigures in these ways the later more elaborate design by Diocletian.

The description of the elevation of Gordian in the collective biography of the three Gordians in the *Historia Augusta* is that the boy 'was hurried to the Senate and then taken to an Assembly, and there they clothed him in the imperial garments and hailed him as Caesar'. Relying on the *Historia* is hazardous, but this would seem to be a description of either what did happen on the accession of an emperor or what was thought to have happened. That is, the author is describing in general terms the process of investing a new emperor at Rome: first at a meeting of the Senate where he would be voted into office with the specified imperial powers, then at a meeting of the citizens (the Assembly) where he was acclaimed, and finally being clothed in a purple robe. The significance of the purple robe is crucial, and donning it was the definitive moment in the acclamation of both Maximinus and Gordian I. The least likely event is the meeting of an Assembly. This is the only example of such a meeting that is known since the time of Nerva, though some sort of public presentation of the new ruler seems to have been required whenever the installation took place in Rome. Apart from the purple robe, the ceremony was not very different from that at the accession of Tiberius. The first essential, however, was the Senate's approbation, indicated by a vote in the full House. This is what was missing for Maximinus, at least until sometime after he took the powers himself. The proclamation of emperors by the army had similar elements: the urging by the officers was followed by acclamation by the soldiers, an event that may have substituted for the popular Assembly; the soldiers, after all, were citizens (though this is hardly a meaningful distinction by the mid-third century). Then came the purple robe, which was now the ratifying moment.

The Guard had been thoroughly humiliated in all these events, and was now allied with II *Parthica*, which had originally been placed at Alba by Septimius in order to act as a control over the Guardsmen. It would also be clear to every soldier that the new regime, owing nothing to the soldiers, would be unfavourable to them, though Gordian I had promised a large donative and Pupienus promised one at Aquileia. The new rulers had also brought in a group described as 'Germans' to act as their bodyguard, which were presumably the men who Pupienus had summoned to his assistance from the Rhineland forces. This can only mean they were afraid of what the surviving Guard and the legionaries might do. This was an accurate fear, for the Guard in Rome invaded the Palace. The two emperors were murdered when the Germans attempted to come to their rescue.

This assassination was as well-planned as the Senate coup had been, for once in the history of the Guard's politics. There was already a successor in place, once Gordian III had been installed. The Guard located the young Gordian, proclaimed him emperor and took him off to their camp. This was the only occasion on which the Guard successfully installed an emperor, but it will be noticed that he had already been selected and promoted by the plebs of Rome and the Senate before the Guard became involved.[18]

This was the final act of the political upheaval that took place in 238. Superficially the killings of Balbinus and Pupienus, following on that of the two Gordians in Africa, were defeats for the Senate by the Guard acting on behalf of the army and in revenge for Maximinus. Yet the events of the year had shown quite firmly and clearly that the influence and authority of the Senate was still very powerful. The reaction of Rome and Italy had been very strongly favourable to the Senate's actions, as was that of the Eastern provinces and parts of the army, especially in Germany; the Pannonian army commanded by Maximinus had gradually come to realize this. The senatorial emperors Pupienus and Balbinus were widely accepted by other sections of the army and by many of the governors in provinces outside Italy. Also, despite the killing of four emperors of the senatorial group in only a few months, it was nevertheless a senatorial nominee for the throne who eventually emerged as the sole emperor. There were also, of course, good opportunities for senatorial influence in the enthronement of a teenage boy, as had been seen earlier with the reign of Alexander Severus.

Of the programme that the Senate seems to have followed, the idea of a double emperorship was discarded for the present, as was their preference for elderly men on the throne. In fact, it was partly the fact that the two emperors could not agree with each other that contributed to their deaths since their disagreement fatally delayed the summoning of Pupienus' German guard to their defence when the Guard invaded the Palace. (Balbinus was suspicious that Pupienus would use his control of the German guard to seize sole power.) This sort of disagreement would ultimately have led to a political paralysis as, in the time of the Republic, it was intended to. It is also noticeable that the two oldest emperors of the year – Gordian I, who was about 80, and Balbinus, over 70 – left the more energetic work, such as commanding armies, to their younger colleagues.

This unexpected but clear revival of the Senate's authority had led to the removal of an emperor whose sole support was his own army; support that had proved to be all too fragile. The events of 238 had shown, yet again, that it was necessary for an emperor to have substantial support in both the army and the Senate if he was to govern successfully and for a decent length of time. The year 238 was, in a sense, a counter-revolution, the undoing of some of the effects of the *coups d'état* that had put Septimius Severus on the throne almost half a century earlier, and had in effect been repeated by Maximinus. These coups had relegated the Senate to a distinctly secondary role in deciding who should be emperor, a reduction in influence that operated for much of the period following. It also undid part of the methods of succession that had operated from the time of Trajan. The plot to enthrone Gordian I and the elevation of Pupienus and Balbinus were in many ways similar to the Nervan conspiracy against Domitian. The great reduction in the Senate's influence since 97, however, was not wholly reversed: 238 had proved that the army was not the absolute paramount influence in the State, and the actions of the Guard showed that it also had to be taken into account, though its actions were almost consistently negative. The balance of power had reverted, perhaps, to the condition of the first imperial century, but the army was not to forget its basic political power.

In an even longer context this was a new phase in tension that had been set up by the result of the civil war that had ended the Republic when Octavian, the controller of the only army left, tried to restore the Senate's work without resigning his own position. By the mid-third century, two and a half centuries since Augustus, much of the damage inflicted on that system by Septimius and before him by Trajan was irreparable. It was the unpopularity engendered for Maximinus by the necessity of taxing harshly to fund the military establishment of the Empire that brought about his downfall; and that necessity was a direct result of Septimius' extravagant favouring of and his and his son's generosity to the army. Now the Senate had revived, and the next half-century would see the contest between them continue.

The Licinian Near-Dynasty

Trebonianus Gallus (251–253).
(*Sailko via Wikimedia Commons*)

Gallienus (253–268).

Aemilianus (253).

Valerian (253–260).

The Gallic Empire

Postumus (260–269).

Victorinus (269–271).

Tetricus II (271–274). (*CNG via Wikimedia Commons*)

Chapter Ten

The Consequences of Gordian (1): Successful Emperors

One of the results of the events of 238 was to emphasize once again the possibility that a man might, by rebellion, make himself emperor. The events of 68–69 and 193 had already done so, and more recently in Syria Elagabalus had successfully seized power by rebellion.

A distinction must be made between the rebellions of Elagabalus and Gordian against the actions of other emperors in killing or acting against an emperor and taking his place, as Maximinus and Macrinus had done most recently by *coup d'état*. A rebellion was mounted away from the court and required an army to march on the capital. The most successful recent example was Septimius, but Gordian clearly intended to do the same; ironically, one result of his rebellion was that the Emperor Maximinus ended up in the posture of a rebel marching on the city.

The events of 238 were so widespread, involved so many groups and were so widely broadcast that the possibilities became much more appreciated. This was clearly one of the reasons why the next half-century saw a great number of pretenders and rebels to add to the confusion generated by the rapid turnover of 238, the 'year of seven emperors'. Yet this was a time when the Empire went through an agonizing and extended period of foreign invasion and monetary inflation, and the rebels and pretenders were all part of that overall problem; at once cause, consequence and solution. The confusion was such that it is not too much to say that the Empire had collapsed.

The rebels are often pushed aside or out of consideration, so that the main story of the 'legitimate' emperors is usually that which is told, and it must be said that story is certainly complex enough even without the rebels. Here, however, rebellion is central to the concerns of this study, and so we shall consider the rebels as a separate group in the next chapter. Previously (in Chapters 6 and 8) they have been included in the main account, but they are so numerous in the mid-third century that they deserve a more detailed discussion. This chapter, therefore, will look at the 'legitimate' emperors – those generally supposed to be so, that is – and their modes of succession.

From 238 to 284 a superficial consideration of Roman politics might suggest that it was the Roman army that determined who should occupy the imperial throne. The emperors were certainly usually proclaimed by their soldiers, who had often murdered their imperial predecessors, hence the term 'military emperors' or 'military monarchy' which is sometimes used for this period, but such a description is not necessarily accurate. After all, the basis of Augustus' power, and hence of every later emperor, was control of the army.

Also, the revival of senatorial influence during 238 cannot be ignored. After all, influence was the only power ever wielded by the Senate once the imperial system had been installed. Only in the case of Nerva before the Gordians had the Senate's choice of emperor been free of outside pressure, and Nerva and the Gordians had scarcely been the most effective emperors. In all other cases the Senate had, sometimes after debate, accepted a candidate put forward from another authority: from the former emperor, the current emperor, the army, even on one recent occasion from the Guard. That is, the role of the Senate was to ratify a candidate nominated by one or more of these authorities, and at times (as with the crisis following the death of Gaius) the senators had to choose between several possible candidates. The basic reason, of course, was that the Senate itself controlled no armed force; its influence came from its collective experience, and this was not enough in some cases. Yet it is clear that in 238 it was able to use that influence and experience with success.

The reassertion of senatorial authority in 238 remained effective for some decades. Gordian III died in the war in the East in 244, killed by some means now quite unascertainable but probably in battle or by accident during a battle. One of his Praetorian Prefects, M. Iulius Philippus, recently appointed, was, after some delay and confusion, made emperor by the army on the urging of his brother, Priscus, the other prefect. This army was a major expeditionary force, so Philip's elevation had powerful authority. Philip rapidly made peace with the Persians and removed his army to safety and himself to Rome, just as Hadrian had done in 117, and as Macrinus had failed to do in 217 or Maximinus in 235. The Senate's endorsement of the army's nomination was clearly of the first importance to him, even more than achieving victory in the war in the East. He had also, presumably, learned the lesson of Maximinus' fate: that the Senate's clear and willing acceptance of the new emperor was necessary.[1]

Philip succeeded in his endeavour, and soon his son was made Caesar as well. It may be that it was the fact that he had a son, about 7 or 8 years of age, and so was able to found a dynasty, that was one of the reasons he was promoted to the post by his brother. He reappointed Priscus as Praetorian Prefect and then as Corrector of the Eastern Provinces, a sort of super-governor. His brother-in-law Severianus was appointed to a similar position in the Balkans for a time; these were the two really troublesome areas, militarily speaking, at the time. These measures may be seen as revivals of similar emergency measures going back to Augustus' use of Agrippa in various areas, or Avidius Cassius by Marcus Aurelius in the East. (For the family, see Genealogical Table XIII.)

XIII   The Philippian Dynasty.

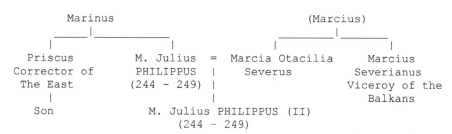

```
            Marinus                        (Marcius)
        _____|_____               _____|_____
       |               |             |               |
    Priscus       M. Julius    =  Marcia Otacilia   Marcius
  Corrector of     PHILIPPUS   |    Severus        Severianus
   The East       (244 - 249)  |                 Viceroy of the
       |                       |                    Balkans
      Son            M. Julius PHILIPPUS (II)
                          (244 - 249)
```

A revolt broke out in the Balkans and Philip at once consulted the Senate. The rebel was Pacatianus, who was the successor of Severianus in overall command in the Balkans. Philip sent a senator, P. Messius Decius, who came from that region, to deal with it. Decius had demurred at first, arguing that the rebellion there would soon end and, sure enough, he achieved its suppression with little difficulty. He was a man of some experience, a former governor of Moesia Inferior and of Tarraconensis, and he had been City Prefect at Rome when Philip appointed him to suppress the revolt. However, it was his behaviour in the crisis of 238 that seems to have been the key to his general policy and attitude: as governor in Tarraconensis he was loyal to Maximinus until that emperor's death. He presumably then made his peace with those who succeeded him, namely the regime of Gordian III, though Spain had remained resistant to Gordian's authority for some time.[2]

Having won a battle with invaders who sought to exploit Pacatianus' revolt, Decius then organized his own proclamation as emperor as soon as he had finished his campaign. The story as it is usually told leads directly from

Decius' suppression of the rebellion to his proclamation by his soldiers, and so to the battle in which he defeated and killed the Emperor Philip, but the events were more spread out than that version implies. The original rebellion by Pacatianus began late in 248, and was suppressed, judging by the coin evidence, by April of the next year, 249. The Battle of Verona, in which Philip died, did not take place until September 249. In other words, Decius spent several months in his province before he was made emperor, and several more months passed before the decisive battle. It is said that Decius corresponded with Philip over the problem they faced. It seems that Philip had been depressed by the rebellions against him (there was another in the East at the same time) before sending Decius north. Perhaps Decius believed that Philip would now resign. He did not, and Decius had to invade Italy. They met in battle at Verona and Philip, fighting apparently in the front rank of the army, was killed. It may well be that he was still depressed, even suicidal.

Decius, however, though a senator, was of the persuasion of Maximinus in regard to governing the Empire; that is, he insisted on the primacy of the needs of the army over those of the taxpayers. He was supported by his own soldiers, and by those who had supported Pacatianus. This second group of men were afraid that they would be punished for their rebellion, and the two groups had joined together to make Decius emperor. He was clearly not unwilling, and the length of time that passed between his victory and his proclamation suggests that he was using the time in a search for other supporters, as well as, perhaps, negotiating with Philip. One source roundly says he plotted his way to the throne. One measure he appears to have taken was to contact the Guard in Rome, where Philip's son, now Augustus, had been left when the emperor marched north. As soon as news arrived that Philip was dead, the boy was killed, having apparently been kept in the Guard's camp. This was surely prearranged, with the murderers hedging their bets by agreeing with Decius in advance that they would act in his support only if the elder Philip died in the fighting.[3]

Decius returned to Rome, where he spent some time. He was invested by the Senate in the normal way, but his reign was less than successful. He claimed a military ability that he did not in the end display. He promoted his son Herennius Etruscus as Caesar, which was once again an attempt to found a ruling dynasty. It was perhaps more likely to succeed than Philip's, whose son had been killed while he was still a child. Decius himself was in his 60s and Herennius was an adult in his 30s. There was also a second son,

Hostilianus, who was much younger than his brother and who remained in Rome when the Augustus and the Caesar went off to war in the Balkans once more. (For the family, see Genealogical Table XIV.)

XIV   The Messian Dynasty.

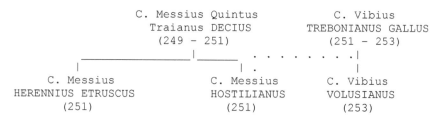

```
            C. Messius Quintus              C. Vibius
            Traianus DECIUS          TREBONIANUS GALLUS
              (249 - 251)                (251 - 253)
       _____|_____  . . . . . . . .|
              |                  | .                |
        C. Messius          C. Messius          C. Vibius
   HERENNIUS ETRUSCUS       HOSTILIANUS         VOLUSIANUS
       (251)                  (251)               (253)
```

Despite his time in Rome, nothing Decius did indicated any affection for the Senate. He clearly despised Philip, and his speech as recorded on the occasion of the debate about Pacatianus is a thinly-veiled attack on the emperor's indecision, which may actually be an attack on the process of consulting the Senate. He had supported Maximinus against the first two Gordians and against the senatorial emperors in 238. While he was on campaign in the north, and despite the presence in Rome of Hostilianus and the boy's guards, a senator, D. Iulius Valens Licinianus, staged a coup with the support of the plebs in the city. He may also have had senatorial support, in a mild way, but he was quickly suppressed, presumably by the Guard. This event was a clear sign of Decius' unpopularity, however, and it has all the appearance of an attempted coup on the pattern of those against Maximinus.[4]

The war in the Balkans resulted in the deaths of both Decius and Herennius Etruscus. They were succeeded by an army colleague, C. Vibius Trebonianus Gallus, governor in Moesia, who the army chose as emperor as soon as Decius was dead. Like Philip, he headed straight for Rome, having made a rapid and generous peace with the invading Goths first; the same sequence of events that occurred when Philip succeeded Gordian III. Here was another indication of the new potency of the senatorial investiture process, in that it was considered necessary for a new emperor to report to the Senate first. Gallus adopted Decius' son Hostilianus, and made both him and his own son Volusianus Caesars. He even put Hostilianus first, before Volusianus, for he had been Caesar under his father already. (Gallus was from Etruria; Decius' wife was also from Etruria; it may be that she and Gallus were related, hence the adoption, which is otherwise difficult to explain.)[5]

The whole dynastic scheme quickly collapsed. Hostilianus died, apparently of disease – it was a plague period in the Empire – and rebellions broke out, both in the East and in the Balkans. Gallus commissioned P. Licinius Valerianus, governor in Germany, to cope with the rebellion in the Balkans, which was led by a man called Aemilius Aemilianus.

In Italy the soldiers were now operating a system of improvisational election, with a fearsome penalty for the defeated candidates. Gallus and his son Volusian led an army to face Aemilian, while Valerian brought a third army south from Germany. Instead of fighting, the several armies – or rather their commanders – consulted. Out of it Valerian emerged in power, while each of the other armies killed its own emperor.[6] There was, apparently, no actual fighting. The army was acting as a political constituency, nominating an emperor, and its choice was ratified by the Senate. Gallus had been Decius' heir, and Decius had been a Maximinist; that is, Decius, Gallus and Volusian were relying wholly on the army as their basis of power with no regard for the Senate, disdain for which Decius had earlier made clear. The same was the case with Aemilian, who is said to have written to Gallus offering to share power with him; in other words, he also had no regard for the Senate's preferences and prerogatives.

Valerian, on the other hand, was a senatorial candidate. He had been in Africa in 238 and had been one of Gordian's messengers to Rome, probably of consular rank even then. He was about 60 in 253, with an adult son, Gallienus, and the year before he had been in Rome and associated with Hostilianus, perhaps as his guardian, while Decius was on campaign. He therefore straddled both parties: the militarist (Maximinus, Decius and Gallus) and the senatorials (the Gordians and Philip). His age commended him to the Senate, which always preferred elderly candidates, and his adult son reassured those seeking the stability of dynastic continuity, while his military experience and ability recommended him to the soldiers, who had demonstrated their preferences in the most drastic style. (Valerian's wife was Egnatia Mariniana, and seems to have been a relative of the frightened 'competitor' of 193, Triarius Maternus.)

Valerian's position in the army/Senate conflict permitted him to be invested by the Senate and still spend much of his reign away from the city, while his son Gallienus operated there. Yet it was in his time that the role of the Senate in public affairs was potentially reduced to a largely ceremonial and deliberative one by legislation. The repeated rebellions and invasions had emphasized the necessity for a reform of the army, and this was undertaken by the joint emperors Valerian and Gallienus. One result was to remove senators from military commands; only emperors who were well entrenched in the goodwill of the Senate could have done this, for an army man might advocate the reduction of senatorial involvement in affairs, but would inevitably be accused of partiality. The new system left to the Senate the consulship and the government of several of the provinces, but put into the hands of the professional soldiers the control of frontier provinces and the command of the legions and armies.[7]

This was done principally by the work of Gallienus, who remained in command in Italy and the West while his father campaigned. Senators were thus to be deprived of the experience their forebears had gained while commanding legions and governing provinces. It was not a change done suddenly, for in many ways it was only a recognition of the preferences the senators had shown by their earlier unwillingness to take up these more arduous posts, and senators are still found later at times in command of armies and military provinces, but their exclusive role had gone. The Senate did retain its great prestige for some time, of course. Senators were always wealthy – it was a condition of membership – and the Senate was a legitimate and legal body, but inevitably the promotion of non-senators to the most important military and administrative positions gradually degraded its importance; by refraining from those forfeited positions, senators ceased to be listened to. It was still possible for senators to be employed as commanders and governors, but this was now at the discretion and choice of the emperors, not by right or by election or appointment by the Senate. The result was a divorce of senatorial competence from the reality of the Empire. For another generation there were in the Senate men who had governing and command

XV   The Licinian Dynasty.

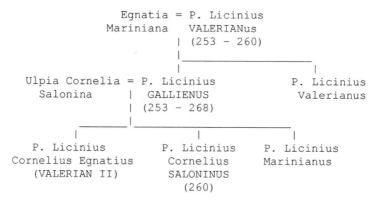

```
                      Egnatia = P. Licinius
                     Mariniana   VALERIANus
                             |  (253 - 260)
                             |_____
                             |                    |
    Ulpia Cornelia = P. Licinius            P. Licinius
       Salonina    |  GALLIENUS              Valerianus
                   |  (253 - 268)
          _____|_____
         |                    |             |
    P. Licinius          P. Licinius    P. Licinius
 Cornelius Egnatius       Cornelius     Marinianus
   (VALERIAN II)          SALONINUS
                            (260)
```

experience, but as they died off, the Senate as a whole ceased to have a direct role in governing the Empire, and this applied as much to its role in installing emperors as it did to its function as a legislative and consultative body.

Valerian went east to deal with another Persian attack, and Gallienus placed his own son Saloninus as Caesar in nominal command of the Rhine frontier at Cologne. Once more a dynasty was in the process of formation, and Gallienus had a second son, another Valerian, available as well. Dynastically, however, the family failed: Valerian the elder was captured by the Persians; Saloninus and the younger Valerian were murdered; and eventually Gallienus, apparently for failing in all his policies, was murdered by a cabal of his generals.[8] (For the family, see Genealogical Table XV.)

In the meantime the capture of the emperor precipitated a collapse of the Empire. The westernmost provinces were detached from Gallienus' authority by the governor of Germania Inferior, M. Cassianus Latinius Postumus, who killed the boy Emperor Saloninus and made himself emperor in his stead. His programme was the defence of Gaul, which Gallienus had done much to improve already, but which he had then left in the hands of his adolescent son and his adviser. Postumus gained control of both Germanies, and of their frontier armies, of the Gallic provinces including Narbonensis, and the Spanish and British provinces as well, which also held armies. He took the full panoply of imperial titles – *imperator*, Caesar, Augustus – but made no serious attempt to take over the rest of the Empire. From the point of view of this study, it is especially interesting that Postumus also organized a Senate, which sat presumably in one of the cities close to the German frontier, and held elections to the usual Roman magistracies. When Postumus was killed by his troops at the instigation of a usurper in 269 – this was indeed a true version of the Roman Empire – he was succeeded by a former consul who put down the murderer and another usurper, and in turn was succeeded by another senatorial governor.

The 'Gallic Empire' is conventionally regarded as a case of the secession of a section of the Roman Empire, which was therefore ruled by rebels, but this interpretation is difficult to maintain. Postumus seized power by murdering his predecessor, or having him murdered, certainly, but this was almost normal in the century of Commodus, Caracalla, Maximinus and many other such murderers. He was acclaimed as emperor by his army, was accepted without serious demur by the people of his part of the Empire, and he was able to assemble a group of wealthy men to form a Senate – many of them would have had senatorial rank already – and he himself took up the office of consul five times. It was a process very like that of Galba two centuries before, except that Postumus did not immediately head for Rome. The only element in the usual array of imperial powers that is absent is therefore possession of the city of Rome, but 'legitimate' emperors such as Macrinus and Maximinus did not visit that city either.

It is best to see Postumus and most of his successors as normal Roman emperors, though there are some of his successors to whom such recognition cannot be extended. Postumus was killed by some of his soldiers, who proclaimed one of their commanders, Marcus Aurelius Marius, as the new emperor. He must be considered 'legitimate' since he would seem to have ruled for some time, perhaps three months. On the other hand, Ulpius Cornelianus Laelianus may be regarded as an unsuccessful rebel, for he did not command much beyond his province, which was probably Germania Superior, and he had been suppressed by Postumus just before the emperor himself was killed. Marius was himself killed by Postuman loyalists, headed by M. Piavvonius Victorinus, a former high official of Postumus', and his colleague in the consulship on one occasion. Victorinus was clearly Postumus' successor, and was successful in holding his empire together, ruling for more than two years.

The justification for the secession led by Postumus had been the defence of Gaul against barbarian attacks, and the rulers had accomplished that; at least, there were no records of any attacks after Postumus won victories along the frontier in 263 and 264. However, the murder of Victorinus in 271 – supposedly at the hands of an outraged husband – brought collapse. No successor had been chosen in advance of the murder, which rather confirms its spontaneity and personal nature. Victorinus' mother Victoria took control, persuading the army to wait for the arrival of the governor of Aquitania, C. Pius Esucius Tetricus. He was duly proclaimed on his arrival, but Spain seceded from the secession and rejoined the main Empire, which was now under the rule of the Emperor Aurelian. Barbarian invasions penetrated once more into Gaul, and Aurelian invaded in 273. Tetricus, in the usual style, had his son made Caesar, but either lost heart in the face of Aurelian's invasion or lost the decisive battle.

Between them, Postumus, Marius, Victorinus and Tetricus ruled a quarter of the Roman Empire with some success for fourteen years. Postumus' reign of nearly ten years was the longest, except for that of Gallienus, between Alexander Severus and Diocletian. Aurelian's recovery of control of the West was marked by the reception of Tetricus and his son into the Italian governmental system, and no doubt into the Roman Senate, so their Gallic senatorial colleagues can have achieved no less. The Gallic emperors were in truth true Roman emperors and Aurelian's treatment of the last of them confirms this. The 'Gallic Empire', in fact, in most respects looks like a version of the Roman Empire before the reforms of Gallienus, and maybe this was one of the sources of Postumus' support; that is, it represented a conservative reaction against those reforms. This would in part explain his constitution of a regional Senate, and one in which the reforms were resented. Yet it was Gallienus' reforms, in the army and in the government, that were the future for the Empire. Just to remain the same, in a conservative way, as was the aim of the Gallic emperors, was no longer enough.[9]

Gallienus had clearly alienated many men by his reforms, and perhaps by his apparent legitimacy as emperor. His generals in the end conspired to kill him; the Senate may well have been dismayed by his reforms, and his reputation has suffered by the accounts of the ancient historians, though moderns have been more indulgent. He had, above all, ultimately failed as emperor: the West had gone to Postumus and Gallienus had failed to regain it; in the East his father Valerian was defeated and captured by the Persian invaders in 260. The whole East had then gone first to the Persians, then to the Palmyrenes, who were claiming to restore the Empire, acting as local emperors in the same way as Postumus and his successors. Gallienus' fall was triggered by the rebellion of one his generals, Aureolus, in northern Italy, perhaps in concert with Postumus. It was this rebellion that finally provoked Gallienus' killing.

The rebel Aureolus was swiftly disposed of, fighting a final battle after he had despairingly proclaimed himself emperor.[10] The army – that is to say, the generals – chose one of their own number to be the next emperor, M. Aurelius Claudius, called 'Claudius II' or 'Claudius Gothicus'. The ordinary soldiers were unhappy about the change and the Senate was persuaded to deify Gallienus to mollify them. That is, Claudius turned to the Senate, as had his predecessors, for the validation of his election by the generals.[11] Gallienus had carried through a reduction of the Senate's powers, but they had not yet seriously affected its prestige, and the institution of the Senate in Gaul told the same story: a Senate, even one as speedily recruited and provincial as that in Gaul, was required if a regime was to be seen as legitimate. It was the same measure as that taken by Galba two centuries earlier.

Claudius had a brother, M. Aurelius Claudius Quintillus, who was given some sort of authority, but not, so far as can be seen, the title of either

Caesar or Augustus. When Claudius died of disease in 270, after a reign of only two years, however, Quintillus assumed the imperial power as of right; the dynastic principle was once more in operation. He did not have much support in the army, not apparently being a military commander, nor did he have time to secure recognition in the Senate. After a reign of less than a month, just long enough to have coins minted in several mints and to give a good impression to the Senate, as the later senatorial historians show, but not being vigorous enough to be acceptable to the army, he ceased to reign. He had initiated some negotiations with Claudius' commanders and probably with the Senate, but the proclamation of a more widely acceptable man disheartened him. He was either killed or committed suicide, probably the latter.[12]

The army's new choice was L. Domitius Aurelianus. He was proclaimed somewhere in the Balkans where the army was on campaign, marched by way of Aquileia (where Quintillus had died) and on to Rome for the senatorial ratification. This was apparently willingly given. He was a well-known and energetic military man who had been one of Gallienus' senior commanders (and one of his murderers, as was Claudius, probably) before becoming one of Claudius' senior generals. He was in the line of emperors from Gordian III and Philip who had been keen to seek the support of senatorial opinion, perhaps in some cases too much so for the taste of the senior soldiers. The generals who killed Philip and those who killed Gallienus were clearly convinced that they could do a better job of defending the Empire than them, just as Aurelian and his soldiers were convinced that he could do it better than Quintillus. Those generals – it is a characteristic of the species – were also quite certain that they did not need support or interference from the senators. That is, within the army there was always a Maximinist persuasion, yet each time an emperor was struck down, his successor rapidly came to the conclusion that the support of the Senate really was necessary. It had happened with Claudius, it was happening with Quintillus when he died, and now with Aurelian.

When Gallienus was killed, the rank-and-file were very displeased and the participation of the generals in the killing was hushed up, both at the time and in the later histories. The rank-and-file were thus of the opinion that the Senate's accolade was necessary. So Claudius sought Gallienus' deification, and Quintillus and Aurelian headed for Rome as soon as proclaimed, though only the latter actually arrived. So for the time being the men called 'Maximinists' by the author continued to be out of power;

like the Guard in earlier years they were able to kill or remove emperors, even to put one of their own in his place, but the successors had immediately become 'senatorials'. This may well be the reason that the decision as to who should be the next emperor when Aurelian died was left to the Senate.

This, of course, was not the way it was normally done, for the Senate did not usually do more than ratify a candidate chosen elsewhere, either by the previous emperor or by a cabal of generals (or in the occasional case by the Roman plebs). The normal method was for the army to nominate one man, as had been the case with Aurelian. This made sense, since his main task at this time was to lead the army into battle and he had to be able to command it. The days of a mainly civilian administration were now, at least for the moment, over. The Senate was no longer qualified to select such an emperor, and as those senators with experience of commanding government died off, it would become decreasingly capable of correct military judgement. However, the army now insisted that the Senate select the new emperor – or at least the army commanders did so – and the rank-and-file acquiesced. This is not really surprising, given the rapid requirement of senatorial acceptance shown by the emperors since Gallienus' death. Indeed, if the reaction of the troops after Gallienus' death is anything to go by, it was their attitude that insisted on it. The army by now was seeing itself once more as a representative of the citizens, and 'Senate and People of Rome', inscribed on their standards, was clearly being taken seriously by them.

Aurelian was murdered in a plot involving court officials and disaffected officers, but the plotters did not have a replacement emperor ready to hand, suggesting spontaneity and panic. It was clearly the absence of a candidate, and perhaps paralysing rivalry among the generals, that compelled the commanders to involve the Senate. The sources imply that the subsequent negotiations between the generals and the Senate lasted some considerable time, and indeed, there was a period of several weeks with no emperor. The Senate finally nominated M. Claudius Tacitus. He was probably another old soldier; certainly he was old, he showed a certain command ability during his short reign, and he was acceptable to the army. The senators had thus shown good sense in choosing a man likely to be liked by the troops; or rather perhaps it was a case of each side blocking the other's selections until Tacitus' name became a compromise choice. His age was no doubt one of the main recommendations from the Senate's point of view.[13]

Tacitus, as it turned out, did not last long, nor could he be expected to, being too old for the vigorous life required. He was probably in his 60s – if not actually 75, as one source says – and so was a fairly typical choice of the Senate. He died while moving the army eastwards in pursuit of some of the murderers of Aurelian. Whether his death was from disease, as a result of an accident or murder is not clear, though given his age a natural death is the most likely. He was succeeded by his half-brother M. Annius Florianus, who had been his Praetorian Prefect, apparently by acceptance by the army in the Balkans where he commanded, and then by the Senate. It was a succession by dynastic right, and it would appear that Florian was accepted throughout the Western parts of the Empire without difficulty.[14]

Another general, M. Aurelius Probus, was proclaimed by the army in Syria, where he commanded. The situation was reminiscent of the Quintillus/ Aurelian dispute and came to the same result: the general triumphed over the heir, mainly due to Florian's army being damaged by disease which broke out when he allowed himself to be blocked up in Tarsus in a siege. Probus' forces did little actual fighting, and it was Florian's army that finally ended the matter by killing their man.[15]

It is worth noting that frequent disputes between commanders nominated by different parts of the army only rarely resulted in serious fighting. The armies of Philip and Decius had fought a battle, though perhaps only doing so until Philip was killed; in later cases the result was often achieved when one army eliminated its own candidate, either because it faced unwelcome odds or when it was persuaded that the opposing candidate was a better man for the job. So Valerian did not have to fight to triumph over Aemilian and Gallus; when Gallienus did get involved in a siege against a rebel he was removed (and so was the rebel); Quintillus' army peacefully accepted Aurelian; and Florian's army accepted Probus. Actual and prolonged civil war between these forces was therefore very rare. The only serious exception was the secession of the Gallic Empire and of the East under Palmyra, both of which are rather different situations, and even in the case of the suppression of the Gallic secession, it was not clear that there was serious fighting; the final battle may not actually have happened. These Eastern and Western events were not disputes over the succession so much as disputes over the integrity of the Empire. The unity and defence of the Empire was the basic programme of the army, and this was the justification for all the political manoeuvring and murders of the armies and the Guard.

Probus went to Rome for his formal senatorial investiture and made a good impression, by all accounts.[16] He faced rebellion and invasion during much of his reign. The *Historia Augusta* is eloquent on the Senate's favour towards him, but the passage must be judged an invention. Nevertheless, Probus' reputation is of an emperor in alliance with the Senate, and his employment of a senior senator, Virius Lupus, as governor in Syria would suggest that this reputation was in part earned by a decision to employ senators once more in government positions. He was killed by his officers, apparently because of an offhand remark he made that he had been so successful in pacifying the Empire that he might soon be able to do without soldiers. The implication was that he would be able to reduce costs to the civilians of the Empire by at least reducing the number of soldiers and therefore their wages. He seems also to have annoyed his soldiers by making them work on construction projects. This gave his Praetorian Prefect, M. Aurelius Carus, a platform. The troops under Carus' command hailed him as emperor, and then the soldiers sent to suppress him joined in. Probus was then murdered.[17]

Carus took power smoothly when Probus died. He was one of those emperors who did not go to Rome for the investiture, and the fact that his son Carinus did so a year later was no substitute. Given the circumstances of his coup and the men who supported him, this must put Carus and his two sons into the party of the Maximinists, the believers in a purely military organization of the Empire; Carus promoted himself and his sons to the rank of Augusti and simply reported his elevation to the Senate with the implication that it did not really matter whether the Senate approved of him or not.[18]

Carus died on campaign in the East; his younger son Numerian followed him, perhaps killed by his Praetorian Prefect; the elder son Carinus faced rebellions by a local commander, M. Aurelius Iulianus, in Venetia in northern Italy, and by the generals in Numerian's army, who proclaimed C. Aurelius Valerius Diocletianus as the new emperor. Carinus destroyed Iulianus in a battle near Verona, but was then killed by some of his own men during the battle with Diocletian's army. Diocletian then publicly cut down the man accused of the murder of Numerian.

This confused set of coups, murders and battles is difficult to sort out. If Carus represented the militaristic (Maximinist) tendency, as his disdain for the Senate implies, then Iulianus should perhaps represent the senatorial party, and since he was operating as a governor, he was one of those senators who still played an active governmental role. His suppression by Carinus does indicate, besides his rebellion, that he was a political enemy of the Maximinists. Carinus in turn had referred to the Senate in dictatorial terms rather than with the more traditional request for confirmation of authority.

So the deaths of Carus and his sons might be seen as coups on behalf of the revival of the Senate's power.[19]

This may well have encouraged the senatorial party, but Diocletian proved to be just as unwilling to engage with the Senate as Carus had been. Probably Diocletian visited Rome, but only for a very brief visit; there is no sign of the Senate's attitude to him. Probus had been conciliatory towards the Senate, but he was the last emperor to be so. After him, none of the emperors felt much need to gain the Senate's approbation. The acceptance by the emperors of the refusal of most senators to engage in the government of the Empire had resulted inevitably in the emperors' engrossing of powers to themselves, including the power of making a successor; the Senate had moved on to irrelevancy.

The accession to power of Diocletian proved to be the turning-point. The new system he constructed proved able to control the Empire and to ward off its external enemies but, of course, at the cost of increased autocracy. He was reacting against the political system that had existed before his seizure of power, and had existed during the preceding chaotic half-century. The balance of power that had been established by the upheaval of 238, between the Senate and the army, was perceived to have actually promoted disorder.

Such a balance had proved very difficult to maintain. There were always groups in the army who were liable to advocate a return to Maximinus' disdain for the Senate and others who were much more willing to have the Senate taking a central role in the political and governmental process. The circumstances of the deaths of emperors, invariably with the army on campaign, whether by disease or assassination and invariably in the midst of a crisis, meant that it was always urgent for a new emperor to be chosen as quickly as possible. The command of an army by a single ruler was the only way of keeping the Empire united. The Senate was then invited to ratify the army's choice, but not always. Mainly it did so, because the army and the new emperor made efforts to be considerate, but there were always those who despised such considerations and manoeuvres.

On the whole, the system had operated successfully. The mid-third century is regarded as confused and confusing, but this is largely a product of the few sources, which are late and difficult, together with the repeated barbarian invasions. Yet the succession of emperors was generally achieved by agreement until the dynasty of Carus (and dynastic succession was repeatedly attempted). We can see, therefore, that beyond the apparent confusion, the same factors in determining the succession were operating as in the previous centuries: the previous emperor's preference, if he had indicated one, the army and then the Senate, in that order. The balance between these shifted for five decades, and it seems to have been very largely the Senate that predominated, even if the army tended to be the source of each new emperor. Finally the balance tipped and power came down on to the army and on dynastic succession, very largely cutting out the Senate. This was in part due to the governmental reforms of Gallienus, which reduced the role of the senators in public affairs. Yet the Senate survived, and its ambitions were undimmed.[20]

However, it was not simply a matter of the previous half-century, but of the previous two and a half centuries. For what had collapsed during the period since 238 was the system of selecting an emperor that had been developed by Augustus. This had, in a variety of ways, operated since his death. It had been altered in the course of that long period, as the basic military situation of the Roman Empire gradually obtruded itself. This was realized first by Vespasian, then by Trajan, and brought to its fully military refinement by Septimius. Changes such as this is what one would expect from any system, and the fact that it had operated for almost two centuries with only minimal changes was a tribute to its originator and to those who operated it. Nevertheless, it failed and its failure produced the chaos of the middle of the third century. It was Diocletian's achievement to realize that tinkering with the system was no longer an option.

Odainathos (250).

Zenobia (270–272).

Vaballathus (270–272).

Balista (c.260).

The Restorers Of Unity

Claudius Gothicus
(268–270).

Quintillus (270).

Aurelian (270–275).

Tacitus (275–276).

Florian (276).

Probus (276–282).

The House of Carus

Carus (282–283). (*Met Museum of Art / Public Domain*)

Carinus (282–285).

Numerian (282–284).

Chapter Eleven

The Consequences of Gordian (2): Unsuccessful Emperors

The problem of rebels and pretenders aiming to replace existing emperors has been touched on twice so far, in Chapters 6 and 8, in which one and nine cases respectively were commented on. This covered the period up to the death of Maximinus. In the following fifty years or so, there was a much larger number of such men: perhaps forty of them known in some way, and there were probably more. This is such a huge number, about four times the number of 'legitimate' rulers, that it is necessary to investigate them as a group and to separate them from those in power at the time.

The difficulty at the root of all this, as so often happens, is the source material. The most comprehensive source is the *Historia Augusta*, which is also probably the least reliable of all the ancient sources, except perhaps for the Chronicle of John Malalas. It has a chapter on the 'Thirty Tyrants', in which thirty-two are actually named, and another chapter on four other usurpers from the same period; much of the information it purports to purvey is inaccurate or simply invented. Further, the classification of men as 'tyrants' is very misleading: the word had lost its original meaning and now it really meant pretenders or usurpers. Several of them were actually simply rebels, with no pretensions to imperial power. It is therefore one of the purposes of this chapter to winnow the collection and remove those that were not pretenders to imperial power. Then the actual authenticated cases can be looked at for the purposes of classification, particularly in connection with how men became emperors.

Some of these have been considered already in the last chapter, especially those who ruled the 'Gallic Empire' from 260 to 274, whose length of time in power makes it impossible to regard them as pretenders at all, though if you stand at Rome, as most ancient historians do, they must be seen as rebels. In the same way this author prefers to distinguish between successful emperors, who clearly included Postumus and his Gallic Empire successors, and those who were unsuccessful; hence this chapter title. Their lack of success is also a judgement, of course; however, it is founded not on a subjective decision as to their 'legitimacy', but generally on their longevity as rulers. It is difficult to see a man such as the Gallic Emperor Postumus, who ruled a major portion of the Roman Empire for nearly a decade, as a pretender or even as a rebel. He was clearly a successful ruler, and to classify him as anything but a ruling emperor is to judge him from the viewpoint of his enemies. At this distance this seems both unfair and pointless. Also why do we accept Macrinus as a 'legitimate' emperor? He lasted only a year, was clearly unsuccessful in his policies, and fled the scene at the first sign of real opposition. So only the criteria of extreme localism and brevity of tenure are worth considering in classifying such men as pretenders, usurpers and rebels. The two together imply that they were quickly suppressed by someone stronger, as clear a mark of lack of success as can be devised.

It is worth noting that a large proportion of the third-century emperors who are counted as 'legitimate' were in fact rebels when they began. Gordian I and Decius both rebelled against the legally-constituted emperor of the time, to whom they had sworn an oath of obedience and loyalty: Claudius, Aurelian, Probus and Carus also began the same way, by rebelling and killing their predecessors, as did Diocletian. 'Legitimacy' therefore has little or no meaning in the context of Roman emperors; if a man claims to be emperor, all it takes for him to be 'legitimate' is for one man to obey him and call him emperor. There was no obvious mechanism, other than recognition by the Senate, for legitimizing a pretender and, as we have seen, several well-regarded 'legitimate' emperors were never given senatorial recognition.

Of the *Historia Augusta*'s thirty-six unsuccessful aspirants to empire between 238 and 284, one is a recognized emperor, Aemilius Aemilianus, though he lasted only three months, and six were the rulers of the 'Gallic Empire', four of whom must be regarded as successful. Of the remainder Trebellianus is classified by the historian as an 'archipiratus'; he operated in the Isaurian Mountains of Anatolia and was in fact simply a brigand.[1] Mariades was another brigand, who was chased out of the Empire and then joined the Persians in their invasion of Syria, guided them to the capture of Antioch and returned with them to Persia, no doubt enriched by his share of the loot of the city, which would have been his aim all along. He was hardly an aspirant to the imperial throne; if, indeed, the story is not simply a fiction.[2] Felicissimus was the mint master at Rome, who mounted a rebellion in the city against Aurelian; he also was not aiming at the throne. Indeed, his name suggests that he may well have been a slave or perhaps a freedman; his

Table II: Rebels aiming at the Throne, 238–284.

Date	Emperor	Challenger		Region
238	Gordian III			
240		Annius Sabinianus		Africa
244	Philip			
		Iotapian	Syria	
		Pacatian	Pannonia	
249	Decius*	Silbannianus, Sponsianus		Gaul, Dacia
251	Trebonianus Gallus	Priscus	Thrace	
		Valens	Rome	
253	Aemilian/Valerian + Gallienus	Uranius Antoninus		Syria
		Regalian	Pannonia	
		Macrianus, Valens		Syria, Greece
		Ingenuus Mussius		Pannonia, Egypt
260	Gallienus (alone)	Piso	Postumus (Gallic Empire)	Greece
		Aureolus		Italy
268	Claudius II*		Marius	
			Laelian	
270	Quintillus/Aurelian	Zenobia	Tetricus	Syria
		Septimius		Dalmatia
		Firmus	Domitianus	Egypt
		Urbanus	Faustinus	Moesia
			Tetricus II	
275	Tacitus			
276	Florian/Probus	Bonosus, Proculus		Germany
		Saturninus	Syria	
282	Carus*			
283	Numerian			
284	Carinus	Iulianus	Italy	

(* These emperors began as challengers)

rebellion was more in the nature of a labour dispute.[3] These three may be discarded at once.

Several men on the list are no more than names. The suspicion must be strong that the *Historia* author was so keen to make his number up to thirty (a number lifted from an episode in Athenian history) that he counted not only the rebels and brigands mentioned already, but filled out the total with inventions. Even if they existed, several of these – Celsus, Sponsianus, M. Silbannianus, Memor and Censorinus[+] – are so unimportant that there is no point in considering them. The ingenious and fertile mind of the author betrays them by a complete lack of authenticating external references, by the sheer exuberance of his invention, and by the total lack of any accompanying worthwhile information. Silbannianus, however, minted coins, and appears to have operated in Gaul, and Sponsianus in the Balkans, but more than that is not known.

We are therefore left with twenty-one clear cases of actual rebellion; that is, of men who claimed the right to be called emperor, wore the purple and were obeyed for a time by their subjects. The chronological spread of these cases reflects the overall problems of the Empire, for they tended to appear in sets when the Empire also faced other troubles, often in exactly the same areas. There is one example in 240 in the reign of Gordian III, in Carthage; two in the reign of Philip the Arab; two in that of Decius, including the Palmyrene uprising; and one in 253 in Syria in response to the Persian invasion; five came in 259–260 (not counting the Gallic Empire of Postumus) when the Emperor Valerian was defeated and captured by the Persian army; one came at the end of Gallienus' reign when there was much confusion over who should be emperor; five in Aurelian's reign; and four in the early 280s. (These are tabulated in the chart, Table II.)

Their geographical distribution is equally a reflection of the distribution of power in the Empire, and a reflection of the most troubled regions. The most heavily garrisoned areas were the most likely to see rebellions, not surprisingly, since the first step to power was always to gain control of part of the army. It is also necessary to factor in the size of the external threat. The well-garrisoned provinces that were not under heavy threat saw few or no rebellions; Britain is notable, with no known attempts in this period. Syria, on the other hand, was the scene of at least five, to add to those noted already under the Severans (and that of Avidius Cassius even earlier); there was something more than simply men with an ambition to be emperor here. The Danube frontier was the scene of three attempts, and the wider Balkan area adds three more. These were always dangerous, since the Pannonian army was the closest of the major Roman forces to Rome; Vespasian, Septimius and Maximinus had all launched invasions of Italy from that province. The Rhine frontier was the basis of the Gallic Empire's power, which began as a rebellion against Gallienus' regime, and there were two later attempts in that area after the regime collapsed. Egypt and northern Italy saw two attempts each, though one of the latter could really be counted as Pannonian. Rome was the scene of just one. The complete absence of risings in Spain and Gaul and most of Anatolia is presumably due to the absence of sufficient forces in those areas to support an attempt at the throne, yet Greece was the scene of two of these events, and it was also virtually ungarrisoned.

However, these comments are only statements of the obvious. It is necessary to look more closely at the individual actions to see what it was that motivated the rebels in their attempts. It will be sensible to consider them in chronological order.

The first case, of Annius Sabinianus in about 240, is unusual in several respects: it took place in Carthage, it happened early in the sequence, and its leader is difficult to identify. He was probably M. Annius Sabinianus, governor of Africa, Gordian I's successor. His rising took place only two years after the Gordians rose against Maximinus in the same province, and it is difficult to avoid concluding that there must be a connection. Gordian III's government had disbanded the III *Augusta* legion which had defeated and killed his uncle and grandfather, but local forces were still available to put down Sabinianus; note that he was actually rebelling against the government of Gordian III. It all suggests a local affair without much wider significance; perhaps a rising by elements of the former legion, hoping to be reinstated.[5]

The rising of Iotapian took place in Syria in 248, a response, so the sources claim, to the heavy taxation imposed on the Eastern provinces by Priscus, the brother of the Emperor Philip, who had a wide responsibility over the whole region. Priscus may well have been an early casualty of the rising for he vanishes from all records about this time, and he would have been expected to contest Decius' success against his brother in 249 had he been alive and in a powerful position. The name of the rebel, which is not known completely but is recorded as M.F.R. Iotapianus, is reminiscent of the queens and princesses called Iotape who were members of the defunct Commagenian dynasty. He claimed descent from Alexander the Great, which is part of the mythology of that dynasty, by way of its connections with the Seleukids. This may well have been seen as a helpful point in Syria, and it carried echoes of the ancestry of Avidius Cassius as well. Iotapian did not, however, last long, the forces in Syria being loyal to Philip, who was also a local boy, of course; he built up the village he came from into the city of Philippopolis, though it seems to have faded away soon after he died.[6]

In the same year in the Balkans the governor of either Moesia or Pannonia, or perhaps both, Ti. Claudius Marinus Pacatianus (mentioned earlier in connection with Decius' rebellion) was disgruntled at the policies of the Emperor Philip towards the barbarians who were threatening his territory. He appears to have had himself proclaimed as emperor, and to have gained the support of at least some of the legions on the Danube frontier. This act led indirectly to the defeat and death of Philip (see Chapter 10), but Pacatian himself did not last more than a few weeks, being killed by his own soldiers when Decius arrived to suppress him. However, Pacatian was, like many of the other rebels in this section, a prominent man, the son of a senator. It took some effort in such a man to rebel, and is an indication of the scale of the problem faced by Philip. It was a reaction by Pacatian to his frontier problem that appears to have been his motive; that is, his rebellion was in favour of a more active frontier policy.[7]

Three years later the Emperor Decius found that one of his rear commanders, Licinius Priscus, was proclaimed emperor briefly in Thrace. This came in the midst of the war against the Goths that Decius had to wage as a result of his own seizure of power (this was, no doubt, Pacatianus' problem). Priscus was governor of Macedonia. His elevation took place in very confused circumstances and was not necessarily voluntary. (He may be the same as T. Iulius Priscus, known from milestone from Serdica). He died soon, and his rising was of minor importance, though no doubt disturbing at the time. It came from the same basic cause as that of Pacatian, the dissatisfaction with the policies of the government in Rome towards the provinces, and it was a response to the temporary problem of the barbarian invasion, whose size is thus suggested.[8] It is noticeable that both these Balkan rebellions took place after the brief super-governorship of Philip's father-in-law Marcus Severianus. He is not mentioned in the events, and had possibly ceased to rule in the region before they took place. What effect his rule or its ending had is not known, but it is unlikely to have been without some effect.

In Rome, Valens – full name Iulius Valens Licinianus – had himself proclaimed emperor, also in 251. He was a senator, and he seems to have had some senatorial support in reaction to the military and austerity policies pursued by Decius; he is also said to have had some popular support. He was killed within a few days, but by who is not stated, though it was probably the Guard. Just as the support of a single legion of the army was often not enough to topple an active emperor, so support of the Senate alone was insufficient.[9]

Uranius Antoninus was a priest at the Emesa, who emerged in 253 at the head of a locally-recruited army with which he contested the Persian invasion of Syria. This force won a battle (later improved in one account to include his killing of the Persian king), and Uranius was proclaimed emperor by his troops as a result. He appears as 'Imperator Caesar L. Iulius Aurelius Sulpicius Uranius Antoninus Augustus' on coins minted in his name, but after his victory he is heard of no more. Later historians claimed he was connected with the Severan dynasty and/or with that of the old kings of Emesa (he was actually referred to as Samsigeramus, the name of the originator of that dynasty, by one source), but this is probably because he was, as they were, also the chief priest in that city.[10] He bore the same name as an earlier rebel from the same region, unless the earlier story is his simply repeated for a different date. At least the 'rebel' of 253 is well attested outside the pages of the *Historia Augusta.*

Two curious events – it is difficult to classify them as rebellions, though that may be how the central government thought of them – with very local effects appeared about the same time. Two men issued coins bearing their names and images. Silbannianus' coins turn up in Gaul, Sponsianus' in Dacia, but, as already noted, nothing is known of either. It has been suggested that they were using their coinage to recruit help from the trans-frontier peoples.[11] Their coins do not suggest they were pretending to the throne, though coining was in theory an imperial monopoly. They are purely local and could only be made while the central government's attention was directed elsewhere and at bigger problems.

This is a group of unsuccessful emperors whose only link is that they made their appearances within the space of five years (248 to 253). Otherwise, they seem to have nothing in common but that they were local men, acting as they did in order to defend their society or their city. The threats they faced were different: Iotapian was resisting the imposition of taxation which the central government clearly felt was necessary; it was thus the same reaction that the Senate had had to the same policy of Maximinus. Uranius Antoninus, Pacatian and Priscus were fighting foreign invaders; that is, they were defending both their communities and the Empire. These men's rebellions were therefore the results of local problems and all of them were very brief. Decius is said to have commented on the debate in the Senate that Pacatian's rising would not last long, and this was true of all of them. The usurpation of Valens, having taken place in Rome, might have been more serious, but he gained no armed support. His complaint was similar to that of Iotapian, about the policies of the ruling emperor.

These events may therefore be provisionally classified. Most were responses to local problems, notably invasions; others were essentially complaints about government policies at a time when it was clear that the emperor's policies were being imposed without any consultation and without consideration of those local problems. They were pleas by neglected, troubled communities for help, which would have been forthcoming in earlier periods.

None of these rebels grasped at imperial power primarily for personal ambition, so far as can be seen, though no doubt it was part of their motivation. All were suddenly elevated, in the midst of crisis, invasions or threats to the concept of what they thought was right. None of them lasted more than a few days, weeks at the most. They were all prominent men, senators or similar, and all must have known that their proclamation as emperor was only the beginning of a long troubled road, even if they succeeded in negotiating the early and violent reply of the central government to their complaints.

There were both similarities and contrasts between this group and those that were noted earlier. The Syrian area was prominent again, Iotapian and Uranius Antoninus following on from Avidius Cassius, Seleucus, Taurinus and the earlier Uranius Antoninus, if he existed. Yet there were no direct attacks on the emperors in the manner of Sallustius, Magnus or Quartinus, and these later rebels do not seem to have been aiming at control of the whole Empire; Valens in Rome was the only possible exception. We need therefore to distinguish between these purely local crises and those that seem to be more serious, at least as seen by the imperial government. Note that the Pannonian example – Pacatian – was not regarded as serious in the Senate, and that Pacatian himself seems to have made no move towards Italy. His complaint was local to Pannonia.

These general conclusions are borne out by the next wave of rebellions. There was a gap of five years in the sequence after Uranius Antoninus, which suggests a distinct improvement in affairs, no doubt because of the stability brought by the Emperor Valerian. Most of the next set of rebels/pretenders/usurpers happened as a reaction to the capture of Valerian by the Persian King Shapur in 260. This triggered a crisis of empire-wide dimensions, despite the fact that he left an adult and vigorous son (Gallienus) as Augustus in office, and a number of male relatives, sons and grandsons, who were also in offices from which the government could be continued.

There had in fact been an earlier attempt against Valerian by a governor of Pannonia called Ingenuus in 258. His was apparently reacting to the installation of the junior emperor, Valerian II, Gallienus' youngest son, as titular over-governor for Illyricum. This was the general name now being used for much of the Balkan Peninsula, and the arrival of the Caesar Valerian, only a child, may well have meant a closer supervision of Ingenuus than he was accustomed to or liked. The Caesar certainly died in 258, and had only been installed that year. Ingenuus did not actually claim the throne, so it looks to have been a personal problem. He was defeated in battle by Gallienus at Mursa and died.[12]

The Emperor Valerian was captured by the Persians in March 260, and several rebellions all seem to have followed from it. In the East the army led by the emperor was defeated and suddenly leaderless, and the Persians were invading Mesopotamia and Syria. General collapse is not surprising, but locally this was resisted. Two of the leaders of that resistance were high officers of Valerian's army, and so they were endeavouring to reassert Roman imperial control over the invaded land. One man, Callistus (or Ballista, according to the *Historia*'s author's sense of humour) is an example. He was working with another official, Fulvius Macrianus, who was *rationibus Aegypti et praepositus annonae* (a logistics official), and he gathered military support. Macrianus had his sons proclaimed as emperors: T. Fulvius Iunius Macrianus and T. Fulvius Iunius Quietus. Under this authority, he and Callistus were able to fight off the Persian forces, who by this time were heavily burdened by loot. He then set off with one son, presumably the eldest, Macrianus, to expand his reach into Anatolia and the Balkans, while the second son, Quietus, remained at Emesa, a curious choice of headquarters (but Antioch had been captured and sacked by the Persians, as had other cities in north Syria.) All three of the family soon died, Quietus at the hands of the Palmyrene prince Odaenathus acting (eventually) in the name of Gallienus, who awarded him the title *corrector totius orientis*. The other two, father and son, died after their defeat in battle by Gallienus' cavalry general Aureolus in Pannonia.[13]

As the wars spread, other frontiers became active. On the Danube, damaged already by the rebellions of Pacatian and Ingenuus, the new governor of Pannonia, P.C. Regalianus, fought invading barbarians and for his success was proclaimed emperor by his soldiers.[14] At much the same time, and for much the same reason, Postumus killed Gallienus' son Saloninus at Colonia Agrippina and made himself emperor in Germany, Gaul, Britain and Spain.[15]

Postumus and his Gallic successors may be seen as either rebels or legitimate emperors but they, Regalian and Macrianus and his children were all acting from similar motives. They may well have proclaimed themselves emperors in apparent opposition to Gallienus, but they did so in order to defend their province or city, and so the Empire. Macrianus was in effect Valerian's military successor in Syria, picking up the pieces after the defeat and capture of the emperor and resisting further invasion; Regalian was fighting to defend the Danube frontier, following Pacatian and the rest; Postumus was acting to defend Gaul and the Rhine frontier. Postumus and his successors on the German frontier were different from the others in that they organized a fully functional quasi-imperial system to back them up: Senate, consuls, mints and all. There is no sign that Macrianus or Regalian did this, and it was not just that Postumus had more time. Macrianus and his sons held power in the East for several months, maybe a full year, yet the only sign of their governing system is the production of coins to pay their troops; they also made a serious attempt to seize the whole Empire. Neither Postumus nor his successors apparently ever did, and since this was the proximate cause of Macrianus' fall, Postumus' decision was clearly sensible. Macrianus and his son took a substantial part of the army away from Syria to fight Gallienus; any professions they had made of defending Syria rang somewhat hollow once they were through the Cilician Gates and marching away through Anatolia. They had, of course, no chance, once it was clear that they were regarded as enemies by Gallienus.

The effect of the difference between the regimes of Postumus and Macrianus is seen by the reactions of their subjects to their defeat. Postumus was beaten by Gallienus but his regime survived; Macrianus and his son died in the battle in the Balkans when his forces gave up as soon as they were faced by a resolute opponent defending the throne of Gallienus, even though they had gained the additional support of the Pannonian army, still smarting from the defeat of the rebellion of Regalian (and perhaps those of Pacatian and Ingenuus). Macrianus' regime, now headed by Quietus and supported by the capable Callistus/Ballista, was still in place in Syria, but it crumbled at once on the news of the deaths of the Macriani and the several cities they controlled (throughout the East from the Bosporus to the Nile) opted back into the regime of Gallienus. One result was that the Palmyrene Odaenathus was able to remove Quietus and Callistus without difficulty. There was, in other words, no political basis for the regime of Macrianus but his army, which is presumably why he was so keen to get to Italy, so as to acquire the legitimacy that only the Senate could bestow; having his own Senate and apparently strong local support, Postumus did not need Italy.

The Prefect of Egypt, L. Mussius Aemilianus, is listed as a usurper here and there, but it is not certain that he really was one. The authority of Macrianus and Quietus extended into parts of Egypt for a time, and Gallienus sent a fleet under one of his generals, Theodotus, to recover it. Mussius meanwhile would seem to have retired upriver in the face of Macrianus' usurpation but remained loyal to Gallienus. The story in the *Historia Augusta* is a product of the author's imagination and cannot be believed, though it seems that Mussius was later believed to have had himself proclaimed as emperor after Quietus' death. This may have happened, in which case Theodotus had to recover Egypt from its legal prefect. Mussius did not issue any coins, though the Alexandrian mint was a huge and busy one and responded quickly to political changes. Mussius will have to be put into the doubtful category; even if he seized the imperial name and title, he survived as such only briefly.[16]

Another doubtful case is that of a second man called Valens, who, according to the *Historia Augusta*, was proconsul of Achaia. Apart from a passing reference by the historian Ammianus Marcellinus a century later, there is no other evidence for him and no reliable dating. This story is mixed in with that of another local governor named as 'Piso Frugi' and claimed as the descendant of the ancient family of those *cognomina*: serial plotters against Domitian, Nerva and Trajan. It may be that both were involved in Macrianus' attempt, either by resisting him or by helping him. They were not successful, and their claims to the Empire are doubtful. That of Valens may be less doubtful than that of Piso, and it is worth noting that he was claimed to be related to the Valens who had tried a rising in Rome against Decius. The possibility must remain open that the ingenious author cobbled together the details and so invented another rebel to make up his targeted number of thirty, or possibly they were local governors who were on opposing sides in Macrianus' adventure into the Balkans. Either way, in whatever aspirations they had, they were unsuccessful.[17]

The usurpations that followed the news of the capture of Valerian were all, once more and without exception, the products of local crises. That of Ingenuus, which preceded the emperor's capture, is best seen as a personal matter and may perhaps best be seen as a rebellion rather than a usurpation. Regalian, Postumus, Macrianus and his sons were all reacting to threats to their provinces from outside the Empire; so also, if they existed, were Valens and 'Piso Frugi' and perhaps Mussius in Egypt, though the threats here came from within the Empire; they may, in fact, have been loyalists resisting rebels. Of these the only one who made any attempt to expand his authority beyond the original provincial base was Macrianus. His failure shows how very fragile his support was. Postumus in Gaul showed the most political sense by sticking to his proclaimed intention of defending Gaul, in refusing to make any attempt to expand, and in recruiting his own Senate to provide him with some legitimacy beyond those ideas. Regalian may have had similar intentions, but he died on the swords of his own troops during the barbarian invasion in which he had seized power to fight, so we will never know.

These rebels were thus all at base imperial loyalists, seeing the great imperial problems of the time through their provincial lenses. It is difficult to apply the term 'usurpation' successfully to their conduct, for, like many of the earlier groups, most of them showed no intention of combating the 'legitimate' emperors; perhaps 'provincial emperors' in the pattern of Postumus would be more appropriate. Most did not last very long, and the reason is that their subjects saw through their imperial pretensions and failed to provide any support; the exception as always is Postumus. The Roman army and the citizens of the Empire were loyal to the Empire as a whole, and were not to be easily gulled into anything less.

The Gallic Empire seemed stable while Postumus (260–269) and then Victorinus (269–271) ruled, but under Tetricus (271–274) it began to fail. Spain reverted to loyalty to the Italian regime of Aurelian when Tetricus became emperor. The Gallic emperors also suffered from their own rebels, by Ulpius Cornelianus Laelianus near the end of Postumus' reign, and by at least two men who attempted rebellions against Tetricus: Domitianus, known only from a couple of coins and a brief reference; and Faustinus, who may or may not have claimed the imperial title. None of these attempts lasted long, but their activities certainly indicated unrest.[18]

Gallienus' various attempts to suppress the Gallic regime failed, and this may be the background to the context in which his general Aureolus rebelled. Aureolus had been a successful commander and Gallienus' instrument in the suppression of both Ingenuus and the Macriani. He was thus conspicuously loyal, until his rebellion. He was intercepted by Gallienus' army as he was heading for Rome and was driven into Milan. He proclaimed his loyalty to Postumus, who did not respond. After Gallienus' murder, Aureolus proclaimed himself emperor but died in the fighting soon after. It has always been difficult to account for Aureolus' rebellion, though perhaps personal ambition was involved. The actions of generals in killing

Gallienus suggest that Aureolus was only a little premature in his rising; discontent was clearly widespread among the generals. His appeal for help to Postumus also suggests that, even if he was a notable commander, his political sense was not of the best. His claim to the imperial title was clearly a last desperate hope rather than his original intention.[19]

The rise of the family of Odaenathus of Palmyra to prominence was a home-grown Syrian event, but also it partook of the same basic imperial loyalty as the other 'rebellions' of the time. The rise of the family to predominance and the appointment of the elder Odaenathus to authority over the whole Eastern part of the Empire by Gallienus was a good example of imperial loyalty rewarded. The elder Odaenathus gained his reputation by defeating Persian invaders and then by suppressing the usurper Quietus after the death of his father and brother. After the elder Odaenathus' murder in a private quarrel, his son was promoted as emperor by the ambition of his mother Zenobia. Their success in briefly gaining control of the whole East from the Propontis to the Nile was, like that of Macrianus ten years before, merely momentary, being founded on sand. The Roman soldiers and the great cities were not really interested in a regime run by a woman from Palmyra in the name of a child. The victory of the Emperor Aurelian over Zenobia's forces was easily gained. As a throw for the Empire, the Palmyran attempt was brief and spectacular, and almost any Western emperor could have suppressed it without any difficulty.[20]

The scene of these events was Syria, with extensions into Egypt and Anatolia. The agony of Syria in the third century is clearly the source of the frequency of the appearance of rebels there, from the time of Macrinus and Elagabalus onwards. They were, however, almost invariably loyal to the Empire as an idea; even Zenobia's coins had Aurelian's head on one side. Her husband had had much the same position as overseer of the Eastern provinces as a series of previous officials, going back at least to Agrippa and Germanicus under Augustus and Tiberius, and even to Pompey the Great. The East was simply too far from Rome to be governed directly with ease unless it was content, hence large responsibilities were regularly given to selected trusted men, whose loyalty at times broke down. The third-century problem arose because of the new aggressiveness of Persia under Sassanian kings; the local emperors, even Zenobia, grew out of that local problem and they were almost always basically acting in defence of the Roman Empire. Most of them stayed in Syria; only Macrianus and Zenobia strayed outside that land and both of them suffered rapid defeats as a result.

The disturbances in the East did not end with the capture of Zenobia and the defeat of her armies, but none of the subsequent troubles – Firmus' suppression of riots in Alexandria, Antiochus and Achilleus' rebellion in Palmyra[21] – were serious attempts at seizing the imperial power, but rather local attempts to revive the Palmyrene regime. The leaders were men who had hitched themselves to Zenobia's wagon and would suffer whether or not they continued in rebellion.

Unconnected with either the Western or Eastern crises was the rebellion of a man called either Septimius or Septiminus in Dalmatia, mentioned along with Urbanus and Domitianus by Zosimus and noted by another source as well. This juxtaposition implies an event late in Aurelian's reign, but little more can be said. Dalmatia was not a province at this time severely threatened by barbarian invasions. Septiminus was killed by his own men, having clearly failed to appreciate their primary loyalties. A man called Urbanus who was linked with him is just as obscure – even his location is not certain – and he was just as rapidly suppressed. It has to be said that the occurrence of the attempt of Scribonianus in Dalmatia under Claudius and the similarity of 'Urbanus' to 'Uranius' gives rise to considerable suspicion of invention and duplication, though Zosimus is much less liable to such a practice than the author of the *Historia Augusta*.[22]

Syria and Gaul continued to be sources of trouble for the central government for the next decade after Zenobia's suppression. Another appointment of a man to the wide authority in Syria by the Emperor Probus produced yet another attempted coup in that area. This was in 280, by Iulius Saturninus, said to have been a friend of Probus and whose attempt was suppressed by his own soldiers. Saturninus is identified by some sources as an appointee of Aurelian's, which would mean he had been in office in the East for at least five years when his rebellion began. No doubt he had been there since the defeat of Zenobia, maybe even with the same responsibilities as Odaenathus. He was also connected with Egypt, and if he had authority over both Egypt and Syria his position was the same as that of Avidius Cassius, Macrianus or Zenobia.[23] The extent of such authority could well breed ambitions in any man, and changes in the person of the emperor might then be seen as a personal threat, triggering a defensive *putsch*.

In the former Gallic Empire the suppression of Tetricus in 274 had not quietened the desire there for close and constant imperial attention to the frontier. Aurelian had brought the Gallic legions back into the army and had at once used them in a raid into the barbarian lands; a sensible move that no doubt killed off some of the men and at the same time employed them to do the work that had been the main justification for the Gallic Empire's existence. Probus attended to the same frontier in 277–278, but found a problem arising in Britain, where a governor (probably of Britannia Superior, in the north) was thought to be contemplating trouble and was suppressed by the advisor of the emperor who had originally recommended him for the post, using German prisoners who had been enlisted after his German campaign; that is, without much difficulty.[24] He clearly did not get far, but this might be seen as part of the aftermath of the suppression of Tetricus and as a precursor to the trouble Britain would cause in the next century or so. The British army had been the only force of some size that had not so far produced an emperor; the Syrian, the Pannonian and the Rhine armies had done so repeatedly.

Probus by the late 270s was in the East, where the tedious siege of Cremna in Pisidia took a long time and where Saturninus rebelled in Syria. While he was there, two men, Proculus and Bonosus, were successively proclaimed as Gallic emperors. The *Historia Augusta* tells us a long and strange story about Proculus (he was supposed to have been hen-pecked into rebellion by his wife, a virago) but it does imply that he had support in Gaul, at Lugdunum and at Colonia Agrippina, and that he conducted wars against the Franks and the Alamanni. His seizure of power was not, therefore, merely momentary, but must have lasted some time, at least a few months. Bonosus is said to have been the commander of the Rhine fleet before his seizure of power, so again we have a connection with the defence of the frontier.[25] The example of Postumus and his successors would seem to have continued to have influence.

The last of the pretenders to be discussed here is M. Aurelius Iulianus Sabinus, already mentioned as the opponent of Carinus. He was given offices unknown at this time by later sources, but he did command a worthwhile army and minted coins at Siscia, the main centre for Illyricum. He is said to have had support in Italy also, and this can be interpreted as a reaction in the West to the deaths of Carus and Numerian in the East. Iulianus' proclamation happened before the news arrived of the coup carried out by Diocletian; he lasted for some months, judging by the coinage, but he did not get to Rome for a senatorial installation, no doubt because he found himself threatened at once by the forces of Carinus, by which he was indeed defeated and killed in the spring of 285.[26]

This is best seen as an attempt to pre-empt the main army in the East by elevating a senatorial candidate to replace or discipline Carinus, who was certainly unpopular among the senatorial class. Yet Iulianus' attempt was also in the tradition of local uprisings in the Pannonian region by Pacatian, Regalian, Ingenuus and others, and even by Septimius Severus, Trajan and Vespasian. This was one of the places that had repeatedly produced pretenders during the third century, the others being Syria, especially Emesa and Antioch, and the Rhine frontier, notably Colonia Agrippina. The source of antagonism in Syria probably goes back to the family of the Severi, if not to Avidius Cassius, that of Gaul certainly to Postumus and perhaps earlier, and the main Pannonian memory was surely the success of Septimius Severus himself in 193.

One of the most remarkable things about most of these disturbances is how easily they were suppressed. Some were certainly relatively long-lived and had spread widely – Postumus and his successors in Gaul and the West, Zenobia and Macrianus in the East – but the rest lasted from a day or two up to a month or two, and rarely extended beyond their own province, and it turns out that these brief attempts were frequently stopped by their own soldiers.

This is one contrast between those who aimed at the whole Empire (very few), and the majority who were reacting to a local problem. The other contrast is between the Gallic Empire and all the rest. The Gallic stability was due to the careful work of Postumus, who ensured that he had the support of his Rhine army and of a local Senate, and put out a propaganda effort that insisted on his role as the defender of his provinces and one which he then adhered to, even when tempted, as he surely was, to take advantage of Aureolus' rebellion in northern Italy. The other pretenders regularly overestimated the support they could expect, particularly among their troops. If they were serious in their aim to seize the imperial power, they obviously believed that they could attempt to gain control of the whole Empire without a firm local political base and with only army support. As soon as they made a wider attempt, such local support as they had assumed failed them.

These rebels, therefore, were in most cases of only minor and local significance. They were, as noted earlier, normally local to a particular province or even a single city, and usually they were responding to a local problem. Above all, none of them made any attempt to damage or break up the Empire; they were seizing power in order to defend the Empire in the same way as the many 'legitimate' emperors of the time were eliminating their predecessors in the belief that their own abilities in command were required. In their aims, therefore, there is no essential difference between those considered as usurpers and rebels and those who are counted as legitimate emperors. It was one of the results of the autocracy imposed by emperors that every problem became an imperial problem and was expected to be solved by the emperor; if the recognized emperor would not or could not do anything, one solution was to erect an emperor of one's own.

There is a paradox, therefore, in that local problems were the sources for rebellion in which the leaders claimed to be emperors, but as soon as they attempted to make that claim wider, they failed. However, they knew that by staying within their local area they would suffer attack and be defeated. Having claimed authority, their only solution was to impose it on everyone, and in this they normally failed. The basic tension was between local needs and imperial resources. Any politician in any age has confronted the same problem. At the same time those who put their local problems so high that they attempted a rising were also loyal to the Empire as a worldwide political entity. A real secession, even by Postumus and Zenobia, into independence and separation, was not a serious option, though expulsion, as with Dacia in Aurelian's reign, certainly was. Attempts at reconciling these differing political concepts underlay much of the politics of the time.

There is, however, another aspect. Several of the legitimate emperors of the third century began in rebellion. Septimius, Elagabalus, Gordian I, Decius and Probus all began as rebels against an established emperor, while Macrinus, Maximinus, Gordian III, Valerian and Claudius became emperors by the device of accomplishing the murder of their predecessors. That is, enough men succeeded in seizing the imperial throne by violence and rebellion to make it a worthwhile target for others. Rebellion when it prospered became legitimate; only when it consistently failed would attempts cease. Once again, the absence of a legal succession framework, established by law and respected as such, was a basic cause of imperial instability.

Part IV

Heredity and Absolutism

The Tetrarchy

The Tetrarchs hang together.

Maximian (286–311).

Diocletian (285–305).

The British Secession

Carausius (286–293).

Allectus (293–296).

Constantius I
Chlorus (305–306).

Chapter Twelve

The Tetrarchy

The new ruler who seized power in 284, Diocletian, benefited from the hard work of his recent predecessors, notably Probus and Aurelian but also Gallienus, and even the senatorial emperors of 238. One of his major achievements was to stay alive and in power for the next twenty years. (It was an even greater achievement to retire and then to die a natural death several years later; a unique pair of achievements for a Roman emperor, except for Tetricus.) It was the facility with which emperors had been murdered that had been one of the root causes of the imperial instability in the recent past, and one of the reasons for that was their practice of living in the midst of their forces and appearing in public audiences. Diocletian survived in part by removing himself from such soldierly temptation; he appeared relatively little in public and inhabited a palace rather than a camp. He was a soldier, of course, though not a great one, although he was able to find and appoint capable generals to command in his name, and he slowly devised a method of organizing the imperial succession.

His own accession was particularly brutal and intimidating. He was a senior officer, called at the time Diocles, in the army of Carus and Numerian in the Persian War. Carus died and was succeeded by his son, but Numerian was dominated by his father-in-law Lucius Aper, his Praetorian Prefect. Numerian died, probably by Aper's hand, and when the death was discovered, the soldiers at once arrested Aper; he had been the one with access, after all. However, it is probable that Diocles the general was also involved, at least in the arrest.[1]

The army consulted over a successor. Diocles had convened the council of senior officers and he was their choice as emperor. The army was paraded. He was loudly acclaimed by the troops, and the purple cloak was placed on his shoulders. He swore by his gods that he had had no hand in the death of Numerian (which implies that he had been accused of it). He brought Aper forward and accused him of the murder, then personally stabbed him to death. As an accession to power it was a display of vengeance and a warning to plotters quite magnificent in its brutality. It also conveniently silenced Aper.[2]

This gave Diocletian, as he now called himself, control of the Eastern half of the Empire through the army he had inherited from Numerian. Carinus, Numerian's brother, still controlled the West. The two met in battle at Margus, near Sirmium. Carinus' army was winning the fight when Carinus himself was murdered by one of his own officers, who had a personal grievance against him. Carinus' army then stopped fighting and at once acclaimed Diocletian.[3]

This was one of the most difficult and dangerous imperial accessions since that of Septimius in 193–197. It was a long time since two Roman armies had fought a set battle. As a seizure of power it was messy and costly, and if anything was able to convince the new ruler that he was lucky to have survived it was this. The complexity and unpleasantness of this were the background to the reforms introduced by Diocletian and the new and extraordinary system of succession that he designed.

This system did not emerge fully grown, but was developed piece by piece in response to events. As such, it was reminiscent of the way Augustus' system had developed. It was a sensible response to the problems that had brought the Empire close to collapse, but it was so complicated that it soon became a hindrance. The pressures on the frontiers as a result of the continuing internal problems of the Empire had become incessant, from Hadrian's Wall to the Upper Nile, from the Crimea to Morocco, and it was physically impossible for the emperor to cope with them all. Expedients devised in the past had included joint emperors and super-governors, and Diocletian used them, as well as dividing the larger provinces into smaller sections that could more easily be directly controlled and would reduce the immediate armed support available to a potential usurper. At the same time the lack of resources of a local governor made his province the more vulnerable and demanded the creation of super-governors with wide regional authority; this could well produce even more powerful usurpers.

The real problem, though, was not the administrative system but that the barbarian invasions were actually in most cases a response to trouble within the Empire. In 284–285 four emperors and a pretender died, and Roman armies twice fought each other; not surprisingly, there was now trouble on the Danube and the Rhine, in the East, in Africa and in Britain. The secession of the Gallic Empire had been explicitly intended to defend Gaul against barbarian attack, but the Gallic go-it-alone solution would not work in the long run. The rise of the Palmyrene power in the East was a response to the Persian invasions that had briefly conquered large parts of Syria. In turn, the occurrence of rebellions was in almost every case a local response to local trouble – an invasion, usually – which the central government was unable to combat. Diocletian learned this lesson also, but the only way to solve this problem was to stop the internal dissent, a task that was by no means easy. At the time it was particularly acute in Gaul, where there was a widespread insurrection by people referred to as *bacaudae*. Diocletian's attempted solution to the problem of imperial power and succession is a major element in tackling the problem.

He began by adopting an old solution, one that went back to Augustus and Agrippa or even in a sense to the consuls of the Republic: he appointed a Caesar, M. Aurelius Maximianus, a friend and fellow soldier, as emperor of the West. He was explicitly to deal with the *bacaudae*. Two of their leaders, perhaps as a last resort, like Aureolus, claimed the title of Augustus but only briefly before their destruction.[4]

Maximian's fleet commander in British waters, M. Aurelius Carausius, seized control of Britain and part of northern Gaul in 286, after Maximian's successful campaign against the *bacaudae*. Carausius had gained a substantial reputation in his military post and no doubt he was well-liked in Britain for his campaigns against Frisian and Saxon raiders, who were always stigmatized as 'pirates'. His seizure of power came as a result of his belief that Maximian intended to arrest him. Carausius' regime was stable for several years, possibly because he portrayed himself as a colleague of Diocletian and Maximilian, though this was not an interpretation of the situation that they shared.[5]

It may have been Carausius' seizure of power locally or the spectre of *bacaudian* Augusti fighting a 'legitimate' Caesar, but in April 286 Diocletian raised Maximian to the rank of Augustus,[6] theoretically therefore Diocletian's equal, though Maximian was clearly the junior of the two for it was Diocletian who raised him to Augustus. The title of Caesar implied in the old scheme that Maximian was Diocletian's heir, a matter that also led to the assumption that he had been adopted as Diocletian's son. This might be all the more cunning since Diocletian had no sons of his own. Maximian's promotion to Augustus happened in the aftermath of a victory over the *bacaudae*, rather as, back in the defunct Republic, soldiers saluted a victorious consul as *imperator*. The two men trusted each other, and neither of them succumbed to plots or seems to have intended plots. These various moves were all within the repertory of the imperial government as conducted over the previous three centuries.

Maximian was defeated in 290 in one of the various attempts to suppress Carausius, and this provoked further thoughts about the system that Diocletian was organizing. The two Augusti met in conference in Milan in 291. A public display of amity and unity was put on, the two men riding cheerfully together through the city. Diocletian had come west to display his support for his colleague after his defeat, and Maximian certainly had the more difficult task. His defeat by Carausius was a dangerous moment that would surely encourage invasions and plots if precautionary measures were not instituted. This was a situation that had happened in the previous half-century, after all; more frequently than most would care to recall. It was the very situation that normally provoked an army to look round for a new commander. Diocletian's visit west was thus a pre-emptive move, designed to show that he and his forces would support Maximian despite his defeat.

Diocletian's was the political brain and it was presumably he who devised the next development. Again, he only needed to drop back into the Roman imperial past to find precedents. Augustus had employed Agrippa and Tiberius as his military arms, and Tiberius had used Drusus and Germanicus in the same way. The purpose had been to allow Augustus – never an outstanding commander in the field – to control matters in Rome and avoid the danger of defeat, while more competent commanders took on the military problems. It also, of course, allowed Roman power to be projected even when the emperor was elsewhere. It was, in fact, only since Marcus Aurelius that emperors had regularly commanded the armies in the field, the only real exception earlier being Trajan.

Diocletian and Maximian were both commanders and emperors; defeat in the field would therefore damage or destroy the prestige of both of them. The answer was to separate, as in the past, the two imperial roles. So the two men set about developing plans for distancing themselves from campaigning; instead they selected deputies who would do that for them. The defeat of a deputy would be much less politically damaging than the defeat of an Augustus, and to show that the deputies were junior they were given the title of Caesar.

The plan was put into effect in 293. Maximian chose M. Flavius Constantius Chlorus as his deputy. Constantius was an experienced soldier, a former governor of Dalmatia (who may well have deserted Carinus for Diocletian in 285), and had been Maximian's Praetorian Prefect; he also became Maximian's son-in-law. Diocletian chose C. Galerius, who divorced his wife and married Diocletian's only daughter. The two deputies were then given the title of Caesar and proclaimed *principes iuventutes*, even though both were hard-bitten soldiers not all that much younger than the two Augusti.[7] The whole scheme is perhaps most closely parallelled by the brief period in 238 when there were two Augusti – Pupienus and Balbinus – with Gordian III as Caesar; if this was in Diocletian's mind one wonders if he noted the irony, for he was wholly dismissive of any senatorial pretensions to power.

There are here echoes of past succession methods, with more or less subtle changes, but how else was the public to understand the situation unless it had been wrapped up in familiar terms? The essential difference from the past was that this was all done, so far as can be seen, with no reference at all to the Senate. The crucial meeting between the emperors took place in Milan, a convenient city in which the rulers of the East and West could meet and not be too far from their separate responsibilities and their frontier problems. It was actually more convenient for Maximian but then it was his military and political problem that was at the heart of the crisis. The designation of the two middle-aged Caesars as 'princes of youth' may have been rather entertaining, but it was another title that had been detached from its literal and original meaning. Such titles' connections were, however, clear: the successors of emperors had often had such titles and Diocletian was organizing a new system of succession under the old titles.

The absence of consultation with the Senate as a body does not mean that senators were not involved. Diocletian had deliberately chosen a senatorial colleague as his partner-consul when he first seized power, and at Milan there were enough senators present as individuals to have held a Senate meeting if it had been felt necessary. These were further traditional gestures to the past but with a Diocletianic twist: this time the senators attended on the emperors, whereas before the emperors had headed for Rome to be invested by the Senate. Diocletian probably did not visit Rome until nearly the end of his reign (though he did rebuild the Senate House when it burned down in 285, and he just might have been in the city in that year).

Carausius had therefore twice provoked major crises and changes in the Diocletianic regime, first in 286 by provoking the promotion of Maximian to Augustus, and then again in 293 and the appointment of new Caesars. The Caesar Constantius justified his promotion at once by clearing Carausius' supporters and forces from northern Gaul, and then besieging and capturing his main continental base at Gesoriacum (Boulogne). This opened the way for the invasion of the island. Carausius himself died at about this time, though how, where and why is not known. His successor was Allectus, otherwise wholly unknown, said to have been one of Carausius' financial officials. He is assumed, without much evidence other than later assumptions, to have been responsible for Carausius' death.[8] In fact, he held on to the island empire for three more years and finally succumbed to an invasion commanded by Constantius in 296.

The length of time this 'British Empire' lasted – ten years – was due entirely to the command with which Carausius began: the local Roman fleet. He will also have been able to persuade the army in Britain either to support him or to acquiesce in his pretensions. Similarly, Allectus clearly had the same sort of local support. However, without acceptance by Diocletian, the senior emperor, it would be impossible for the regime to last long, and Carausius' method of promoting himself, by usurpation and self-proclamation, was exactly what Diocletian, having achieved power by those very means, was determined to prevent. Carausius' regime lasted ten years or so in part only because the emperors on the continent were busy with other affairs.

The 'Tetrarchy', as the Rule of Four Emperors is known in modern historical studies, was devised in 293, and so it lasted for twelve years, until Diocletian retired in 305. Its success was due in part to the military victories of its members, but above all, to the fact that the former rulers all survived long enough for their work to become embedded and generally accepted. The Caesars were given territorial responsibilities, so that all the several frontier areas were covered. (See also Genealogical Table XVI.)

This government system, as it had developed by 293, was the result of a series of expedients devised to cope with crises that threatened the regime. The most serious, in the sense that it was a direct challenge to the legitimacy of Diocletian's rule, was the rival imperial regime of Carausius. Carausius tried to muscle in onto the wider scheme, and had to be excluded for that very reason. The British challenge was a most threatening one for the ruling emperors, for this rival regime, first under Carausius himself and then under his successor Allectus, laid claim to an equal legitimacy with that of Diocletian and Maximian, and it is best, as with the similar Gallic regime initiated by Postumus, to see it as a normal Roman government; it had originated, after all, in a military *putsch*, just as had Diocletian's regime. In terms of origin, the two were the same. Yet it could only be regarded by Diocletian and Maximian as illegitimate, because it was of an origin independent of them; hence its importance and the necessity of its destruction.

This is not necessarily how we should regard them. To take Caurausius as a normal Roman emperor of the type of Postumus is not a plea for the belated

XVI   <u>The Tetrarchs</u>.

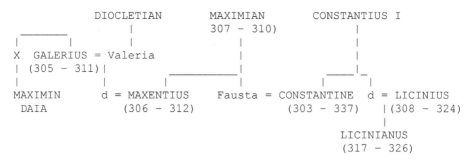

```
              DIOCLETIAN      MAXIMIAN         CONSTANTIUS I
_____            |         307 - 310)            |
|         |         |              |                |
X  GALERIUS = Valeria             |                |
|  (305 - 311)|                   |            ____|_
|         |         |             |           |    |
MAXIMIN     d = MAXENTIUS    Fausta = CONSTANTINE  d = LICINIUS
  DAIA         (306 - 312)             (303 - 337)  |(308 - 324)
                                                    |
                                             LICINIANUS
                                             (317 - 326)
```

installation of these men as 'legitimate' emperors, but a suggestion that to classify one group as legitimate emperors and another as usurpers is, as ever, pointless, especially at this distance in time. It is more useful to look at what they did, what their authority was, and at the way they made themselves into emperors. For if a man could maintain himself as emperor over several years, have soldiers and civilians obey him over a relatively geographically extensive area and pass on his power and position to his successor, he was actually as much a 'legitimate' ruler as any other.

The question of legitimacy is, of course, at the heart of the problem. In the Empire, any man who claimed the throne in defiance of a ruler was automatically a rebel, until he won. So Diocletian, to Carinus, was a rebel, until the battle of Margus and Carinus' death; and Carausius was a rebel or a rival to Diocletian, though he was clearly not so to his British subjects. The only indication between 285 and 305 that a ruler had 'legitimacy' was by his acceptance by Diocletian as a colleague. However, in the decade before Diocletian, and for Diocletian himself at the start of his reign, it was acclamation by the army that counted, together with installation by the Senate. Both before then and after, it was inheritance and designation by a blood relative that were crucial. The criteria for legitimacy therefore altered with the changes in actual power – this was one of Diocletian's achievements – and these changes means it is wasted effort to distinguish rulers into legitimate emperors and usurpers. The case of Carausius and Allectus is to the point, for between them they maintained a successful Roman imperial regime for a full decade, rather longer than most third-century 'legitimate' emperors. To their subjects, from whom they collected taxes and to whom they dispensed justice and provided defence, they were clearly legitimate rulers.

Diocletian himself in the East was faced with a great revolt in Egypt that began in 297. In the course of it the Alexandrians promoted one of their leaders, L. Domitius Domitianus, to the position of emperor. He and the city were then subjected to a grim siege and assault by Diocletian, who was angry at what he may well have seen as treachery in his rear as he was about to launch an attack on Persia. (He may also have been annoyed that the Egyptian rebellion blew up just as the British problem was solved.) Domitianus vanished from the scene fairly early on, after a reign of only four or five months, and the Alexandrian resistance was then led by a man called Aurelius Achilleus, who had been *corrector* of Egypt under Domitianus. He apparently did not take the imperial title, though he and the city held out until the spring of 298. His regime seems to have had deliberate reminiscences of the old Ptolemaic kingdom.[9]

The reasons for the revolt were, suitably enough given the curious Ptolemaic ideology, almost entirely backward-looking. Diocletian was engaged in a widespread programme of reforms, a process that always upsets people whose positions and/or comforts are threatened. Part of those reforms involved a new census for the purpose of bringing the taxation system up to date.

Table III: Unsuccessful Emperors, 284–330.

Date	Emperor	Challenger	Region
284	Diocletian		
285	Maximian	Bacaudae	Gaul
		Carausius British Empire	
293		Allectus	
297		Domitius Domitianus	Egypt
		Achilleus	Egypt
305	Constantius/Galerius		
306	Constantine I, Maxentius		
307	Maximian		
		Domitius Alexander	Africa
312	Constantine/Licinius		
324	Constantine (alone)	Valens	Balkans
		Martinianus	Constantinople

That is, the reforms were going to be more efficient at extracting tax revenues, and the population as a whole quite reasonably did not like the idea. This seems to have been the basis of the revolt in Egypt, though which came first, the city revolt or the claim of Domitianus to the throne, is uncertain. The revolt and the regime it set up fell to pieces during Diocletian's vengeful siege and capture of Alexandria, a fate that also affected a considerable area of the city. The appearance of a local Roman emperor in the city had therefore little to do with the revolt, and he posed no real threat to the wider imperial regime. Yet again, this was merely a local matter, even though it was apparently triggered by a tax dispute. Yet it was exactly these local disputes that had so destabilized the Empire during the previous half-century, and Diocletian's rage at Alexandria was perhaps a response to this localism and his way of making clear that such disputes were not to be the source of revolts. Its failure permitted the Diocletianic reforms, including the census, to go ahead. (See Table III for the rebels of this period.)

Two other events that have been classified as 'usurpations' took place in Syria and nearby in 303. Neither is well-attested. One took place at Melitene (modern Malatya) in the province of Armenia Minor, but that is all that is known about it; the Church historian Eusebius claimed that it was a danger to the Empire, but what it amounted to is quite unknown. The other problem was an attempt by an army unit stationed at Seleukeia in Syria, where the commander, Eugenius, was proclaimed emperor by his men and then led them on a march against Antioch. This is better attested, and was, given the army involvement, rather more serious than that at Melitene. It was quickly defeated. Both of these revolts took place in 303, and it is perhaps best to associate them, as Eusebius does, with the imperial orders designed to suppress Christianity that were issued that year.[10] Diocletian was more concerned over a fire in the imperial palace at Nikomedeia, and did not allow himself to be diverted by these events from a projected visit to Rome. His estimate of the importance of the events in Syria seems to have been quite accurate.

Of the rebellions during Diocletian's reign, therefore, only that of Carausius (and Allectus) was of any real political importance. Like the Egyptian rebellion, it was in all likelihood essentially a resistance movement devoted to preventing Diocletian's reforms from having local effect; the Syrian and Melitenean risings, if at base connected with Diocletian's anti-Christian policy, were thus also essentially resistance to unwelcome imperial measures. Diocletian nevertheless succeeded in imposing those reforms, and in recovering control in Britain and Egypt by main force; this was, of course, the most effective way of discouraging future attempts, and the damage to Alexandria was a graphic warning to others. So far as can be seen, the reforms were also imposed by ignoring the Senate, though the succession scheme might have been a worthwhile subject for senatorial legislation, particularly one as formal and prescriptive as that Diocletian apparently intended to leave behind.

So, amid wars and campaigns, the Empire remained in the grip of Diocletian and his system of Augusti and Caesars until Diocletian fell ill in 304. The Rule of Four Emperors, two Augusti and two Caesars, had worked well for more than a decade, and had been instrumental in recovering rebellious provinces and defeating invaders. The system, however, had been developed in response to particular political crises, notably the problem of how to deal with Carausius. Exactly when Diocletian realized that he also had devised a system by which he could hand over power and ensure a peaceful succession system is not clear. It seems highly unlikely that he thought of the Rule of Four as a scheme of succession at the beginning, but he certainly saw it in that light later.

He had floated the idea of retirement sometime before his long and serious illness, which began in late 304. Once it was in the air, of course, the question of the succession automatically became urgent, but in this case it was not the question of his immediate successor that was at issue but who should be his next successor but one. He persuaded a reluctant Maximian to retire with him, so that their Caesars should inherit full power as the next Augusti, but first it was necessary to pick two new Caesars. Like Augustus and Hadrian, Diocletian was clearly intent on organizing the succession for the foreseeable future; that is, for at least two more generations. If his immediate successors could reign for twenty years as he and Maximian had, and if their successors could then do so as well, he was envisaging the organization of the succession for at least the next forty years.

So on 1 May 305, Constantius and Galerius each moved up to the rank of Augustus, the former as the senior of the two, and each of them was given a new Caesar. The whole process was yet again reminiscent of several earlier occasions, going back to Augustus and Tiberius, but also to the second-century emperors, whereby it was supposed the emperor would select a suitable successor and adopt and train him. Only after a careful investigation does it turn out that in most of these cases the suitable successor proved to be a very close relative of the emperor who selected him.

The new Caesars were not the sons of any of the various emperors. Constantius had an adult son, as did Maximian: Constantine and Maxentius respectively. They were the obvious candidates to be Caesars, but neither was chosen. They had none of the experience that the promoted Caesars had had ten years before when they took the office. In particular, no one except Maximian and Maxentius himself was impressed by Maxentius, and if the son of one emperor was to be excluded, the other would have to be as well. It might also be that Diocletian, who had no son of his own, was intent on avoiding the dynastic principle, though this seems less likely when the various marriages between the four emperors are taken into account.

This idea of the careful selection and judicious weighing of merits in potential successors is, of course, untenable, for it was necessarily a personal decision made, it appears, by Diocletian, partly under the influence of Galerius. They chose men they knew, and tried to impose their choices on their colleagues. The two new Caesars of 305, Severus and Maximin Daia, were both in fact associates of Galerius: Maximin was his nephew and Severus was a military colleague, possibly his Praetorian Prefect. This would seem to be a coup for Galerius, and Constantius clearly felt that he could not rely on his new Caesar, Maximin Daia, in the way that Maximian had been able to trust Constantius. Also, of course, the scheme took no heed of either human mortality or of the deeply-ingrained Roman (and human) affection for heredity.

The whole scheme has all the hallmarks of one that was bodged together out of emergency measures developed to deal with problems as they arose, and based on a set of half-remembered and only half-understood historical memories, just like other aspects of Diocletian's imperial 'scheme', developed in response to events rather than being organized from particular principles. The old Roman preference for double magistracies, the supposed Antonine preference for adoptive succession, the idea of selecting experienced men from a pool of eligible candidates, all are involved, but none of these really existed during the imperial period at any time. No pairs of emperors were ever equal, adoption was only resorted to in emergencies (as with Nerva and Trajan) or when direct family succession failed.

Beyond this, the scheme was unworkable without the authority of a senior emperor with the personal force and power of a man like Diocletian to enforce it, and it actually failed within a year of his retirement. Neither of the passed-over sons of the emperors was prepared to submit to rejection.

Chapter Thirteen

The Crises of 306–312

T he scheme of succession organized by Diocletian lasted for only one year after his retirement, yet it was sufficiently robust that it broke down only slowly, though this was partly because Diocletian, though retired, was still alive. Within two years of his retirement in 305 three men who had been excluded from his scheme were contending for the control of the Western part of the Empire, two men who he had included were dead, and a civil war – which is what the scheme had been designed above all to avoid – was being fought. It had been, as it proved, essentially a personal creation of Diocletian's and it was only his continued existence that ensured it lasted that long. When he was dead it was finished.

The first break came in 306, when Constantius I died at York. His eldest son Constantine was acclaimed by the army there and he was assumed to have been designated heir by Constantius. The acclamation was led by the Alamannic contingent and their king Crocus, who had been defeated by Constantius years before and then enlisted into the Roman forces. The designation as heir may or may not have happened; later it was so claimed, but it is not reported at the time.[1]

However it took place, whoever organized it, whatever construction was later put on the events at York and whether or not Constantius would have approved, it was nevertheless a *coup d'état*, one of the old sort. Constantine had no official position and his promotion had been explicitly refused in a conference of emperors held only the year before, where Diocletian had organized the succession and then he and Maximian had retired. If Diocletian's scheme of succession was taken as the law of the land, Constantius had no legal right to designate the successor to his position in the absence of agreement with his brother emperors; the fragment of the army that was with him had no right to acclaim him, and it was certainly not the place of a tribe of barbarian auxiliaries to do so. However, going back a couple of decades, there were precedents for Constantine's actions aplenty.

It was done, and quickly, immediately it was certain that Constantius was dead. Furthermore it was done in the midst of the whole family, including

Constantine's several half-brothers. These men must have approved and must have been consulted. This is another unusual matter, for Constantine was Constantius' eldest son, but his half-brothers were the children of Constantius' later marriage to Theodora, daughter of the Praetorian Prefect Afranius Hannibalianus, adopted by Maximian.

Constantine's mother was Helena, who may not have been married to his father, and was said, in the usual way of hostile propaganda stories in politics, to have been a tavern-girl and so not of a suitable class to be married to a man of Constantius' rank (but then all the tetrarch emperors were originally of peasant stock). Constantine's illegitimacy was not a serious bar to his ascension to the throne. Constantius' other sons were thus much younger than Constantine, their parents having been married no earlier than 289, and so the eldest was only a teenager in 306. The fate of the whole family at the hands of Constantius' successor, Severus or Maximin Daia, was unlikely to be pleasant after Constantius' death, for they could put forward claims to the Empire that many might accept. All in all, it seems most likely that Constantius himself had organized the coup before he died and that it happened like clockwork. It would certainly be assisted by taking place at York, a place as remote from the centres of imperial political power as could be found. No hostile reaction was likely for months, and at the least Constantine would be able to control the province of Britannia, just as had Carausius. Constantius was of the same generation as Diocletian and Maximian, and had waited a long time for his imperial promotion; he could also remember how things had been done in the 270s and 280s. The provinces of Britannia and Gaul, in fact, rapidly signalled their acceptance of Constantine's enthronement, and the swiftness of all this is surely a good indication of the preliminary planning that had been done.

This was the crucial blow to Diocletian's scheme. He had deliberately removed heredity as a determinant, preferring the selection of mature men, men of experience, who were then linked into the scheme of rulers by marriages; at least if there were daughters available. Constantine's coup was a direct challenge to all that, though he did involve himself in the remains of the scheme by marriage later. His claim to power was a claim to succession by inheritance, and a direct refutation of Diocletian's aims. He got away with it partly because the armies in Britain and Gaul accepted him quickly – and Carausius had shown that Britannia might hold out against a continental army if it had control of the local Roman fleet – and partly because at York he was unreachable by any other ruler, for it would take weeks for the news to reach the other centres of imperial power and further weeks for any condemnation to arrive; by then his local support was firm. In addition he was almost at once copied in seizing power by another disinherited imperial son.

Constantine's coup in July 306 was followed by that of Maxentius in Italy in October. He had been living on an estate a day's journey from Rome; his father Maximian, disgruntled at his compulsory retirement, went off to live on another estate in Campania or Lucania. Neither was happy at their demotion. Maxentius' assumption of power, like Constantine's, quite deliberately also harked back to the old methods. He was asked by the remnant of the Praetorian Guard that was still in Rome to become emperor, and he was supported by a considerable section of the Roman population, by which we may understand the plebs, and by a considerable proportion of the Senate. Two tribunes and one of the city food officials are said to have supported him; the City Prefect opposed him and was killed.[2]

Superficially, this looks like a reversion to the old first-century method of proclamation and succession, an impression deliberately reinforced by Maxentius' use for a time of the outmoded title *princeps* – just as Diocletian had used similarly old titles – rather than either Caesar or Augustus. Closer examination suggests other reasons and motives. The reasons for the Guard's action in seeking their own emperor were that their privileges were being reduced, their numbers were declining and they were in the process of being abolished. Similarly the support of the Romans, who are always identified as 'the people', was due to the imposition of taxation on the city. Parts of Italy had been subjected by Diocletian to taxation for the first time since the Republic; now the new Caesar Severus, who had Italy in his section of the Empire, was extending this to Rome itself and to southern Italy, both hitherto exempt, and the preliminary census had been taken. So the resort to Maxentius as their emperor was a way of attempting to retain their tax-free privileges, just as the Guardsmen wished to hold on to theirs. (We may note, without surprise, that in the troubles of the next few years, Maxentius was compelled to impose taxation on his tax-shy supporters.) The reasons behind Maxentius' usurpation were thus very similar to those of many other such rebellions, notably the Egyptian risings under Diocletian only nine years before. Maxentius never had much support outside Rome and southern Italy, even or especially when his father came out of retirement later in 306 at Maxentius' request and resumed his position as Augustus.[3] In this, Maximian was also in a sense rebelling against change, the change of emperors.

Severus, who had moved up from Caesar to Augustus on the death of Constantius and whose military base was in the Balkans, marched on Rome to suppress Maxentius. He came up against the old professional Maximian, who effortlessly induced Severus' army to change sides and then put Severus himself in prison. Technically, Severus abdicated and was soon afterwards killed, or else committed suicide. In the meantime Maxentius prevented any action being taken by Severus, Galerius or Maximin Daia against Constantine, though this intervention was probably inadvertent, even though the aims of both were aligned for the moment. Constantine was therefore able to consolidate his position in Britain and Gaul, by which he gained command of the two major armies in the West. Galerius perforce recognized him as Caesar, but Constantine, though he accepted this investiture, went on calling himself Augustus. Galerius' reluctance to accept this was palpable and he seems to have withdrawn his recognition later.

The main problem for Galerius, now the senior emperor, was not Constantine but Maxentius and Maximian. The latter in particular was not acceptable to anyone, and he even fell into dispute with his son. He had attempted to bolster his position by a marriage alliance with Constantine and by awarding him the title Augustus, which was not his to give and which Constantine already used anyway. When Maximian quarrelled with Maxentius, he found that the army preferred the younger, more generous man, and he fled to his new son-in-law, who was not pleased to have him as his guest.[4]

As a further result of this break, another pretender appeared, this time in Africa. This was a man called L. Domitius Alexander, who had been *vicarius* in Africa since at least 303. In effect he was protesting at the revived Emperor Maxentius and was able to prevent the despatch of food supplies to Italy. Alexander is universally described as old and lazy, but he cannot have been all that indolent for he managed to develop a navy and to gain control of Sardinia, where his authority is noted on at least one milestone, and so he ruled as emperor there and in Africa for some months at least. He had himself proclaimed as Augustus in 308. However, he did not have much in the way of military forces, and like Maximian he attempted to bolster his position by soliciting an alliance with Constantine, who did not respond. He was eventually defeated by 'a few cohorts' sent by Maxentius from Italy in 311, though the size of the invading army was much greater than is implied. This all suggests that Alexander had had substantial local support, and at least the tacit support of the other nearby governors, who had more substantial military forces at their disposal than he did. He had operated as emperor for perhaps a year; he must be accepted as an emperor, just as Maxentius and Carausius were. The victorious army of Maxentius sacked Carthage and Cirta and conducted a brutal purge of Alexander's supporters. Alexander himself was killed.[5]

All this activity in Italy and Africa effectively left Constantine some years for consolidation. For Galerius, based in the Balkans, and for Diocletian, living in retirement at Salonae in Dalmatia, events in Italy were more important, particularly since Constantine busied himself with frontier wars. For Maxentius it was the secession of Domitius Alexander in Africa that was important, since the spring of Alexander's action was resentment at Italian demands on food from Africa and his blockade of food supplies had to be broken. Restoring these supplies was clearly a priority for an emperor dependent in some degree on Roman support.

By 309, therefore, the number of emperors had grown from four to six. In addition, Diocletian intervened occasionally from his retirement, and in a conference at Carnuntum on the Danube in November 308, he replaced the dead Severus with a new Augustus, Valerius Licinianus Licinius, and browbeat Maximian into agreeing to go into retirement again, which turned out to be even briefer than the earlier one.[6] In 309, Constantine gained control of Spain and Maxentius suppressed Alexander. This was to be the pattern: jostling for position and territory, suppressing or replacing the weaker rivals. The older generation was dying off: Galerius died in 309 or 310; Diocletian probably in 311. Maximian again returned from retirement, but was at last defeated; he committed suicide in prison.[7] By 312 Constantine was ready to take on Maxentius, who had meanwhile forfeited much of the support within his territories.

Maxentius in fact made a good fight of it, demonstrating that it might well have been sensible to have set him up as Caesar in the original scheme. However, Constantine was faster, tougher, more ruthless, a more adroit politician and a better general. He defeated Maxentius at the Battle of the Milvian Bridge in 312, at which Maxentius died.[8]

Between them, Constantine, Maxentius and Maximian had struck wounding blows at Diocletian's governing scheme and had destroyed his scheme of organized succession. They had based their claims to power and authority on competing bases: Constantine claimed the Empire by hereditary right, as the son of an emperor; Maxentius based his claim on the older bases of people, Senate and army, though, of course, he was also the son of an emperor. In the past this combination could have been unbeatable, but Diocletian had destroyed the validity of that set of legitimizers. Now the only claim that counted was armed victory. The usurpers had undermined Diocletian's scheme; Constantine had revealed its fragility, and in so doing he also enforced heredity as the crucial element in a succession. Constantine's victory was therefore a victory also for his hereditary claim and for that as an organizing principle in the imperial succession.

In fact, the whole Diocletianic scheme, developed piece by piece over twenty years, was unworkable without the master's touch on the controls. It was only his interventions that kept it going for a few years after his retirement. (When he persuaded Maximian to retire a second time, his appointment of Licinius angered Maximin Daia; the Diocletianic scheme not only ignored hereditary emotion, it ignored human pride as well.) It was not reasonable to expect that emperors with sons would ignore their posterity in favour of choosing other men. Diocletian, of course, had no son.

There was also another aspect to be considered. The emergence of Constantine and Maxentius demonstrated that the selection system devised by Diocletian was very likely to pass over the most capable candidates. The new Augusti as they were promoted were supposed to choose new Caesars, but they would not wish to select men more capable than themselves for they would not wish to be outshone by their deputies. Nor was it sensible that a group of generals – for it was high military command that Diocletian saw as the necessary qualification for imperial office – should be in control of the system of succession since, as Probus had remarked in that unguarded and fatal moment, if the generals were successful, then they and their armies would become unnecessary. That is to say, the new emperors would require different skills and abilities to the military – civilian ones – and generals were not the best-suited men to divine such non-military qualities. As a skilful political operator, Diocletian really should have understood this.

Diocletian's solution to the succession problem was in fact a personal one, and one that would therefore not outlast its author. Nor was it possible to go back to the old system of army election followed by ratification by the Senate. Maxentius tried that, but rapidly discovered that a conservative reaction was a poor basis for his power, and the maintenance or restoration of old privileges was actually an obstacle to effective rule. Further, election by one army automatically provoked jealousy in others and could all too easily result in multiple claimants. It was in fact inevitable that the emperors would revert to a system based on heredity. Constantius' (presumed) organization of the proclamation of his son as he lay dying had therefore decisively broken Diocletian's whole scheme in one blow.

Maxentius' emergence as *princeps* – he soon upgraded himself to Augustus – came with his father's blessing, but he was only a candidate because he was Maximian's son. Diocletian's scheme had in fact been a substitute for that process of imperial selection that is called civil war; without Diocletian's control, or rather his power and personal influence, it quickly reverted to civil war once more. It could not prevent the emergence of competing candidates who were wholly detached from the scheme.

In the process of his tinkering, Diocletian had finally removed the Senate from the system. Only Maxentius made a claim to installation by the Senate, and that was unconvincing to the rest since his support was no less local than that of the Syrian rebels defending their province against the Persians, or the Gallic emperors claiming to protect Gaul from German invaders. Maxentius was claiming to protect Rome and southern Italy against the imperial government's tax demands. This was no more a defensible position than that of the Alexandrians, and by lending itself to his policy, the Senate was only making itself as local as he was.

This was the final result of the long process of senatorial sidelining that had begun with Septimius, or even Trajan, and whose influence had only revived to a degree with the Gordians in 238 for a single long generation. Carus had not even bothered with senatorial acceptance, nor had Diocletian. Now that the Senate was removed from exercising any influence and Diocletian's odd and unworkable system had collapsed, all that was left was heredity and military power. Constantine's claim to be Augustus was based on inheritance, plus the support of his army. The net result of Diocletian's meddling was to impose an hereditary succession system on what had, in origin, been a military elective system, but it was actually the final working out of the system set in place by Augustus that had combined heredity, the army and the Senate, a combination which had, in the end, proved to contribute to disaster and civil warfare. It was entirely appropriate that Constantine should have begun to style himself Augustus from the moment he was proclaimed.

The Tetrarchy – The Caesars

Galerius (305–311). (*Shinjirod via Wikimedia Commons*)

Severus (306–307).

Maxentius (306–312). (*Jean-Christophe Benoist via Wikimedia Commons*)

Constantine and his Enemies

Constantine 'the Great' (306–337).
(*Shakko via Wikimedia Commons*)

Maximinus Daia (311–313).

Licinius (308–324). (*Adobe Stock*)

Chapter Fourteen

The Consequences of Constantine

onstantine's progressive elimination of those emperors who had been set in place by Diocletian's scheme took a decade and a half, from 308 to 324. His territorial expansion of authority involved a series of civil wars, the very sort of fighting that Diocletian's scheme had been intended to avoid. Constantine was the cause of many Roman and imperial deaths, but he was also powerfully assisted by Licinius, who defeated and killed Maximin Daia in 313 and then also set about eliminating any claimants he could reach: Galerius died in 311, and his wife Valeria (Diocletian's daughter) and son Candidianus, Diocletian's widow Prisca, Severus' son, and Maximin Daia's son were all killed soon after. Diocletian had probably died in 311 and this seems to have been the signal for all this bloodletting. Licinius and Constantine fought their first war in 316 and Licinius lost. He promoted Aurelius Valerius Valens as his colleague for a time during the crisis, but then executed him at the peace. Eight years later, he faced another defeat and this time promoted a man called Marcus Martinianus, who again lasted only until Licinius' new defeat. Both of these were Augusti; both Licinius and Martinianus were then executed by Constantine later in 324. Constantine finally cleared the board, copying Lucinius in his executions.[1] This was the most prolonged period of civil warfare since the end of the Republic.

When Constantine had finished, in 324, he then had to devise a replacement for Diocletian's system. Given that he had become emperor by a device of his father, in order that the son should succeed the father, it is no surprise that his own preference should be for hereditary succession. This had become clear by 310, when he 'revealed' that he was descended from the Emperor Claudius Gothicus (268–270).[2] In other words, he claimed not to owe his throne merely to his selection by a previous Augustus, but to being the son and grandson of emperors. Furthermore, Constantine, almost unique among Roman emperors, had the children to make such a scheme work, or so it seemed.

Heredity had, of course, been in the background of every development or change in the system of succession since Augustus. Every emperor with children had intended to be the founder of a dynasty. Until Constantine none had succeeded beyond a single generation in a direct line, though it was certainly the case that several dynasties of a very complicated constitution can be discerned. These constructed dynasties, however, were more the product of ambition among relatives than procreation.

Augustus, Vespasian, Marcus Aurelius and Septimius had all established their families on the throne and passed it to their chosen family successors, but after one more generation the line had failed. (None of Augustus' 'dynasty' ever even succeeded in delivering the throne to a son, and it is only with some expansion and manipulation of the family tree that his successors can be described as a dynasty; see Genealogical Table I.) The deaths of Domitian and Caracalla ended their direct lines, and it is very difficult to see the later Severans as being of a single family linked to Septimius (see Genealogical Table XI). During the rapid turnover of emperors in the seven decades between the death of Alexander Severus and the accession of Constantine, several other dynasties began, such as the Gordians (Genealogical Table XII), and the Licinians (Genealogical Table XIII) lasting several years, but others quickly failed without having really got started: those of Philip, Claudius II, Carus and Tacitus; in several cases, it seems as though a particular man was made emperor because he had a son who might inherit. In other words, dynasticism was frequently the preferred system, though if a family became established as rulers, this would exclude others and this prospect helped to arouse opposition.

These families do, in fact, often look more like a sequence of pseudo-dynasties rather than an actual dynasty. This must be seen as typically Roman, or rather, perhaps, as the imperial Roman version of dynastic succession. The aim was often direct succession from father to son, but the achievement was always actually a sequence of rulers who were linked by blood, adoption or marriage but only rarely by direct succession. If these more diffuse connections are included then we can see a succession of such dynasties: Julio-Claudian-Antonian-Domitianic, the Antonines from Nerva to Commodus (Genealogical Table VIII), and the Severans from Septimius to Alexander. Further, there was often a tendency to seek links backwards in time, as when Septimius adopted himself retrospectively into the Antonine dynasty, or when Elagabalus and then Alexander were announced to be the sons of Caracalla. Constantine's retrospective recruitment of Claudius Gothicus into his ancestry was part of a Roman imperial tradition, therefore. It seems unlikely that such manipulations of ancestry were ever very convincing, either to the manipulator or to anyone else.

In this sequence, it is the Flavian dynasty that stands out as anomalous, in which two generations, the father and his sons, ruled in succession. Yet even here, had the dynasty continued, Domitian's eventual chosen heirs were his second cousins and so at some considerable distance, genealogically, from him. So the family's anomaly is the result of brevity, not success. (Of the other direct succession, Marcus to Commodus lasted only a little longer than the Flavians: thirty-one years to 27; the Severans, Septimius to Caracalla lasted twenty-six years; the Licinians lasted only fifteen; the family of Carus only three.) Hereditary succession was always the preferred system, at least among the emperors, but it was too often frustrated by those who would therefore be excluded from the possibility of succeeding. Nevertheless it was hereditary succession that was the norm in the wider society and it is hardly surprising that it eventually emerged as the preferred imperial system. The surprise is, perhaps, that it had taken so long.

It was, perhaps, another old Roman tradition that contributed to the long delay. Access to Roman magistrates in the Republic had been easy: they could be intercepted in the street, they could be visited in their homes, or they could be interrogated on the public platform. This openness continued under the Empire, making it all too easy to murder or assassinate emperors. Even the paranoid Domitian had fallen to a fairly obvious conspiracy involving Guardsmen, consuls, senators, officials and servants; the same may be said of Commodus, Caracalla and others. All these plotters had easy access, which they abused. When the military monarchy of Trajan emerged, the danger was surely all the greater, for being surrounded by men carrying arms is hardly the safest place for a ruler to be. Given this social condition it is perhaps surprising that any emperor lived out a natural term. One of Diocletian's necessary innovations, therefore, was to inhabit a palace in which physical access to him was severely restricted.

So Constantine's claim of an hereditary right because of his invented descent from Claudius Gothicus and his actual descent from Constantius I fitted in well with the preferences of Roman society. Not only that, but his actual relationship with Maximian – he married his daughter – and his marriage alliances with other contemporary emperors eventually fitted him into the Diocletianic dynastic scheme, even while he was busy subverting it. When the Tetrarchic dynasty is examined as a whole, it becomes rather more like the confusion of the Julio-Claudian 'dynasty' than the straightforwardness of the Flavians.

Constantine also, of course, set up a new governing centre for the Empire, at Constantinople. Here he was again following the route blazed by several of the third-century rulers, most of whom had not been able to spend much time in Rome. Given the frontier problems they faced, the old city was an inconvenient centre for military command, though geographically sensible from a governing point of view. It also contained the awkward Senate and a city mob liable to riot, and both had supported Maxentius. The use of Milan in northern Italy and Nicomedia in North-West Asia Minor as imperial centres by Maximian and Diocletian was the first real sign, however, that a permanent shift of the imperial capital was becoming likely. The selection of Byzantium to become Constantinople was thus only the last stage in a century-long process of restless movements and temporary halts by third-century emperors. Constantine, in fact, was able to plant his new centre at Byzantium because of this work done by his immediate predecessors and enemies, just as devotion to dynastic succession picked up on a theme that has been evident all through imperial (and Roman) history. Constantinople was, perhaps, a little more convenient for some of the frontiers – though not much, and decidedly unhelpful for ruling the West – but, above all, it was not Rome.

Emperors from Alexander Severus and Maximinus Thrax onwards were clearly disenchanted with the old city, both as a governing centre and as a place with old and very powerful political and religious associations. Constantine could also claim that his new city was a Christian city from the start, which for a time made Rome a stronghold of paganism. However, detaching the imperial regime from Rome had already in effect been done by his pagan predecessors during the previous half-century, and they had often preferred other gods to those of Rome, Sol by Elagabalus and Aurelian, for example. The foundation of Constantinople was the result of casting loose from Rome, and would in all likelihood have occurred even if Constantine had never become emperor and if Christianity had never succumbed to the imperial embrace, but the actual capital might not have ended up exactly there.

One of the elements at Rome from which the emperors detached themselves by the removal of the seat of government was the Senate. It was therefore to a degree paradoxical that Constantine should establish a new Senate in his new city. Yet it was always a useful legislative and judicial body, though the very fact that it was the emperor who founded it and selected its members devalued the institution from the start. Power now resided wholly in the imperial palace, modified to some extent by the authority of bishops and holy men; and the succession, thanks to the sequence of Carus-

Diocletian-Constantine, was now hereditary, leaving no role for the Senate. The imperial succession was now wholly outside the Senate's competence.

Like his father, Constantine was twice married and had sons by both wives. He also had a considerable number of male relatives, half-brothers and their children. Daughters were married off to convenient political allies, sons were trained up as governors of parts of the Empire and, by implication, as possible political heirs. In total, when Constantine died in 337, there were three sons, three half-brothers, a grandson and four nephews (sons of his half-brothers) all available. (See Genealogical Table XVII.) In the circumstances it would have been astonishing if the succession had been achieved without a problem; in fact, it rapidly became another process of elimination by murder, another habit recalled from the imperial past.

XVII   The House of Constantine.

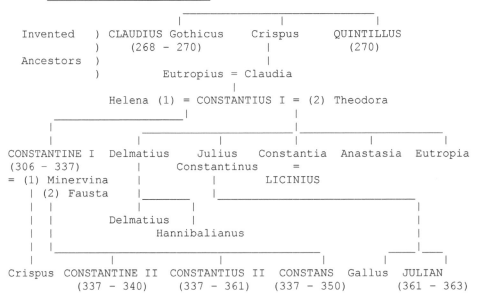

Constantine himself had begun the process of culling and elimination. His eldest son, Crispus, had been made Caesar in 317 when he was about 16 or 17; he promised well, and in 324 proved to be an accomplished commander in the last of the civil wars against Licinius; in 326 he was executed – or murdered – by his father.[3] Constantine's three sons by his second wife were then promoted successively: Constantine II in 317, Constantius II became Caesar in 330 and Constans in 333, no doubt as each of them reached adolescence. He also promoted two of his nephews: Delmatius became

Caesar in 335 and his brother Hannibalianus was 'King of Kings' in 337; two of his half-brothers held high posts in the administration; Delmatius (the father of the two nephews) and Julius Constantinus were respectively referred to as 'the censor' and 'the patrician'. (The elder Delmatius was responsible for the suppression of an obscure rising on the island of Cyprus in 334. Its leader was Calocaerus, who 'usurped power'; it was clearly not a serious threat, though the words used suggest that Calocaerus did attempt to make himself emperor.)[4]

The sons of the emperor were posted to various parts of the Empire as regional governors; his half-brothers largely remained in the capital. The provinces assigned to his relatives were changed as new members of the family grew up and were promoted. As a result, when Constantine died in 337 Constantine II was in Gaul, Constantius II in the East, and Constans in Italy; of the nephews, Delmatius was on the Danube front, and Hannibalianus had been made 'King of Kings' in preparation for a new Persian War, during which he was to be enthroned as king in (probably) Armenia, or even (much less probably) Persia itself.

If Constantine had designed it, he could scarcely have guaranteed more obviously that there would be a civil war and a family bloodletting following his death. Perhaps it was just as obvious at the time. When the news of his death emerged, the army in and around Constantinople staged a sort of coup, proclaimed that only the sons of the emperor should rule, and then proceeded to kill off all those collateral members of the family who were within reach.[5] The result was the survival of just the three sons – Constantius, Constantine and Constans – and the two sons of Julius Constantinus 'the Patrician', Julian and Gallus.

Constantine's governmental policy was reminiscent of Diocletian's practice of assigning parts of the Empire to his colleagues, the difference being that the several rulers were of the same genetic family. The result was also the same: a war among the inheritors, with one survivor. Power is addictive, as he himself should have recalled. Constantine himself had never been content with what he had when part of the Empire was ruled by another. This attitude was inherited by his sons and nephews.

The deaths of the half-brothers Delmatius and Hannibalianus were clearly the work of the army, but Constantius II was in the city as it all happened and it seems likely that he was the organizer of the killings. He was clearly a man quite unwilling to see the Empire divided; a real chip off the old block. The three brothers met a month later at the Viminacium in

The Sons of Constantine

Constantine II (337–340).

Constans I (337–350).

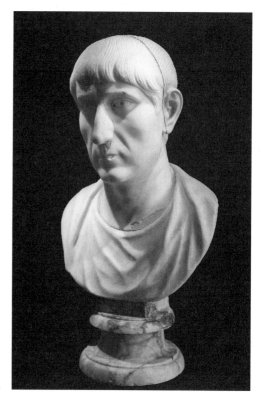

Constantius II (337–361).

The End of Constantine's Dynasty

Magnentius (350–353).

Julian (361–363).

Jovian (363–364).

Pannonia and agreed on a new division of the Empire: not long afterwards Constans and Constantine II quarrelled and the latter died in an invasion of the former's territory.[6] So from there being six emperors in 337, there were just two in 340 – Constans in the West and Constantius in the East – which was very similar to the situation between 306 and 324. Constans died in 350, killed by the followers of an enemy. Then there was just one: the family of Constantine I was reduced to a single Augustus and his two nephews, Julian and Gallus, within little more than a decade.

For nearly half a century there had been no imperial rebels to threaten the dynasty of Constantine (Calocaerus excepted). Then from 350 there was a sudden rush of them, as though they sensed that they were in at the last years of the dynasty's life and the position of emperor was once more about to become open. This might suggest that rebels tend to appear in the period when a dynasty was visibly failing, and the reduction of the family to just three members would have suggested near-failure. In fact three of the four cases of rebels between 350 and 353 are interconnected, and the fourth was an attempted restoration of the dynasty of Constantine after it had officially expired. (See Table IV.)

The first of these risings took place in Gaul. Magnentius was a high-ranking soldier of Frankish/British ancestry, popular with the soldiers. He capitalized on widespread enmity in the West towards the behaviour and policies of Constans to launch a serious and sustained bid for the Empire. At a dinner held at Augustodunum to celebrate the birthday of the son of Marcellinus, Constans' *comes rei private*, Magnentius left the room briefly and then returned wearing a purple robe, at which the assembled diners hailed him as emperor.[7]

This was clearly a well-prepared coup. One does not have a purple imperial robe simply lying around, particularly at a time when mere possession of purple cloth by an ordinary person was considered treasonable. The diners were also no doubt well primed for the event. Constans found that his support in Gaul fell away as the news of Magnentius' action spread. All this strongly suggests that Magnentius had prepared the ground throughout Gaul in advance. Constans fled south, to be caught and killed at a small town in the Pyrenees. Magnentius was accepted as emperor in Britain, the Germanies, Gaul, Spain and Africa, apparently with no resistance.

The sources of support for Magnentius are obvious from the account of his actions: Marcellinus was in charge of the imperial administration, Magnentius himself was in command of the legionary forces, the *praetorians* attached to Constans' court were disaffected, and a unit of cavalry that was stationed near to Augustodunum at once joined the rebel. He was also acclaimed by the people of the town. This was, in all, a good facsimile of the accession of any emperor in the fourth century, perhaps better recorded by the fact of his rebellion, possibly as a result of deliberately publicizing the events in earnest of the legitimacy of his accession.

Table IV: Unsuccessful Emperors 350–425.

Date	Emperor	Challenger	Region
350	Constantius II	Magnentius	Gaul, the West
		Vetranio, Nepotianus	Pannonia, Rome
		Silvanus	Germany
361	Julian		
363	Jovian		
364	Valentinian/Valens	Procopius	Constantinople
		Firmus	Mauretania
375	Valens alone		
378	Gratian/Valentinian II	Theodosius I	
383		Magnus Maximus	Britain, Gaul
		Eugenius	The West
395	Arcadius/Honorius	Marcus, Gratian	Britain
		Constantine III	Britain, Gaul
408	Theodosius II	Maximus, Priscus	Spain
		Attalus	Visigoths
		Jovinus/Sebastianus	Germany
		Maximus/Gerontius	Spain
421	Constantius III		
423	John		
425	Valentinian III		

Magnentius was faced by rival and opposing competitors. In Pannonia an old general called Vetranio was also proclaimed emperor. This, however, was not his own idea but that of Constantia, a sister of the dead Constans and of the living Constantius II. She was apparently present at the acclamation and prodded Vetranio into action to pre-empt the further advance of Magnentius, who might have persuaded the Pannonian army to join him; with its own emperor that army was not committed to Magnentius.[8] In Rome another scion of Constantine the Great, Nepotianus, led a rising that was briefly successful in seizing the city, but was soon beaten down by a detachment sent by Magnentius under Marcellinus' command.[9] Both Vetranio and Nepotianus had decked themselves out in imperial garments but both were self-proclaimed Constantian loyalists.

Magnentius attempted to bolster his position by appointing his brother Decentius as Caesar and by marrying Justina, an aristocratic girl, probably about 12 years old, whose family was part of a wide aristocratic network throughout Gaul. Even more significantly, she was the daughter of Galla, the great-niece of the great Constantine. Magnentius thus became a marital member of the imperial family, a move that might have been intended to counter the promotion of Vetranio.

Constantius II marched from Syria, where he had been fighting the Persians; a preoccupation that Marcellinus and Magnentius no doubt had in mind at the time of their proclamation. He addressed Vetranio's soldiers, who acclaimed him, and Vetranio gracefully retired, with a pension, obviously by pre-arrangement. However, the armies of Constantius and Magnentius then met in a ferocious battle at Mursa, with both sides losing many men. Constantius was the marginal victor, then slowly hunted down Magnentius, who finally died by his own hand in Gaul in 353, his control of the West having crumbled section by section.[10]

Magnentius is normally, like so many others, regarded as a usurper, but also like so many others this is a judgement that results from adopting the viewpoint of his enemies. Constans had become highly unpopular in Gaul in particular, and few if any of his subjects were prepared to stand with him when he was challenged by Magnentius. Magnentius himself went through a reasonable facsimile of an imperial acclamation, not unlike that of Constantine in York or Gordian I in Thysdrus and Carthage. He was able to establish his authority very quickly over the West, and even in Italy. For three years he ruled the Western half of the Roman Empire. By all normal criteria, except that of his enemies and his defeat, he was a Roman emperor.

The other rebel of this mid-century group was Silvanus. Like Magnentius he was a soldier, of Frankish parentage. He had been a tribune in Magnentius' army, but had changed sides just before the Battle of Mursa. For this he was rewarded with promotion to the command of an infantry force and posted the Colonia Agrippina. The historian Ammianus Marcellinus tells of a complicated intrigue in which Silvanus was a supposed innocent victim, but which resulted in his seizing power at Colonia and being proclaimed emperor.[11]

The story is one in which Ammianus himself was personally involved, and this has tended to distort his account, though he clearly undertook extensive researches into the preliminary intrigues. Silvanus had a good deal of local support in Germany. He had acted on impulse, it seems, feeling threatened, and he collected purple garments by stripping the purple decorations from the military standards, which could only have been done with the soldiers' acquiescence. His seizure of power was a fairly formidable affair, perhaps fuelled by the extreme and brutal reprisals indulged in by Constantius in Gaul in the aftermath of the suppression of Magnentius. However, Silvanus' support collapsed, as had that of Magnentius and Constans, and he was killed by men who had been lukewarm in his cause and had been persuaded to return to the side of Constantius by timely bribes.[12]

Silvanus' support was very narrowly based, and his coup was clearly poorly prepared in clear contrast to the relative success of Magnentius in the same region. Both ultimately failed because Constantius II had the better army, but also because he was a ruling emperor, the son of Constantine the Great, and had been emperor already for a decade and a half. Magnentius had in fact been negotiating for recognition by Constantius for a time before the Battle of Mursa, but Constantius, once assured of the support of Vetranio's Pannonian army, refused him. What was clearly required for success was all three elements: support from the army (which both rebels gained), general acceptance by the officials and governors (which Magnentius gained), and recognition by the senior Augustus. Only if there was no Augustus could a man make himself emperor by the support of just the army and the officials. Constantius as the direct heir to Constantine could use the crucial element of loyalty to the dynasty, but the failure of Constans was a clear sign that this was something with only a limited value.

Such loyalty was also dependent on the dynasty continuing. One of the elements in the background may well have been the likely early extermination of Constantine's family. None of Constantine's sons had sons of their own, though Constantius eventually had a daughter. Crispus had a son, but he was never considered; perhaps he died young. The only other members of the family were the sons of Constantine's half-brother Delmatius, who had been killed in 337. The boys had survived because Gallus, the elder, was thought too sickly to live, and Julian is said to have aroused the pity of the soldiers designated to kill him because of his youth. Gallus was now (in 351) made Caesar and sent to the East while Constantius II coped with the rebellion of Magnentius in the West. This was in part a reassurance to the Syrians that his move to the West was not a desertion, and also a signal that the Constantinian dynasty was still active and that even if Magnentius won in the West, there were still other members of the dynasty he would have to face. However, having suppressed Magnentius, Constantius then had to deal with the misbehaviour of Gallus at Antioch. He was executed.[13] The one remaining Constantinian, Julian, was then appointed as Caesar and sent to the West. Constantius was clearly unconcerned about the continuity of his dynasty.

Julian, after a successful campaign in Germany, was made Augustus by his soldiers in 360. He advanced slowly eastwards to challenge Constantius' rule, meanwhile negotiating for acceptance. Constantius died before they could meet; Julian became sole emperor from being a condemned rebel. The difference between his and Magnentius' conduct is invisible. He was killed in battle against the Persians in 363.[14]

So the family of Constantine became extinct, apart from some distant connections. This first Christian dynasty had behaved in the same way as its non-Christian predecessors: it had not only failed to reproduce itself, but its members, particularly Constantius, had then compounded that failure by all too readily resorting to killing other members. There was just one survivor, the daughter of Constantius II, Constantia Postuma; the dynasty had in effect expired.

On the other hand, this was the first dynasty whose rule in the Empire had lasted more than half a century since the death of Nero (discounting the second-century rulers as a non-dynasty). Counting from the promotion of Constantius I as Caesar in 293, the family had ruled for seventy years and had lasted through three generations. (The fiction of the descent of the family from Claudius Gothicus could be said to have extended this to ninety-five years and five generations.) Constantine's dynastic programme, if it may be called that, had certainly replaced Diocletian's curious scheme and he had re-established dynastic inheritance as the appropriate method of delivering the succession in the Empire. Constantine had not actually solved the real problem, which was that no Roman imperial dynasty, except the first (if the Julio-Claudians may be counted as a single dynasty) had lasted into the fourth generation. He had made an attempt to train up his sons, but was then partly foiled by the army he had also trained, and by the mutual suspicions and ambitions of those very sons, who feared each other as much as any outsider.

The hereditary principle that Constantine had been at such pains to implant could only survive if there were dynastic members available; it also required a certain trust between the several members. Failing those qualities, the problem of choosing a successor devolved elsewhere. The army Julian was commanding at the time of his death was deep in Persian territory and under imminent danger of attack. The problem of the imperial succession therefore automatically devolved once again on to the army which required a new commander who must be an emperor. So once more the method of choosing a successor was to be decided in an emergency situation, the previous emperor having been deficient in his duty either to father an heir (Julian's only son had died the year before) or to nominate a successor.

Finding a successor for Julian was the subject of extended discussion. For once we have a detailed description of what happened. A council of army commanders met in order to choose the successor. Ammianus Marcellinus, who was with the army at the time and may even have attended the council itself, recorded an account.

The men at the council were the legionary commanders, the commanders of the cavalry squadrons and a number of court and administrative officials who were also present with the army. This must have made for a fairly numerous gathering. There were two groups with definite ideas as to whom to choose and a considerable number without a programme at all. One group wished to choose a man from among Constantius' palace officials, that is, a bureaucrat; the other group wished for a soldier. It was much the same division as had been visible when Macrinus killed Caracalla, and similar in a way to the parties that had followed Maximinus and the Gordians through the third-century crises, or as personified in the confrontation between Diocletian and Aper, and even further back the decision required by the army commanders in Pannonia when the news of Nerva's accession reached them. In this case, curiously, each group cancelled out the other and a compromise candidate was agreed on: Salutius Secundus, the Praetorian Prefect.

However, Salutius then refused and persisted in his refusal even when one of the soldiers suggested that he take command only until the army had been conducted to safety. The Praetorian Prefect by this time was an administrator and legal expert rather than a soldier, so it looks as though the 'compromise' came down on the side of the Palace officials. Salutius, of course, as the prefect, was the senior man in the camp, more senior than any of the military men. It also looks as though the soldiers' suggestion of a temporary command was sarcastic, made in order to persuade Salutius to refuse. His refusal now left the way open to the ordinary soldiers, who were impatient at the long delay by their superiors and who now put forward

Jovian, the commander of the household troops, as their candidate. He was young, fairly junior, but to have reached the position he held at his age he was clearly a coming man. He also had a young son.[15]

Jovian was acceptable to the Palace party perhaps because of his youth and comparative lack of experience, and to the senior officers because he was a soldier. He was, that is to say, another compromise candidate, just as Salutius had been. He was successful in extricating the army from its difficult position and in making peace with the Persians. Then he died in some mysterious way – supposedly suffocated by the fumes from a stove – during the march towards Constantinople, having reigned for only a few months.

The army officers' council met again at Nikaia, across the Propontis from Constantinople. Salutius was again suggested as emperor and again refused. Others were then considered. One was Aequitius, commander of the targeteers' regiment; another was Januarius, a relative of Jovian, also an official. Both were rejected for odd reasons: Aequitius because of his boorishness; Januarius because he was too far away. This seems an unlikely reason, for the man who was actually chosen was in Ankyra at the time, far enough off in all conscience. It looks like a discussion in which each candidate who was put forward was vetoed by the rest. (The details of the meeting are much less clear than that in which Jovian was chosen; Ammianus was not present this time.)

In the end, and yet again, a man below the top ranks was chosen. It seems evident that the senior officers could not agree on one of their own number, perhaps because all of them wanted the job, and so all combined to deny it to anyone else. This time the choice fell on a man called Valentinian, who was of a higher rank than Jovian had been and at 43 was somewhat older. He was an active and moderately well-known officer, who had been involved in the suppression of Silvanus' rising in Gaul a decade earlier. He was summoned from Ankyra – two or three days' ride away – and then at Nikaia he took a day or so to think about it (using the excuse that it was an unlucky day in the Roman calendar). It was clearly possible for him to refuse, as Salutius had shown. The senior officers meanwhile found it difficult to control the army, and when Valentinian was presented to the rank-and-file, they began to demand the appointment of a second emperor as his colleague.

This made sense, since the destruction of the dynasty of Constantine and the deaths of three emperors in the last three years had demonstrated the awkwardness of the method being used. It had also become customary, for at least the last century, to have a second man invested with the post of either Caesar or Augustus who could take over at once when one emperor died. The soldiers' demand was therefore sensible and Valentinian heeded it, though not immediately. He was advised to choose someone not of his family, but since that advice came from one of the disappointed generals, it was scarcely disinterested and was possibly a bid for the post that he had already implicitly been refused in the conclave. None of the obvious candidates who had been at the council could be chosen, for this would immediately annoy all the rest and cast doubt on the validity of his own selection. Valentinian met with his younger brother Valens as soon as possible and installed him as joint Augustus. It was only close relations who could be trusted and even then not always, as the debacle of the Constantinian family had shown.[16]

This choice of an emperor was clearly a fairly orderly process. It also took some time, for the ordinary soldiers became impatient, specifically at the delay; if a candidate had been agreed quickly, the soldiers would clearly have accepted him and it was Salutius' obstinate refusal to take the post that caused the delay. There was obviously a considerable degree of discussion involved and a wide variety of candidates were considered once Salutius refused, perhaps even before. There is no doubt that several men in the council hoped to be chosen; the putting oneself forward was evidently not acceptable. It is obvious also that once a decision had been made they generally fell in line and accepted the chosen man.

The range of candidates would appear to be fairly wide, and included the senior men of the army and the court administration and army officers down to Jovian's rank, which was the equivalent of a modern regimental colonel. It was also possible for a man to refuse without incurring danger to himself. Salutius continued working for both Jovian and Valentinian.

How far this council was typical of early and similar crises is difficult to say. Earlier cases of emperors dying on campaign were usually the result of murder (Caracalla, for instance) – Gordian III and Numerian may have suffered more natural deaths – or there was an obvious candidate in office or nearby (Valerian, Trajan and Philip the Arab). Further, it was a long time since a similar situation had arisen. The councils periodically convened by Diocletian were the obvious precedent rather than the swift and pre-arranged elevation of Constantine. It seems probable, therefore, that the councils in 363 and 364 occurred because no immediate or obvious successor existed. Probably Salutius was the convener of the council and the dominant member; in that case one can see the logic of the council's original choice.

The participation of the ordinary soldiers, in putting Jovian forward and then insisting on the appointment of a joint emperor, is notable. No doubt Jovian was acceptable to the senior officers, and the soldiers' initiative might well have been cleared with them first; a second emperor was clearly a good idea, so men and officers could be seen to have been thinking along the same lines.

The whole process of selection in this case has the appearance of a distorted version of an old Roman election, with the candidates being discussed in a council of magnates (a pseudo-Senate), and the decisions made there being subject to popular acceptance (a pseudo-Assembly or *comitia*). What is actually very clear is that neither the Senate (that in Rome or that in Constantinople) had any input, nor was even considered. Nor, of course, were the generality of Roman citizens considered or consulted, but that was scarcely new.

Jovian had made a start at founding a dynasty when he appointed his infant son as consul. Appointing a grown brother, as Valentinian did, made rather more political and military sense, and the two brothers worked well together; or rather separately, for they tended to operate at opposite ends of the Empire. Valentinian had an adolescent son and Valens soon had an infant son, which seemed to take care for the moment of their heredity and were the foundation for a new dynasty.

XVIII   Dynastic Connections between the Houses of Constantine and Valentinian.

(See also Genealogical Tables XVII and XIX).

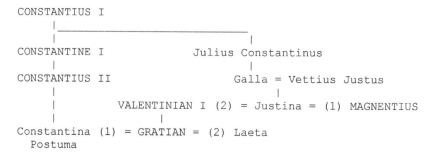

CONSTANTIUS I
  |
  |_____
  | |
CONSTANTINE I   Julius Constantinus
  | |
CONSTANTIUS II   Galla = Vettius Justus
  | |
  | VALENTINIAN I (2) = Justina = (1) MAGNENTIUS
  | |
Constantina (1) = GRATIAN = (2) Laeta
  Postuma

Valentinian at some point divorced his first wife and married Justina, the widow of the usurper Magnentius and the grand-niece of Constantine I. She was married to Valentinian in 371, having been a widow for eighteen years, though it seems that her liaison with the emperor had begun rather earlier. They had three daughters and a son; thus the new dynasty was joined to that of Constantine. (For the connections so formed, see Genealogical Table XVIII.)

This marriage, with its retrospective connections to the previous dynasty, was similar in its effects to Constantine I's claim to be the descendant of Claudius Gothicus; or perhaps a better comparison is with Septimius' retrospective self-adoption into the Antonine family. In the same way Valentinian's eldest son Gratian was married to Constantina Postuma, the daughter of Constantius II, and then to Laeta, another sprig of the old imperial nobility in the West. These political marriages indicate the continuing importance of the Western nobility, particularly in Italy and Gaul, but also the need for the new imperial family to acquire some of the lustre of the family of Constantine. This was all typical marital behaviour of any dynasty, of course, royal or otherwise.

The need for such support had become clear soon after the new family had acceded to the throne. In 365, only a year after their elevation, the Emperor Julian's cousin Procopius seized control of Constantinople, claimed the throne and emphasized as strongly as he could his relationship with the dynasty of Constantine. This connection was, it has to be admitted, rather distant; he was the son of Julian's mother's sister, thus his first cousin, but on the female side. It was perhaps no more distant a relationship than some of those among the family of Augustus, or in that of the later Severans, though normally a clear blood connection was expected. It was the same sort of relationship that was provided to Magnentius by his marriage to Justina and it was potent enough for Valentinian I and Gratian to repeat it by their own marriages. Yet such a relationship is only, as it were, enabling; to make it effective, the claimant had to show ability as well. What Procopius' attempt reveals is the strength of the dynastic impulse that had now developed. Also, if such a distant connection was accepted as legitimate, it would open the gate wide to the many other claims.

Procopius was acceptable in part because of his culture and sophistication, particularly to the city's elite, but this cut no ice with the army, at whom the family connection with Constantine was clearly aimed. Valentinian had moved off to the Western provinces by the time Procopius emerged and Valens took his time to deal with the problem, spending the winter of 365–366 watching, waiting and gathering support. He was so successful that Procopius' support gradually crumbled. He finally marched against Valens, rather desperately, but one of his generals switched sides during the fighting and the revolt was over. Procopius fled but was soon captured and executed. A relative of his, Martialis, 'seized the shadow of a failing principate', as Ammianus puts it, at Nikaia, but after a fairly short time he was seized by some soldiers sent by Aequitius, scourged and executed. His claim to the throne depended on his relationship with Procopius, who claimed it by a supposed but remote relationship to Julian. Only Procopius had any success, largely perhaps because he claimed that Julian had secretly made him his designated successor. The story was thin to the point of transparency, but the lesson was clearly not lost on Valentinian at least, whose first moves to gather Western aristocratic support came in the year after Procopius' collapse with the marriage of his son Gratian to the daughter of Constantius II.[17]

Procopius and Martialis had tried to claim the throne by right as members of the royal family. The other rebellion against Valentinian and Valens was rather different. An internal tribal dispute in Roman Mauretania pushed Firmus, a claimant to the local kingship of his father, into rebellion. Valentinian I sent his general Count Theodosius to suppress it, which he did over a period of two years or so, campaigning in the very difficult terrain of the Atlas Mountains. Theodosius had successfully recovered control of Britain in 367 after a series of barbarian invasions. Firmus' support steadily dropped away, and finally he came out dressed in a purple cloak, exhorting his enemies to rebel against Theodosius, whose discipline he derided. When this did not work, Firmus committed suicide.[18] (For these pretenders and rebels, see Table IV.)

As an imperial pretender Firmus was clearly a non-starter: his aim was always to achieve his father's local position, though he was also capable of exploiting local grievances such as the perennial complaints about taxation. His final actions are reminiscent of the last desperate measure used by Gallienus' general Aureolus, who also came out in a purple cloak as his rebellion was failing, or of the *bacaudae* leaders fighting Maximian. These men clearly over-estimated the effect they expected to have, but it is at the same time a mark of the power of the purple cloak; for it to be over-estimated, an effect has already to exist.[19]

The fourth century, therefore, witnessed true dynastic succession in the Roman Empire for the first time since the brief Flavian dynasty in the first century and perhaps the Severans, and when the direct Constantinian line finally died out with Julian, a new dynasty was soon in place, which, though it tended to break up towards the end, and though it needed an infusion of reinforcement, lasted even longer. One factor in its relative success was the

Valentinian dynasty's marriage connection back to the family of Constantine. (See Genealogical Tables XVIII and XIX.) These, and the appeal made by Procopius, are testimonies to the continued reputation of Constantine and his family.

Paradoxically, of course, the emergence of two successful and successive dynasties raised the stakes of power even higher, for if a man could become emperor he now stood a much better chance than ever of founding a dynasty. The intentions of Augustus had finally been realized. This development had been in question all through the history of the imperial system. Its final emergence added one more element to the succession system. Now there was a perception that the succession would go normally to a member of the imperial family, if a close relative of the former emperor existed. Both the army and the Senate had been effectively removed from the process.

The House of Valentinian

Valentinian I (364–375).

Valens (364–378).

Gratian (375–383). (*Sjuergen via Wikimedia Commons*)

Valentinian II (375–392).

The House of Theodosius

Theodosius I (379–395). (*Marie-Lan Nguyen / Wikimedia Commons*)

Arcadius (395–408). (*Gryffindor via Wikimedia Commons*)

Honorius (395–423).

Chapter Fifteen

The Crises of 375–379

T he dynasty founded by Valentinian in 364 consisted of the two brothers plus Valentinian's children; Valens' son died young and he had no other offspring, it seems. When both emperors died within four years (in 375 and 378), therefore, the dynastic crisis developed into an imperial one.

Valentinian died first, suffering a stroke when he became angry at the unhelpful and insulting answers of a barbarian embassy. He died shortly after the stroke. In the interval he had been unable to communicate with his entourage and could not give any instructions about the succession,[1] though these were not really needed. His brother automatically became the senior emperor and Valentinian's eldest son, Gratian, had been raised to the rank of Augustus in 367 when he was only 8; there were therefore still two emperors, one in the West and one in the East.

The 16-year-old Gratian was just about old enough to be seen as a legitimate and ruling emperor, and he could be regarded as under the distant guardianship of his uncle, Valens. The brothers had taken responsibility for the Western and Eastern parts of the Empire respectively, and Valentinian died at Brigetio on the Danube, while Valens had been in charge in the East from the start, being based at Constantinople, though at the time of Valentinian's death he was actually in Antioch. Gratian was at Augusta Treverorum (Trier) on the Rhine frontier. This geographical separation is crucial to what happened next, for neither of the emperors could bring any pressure to bear on the entourage of Valentinian at Brigetio, which amounted to the main central government authority of the West, overriding Gratian at Trier because of his youth.

Neither Valentinian's son nor his brother could reach Brigetio in less than two or three weeks. Valens was clearly too busy and too distant to attend a face-to-face discussion on the succession, and Gratian was still too young to be heard. Valentinian had been in the midst of negotiations to try to bring an end to the war with the Quadi when he died, and that war was still being fought. It was clearly necessary to be able to conduct the war or negotiations in Pannonia, and only an emperor who was based on the Danube frontier had the necessary authority to do so.

To the men at Valentinian's court it must have seemed urgent to have an emperor in whose name they could carry on the war and the government. Yet there were already two Augusti, and Gratian had clearly been intended to be Valentinian's direct successor; Valens was now the senior of the two, but there was clearly more than this dynastic matter involved in the situation. These quasi-altruistic factors do not, of course, exclude elements of personal ambition among the courtiers at Brigetio; indeed, it may well be that these were actually paramount.

The central figures were ambitious enough. The main engine of events following the emperor's death was Sextus Claudius Petronius Probus of a senatorial family who had, unusually for a man from such a family, made a successful high-flying career in the imperial administration. He was accompanied by Flavius Aequitius, an early supporter of Valentinian's (and a participant in the succession discussions after Julian's death). He had been regarded as a candidate for the throne in 364 at the conclave at Nikaia and had been instrumental in extinguishing the last embers of Procopius' usurpation the following year. Two prominent soldiers were the *magister militum* Flavius Merobaudes and Sebastianus, both out on campaign at the time; there was also Count Theodosius, at that moment just completing his campaign in Africa against the rebel-pretender Firmus. These, as will be clear, were no band of brothers, and it is an indication of Valentinian's power of command that he was able to harness this disparate group into working together.

The men at Brigetio – probably, in fact, Petronius Probus – sent a message to Merobaudes, who was beyond the Danube with the army in enemy territory. The message was in Valentinian's name, though it was sent after his death. Merobaudes was apparently told that the emperor was dead, presumably either by another letter or by word of mouth from the messenger. His first action, before turning back, was to despatch his fellow general Sebastianus far away. Then he returned to the court, which had moved on to Aquincum. Sebastianus was popular with the soldiers, and was therefore seen by Merobaudes as a danger; Merobaudes was thus preparing the ground for an action that would set him against both Sebastianus and possibly the troops as well. That is, neither Merobaudes nor Sebastianus, nor the men in the court at Aquincum, had any intention of simply acknowledging Gratian's and Valens' authority.

The senior man at Aquincum, Petronius Probus, was Praetorian Prefect of Illyricum and Italy, and it is presumably an alliance of Probus and Merobaudes which was the engine that drove events, though the officers with Probus acted before Merobaudes arrived, even if they clearly assumed his agreement. By the time he got back to the court, the plan had been made and put into effect. There was, living near to Carnuntum at an imperial estate called Murocincta (probably the modern Parndoff), Valentinian's other son, also Valentinian, with his mother Justina. Her brother, Cerealis, was with the court. He was sent to her and she and the boy were brought the 100 miles to Aquincum. There the boy was hailed as Augustus.

The proclamation took place on the sixth day after Valentinian I's death. The decision to send for the boy was thus taken very quickly, even before Merobaudes got back to the court, for Cerealis had to travel the 100 miles twice, making the return journey with Justina and the boy in a litter and so fairly slowly. Six days was therefore extremely good going, and suggests that these events had been set in train before Valentinian died, while he had been comatose. It follows that the real decider in all this was Petronius Probus, with the others going along.[2]

Some of the others at the court at Aquincum will certainly have pointed out that Gratian would have good cause for annoyance at these events, but it would be clear to all that he could do little about it since the court on the Danube commanded the major part of the Western army. By the time Gratian heard of it, the new regime would be well-established. Probus, as Praetorian Prefect for Italy and Illyricum, give it a flying territorial start.

This procedure is very reminiscent of that by which Valentinian himself had been made emperor. It was, of course, a *coup d'état*, and if Gratian had objected, Valentinian II would have been labelled a usurper and a civil war might have followed. Valens might also have objected, but he was fully involved in the East and then from 376 he was heavily preoccupied with the Gothic problem on the Danube frontier. As it was, Gratian, or his handlers, did not object and instead, showing the good sense that marked him out, took his half-brother and his stepmother into his own court at Trier.[3] He thereupon effectively nullified the Brigetio coup and acquired control of the new emperor, who could thus be seen as the heir of his own throne but this was at a cost.

The years 376 to 378 were those that led up to the Battle of Adrianople, in which Valens was killed. In the West it was a time of murderous intrigue in the joint court of Gratian and Valentinian II. One outcome was the killing of Count Theodosius who had just succeeded in suppressing the awkward rebellion of Firmus in Africa. It would seem that Theodosius was thought to be a likely enemy of those in control in the Western part of the Empire in the same way that Sebastianus had been feared by Merobaudes and perhaps by Petronius Probus as well.[4] His son, also Theodosius, quickly retired to his northern Spanish estates, got married and settled down; similarly Sebastianus was in retirement in Italy when Valens asked for his services a little later in the Gothic war. The elevation of Valentinian II was thus part of a long-running faction dispute within the court of Valentinian I, which came to the surface when he died and which Gratian, by uniting the two Western courts, had imported into his own entourage. He was clearly not immediately able to control the conflict.

The intrigues of 375–376 against Theodosius in particular, however, rebounded: those factions that compassed his death were themselves soon removed. The younger Theodosius was recalled in (probably) 377, just about the same time that Sebastianus returned to favour and authority with Valens in the East.[5] When Valens died, therefore, in the battle at Adrianople, leaving a chaotic situation in the Balkans, there was an immediate need for a new commander there. Sebastianus would have been the obvious choice, but he had been killed in the battle alongside the emperor. Gratian had been on his way to help Valens when the battle took place, and had to retire to Sirmium in the face of the chaos. The Gothic forces threatened Constantinople, and the whole of the Balkan Peninsula dropped out of the control of any Roman government.

By means of a timely minor victory, apparently against some Sarmatians and so somewhere along the lower Danube, the younger Theodosius came to the notice of Gratian at Sirmium. This brought him promotion, and now he was suggested as the right man for the job of restoring order in the East. No doubt Theodosius agreed with this assessment, but it was not until January of 379, more than five months after the Battle of Adrianople, that he was finally appointed.[6] He had been with the court all that time, clearly available, and the need had been as urgent in September as it was in January. The delay has to be explained.

The answer appears to be that Theodosius insisted that he must be appointed emperor, not just general. (This was sensible of him, for his military ability was only adequate; he would be much more effective as emperor than in direct command of the army.) He already had a number of relatives in prominent positions at Gratian's court: his uncle Flavius

Eucherius was *comes sacrarum largitionem*, and an in-law, Flavius Claudius Antonius, was Praetorian Prefect for Gaul and was then transferred to Italy; Petronius Probus seems to have been a supporter as well, if not an actual relative. All these men would also have had their own men in posts around and beneath them, forming a set of factions that had now coalesced around Theodosius.

Theodosius' insistence on being promoted to emperor, not just *magister militum* or something similar, presumably derived from his father's experience. The older Theodosius had been sent to put down trouble in Africa, just as the younger was being proposed as the man to do that in the Balkans. Having succeeded, he was then arrested and executed in an intrigue of his enemies at court, and some of those enemies were still present (not to mention that the brother of Firmus, his father's enemy in Africa, was still in authority there as governor). This had happened only two years before. The younger man's demand for an authority that would put him out of reach of the court intrigues at Gratian's court and of the knives of vengeance-seeking Africans – and perhaps with the power to wreak his own revenge – is thus quite understandable, though it may well have startled, even dismayed, his political allies, just as it apparently took Gratian aback.

It therefore took several months to convince Gratian, now the senior Augustus, both that another Augustus was needed in the East, and that neither he nor Valentinian II (still only 8 years old) was suitable or available. Gratian at this time had to stand guard in the West, where he had recently attacked and defeated the Alamanni. Finally, he had to be convinced that Theodosius was the right man to be the new Augustus. It clearly required a man with military skills and Theodosius' past victories (and those of his father) suggested that he had them. Nevertheless, Gratian was clearly difficult to convince, though in January he was finally persuaded and Theodosius was installed as emperor.

For the second time in three years, an emperor had died in circumstances that made it impossible for him to appoint an immediate successor. In each case the officials of the court in attendance had put forward their own candidate, and Gratian, senior emperor once Valens was killed, was then constrained to accept him. In both cases the procedure was in fact close to being an internal coup by the court officials and the senior commanders.

The similarities of these intrigues to the choice of Jovian and then of Valentinian I only a decade and a half earlier are clear: the discussions between the army chiefs and the senior civilian officials; their promotion of fairly unlikely candidates (a 4-year-old child and the son of a disgraced general!). In addition, there was the need to either intimidate or persuade the reigning emperor or emperors. Gratian made no objection, it seems, to the promotion of Valentinian II, even though it was done without his authority and clearly with the interests of his backers more to the fore than those of the Empire. By annexing the child, however, he could put himself in a position of control, but it took a long time to get him to accept Theodosius who, of course, could not be dominated. There was no involvement of either the ordinary soldiers or the Senate in any of this, though the soldiers had had some influence in the elevation of Valentinian and Valens.

The promotion of Theodosius, in particular, has resonances from earlier imperial crises: the promotion of Trajan in the face of Nerva's reluctance is one parallel, involving as it does an ongoing war in both cases. It also has references to the Antoninus adoption process at the end of Hadrian's reign, though by this time multiple emperors were normal and actual adoption was not deemed necessary as well as being unseemly, for Theodosius was a good deal older than Gratian. However, the real precedent in the 370s was the elevation of Constantine I in 306 by a court group associated with his deceased father. The promotion of all the emperors from Constantine to Theodosius was the work of similar groups of courtiers and soldiers, and in all cases their candidate was initially unacceptable to the existing emperors, or was a child.

The real innovation in 379, however, was that Theodosius had no obvious connections with the ruling house other than as an official. As an adult with children he was clearly setting himself up as the head of a new dynasty competing with, or perhaps, more politely, complementing the dynasty of Valentinian. It was above all in this that the events of 378–379 constituted a *coup d'état*. As it happened, Theodosius did succeed in establishing his family as a ruling dynasty, but only after something of a struggle. His example was scarcely encouraging for the stability of the Empire, where a general could muscle his way to the emperorship using a minor victory and a crisis as his credentials.

Enemies of the House of Theodosius

Magnus
Maximus
(in the West
383–388).

Eugenius (in Italy 392–394).

Johannes (in Italy 423–425).

The Later Theodosians

Constantine III (407–411).

Theodosius II (408–450).

Constantius III (421).

Galla Placidia. (*CNG Coins via Wikimedia Commons*)

Chapter Sixteen

The Consequences of Theodosius

Theodosius I, made emperor in 379 in such an unexpected fashion, proved to be only a moderately successful commander in the field, though he was a good organizing commander-in-chief; on the other hand, he was a capable politician, able to seize his opportunities, as indeed he had shown in his rise to imperial power. In 383, when Gratian was killed at the behest of the British rebel Magnus Maximus, Theodosius promoted his eldest son Arcadius as a new Augustus, and in 387, when Valentinian II had been driven out of Italy to take refuge with Theodosius in Constantinople, he seized the opportunity to marry Galla, daughter of Valentinian I and Justina, so establishing himself firmly within the family of Valentinian and, through Justina's ancestry, with that of Constantine as well; as a result it is possible to consider the two families of Valentinian and Theodosius as a single dynasty (see Genealogical Table XIX). Finally, in 392–394 Theodosius took advantage of the suicide of Valentinian II and his own victory over the usurper Eugenius to promote his second son Honorius as a second Augustus.

He did have to surmount two serious challenges to his power and position, however, before he and his family were secure, as well as enfolding the surviving descendants of Valentinian I into his dynastic embrace. Two serious attempts to take over at least the Western part of the Empire were made. The first of these, by Magnus Maximus, was the most formidable. He was of a Spanish family, and is said to have been distantly related to Theodosius himself; he had certainly been an officer in the armies led by Theodosius' father in Britain and Africa; it has also been suggested that he may have been involved in the crisis of 378–379 at the court and so a witness to Theodosius' rise. In 383 Magnus was governor of Britannia when he rebelled against Gratian, who was ruling the West from Trier. Like Constans a generation before, Gratian was chased through Gaul, caught and then killed. Magnus quickly, like Magnentius, Postumus and Constantine, gained control of the armies of Germany; once Gratian was dead, he was acknowledged as emperor in Britain, Gaul and Spain.[1]

XIX   The Valentinian/Theodosian Dynasty.

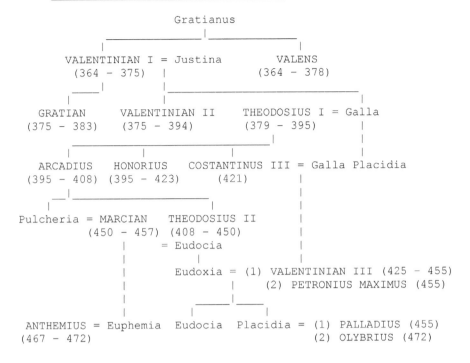

He held this position for five years, but his insecurity was such that he asked to be recognized by Theodosius. This was provided but not until 386, and only on condition that Maximus remain where he was in the West and accept the seniority of the child emperor Valentinian II, whose government controlled Italy. This put Maximus fourth in the imperial rankings of the moment, behind Theodosius, Arcadius and Valentinian. For a man whose motives for seizing power included a grievance that he had not been promoted highly enough, this could not be tolerated for long.

Magnus' position in 386, however, was not unlike that of Constantine. Possibly the history of that emperor was in his mind; he faced an even weaker government in Italy than that of Maxentius and Theodosius' power was scarcely well-grounded in the East. Probably Magnus' major mistake was in having Gratian killed, for that emperor had proved to be very pliable and had clearly been reluctant to accept Theodosius as his imperial colleague. If Magnus had been at the court in 378–379 when Theodosius mounted his successful intrigue, it might be that he had determined to make the same sort of moves for the same purpose. It has even been suggested that he might have been a candidate for the Eastern command at the time, which, if so, would set him on all the stronger.[2]

Magnus' process of elevation is not clear, in part because the exact nature of his British post is in itself not clear. There was no question of an election, though some sources indicate that he was promoted by the will of the army he commanded after victorious campaigns against the Picts and the Scots. Ambitious he certainly was, as well as capable, and he would certainly need acceptance by the army in Britain. Perhaps he rose through a mixture of personal ambition and army enthusiasm, with the story of any resistance to him being a version of the traditional reluctance new emperors were supposed to exhibit.[3]

Magnus invaded Italy in 387 but failed to catch Valentinian II, who escaped to the East with his mother. Magnus did, however, manage to gain control of the whole peninsula, thereby breaking his agreement with Theodosius of the previous year. Theodosius replied by attacking him by sea and land the following year. Magnus was defeated and captured at Aquileia and was then executed after the usual tortures.[4] His imperial career is in many ways remarkably similar to that of Magnentius. Both failed, despite considerable military success, because they were unable to extract serious and permanent recognition from the senior Augustus.

The other usurper faced by Theodosius was challenging in a different way. This was an official of the Palace called Eugenius, who was in fact the figurehead for an attempt by Arbogast, the *magister militum* of Valentinian II, to regain power. Valentinian had been restored as Augustus of the West by Theodosius, with Arbogast in effect ruling for him. However, Valentinian by 392 – he had been emperor since 375 – was impatient to exercise power in his own person, while Arbogast refused to make way for him. After yet another refusal, Valentinian killed himself.[5]

This did succeed in depriving Arbogast of his post, of course, though it was up to Theodosius to decide on his future employment or on his punishment. After some months, it became clear that Theodosius had decided on punishment, and the official story of Valentinian's death was now that he was murdered by Arbogast. In reply, Arbogast pushed Eugenius forward as an emperor. A further complication was the hopes and assumptions of the pagans among the Roman aristocracy that Eugenius might restore pagan worship or at least allow it. However, both the pagans and Arbogast are side issues. Eugenius, like Magnus and Magnentius, could only succeed if he was accorded recognition and acceptance by Theodosius. Yet the involvement of Arbogast and the hopes of the pagans were exactly the factors that would compel Theodosius to refuse any recognition. The support of Arbogast's army and the hopes of many of the senators of Rome were not enough to prevail against Theodosius and his Eastern army.

Eugenius made many of the usual moves: issuing coins recognizing Theodosius, suggesting that they share the consulship and sending conciliatory embassies. All this, together with Theodosius' naval and military preparations, delayed retribution for a year and more, but it was not enough. The rival armies met in battle in northern Italy at the River Frigidus in 394, and Eugenius and Arbogast were beaten; the former died and the latter escaped, but then committed suicide.[6]

Eugenius' rule had clearly been almost as formidable a challenge to Theodosius as that of Magnus Maximus, though he worked from a smaller territorial base. The episode is also noteworthy for the first appearance of a powerful *magister militum* who could manipulate the figurehead emperors. Arbogast was not the first barbarian general to rise to a powerful governmental position but he was the first to be so dominant. No doubt it was partly his barbarian origin – he was a Frank – that recommended him to Theodosius as regent for the child Valentinian II, since a barbarian could not aspire to the throne (as both Magnus Maximus and Theodosius himself had done), but it did not stop such generals aiming at imperial power without the outward trappings.

Theodosius I, by surmounting these usurpations, had therefore succeeded in establishing his dynasty. When he died in 395, he left two sons who had both been made Augusti: Honorius in the West and Arcadius in the East. The latter was just about adult, 17 years of age, but Honorius was only 10 years old. They were scarcely capable of ruling, partly due to their youth but also their extraordinarily sheltered upbringing.

The great weakness of imperial rule in the 380s had been the preoccupation of Theodosius with the East and that Valentinian II was a child. This condition was to be perpetuated into the 390s, after Theodosius' death. Here was the unfortunate part of the dynastic succession, which is just as liable to produce children or incompetents as it is competent men or even the occasional genius. Yet there is also something very strange about the situation between 380 and 410. Imperial children had been brought up in palaces before. They might turn out to be vicious or incompetent – Gaius, Nero and Commodus – but this was the first time that the inheritance had gone to lazy incompetents who were all too easily swayed by insinuating favourites. Gratian had been shaping up well, even if he was perhaps excessively cautious, until he was murdered; Valentinian II was clearly unbalanced and incompetent. With the children of Theodosius, the favourites became the dominating people at court and the effective rulers.

This pattern had in part been set by Gratian's minority – he became sole emperor in the West at the age of 16 – and by Valentinian II, who was the senior Augustus at the age of 8. Valentinian had been dominated at first by his mother Justina, then by his *magister militum*, the Frank Arbogast. The arrival of the emperor at adulthood, therefore, proved to be the real danger point, for in theory the favourite should then gracefully retire to a subordinate role. Arbogast did not intend to, and when he had found that Arbogast refused to obey his orders, Valentinian had hung himself.

This, therefore, was part of the legacy of Theodosius: first, he had acquired the throne by compelling Gratian to promote him; second, he left children as emperors, apparently untrained, and they grew to be incompetent as rulers; and third, he insinuated the practice of employing over-powerful generals, often of barbarian origin, who ruled in place of the incompetent emperors. This combination was one of the main reasons that the Western Empire fell apart. Theodosius, the last emperor to rule the whole Empire (but only for a year), was one of the prime causes of the fall of the Western Empire.

Theodosius died in 395, the year after he suppressed Eugenius and Arbogast, leaving his two sons as joint emperors. Another barbarian general, Stilicho, now came forward to report that he had it privately from Theodosius on his deathbed that he should be the guardian of his two sons.[7] Stilicho was the son of a Vandal father and a Roman mother. He had worked his way up the court ladder, on the way marrying Theodosius' niece Serena; in 394, he became Arbogast's successor. So Theodosius – always assuming, of course, that the deathbed conversation really happened – was organizing the succession in a version of what several previous emperors had done, with the regent to be in place until the child emperor was old enough to rule alone. The precedent came from Augustus, with his plan to make Agrippa emperor-guardian for Gaius and Lucius and then Tiberius for Germanicus. Antoninus Pius had been selected explicitly by Hadrian to be the emperor-guardian for Marcus. Very respectable precedents therefore existed for Stilicho's (and Arbogast's) position. Closer in time Valens had in a sense been emperor-guardian for Gratian, and Gratian had taken the child Valentinian II into his household. So the position of Stilicho (or Arbogast, for that matter) was not wholly unknown to Roman succession practice; if he had been fully Roman by parentage, he could have been emperor, but he was a Vandal, not a Roman, and could not be emperor.

It would not be reasonable to claim that all these precedents were in the minds of the dynastic and imperial organizers when they were making their constitutional and administrative arrangements, but the pattern had been repeated often enough over the previous four centuries that it had become one of the possible arrangements of imperial power for any emperor or regent seeking for a way of coping with incompetent or under-age emperors.

Stilicho remained as governor for Honorius until 408, when the emperor finally ordered his execution. Partly as a result there came the successful invasion of Italy by the Goths under Alaric, the first barbarian occupation of Rome and a rash of opposing imperial nominations in Italy and Gaul. Honorius, moreover, although married twice, had no children. Both of his wives were daughters of Stilicho, and it may be Honorius' distaste for his father-in-law that reduced his appetite for intercourse or, as some contemporaries had it, increased his impotence or even chastity. Whatever the reason, it appeared for a long time as though his brother in Constantinople would be his heir. As it happened this was not to be so, for Arcadius died in the same year that Stilicho was killed.

During the reigns of Theodosius' two sons the Eastern and Western parts of the Empire seriously and, as it turned out, permanently diverged. This was not a new phenomenon of course, for there had been several occasions when two rulers had controlled the East and the West – Marcus Aurelius and Lucius Verus, Valens and Valentinian I are obvious cases – and once more the first example was Augustus, who at one point placed Agrippa as Eastern ruler for several years. This time, however, the division proved to be lasting and attempts to rejoin the two separated sections were much feebler than in the past.

The partnership of Honorius and Stilicho ended with the quasi-judicial murder of the general, which was preceded, accompanied and followed by disasters all over the West. Honorius, having murdered one general, was then constrained to find another, for he was as unmilitary as his brother and his nephew in the East. The man of the hour was Constantius, a capable commander from Pannonia, who was kept busy suppressing rebels and usurpers for several years.

The rebellions came in two groups: one from Britain, the other in Italy and Narbonese Gaul; needless to say, these also overlap (see Table V). The first cases came in Britain, where officials were not unmindful, no doubt, of the previous examples of Magnentius, Magnus Maximus and Constantine. On the last day of 406, a great barbarian invasion came across the frozen Rhine and bands of raiders spread across Gaul and even into Spain. The Roman army in Germany disintegrated and Honorius' authority vanished. In Britain power had already been seized by a man called Marcus, whose other names are not known but who seems to have had some official position, perhaps as commander of one of the forces in Britain, or possibly as the governor of one of the five British provinces. His coup had come before the Rhine crossing, but may have been carried out in anticipation of it. Information about him is thin, other than that he had himself proclaimed as emperor.

Table V: Unsuccessful Emperors, 379–425.

Date	Emperor	Challenger	Region
379	Theodosius I		
383	Magnus Maximus	Britain, Gaul	
	Eugenius	The West	
395	Arcadius/Honorius		
		Marcus, Gratian	Britain
		Constantine III	Britain, Gaul
408	Theodosius II		
		Maximus, Priscus	Spain
		Attalus	Visigoths
		Jovinus/Sebastianus	Germany
		Maximus/Gerontius	Spain
421	Constantius III		
423	John		
425	Valentinian III		

Marcus did not last long, being replaced by a man called Gratian, described as a *municeps* and *tyrannos*, which might suggest a local man, perhaps a major landowner able to command authority. He in turn lasted only a short time and, still in 407, he was replaced by an army officer, Flavius Claudius Constantinus, who was supported in part because of his name (this was possibly a source of support for Gratian also) and in part because he proposed to take vigorous military action to recover Gaul for the Empire and so end the isolation of Britain from the Continent. The implication is that this was not part of the programme of either Marcus or Gratian, and that these two were content, like Carausius, to rule in Britain alone. The further implication is that there was a dispute in Britannia over what to do in the face of the German invasion. Constantine was therefore an imperial loyalist in the pattern of Magnus Maximus and virtually all earlier 'usurpers'.[8]

Constantine was only fairly successful in his expedition, but he re-established an imperial authority in much of Gaul and collected together the remnants of the Roman army in Germany. He was perhaps assisted by local resisters and by the fact that many of the barbarians would have headed home with their loot by the time he was able to take action. Some of them, however, settled down in Gaul and Spain. Having done much of the job he had crossed into Gaul to do, of course, Constantine was compelled to seek recognition for his position from the Western Emperor Honorius, so ending up in much the same situation as Magnentius and Magnus Maximus.

Meanwhile, Honorius himself was beset by the invasion of Italy by Alaric and the Visigoths. Alaric, unable to bring Honorius to any agreement that the emperor would keep, selected a senator called Priscus Attalus as his own candidate as emperor. Attalus was a notable orator and a member of the Senate, an Asian, very rich and a man who had been selected by the Senate itself in the past as its envoy to treat with the emperor over legislation. Alaric, therefore, was not choosing a mere puppet. Attalus made a series of appointments, including Alaric himself as *magister militum* (and therefore as successor to Arbogast and Stilicho). This was all generally pleasing to the Senate and, by implication, to Alaric, but also highly displeasing to Honorius.[9]

Alaric's justification was that he had been quite unable to bring Honorius to an acceptable agreement and therefore he had elevated to the imperial throne someone with whom he could do business. This had been his persistent demand all along since he became leader of the Visigoths, and so he therefore demonstrated yet again that he and his people were members of the Empire and wished to be treated as such. There was an armed group who wished to be permitted to settle inside the Empire; because of this, they were important politically and, like other armed groups that constituted the Roman army – at this point, notably the army in Britain – they claimed the right to nominate or to take part in the nomination of Roman emperors.

When Alaric and Attalus took an army to attack Honorius in Ravenna, Honorius seriously considered co-opting his rival as co-emperor. It would, after all, have been only a rather more blatant example of the way Honorius' own father had become emperor. Events of various sorts intervened, however, and Alaric tired of the game. He wanted an official appointment for himself and to be given pay and land for his people, and only Honorius could provide those. The Emperor Attalus did not collect a wide enough set of supporters to be a serious rival, so when even the threat of a rival emperor failed to bring Honorius to terms, Alaric discarded his emperor and marched on Rome once more. Honorius had retained the loyalty of enough of Italy to undermine Attalus decisively. Honorius was, therefore, regarded as 'legitimate' by the majority of those in Italy who had influence or political power; it was a triumph above all for the dynastic inheritance over Honorius' proven incompetence, treachery and double-dealing.

Attalus was therefore revealed as a puppet after all. He pretended to imperial authority and claimed to make governmental appointments, but he could not carry it off without the armed support of Alaric. His basis of support was thus far too narrow, as with so many brief emperors supported only by an armed force. Having been deposed, he had no option but to stay with the Goths as they marched around Italy and on into Gaul.

Meanwhile Constantine, the British emperor ('Constantine III') had gained a brief recognition from Honorius during that emperor's time of extreme stress, but this was withdrawn as soon as the pressure of Alaric and Attalus on him was reduced. Constantine himself suffered from a rebellion when his general Gerontius in Spain promoted his own son Maximus as a rival emperor during 409, at the same time as Attalus was being elevated by Alaric. The reason Gerontius acted this way is said to have been personal pique, but it was also just at this time that Constantine III's imperial structure was crumbling; Britain, his original base, defected and asked for assistance from Honorius – though none was provided – and in addition the Rhine frontier was under attack once more. Spain was restless after its conquest, occupied in parts by irremovable barbarian groups. Constantine succumbed to his various enemies during 411. The victors, commanded by Honorius' general, the *magister militum* Constantius, went on to Spain, where Gerontius committed suicide rather than be captured. Maximus took refuge with one of the barbarian bands that had taken over parts of Spain as a result of the recent events.[10]

Perhaps as a reaction to the end of Constantine, two of the barbarian kings who had moved into Gaul and had not been removed – Goar, king of the Alans, and Gundarius of the Burgundians – took a leaf out of Alaric's book and persuaded a Gallic noble, Jovinus, to have himself proclaimed emperor at Moguntiacum in 412. This was clearly an attempt to preserve the separation of Gaul from Italy which Constantine had achieved for a time, and which Honorius had ordered for Britain by this time as well in another move to undercut Constantine's authority. Jovinus raised his brother Sebastianus to be his colleague almost at once.[11]

Unfortunately for all these men, Honorius had found in the Pannonian Constantius a general capable of beating his enemies. He had already captured Constantine III and his son Julian and had driven Gerontius to suicide, now first Sebastianus and then Jovinus were caught and executed as well. Meanwhile both Maximus (in Spain) and Priscus Attalus (with the Visigoths) survived, but did so only because they did not attempt to exercise any imperial authority and had taken refuge with barbarian groups. Attalus stayed with the Visigoths and even pronounced an oration at the wedding of the Gothic King Athaulf and the Imperial Princess Galla Placidia, Honorius' half-sister. She was returned to Honorius after her husband's early death and then was married to Constantius.[12] This was another pattern that became standard: the *magister militum* joined the imperial family by marriage. Theodosius I had done so by marrying Galla, the daughter of Valentinian I, and Stilicho had married Theodosius' niece and had given his two daughters in marriage to Honorius.

Attalus was re-proclaimed as emperor later in that year (415), but was then abandoned once again by the Goths; he was mutilated and then exiled by Honorius.[13] Had he not been a rich and important senator he would surely have suffered the fate of Jovinus, Sebastianus, Constantine, Julian and possibly Gerontius: execution after torture.

The settlement of the Goths (formerly led by Alaric) in Aquitania by a treaty with Honorius in 418 largely calmed Gaul, though areas had been taken over by other barbarian groups by that time. (The Visigoths, received thereby into the Empire, were then used as imperial troops against their fellow barbarians.) One of those groups who had settled in Spain in about 420 re-elevated Gerontius' son Maximus as emperor. He had first been proclaimed in 409, making this unimportant Briton the longest-serving rebel emperor in Roman history. His re-emergence led to his swift suppression and execution.[14]

While all this continued in the West, the Eastern part of the Empire had gone through a different succession process that soon had its effect on the West as well. Arcadius had married the daughter of a half-barbarian general who had been brought up in Constantinople. They had five children: a son Theodosius, who succeeded to the throne by hereditary succession in 408, and four daughters. Theodosius II was only 7 years old when his father died and therefore required a regent-guardian. In Constantinople, unlike the West, the regency was largely civilian. The first regent for Theodosius was the Praetorian Prefect Anthemius, and later his own eldest sister Pulcheria. There appears to have been no question but that Theodosius should succeed: he had been Augustus since he was only 1 year old.

The situation in Constantinople was thus superficially similar to that at Ravenna. A child was emperor and a powerful guardian was ruling for him. Furthermore, Anthemius was a member of a family with at least three generations of prominent service in government, and this would continue into the future. The difference was that Anthemius was succeeded as regent for Theodosius II by the emperor's strong-willed sister Pulcheria. The need for a powerful general was staved off in the East for some time by this means. This was therefore a key moment in the divergence of East and West.

Honorius' general, Constantius, had married Galla Placidia in 417, and was promoted as joint-Augustus ('Constantius III') four years later. He then died after a reign of only seven months. He had been a successful subordinate, recovering Gaul and Spain from Constantine III and Africa from another rebel, but he seems to have chafed under the restrictions of his position as emperor. Despite Honorius' decision to raise him to the throne jointly with him, he failed to gain a similar recognition from the government of Theodosius II in Constantinople. How important this was is not clear for Honorius was the senior emperor, but it did have some bearing on the situation.

Constantius was thus emperor for only a brief period, but he and Galla Placidia had been married long enough to have two children: a daughter Honoria and a son Valentinian. Honorius drove Galla Placidia away soon after Constantius' death, and she took her children with her for refuge at Constantinople with Theodosius. When Honorius died in 423, therefore, no member of the imperial family remained in the West. It seems characteristic of the hapless, indecisive and faithless Honorius that not only did he have no children, but he had apparently made no provision for the succession. Constantius' place as the soldier holding up the government had been taken by Castinus, one of Constantius' officers. He was ideally placed to impose his own candidate, and after a pause for thought and to consider his options, he chose a palace official called John as his candidate for the Western throne.[15]

This procedure was not so very different from that which had seen the emergence of Jovian and Valentinian in 363 and 364 or the elevation of

Valentinian II in 375, but in the event it was actually seen as closer to the action of Arbogast in promoting Eugenius in 392. The essential basis was that the new emperor was chosen by the army, in the person of Castinus. There is some evidence that Castinus for a time had been in communication with Theodosius II, but John's promotion was not acceptable in Constantinople. It seems likely that Castinus put up his man as an act of desperation, and then, having done so, and being in control, he tried again to gain the recognition of the senior emperor. This was as necessary for John as it had been for the Western upstarts ten years before. An embassy was sent to Constantinople.

It seems that Theodosius II, by now more or less in control of his own government, had been pondering the idea of reuniting the West with the East, but the news of John's elevation, as well as the disturbed condition of the Western provinces, demonstrated the difficulty of that notion. John and Castinus between them represented the military and civilian elements of the Western government, which by now had little or no connection with those elements in the East. To establish control in the West it would be necessary for the emperor to be there in person, and to campaign for probably several years; but he needed also to be in Constantinople. That is to say, the two halves of the Roman government had solidified into separation, and two emperors were now required. So, if Theodosius II could not do both jobs himself, he had to find a substitute, and if John with Castinus was unacceptable, he had to appoint a man of his own. He appears to have decided right away that John was not suitable, no doubt in particular because he was not of the royal family but also because Castinus would be the real ruler. Instead he sent an expedition under Ardaburius, the *magister militum* in the East, with the mission of removing John (and Castinus), which was achieved, and then of installing his nephew Valentinian III, the son of Constantius III and Galla Placidia, on the throne in Honorius' place. Suddenly Constantius III had become acceptable, especially now that he was dead.

Valentinian III was only 6 years old at the time and had to have someone ruling for him. At first this was his mother, Galla Placidia, and then, eventually, a senior general, Aetius. Once again the pattern reasserted itself, and this time it lasted more than two decades. Valentinian became emperor in large part because of his heredity and in part because of his emplacement and recognition by the senior emperor in the East. The process of the imperial succession in the West, therefore, had not been formalized as it was soon to be in the East, presumably because it had not been possible to create a firm foundation for a clear inauguration process in the absence of a clear hereditary line. One of the reasons for this was that Honorius had not lived at Rome but at Ravenna for much of his reign, but Ravenna was not an imperial capital of long standing. One of John's strengths in Italy may have been the fact that he was living in the old capital.

Valentinian III was appointed Caesar by Theodosius in October 424 at Constantinople and was taken, along with his mother, with the army on the expedition against John and Castinus. The victory had led to his acclamation as *imperator* in the old way, but this was never taken to be the date of his official elevation and installation.[16] This, it appears, could only be done by the authority of Theodosius. Valentinian was installed at Rome, thus trumping John's move of residing in the city, but he was not officially pronounced Augustus until a representative of Theodosius arrived in the city. Theodosius had intended to do this himself, but he fell ill on the journey and left it to an official.[17] It was therefore demonstrated all too clearly that it was by the will of Theodosius that the child emperor was created, which was no doubt the intention. The Senate in Rome was not involved, nor was the army, despite the proclamation as *imperator*. Valentinian's accession was being emphasized as due to his hereditary claims and to his appointment by the senior ruler. The boy was also betrothed to Licinia Eudoxia, Theodosius' daughter. The marriage took place eventually in 437 in Constantinople. Running true to form in the family, they had two daughters but no son.

The legacy of the seizure of power by Theodosius I was therefore ambiguous, to put it no stronger. He had shown how a military man could push his way to the position of emperor, an example followed by Constantius III, and in effect also by the barbarian generals. These men in turn had shown that it was equally possible for them to exercise imperial power without the purple robes on their shoulders, simply by dominating the emperor, especially if he was a child, or, just as well, if he was incompetent, timid or lazy.

That this arrangement could work well enough was shown by the successful survival of the Empire in the East, but there it also depended on a clear line of hereditary imperial succession. This did not exist in the West, which gave much greater scope for the intrusive generals, though, as Arbogast and Stilicho had discovered, they were always in a very precarious situation. Their authority depended in large part on their command of the army, which was by this time largely composed of barbarian recruits; Aetius' position under Valentinian III was strong because he was able to command these men. Such an army was different from that of the classical Roman army; among other changes its men fought for pay and for loyalty to a commander, not as Roman subjects, who were increasingly reluctant to be enlisted. Meanwhile senators in the West insisted on their continuing status as being exempt from service and taxation. Only if they chose to did they take up government posts.

The alternative emperors of the years 406–414 had been the product of the confusion of governmental authority in the West, of Honorius' weakness and of the barbarian invasions. Their claims to authority lay in their command of armies and their ability to win victories. There was little difference between the Visigothic army of Alaric that promoted Priscus Attalus, the army that supported the British Emperor Constantine III and that which was commanded by the *magister militum* Constantius and supported him to an imperial marriage and the Western throne. This was therefore one route to the throne – command of an army – although if the general was barbarian-born he was ineligible and had to be content with the power without the robes. The success of Constantius, brief though it was, and the destruction of the others, highlighted the further requirement: besides command of a loyal army, pretenders needed to be accepted and recognized by an emperor in place. Without such recognition they failed.

The establishment of Valentinian III on the throne in Italy kept Theodosius' dynasty in power, of a sort, for another generation. In the event, the final crisis of the dynasty came first in the East, in 450, when Theodosius II died. He had been surrounded all his reign by women: his sisters, his wife, his daughter; even many of those who were his advisers were eunuchs. As an emperor, like his father and his uncle, he was thoroughly unmilitary; a characteristic for which he was criticized for it was now expected that an emperor should command in the field. One of the contributions of the dynasty to future history was to end that tradition.[18] This did not affect his relative longevity, but the absence of a male heir was just as serious. His son and one of his daughters both died young, and his other daughter, Licinia Eudoxia, was sent to marry her cousin the Western Emperor Valentinian III; in all, not an unfamiliar situation. Theodosius was emperor for forty-two years, so that when he died, after a riding accident, there should have been mechanisms in place to find a new man. It is not clear that this had actually been done, but a clear dynastic process was certainly used to find a successor.

The emperor's eldest sister Pulcheria, one of those who had done much of the ruling for him, selected an officer on the staff of the general Aspar, a man called Marcian, had him proclaimed emperor and then married him.[19] The order of these events was clearly important. Aspar was one of a succession of barbarian generals employed by the Eastern emperors. He was the son of Ardaburius, who had commanded the expedition to remove John and Castinus, and was of Alan descent. By promoting a man from the staff of Aspar the army could believe it was involved; no doubt Aspar really was consulted. Once Marcian was installed, Aspar was clearly in a very powerful position, one that was analogous to that of Stilicho or Aetius in the West. By making Marcian emperor before he was married to the empress, he was clearly being enthroned not because he was Pulcheria's husband but by the will of those who were (at least superficially) involved in the process: the army, the Palace officials and the Senate of Constantinople, even though it seems to have been Pulcheria who was really in charge. Marcian was then presented to the people, who acclaimed him, thereby in theory at least accepting him and ratifying the process of selection. Only then did he marry the empress. By all accounts he was made to promise to respect her virginity; since they were both now well over 50 the matter was perhaps moot in any case.

Marcian was well-connected even before his promotion. His career had been as a follower of Ardaburius, but his daughter (he had been married before) was married to Anthemius, who was the grandson of the former regent for Theodosius II of the same name. In other words, Marcian was in much the same position as Constantius III in the West. (See Genealogical Table XX.)

The elaborate and public aspects of Marcian's selection, coronation and marriage were clearly intended to persuade all that the new emperor was installed by the strictest legal and constitutional formulae. The situation was new. There was no possibility of hereditary succession – note that a ruling empress was not acceptable – and a process like that following the death of Valentinian I in 375 was not available either. The nearest parallel might be the selection and promotion of Theodosius I in 378/379, though that was close to being a coup by Theodosius. It was, no doubt, to avoid a coup that the process of Marcian's accession was devised. It was only because Marcian had no hereditary right that he had to be so widely and publicly proclaimed and accepted. (It is noticeable that Valentinian III, by 450 the only emperor once Theodosius was dead, was not consulted, nor was he involved in the process.)

The sequence of events in this selection became important when Pulcheria died only three years later in 453; her husband was able to continue as emperor without any question over his legitimacy for the post. It was, of course, a sleight of hand; everyone knew that Pulcheria's voice had been decisive and that he was her choice, but the constitutional proprieties were respected, insofar as there were any; perhaps 'invented' would be more accurate. Yet the choice was eccentric and unhelpful. Marcian, though he had been married before, had no son, only a daughter. He was even older than Theodosius and could not have been expected to live long. When he died, the succession problem would recur even more acutely and there would be no more imperial daughters available who could fudge the issue.

XX   Connections of Anthemius.

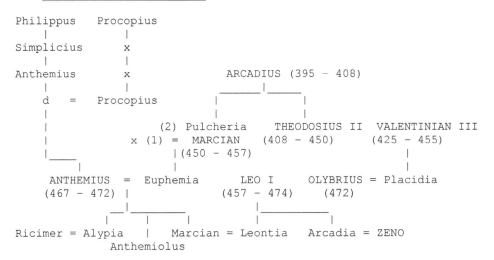

Theodosius I's insistence on being appointed emperor in 378/379 had therefore resulted in the establishment of his family on the Roman imperial throne for nearly eight decades, despite the incompetence displayed by many of the emperors of the family. In the history of the Empire this was fairly good going: only the Julio-Claudians and the Antonines lasted longer. It might be objected that these were scarcely dynasties in the accepted sense of a sequence of blood relations, though they certainly were in Roman eyes; yet the Julio-Claudians, the Antonines and the Severi scarcely can be counted as real dynasties. Then the family of Theodosius also had its own dynastic oddities and the succession of emperors in the West was hardly dynastic: Honorius inherited from his father but his successor was his nephew, and in the East it was only by the marriage of Pulcheria and Marcian that the dynasty can be said to have lasted until 457. (In fact by including Marcian we can also extend the dynasty for another fifteen years by counting Marcian's son-in-law Anthemius, Valentinian III's widow's second husband Petronius Maximus, and her daughter's husband Olybrius, so taking it down to 472. The dynasty that resulted is no stranger than earlier versions. See Genealogical Tables XX and XXI.)

It cannot be said that Theodosius' method of elevating himself to the position of emperor and his policies thereafter had been good for the Empire. His progeny were a set of the weakest emperors the Empire ever had, his use of regent-generals proved to be deeply unsettling and his own example was a constant temptation to ambitious generals and bureaucrats alike. He was successful in the sense that his family provided emperors for three generations, but the Empire required more than just a series of incompetents and children backed up by unstable generals. When the direct line of the dynasty ended, which it did in both East and West rather suddenly and almost simultaneously in 457 and 455 respectively, the methods used to cope with the resulting crises were also his legacy; the different aspects emphasized in East and West are signals, once again, of the different fates of the two halves of the Empire.

Part V

Breakdown

Valentinian III and His Successors

Valentinian III (425–455).

Petronius Maximus (455).
(*CNG Coins via Wikimedia Commons*)

Avitus (455–456). (*NAC via
Wikimedia Commons*)

Majorian (457–261). (*Sailko via
Wikimedia Commons*)

Eastern Emperors After the Theodosians

Marcian (450–457).

Leo I (457–474). (*Marie-Lan Nguyen/Wikimedia Commons*)

Zeno (474–475, 476–491). (*CNG Coins via Wikimedia Commons*)

Basiliscus (475–476). (*CNG Coins via Wikimedia Commons*)

Chapter Seventeen

The Crises of 455–457

Between March 455 and January 457 four emperors died: three in the West, all murdered, and one at Constantinople, in his bed, of old age. The crisis occasioned by the deaths brought the two parts of the Roman Empire to the fatal breaking-point. The actual break took two decades to work through, and had been heralded for a century beforehand. For a polity that had existed in one form or another for almost seven centuries the break was inevitably slow and reluctant. It was the failure of one part of the Empire to produce emperors that marked the end. That is, the processes of choosing emperors finally failed in the West, but in the East the process continued and adapted to events, so the Eastern half really was the Roman Empire's continuation.

The new succession crises began in September 454, when Valentinian III finally reached the stage of homicidal anger with his *magister militum* Aetius, the latest in a line of such over-powerful military ministers. The emperor and his *magister militum* had been at enmity for years, but the break seems to have come with a dispute over the succession. Aetius wished his son Gaudentius to be betrothed to the emperor's younger daughter Placidia; Valentinian had earlier hoped to betroth her to one of Aetius' officers, Majorian. Aetius had reacted by banishing Majorian to his home estate, but it seems that Valentinian maintained his intention, which was, of course, a means of breaking Aetius' power over him. That power had partly been based on his ability to call on Hun troops as reinforcements; men who were his to command and so were a separate force from the army that was loyal to the emperor. The Roman-Hun war in 451–453 had, however, severed that link as the Hun Empire collapsed after the death of the Hun King Attila. The combination of Aetius' imperial ambition, the loss of the Hun alliance and Valentinian's wish to rule alone brought the emperor to the pitch of action.

At the beginning of an audience in the Imperial Palace in Rome that day, the emperor personally killed his great minister.[1] It seems that the emperor had been persuaded that Aetius intended to kill him, which may not have surprised him and may or may not have been true, and he decided to strike first. The intrigue involved Heraclius, one of the officials of the Palace, and a member of the Roman aristocracy, Petronius Maximus, who had been a prominent minister himself for more than thirty years and was a grandson of Petronius Probus, who had been the leader of the coup of 375.

Petronius was a member of an aristocratic network that had branches in Italy and Gaul. Besides being descended from Petronius Probus, he was also the grandson of Magnus Maximus, the Western emperor of 383–388, through his mother; on his father's side he was descended from a long line of consuls. He had himself been twice consul, twice Praetorian Prefect and twice City Prefect. He was thus a very distinguished man, and one who was at the heart of Aetius' and Valentinian's government; at the same time he was an active member of the Italian/Gallic senatorial aristocracy. Presumably as a result of this heredity and these offices (some of them largely honorary by this time and awarded to him because of that heredity), he had developed a very inflated idea of his worth and ability. He was certainly a most persuasive intriguer. His success in getting others to remove Aetius led him to assume he would be able to be the new general of the West, but Valentinian refused to appoint him, intending to rule himself without the intervention of any over-mighty general. Petronius responded with another intrigue by which he encompassed the murder, again by other hands, of the emperor himself.

This time he suborned two of the emperor's guards, 'Scythians' called Optila and Thraustila, who had been dismayed and angered by the killing of Aetius. He promised them revenge and rewards, and they took the opportunity of Valentinian's attendance at a military exercise in the Campus Martius to kill him. The emperor was apparently attended by only a small bodyguard at the time, and they were either in on the plot or were too slow to react. The two assassins also killed Heraclius, who was present as well. Then they ran off to report to Petronius.[2]

There was much uncertainty in Rome as the news of the murder spread. Three men emerged as candidates for emperor: Petronius Maximus, whose role in the killing of the former emperor only slowly became known; a man called Maximian, who had been Aetius' steward and was said to be the son of an Egyptian merchant, though what qualities he brought to his candidature and what support he had is not clear; and Majorian, who had been reinstated by Valentinian and was still presumed to be betrothed to Placidia. Majorian was the candidate supported by Valentinian's widow, Licinia Eudoxia, the daughter of Theodosius II.

The decision regarding who should be the next emperor was taken by a small circle of influential people, and without delay. Besides the empress, these would include Petronius Maximus, the imperial bodyguard, or at least the Guard commander, and the officials of the Palace. There is no suggestion in any of the sources – there are several for these events – that either the Senate or the Roman populace was involved, though Petronius might be considered to be the senatorial candidate.

We may therefore assume that the discussions on the new emperor took place within this small circle and that the three candidates who emerged had different sources of support. Petronius presumably had the Guard's support, and might expect support from the Senate. He won over the Palace officials by bribery and so gained control of Eudoxia herself, compelling her to marry him. This all took place very quickly, for within a day of Valentinian's murder Petronius was installed as emperor. He had clearly seized control of the Palace – where he could 'bribe' the officials and control the empress – and this was decisive. His marriage to the Augusta will have taken place later, thus going through the same sequence as with the accession of Marcian in Constantinople only five years earlier, probably not at all accidentally: the death of the emperor, the installation of the new man, then his marriage to the Augusta, which would give him an independent legitimacy, and finally the ratification by popular acclamation. He appointed his son by an earlier marriage, Palladius, as his joint emperor, and Palladius was then betrothed, or perhaps married, to the empress's daughter Placidia; father and son were thus united, or to be united, with mother and daughter.[3]

We may therefore identify the elements in Rome that were considered to be decisive in determining the succession where a dispute existed as the Guard, the imperial family and the high military and Palace officials. The discussions lasted only a single day. It may perhaps be assumed that Petronius was not the first choice of any of these groups – except perhaps some of the Guard – for his seizure of power clearly had elements of force involved.

Petronius' marriage to Licinia Eudoxia was intended to provide him with the legitimacy that marriage to an Augusta had come to imply. If this was to be the source of Petronius' position, then it was just as necessary to annex Placidia, for her husband would have an equal claim to the throne with that of Petronius himself, and it seems to have worked. Petronius was emperor for only three months, but in that time he was unchallenged. We are not told what Majorian's reaction was to being sidelined from his betrothed yet again.

On the other hand, Petronius' time as emperor was turbulent, according to one source, and if he had to reward the Guard it is quite likely that they took advantage and indulged in 'tumults of soldiers, tumults of allies', which would no doubt be answered by the 'popular tumults'.[4] These do not, however, necessarily imply challenges to the new emperor's position. What he really needed was some sign of recognition from Constantinople. The marriages were a signal that he expected this from Marcian, but he was not in office long enough for that signal to be received. He did not have time, either, to appoint men to offices in Gaul, or no doubt in Italy as well. It is very likely that Marcian would have refused recognition, but certainty on the point is not possible. The issue soon became moot, for the Vandals intervened first.

The Vandal King Geiseric brought an expedition to Rome to gain revenge. He had earlier negotiated the betrothal of his son to Valentinian III's eldest daughter Eudocia, so Geiseric was in the position of an interested relative, for it seems that Petronius may now have refused to allow the match. There is also a story, repeated in several sources, though its authenticity is doubtful, that Licinia Eudoxia was so disgusted at these enforced marriages that she summoned Geiseric to her assistance. We may accept the disgust without necessarily accepting the summons. Geiseric was surely very annoyed at the news without needing to be summoned. He was on his way with the fleet and a full muster of his warriors by April; this news arrived in Rome by May and the Vandal army was camped outside the city by late that month. The Emperor Petronius fled as the Vandals arrived, for the city was virtually ungarrisoned. He was killed by the Romans as he did so, not a great surprise. Then the Vandals took the city, by agreement with the bishop, and looted it at their leisure, finishing the work by also carrying off the members of the imperial family and several other carefully selected hostages; Eudocia was then married to her Vandal prince.[5]

After this there could be no question of finding a new emperor in Rome, for the effect of the Vandal sack seems to have paralysed every interested authority. No doubt those who comprised the groups who had interested themselves in Petronius' elevation – the Guards, the Senate, the army and the Palace officials – were either dead or scattered. Nor does it seem that the Emperor Marcian in Constantinople was able to intervene in the crisis that followed the death of Valentinian III. Valentinian had not been consulted on the choice of Marcian as Theodosius II's successor in 450, though as sole Augustus after Theodosius died he should have been; relations between the two courts were thus already strained somewhat before the new crisis in Rome erupted. However, events moved so quickly in Rome that Marcian scarcely had time to react before another item of news of a new event arrived that had to be factored into his considerations.

There was therefore for a few weeks no imperial authority in Italy. The void was filled from Gaul, where the local *magister militum* of Gaul, M. Macilius Flavius Eparcius Avitus, was proclaimed emperor by the Visigothic King Theoderic at Tolosa. He was then acclaimed, or perhaps accepted, or even elected, at a gathering of Gallo-Roman nobles meeting at Beaucaire (on the Rhône near Arles). He moved to Arelate (Arles) where some sort of installation ceremony took place. All this took some time, about five weeks after Petronius' death. Avitus did not hurry to Rome, eventually arriving in the city with an escort of Gallic soldiers and Visigothic troops around October.[6]

Avitus was a Gallic noble of high descent, who had been active in political affairs for at least two decades already. He had been an associate of Aetius in Gallic affairs and was a former tutor to the Visigothic king. He was at Tolosa on a diplomatic mission on behalf of the Emperor Petronius when he heard of Petronius' death. He was urged to put himself forward as emperor by Theoderic, who, as a federate king within the Empire, ranked high in the Roman command structure and clearly had a right to take part in the nomination process. The obvious precedent, if one was sought, would be Crocus, the Alamannic king who acted in the same way at the acclamation of Constantine but also, more relevantly, that of Attalus, promoted by Alaric.

The failure of the Italians, the Palace officials, the Romans or the army in Italy to do anything about finding a replacement for Petronius for several weeks is curious. It is possible that it was due to shock at the sack of Rome, but it seems unlikely that active politicians would succumb to that for more than a day or two at most. Similarly Marcian apparently did nothing, though he did send an embassy to Africa to try to liberate Eudoxia and her daughter. The explanation may well lie in the fact that Avitus was related by marriage to Petronius. It has been suggested, in fact, that Petronius' first wife (the mother of Petronius' son Palladius, now presumably dead) was Avitus' sister. (See Genealogical Table XXI.) This in turn would make Avitus a relative of the very powerful Anicius family, of which Petronius had been a senior member.[7] Avitus' proclamation at Tolosa happened early in July, whereas the sack of Rome by the Vandals had ended only about three weeks earlier. The news of Petronius' death is unlikely to have travelled much faster than that in the circumstances. So Theoderic's suggestion and proclamation were made almost as soon as the news arrived at Tolosa. The lack of action in Italy and the East therefore may well be due to the uncertainty created by the sack – the list of eminent and royal casualties may have taken some time to be compiled – or to the expectation that Marcian might suggest a candidate and then by the news of Avitus' elevation.

The process of Avitus' elevation is therefore perhaps unusual, but it did contain the normal elements: the acclamation by Theoderic was the equivalent of Avitus being put forward by a section of the Roman army; the gathering of Gallo-Romans at Beaucaire was a meeting of men of senatorial rank; the installation at Arelate was as legal a coronation as those at any of the other cities that had been used as an imperial capital in the previous century, such as Milan, Ravenna, Trier, Cologne, even Arles itself and back to York for Constantine. The only element missing was recognition by the senior Augustus, Marcian.

It was, however, not quite as simple and straightforward as that, if 'simple' is a correct description. The aristocracies of Gaul and Italy may have been linked by marriage, descent and ownership of property, but they were still distinct; the Senate at Rome still had a much greater institutional prestige than any assembly of rich men and senators outside Rome; the Roman army in Italy was also distinct from that of anywhere else, and at this time was a good deal more effective militarily than anything in Gaul (except Theoderic's Visigoths). It would still be necessary for Avitus to conciliate these groups.

Avitus, for the first time in sixty years, was an emperor who was more than a Palace-dwelling figurehead. His previous history would have prepared people for that. After appointing commanders for his forces in

XXI   Connections of Avitus and Magnus Maximus.

```
                    MAGNUS MAXIMUS (383 - 388)
                               |
              Ennodius = Maxima     Petronius Probus
                          |                   |
                        Ennodia = Anicius Probinus     Eparchius
                             |                     _____|__
 Eudocia = (1) VALENTINIAN III |                  |         |
          |    (425 - 455) (2) PETRONIUS = (1) Eparchia    AVITUS
          |                    MAXIMUS  |                  (455 - 456)
          |                    (455)    |
   _____|_____           |         |_____
  |               |           |        |                |
 Eudocia      Placidia = (1) PALLADIUS (455) Ecdicius   d = Sidonius
                        (2) OLYBRIUS (472)               Apollinaris
```

Italy, he returned to Gaul, whose security was clearly vital, though he could be accused of favouring it over Italy. This was not much to the liking of the Romans, who had had little to say in the matter so far, but it was also not to the liking of Ricimer, another of Aetius' former commanders, or of Majorian, who had been passed over for emperor at the death of Valentinian and now again by the advent of Avitus. Between them these two were the commanders of the main Italian forces. Taking advantage both of a victory he had won and of the emperor's absence in Gaul, Ricimer joined with Majorian and they seized power in Italy. Then they defeated Avitus himself in northern Italy and forcibly consecrated him as a bishop, which disbarred him from exercising secular power. He died soon after.[8]

There followed an episode in Gaul which is referred to as the Marcellan conspiracy. This was headed by a man called Paeonius, who seized the post of Praetorian Prefect. The conspiracy, however, bore the name of another man, presumably called Marcellus. Neither of these men is known otherwise, though attempts have been made to identify Marcellus, none convincingly.[9] Exactly what was intended is unclear, though the elevation of Marcellus as emperor seems likely, and it all happened as a result of Avitus' defeat and death. His career and then his death enlarged the estrangement between Italy and Gaul.

Neither Petronius nor Avitus had received the approbation of Marcian, though he could have supplied it had he chosen to. (If Avitus claimed the throne in part because of his relationship with Petronius, then Constantinople's disregard of Petronius would clearly be extended to him; there was also disagreement over policy towards the Vandals.) The Petronius/ Avitus episode is also a moment when the Western emperors were tending towards a greater activism, a change that began with the last months of the reign of Valentinian III. This was not to the liking of the army commanders, whose aspirations, now that Aetius was dead, were to take his place as regent.

Ricimer and Majorian, in charge in Italy, were both former subordinates of Aetius. Ricimer was of high aristocratic barbarian ancestry, the son of a noble of the Sueves and the daughter of the Visigothic king; his non-Roman ancestry, of course, ruled him out as a candidate for emperor. Majorian had a good claim to have been Valentinian's chosen successor and that of the emperor's widow, and he was of aristocratic Italian descent. He was therefore probably the best imperial candidate to replace Avitus.

The situation was, however, confused. In Gaul, the destruction of Avitus had provoked the Marcellan conspiracy, but that had got nowhere. In Italy,

Ricimer and Majorian chose to wait for acceptance by Constantinople before taking irrevocable steps. The final illness of Emperor Marcian no doubt slowed things down, but on 28 February 457 they received their official appointments: Ricimer as Patrician, and Majorian as *magister militum*. The implication was that no emperor would be appointed, but this did not suit them. A month later on 1 April, Majorian was acclaimed by the army as emperor. This was followed, or so it must be assumed, by a formal approval from Constantinople. Finally on 28 December 456, Majorian was installed as emperor by the Senate at Ravenna.[10]

This long-drawn-out process is partly the result of the previous confusion over Petronius and Avitus, and partly the result of changes that took place in the East, where Marcian died early in February 457 and was succeeded by Leo I almost at once (and so at about the time Ricimer and Majorian received their credentials from Marcian). It was also an unusually careful and deliberate process, undoubtedly undergone for good public and political reasons. The deaths of Valentinian and Marcian had ended the direct (and even the indirect) hereditary line from Valentinian I and Theodosius I. Majorian had no hereditary claims on the throne. One complication may have been the problem of the fate of the princesses taken to Africa. The elder was now married to Geiseric's son, but the younger had been promised to Gaudentius, then to Majorian, married to Palladius, and then promised to Olybrius, another aristocrat.[11] During 456 it seems that Olybrius had been sent to Africa to marry Placidia; this removed her from the succession issue (the other suitors were now dead; but Majorian may have been hoping for her release).

The more convincing explanation, if not actually the only one, is the need to see the new emperor installed in the most official, public and ceremonial way possible, so as to ensure that his position and authority – and therefore that of Ricimer as well – should not be questioned. The informality of the accession of Petronius and Avitus and the aspirations of Palladius and Marcellus were to be avoided. This would emphasize Majorian's greater legitimacy than either Petronius or Avitus in the eyes of Italy. It was, therefore, a Western version of the elaborate ceremony that had been staged for Marcian in 450. The army, the emperor in Constantinople and the Senate were all involved in Majorian's installation. There could be no questioning his legitimacy as there could have been with Avitus, and as there certainly was with Petronius. The participants and the ceremonies were clearly designed to legitimize Majorian's assumption of power after the recent uncertainties.

The decisive elements in the process were the approval of the emperor in Constantinople and the acclamation of the army, which meant that in effect the new emperor had been chosen by the high command in Italy, and as Ricimer expanded his authority in the wake of the events of 455–457 he became the high command personified. The whole process was a clear attempt to bolster the authority of the new emperor with a view to restoring the Western Empire itself.

Installation by a ceremony in the Senate did not mean that the Senate as a body had had any say in the matter, but the involvement of the Senate was still significant. The previous emperors Petronius and Avitus, whether or not they had been approved by the Eastern emperor, had been senators. Apart from barbarian nominees like Priscus Attalus forty years earlier, this was the first overt participation of the Senate and senators in the installation of an emperor since the usurpation of Maxentius a century and a half before. It is perhaps a sign of the weakness of the imperial power, at least in Rome, if not in Constantinople, that the Senate in Rome was apparently reviving, though it may be another part of the programme of reviving the Western Empire. The Senate's role had always been more confirmatory than initiatory, but it was a body of extremely rich men and as the scope of political affairs shrank with the detachment of Britain, Africa and parts of Gaul and Spain from the authority of the emperors, the Senate's influence, whose members were still largely Italian-based, would inevitably increase. In the final decades of the Western Empire, the Senate once more became a political player that had to be reckoned with.

The problem of the succession in the Eastern half of the Empire in 457 was slightly different in that only one change of emperor took place. There were no murders, but a dynastically-approved emperor was replaced by one unconnected to that dynasty, as happened in the West. When Marcian died in January 457 he had not named a successor. His own 'right' to the throne had been tenuous, and his second wife, the Empress Pulcheria who had provided the imperial validation, had died in 453. So his failure, or refusal, to name an heir was perhaps due to the acknowledgement of the need for the next emperor to be chosen in a far more public and transparent way, and therefore with wider public acceptance. The matter was therefore theoretically left to the constitutional authorities – the army, the Constantinopolitan Senate, the officials and the people – who had been involved in his own elevation.

In fact the decisive voice was that of Aspar, the *magister militum*, who had also been Marcian's sponsor. He selected another of his tribunes, Leo, who had formerly been the agent for Aspar himself and had the rank of count (*comes*). It is striking that Aspar ignored Marcian's own son-in-law Anthemius (he had been married earlier, before Pulcheria), who was the grandson of the Anthemius who had been regent for Theodosius II fifty years earlier. Anthemius might be thought to have a tenuous dynastic claim and he certainly had some supporters, but Aspar's control of the army was the decisive factor. Aspar's power in the state clearly depended in part on there being no clear dynastic succession that would prevent him from exercising a choice.

By now, perhaps because of the absence of a dynastic succession, a ritual of inauguration had been developed. It had first appeared, in a different form, with Marcian's accession; previously, the accessions of Arcadius and Theodosius too had been private affairs, mere public announcements, but now, first Marcian and then Leo were enthroned publicly. It was a version of the process by which Tiberius had been installed as successor to Augustus over four centuries earlier.

The ceremony took place in the hippodrome of Constantinople, the biggest open space in the city, where the new emperor was displayed to his subjects in the imperial box, which was connected to the Palace by a tunnel. In Leo's case he was dressed in the usual purple cloak, a torque was put on his head, he was raised on a shield and the imperial diadem was placed around his head. There then followed a sequence of announcements in Leo's name, each of which was answered by the assembled officials and soldiers by pre-arranged and possibly rehearsed chants in unison.

This was an eclectic set of elements gathered from a variety of royal traditions. The torque and the shield-raising reflect the fact that much of the army was composed mainly of Germans; the diadem was an inheritance from the Hellenistic past; the purple cloak from the dress of the earlier Roman emperors and before that of the Etruscan and Roman kings; and the chants were a formalized version of the oath-taking that had accompanied Tiberius' accession in AD 14. Note that there was nothing particularly religious here, though the patriarch of the city was present. For later coronations the ceremony was moved to a church, perhaps reflecting Constantinople's self-image as a holy city, or perhaps because it was easier to control the crowd in such a building.[12]

The point about such coronations, however, is that they have to be done in public, preferably before as large an audience as can be assembled. It was both an obvious necessity and an inheritance, once again, from the process of installing an emperor when the Senate and people of Rome were the ratifying agents. These, of course, were not especially Roman processes and the development of a much clearer dynastic succession would convert them into formalities, as had been the case when Arcadius and Theodosius II became sole rulers, but the installations of Marcian and Leo had to be accomplished in a public way, just because they had no dynastic right. This was also the case in the same year with Majorian in Italy, with some popular and senatorial participation to give the clear impression that the popular and legal choice had in fact been made.

The events of 455–457 in both parts of the Empire revealed that the participation of the army in the choice of emperor had evolved further. In 363 and 364 the senior officers had selected new emperors in the emergency of the sudden deaths of others, and again in 375 it had been possible for a group of senior commanders to select an emperor and impose him on the senior Augustus. In a way, this is also what happened with the imposition of Theodosius I on Gratian four years later. There had then followed a series of dynastic successions until the 450s, modified here and there by the co-option of auxiliary emperors such as Constantine III, Constantius III and Marcian. In the meantime, however, there had also emerged, in both parts of the Empire, very powerful military commanders, often of barbarian origin, who could command the loyalty of the army. The army itself was now also largely composed of soldiers of barbarian origin and these men were apparently not loyal to either the Empire or the emperors. So the great barbarian generals – Ricimer and Aspar in this particular crisis, but there were others – were able to dictate the choice of emperor because they controlled the army. In the East, Aspar was sufficiently sensible of the local atmosphere to know that the elaborate open-air coronation brought to the process some participation by the population, though the army was the basis of the choice.

This was, in fact, a new situation with regard to the succession. No earlier successions had taken place with such a man looming over the proceedings, though Arbogast and Castinus had aspired to such a role. Indeed, although such men are often depicted as being characteristic of the West in the fifth century, it was in the East, in the situations of Marcian in 450 and of Leo in February 457, that the power of the barbarian general was first displayed so blatantly in the choice of new emperors. In the West, Ricimer and Majorian seem to have operated as allies, but Ricimer soon developed his power to a similar potency to that of Aspar, and it is these men who became the decision-makers in the next phase of the imperial succession.

Chapter Eighteen

The Consequences of Ricimer and Aspar

After a reign of four years, the Emperor Majorian was murdered by his colleague and *magister militum* Ricimer. This act resolved the differences that had (obviously) arisen between them, and hoisted Ricimer to the supreme political position in the Western Empire, which he occupied for the next thirteen years until his death. He did not act, however, either alone or without advice, for it is noted by one contemporary historian that he was advised in the killing by his council.[1] Whatever the reasons for their differences, it is obvious that future emperors, who were theoretically superior to Ricimer, would scarcely be able to assert themselves in the face of his disapproval.

A replacement emperor was eventually chosen, this time by Ricimer himself. He was a senator from Lucania called Libius Severus. He is almost completely unknown to us, but was a man who was clearly known both to Ricimer and the Senate. More than three months elapsed between Majorian's killing and the proclamation and installation of Severus.[2] This delay might suggest that Ricimer hoped to rule without an emperor, or it may be that he spent the time negotiating, particularly with the Emperor Leo in Constantinople, for a candidate acceptable to both of them. He may also have had to negotiate with the aristocrats and officials in Gaul who had liked Majorian and who had earlier put forward Avitus, and with the Senate in Italy whose role in the succession process had re-emerged recently.

Most such negotiations, if they took place, clearly failed, for Ricimer's candidate was not accorded any recognition from the East, and he was also repudiated by the Praetorian Prefect of Gaul, Aegidius, who had been appointed by Majorian. Libius Severus was so obviously a creature of Ricimer's that Aegidius could apparently not bear to acknowledge him, yet Aegidius did not put up an emperor of his own in competition. The selection of a senator does imply that Ricimer had found support in the Senate, and his choice of a senator may have further enhanced the Senate's new importance. It was a display of mutual esteem, made necessary by the isolation of both parties.

Libius Severus was installed with all due ceremony, including the rituals of acclamation by the army and installation in a formal ceremony in the Senate, just as Majorian had been.[3] The elaboration may be taken as a gesture of defiance directed at those who refused to acknowledge him. Neither of these institutions had had any obvious say in the selection of Severus – who was chosen by Ricimer, not by the Senate – but armies had to be presented with a candidate of reasonable accomplishments and presence and the Senate would have known Severus well. His reign lasted for four years (461–465) but he seems to have had little independent authority and to have been generally inactive. He died either naturally or by the hand of Ricimer, but the general was so unpopular that he would be suspected of murder even if Libius Severus' death was natural.

Severus was never accepted by the Emperor Leo in Constantinople as Ricimer must have hoped. On the other hand, it is likely that Leo's recognition of Majorian had been only very reluctant. When Severus died, therefore, Ricimer had been in power or ruling the West for nine years through the reigns of two Western emperors and without any support from the Emperor Leo. The result had been pretty disastrous: not only was Vandal-occupied Africa unrecovered, but Gaul had in effect seceded, at least the part that had not been taken over by Franks, Visigoths, Alans and Burgundians, while Spain was largely isolated and partly occupied by other barbarians. Majorian's attempt to assert his authority there had been only briefly successful. Ricimer, in effect, controlled only Italy and the nearby islands, all of which were being repeatedly raided by the Vandals.

After Severus died, there was a delay of a year and a half before the next Western emperor was installed. This repeated the gaps in time that followed the deposition of Avitus and the death of Majorian, and was presumably due to the same cause: the need of Ricimer to locate a suitable candidate and to negotiate his elevation with the emperor in Constantinople. His last two appointments having lasted only four years each and the second never having received acceptance at Constantinople, the support of the army in Italy and of the Senate in Rome was clearly only enough for a temporary emperor. Ricimer was constrained to look to the Emperor Leo for a candidate. This was all the more necessary since the territory under his control had shrunk drastically. The failure of the Gauls to elevate their own emperor when refusing to recognize Libius Severus implied that they recognized only Leo; the Vandals were as active and threatening as ever, so to be at enmity with Leo was a burden Ricimer could well do without. Accepting an emperor sent from Constantinople would mark an alliance between Leo and Ricimer and so would bolster Ricimer's own position, and that of Leo for that matter.

Leo had at least two available candidates with family connections back to the Theodosian dynasty. One was Olybrius, the husband of Valentinian III's daughter Placidia; the other was the husband of the daughter of Marcian, Anthemius. (See Genealogical Table XX.) These connections meant that they might well be seen by Leo as threats to his own position as emperor in Constantinople. So for Leo the question was whether it was more dangerous to keep them in the city where he could supervise them or to send them West to establish an independent power base in Italy where, if really ambitious, they might become a threat. Anthemius was the better qualified, genealogically speaking, and he was persuaded to go.

Anthemius was the grandson of the distinguished politician of Theodosius II's reign and the son-in-law of the Emperor Marcian. He could also trace his ancestry back to the pretender Procopius, not perhaps the best of omens but this was also a distant connection with the house of Constantine. He was an experienced soldier and a former consul, and he arrived in Italy accompanied by the near-independent ruler of Dalmatia, Marcellinus, and an Eastern army.[4]

One element of the agreement that elevated Anthemius was that his daughter Alypia should marry Ricimer; the wedding took place a few months after his arrival. Ricimer no doubt hoped this would persuade the new emperor to co-operate with him, and that his children might hope for access to the throne; after all, Anthemius had arrived at the throne by that same route. It also duplicated the method used in the past by Stilicho and Constantius III, and indeed by Marcian.

Anthemius, like all the more recent emperors (except perhaps Majorian), lived in Rome, which comfortably separated him from Ricimer, who was normally resident in Milan. Once again there was a public ceremony of installation. The embassy sent by Ricimer to Constantinople to negotiate for the new emperor had in fact gone technically in the Senate's name, but there seems not to have been any further senatorial involvement. Anthemius was proclaimed emperor several miles outside the city at a place called Brontotas, possibly a military camp. He then sent a messenger, Heliokrates, to Constantinople with the news, and received a final recognition from Leo. The sequence is enlightening: nomination by the senior emperor and then acclamation and proclamation near Rome, possibly with military involvement, though this is only an assumption – but he was accompanied to Rome by his own army – brought recognition by the senior emperor. On the surface, Ricimer was not involved. However, the Senate certainly had been involved, with the embassy operating in its name, the previous emperor having come from its ranks and the new emperor living in the city. The Senate's influence was thus continuing.[5]

Anthemius had several advantages over both Severus and Majorian: he had both the approval of the Eastern emperor and control of a military force independent of that under Ricimer's command. If he had hoped to establish an independent policy, however, he was generally unsuccessful; indeed, separate armies were more a recipe for paralysis than dynamism. Also Anthemius personally seems to have been ineffective and on closer acquaintance he was disliked by Ricimer and by many of the Romans. He attempted, rather futilely, to develop his own policy in competition with that of Ricimer, but he was never in a strong enough position to succeed. He was undoubtedly a capable man as his earlier career shows, so his ineffectuality in Rome must be due to the failure of the local powers – Ricimer and the Senate – to pay any attention to him, and his inability to assert himself. The army he arrived with was clearly not sufficient to give him real independence.

Anthemius had an adult son, Anthemiolus, which could have indicated the beginning of a new dynasty. However, Anthemiolus was killed in an ill-fated attempt by Anthemius' forces (not, it seems, supported by Ricimer) to recover control of southern Gaul.[6] This was a necessary first step, geographically, towards a revival of the Western Empire, and as a properly-appointed Emperor Anthemius might have expected those in Gaul who had rejected Libius Severus (and Ricimer) to accept him, but Gallic conditions had changed, above all in the Visigothic kingdom. Anthemiolus and his forces were defeated by the Visigoths under King Euric, the most competent and ruthless of the Visigothic rulers.

Next year the enmity between Anthemius and Ricimer, evidenced in their failure to work together in the Gallic invasion, descended into civil war and Ricimer besieged Rome. The siege began as a blockade, but after the defeat of the relieving force, Ricimer's men broke into the city and another sack took place, apparently rather more destructive than those of either Alaric or Geiseric.[7]

Into this situation came Anicius Olybrius, the husband of Valentinian III's daughter, Placidia. Olybrius was thus very highly-connected. Through his wife he was emperor material, just as Anthemius had been, and he had been the obvious alternative to Anthemius as Western emperor in 467. However, whether he was sent from Constantinople to replace Anthemius or to reconcile Ricimer and Anthemius, or even perhaps to replace Ricimer, is not clear. He dated his reign from April or May 472, at which time Anthemius was still alive and reigning in besieged Rome so, whatever the original intention, Olybrius had been persuaded by Ricimer on his arrival in Italy to take the throne. Anthemius was killed when Ricimer's forces took the city in July.[8]

Olybrius was the first emperor since Libius Severus to have been installed by Ricimer, though it could be argued that he had in effect been nominated by Leo. With his genealogical connections, he could thus be seen as a legitimate emperor, and with support from both Ricimer and Leo he should have been a unifying figure. The circumstances of his entering Rome, however, probably precluded any ceremony in the Senate, which had also not been needed by Anthemius. It seems clear that the Senate's participation, even after its apparent revival earlier, could still be dispensed with, at least in the short term.

Ricimer brought his nephew, Gundobad, a member of the Burgundian royal family (the Burgundian king was married to Ricimer's sister), to assist him during the conflict with Anthemius. When Ricimer died in August 472, Gundobad succeeded to his position without conflict. Then the Emperor Olybrius also died, in November of that year. All three men involved in the conflict had thus died within six months.[9]

This put Gundobad in a difficult position, particularly as he had been credited, if that is the word, with personally killing Anthemius. It also left Leo in difficulties, since both of his eligible candidates for the Western throne had now rapidly expired. Yet Olybrius had lived long enough to confirm Gundobad in Ricimer's position, so the possibility of future successful negotiations existed.

The situation in the West had now once more diverged significantly from that in the East. Leo had been promoted as emperor, as had his predecessor Marcian, by the *magister militum* Aspar, and Aspar had retained his powerful position, as had Ricimer; again like Ricimer, he aimed to marry into the royal family and his son Patricius was betrothed to Leo's daughter Leontia. The other daughter, Ariadne, was married to an Isaurian chieftain, Zeno, who recruited an imperial bodyguard as a counter to Aspar's Germans. (See Genealogical Table XXII.) In about 470 Patricius had been promoted to Caesar, implying his eventual succession to the throne. This was distinctly unpopular in the city of Constantinople, for Patricius was not only of barbarian descent but he was also attached to the Arian brand of Christianity.

XXII   The House of Leo.

```
                        |                          |
              LEO I  =  Verina            BASILISCUS
          (457 - 474)|                    (475 - 476)
                      |_____
                      |                              |
ANASTASIUS I (2)  =  Ariadne  =  (1) ZENO      Leontia  =  Marcian
(491 - 518)                   | (474 - 475,
                              |   476 - 491)
                              |
                           LEO II
                           (474)
```

Leo, however, was laying a trail to enable him to break free of Aspar's power. When all was in place, when Patricius was seen to be unpopular, when Aspar's son Ardaburius was involved in a sedition and when Leo was certain of his Isaurian Guard, he turned on Aspar and his family, just as Valentinian III had turned on Aetius and just as Anthemius had been about to break with Ricimer. Aspar and Ardaburius died but Patricius survived, as did a third son.[10]

This was the background in Constantinople to the emergence of Gundobad as military leader in Italy the following year. It is hardly surprising in the circumstances that Gundobad, despite his appointment by Olybrius, was viewed askance by Leo. Four months after the death of Olybrius, presumably after attempting negotiations with Leo without success, Gundobad appointed his own emperor, choosing a count of the Palace, Glycerius; once again, this replicated a known pattern: John and Castinus, Ricimer and Severus. The sources are quite explicit that the decision was Gundobad's and his alone.[11] He would no doubt have preferred Leo's approval, but Gundobad was only newly in power and he clearly felt that it was better to have the emperor in whose name he acted owe loyalty to him rather than have one that he could not trust foisted on him. There is no sign of the Senate being involved; indeed, the installation took place at Ravenna, and it may be that Glycerius never went to Rome as emperor.

Leo not only did not approve, he actively disapproved. He had sent Anthemius escorted by an army to take up his post by arrangement with Ricimer; he had sent Olybrius, escorted by another army, to either assist or replace Anthemius; now he sent yet another emperor with an army to displace the unwanted Glycerius. Leo must have been fully convinced of the weakness of the positions of both Gundobad and Glycerius to take the risk, and he was proved right. However, by the time the expedition was under way, Leo himself was dead. Another pair of complex succession crises in East and West had arrived simultaneously.

Anthemius, like Majorian and Avitus, had been too energetic for Ricimer to control properly; Libius Severus and Olybrius were so innocuous as to bring only contempt, and parts of Gaul and perhaps of Spain refused to obey them. Ricimer's problem was insoluble, and he was scarcely helped by the varying policy, or lack of it, of the Eastern emperors. Failure to support an emperor in the West soon led to that emperor's death; sending a man from the East could only damage Ricimer, who had to react to the threat by eliminating the Easterner. It was a situation that had no solution other than a massive Eastern expedition into Italy, which was beyond the strength of the East at the present, and the repeated gaps left between the death of one emperor and the appointment of the next indicate clearly the puzzlement that must have been felt. The simultaneous crisis in East and West that began in 474 proved at last to be fatal.

Imperial Puppets of Ricimer

Libius Severus (461–465). (*CNG Coins via Wikimedia Commons*)

Anthemius (467–472). (*CNG Coins via Wikimedia Commons*)

Olybrius (472).
(*NAC via Wikimedia Commons*)

Glycerius (473). (*Auktionshaus H. D. Rauch GmbH via Wikimedia Commons*)

Julius Nepos (473–480). (*CNG Coins via Wikimedia Commons*)

Romulus 'Augustulus' (475–476). (*CNG Coins via Wikimedia Commons*)

Chapter Nineteen

The Crisis of 474–476

It is perhaps a little misleading to single out the years 474–476 as a time of imperial succession crisis when the previous chapters have shown that there was in the West an almost continuous problem from the time of the death of Valentinian III. However, the removal of Ricimer in 472 and of Aspar in 471 – the former having provided a measure of continuity – had set up a new situation in both halves of the Empire. The rule of Leo in the East and the brief supremacy of Gundobad in the West delayed the next crisis until 474; it was the removal of both these men at much the same time that brought the new crisis to a head; and in the West it was terminal, so the description of the events in the mid 470s as a crisis is surely justified.

At the beginning of 474 the Emperors Leo and Glycerius were in office in Constantinople and Rome, and were squaring up to fight each other; in the next thirty months or so the two parts of the Empire saw seven more emperors or would-be emperors between them, ending with just one in power and he was to be challenged twice during the succeeding decades. This was a final crisis only for the Western Empire; in the East the same sort of brief dynasties punctuated by assassinations and coups continued for the next 1,000 years.

Leo died a natural death in January 474. He had no sons, but he was the father of two daughters: Ariadne, married to the Isaurian chieftain Zeno; and Leontia, who had been betrothed to Patricius, the son of Aspar, and so was at this point, with Patricius in rebellion, neither betrothed nor married. Leo nominated his grandson, the son of Ariadne and Zeno, as his successor (Leo II), but he was only 7 years old. A fortnight after Leo I died, Zeno was co-opted as joint Augustus along with Leo II. (See Genealogical Table XXII.) This was done technically by the young Leo, with the connivance of the Emperor Dowager Verina and the Senate, and the installation took place in public in the hippodrome. Here again, as with Marcian and Leo I, it was necessary for all the political elements – the previous emperor, the Senate and the public – to be involved in the coronation, though the army was not specifically represented.[1] The precedents went all the way back to Augustus' adoption of Agrippa.

Leo II died before the year was out and Zeno reigned alone. He survived for only a month and was in effect driven out by Verina and her brother

Basiliskos, who was then chosen as emperor by a group of 'men of power' in the city, as one source puts it; the group included at least two of the Isaurian senior commanders who might have been loyal to Zeno, but the Constantinopolitans then indulged in a massacre of other Isaurians in the city. Basiliskos had been technically made emperor by the Senate and went through a ceremony of coronation, but this took place inside the Palace, not in the public space of the hippodrome.[2]

Zeno fled from the city with some supporters and a substantial treasure, and holed up in a castle in his homeland. There he was put under siege by his former Isaurian colleagues who had supported Basiliskos. In the city Basiliskos' regime, being both voracious and heretic, rapidly became unpopular and messages went to Zeno from the city promising support. By suborning his besiegers, Zeno broke free and he was able to recover control of Constantinople by August 476.[3]

This confusion, compounded by intrigues by the supporters of both men, prevented the Constantinopolitan government from intervening in the parallel and simultaneous crisis in the West. Leo had sent a new emperor to dislodge Glycerius and Gundobad late in 473. His choice was Julius Nepos, governor of Dalmatia, and a relative by marriage of the Empress Verina. There was no resistance from either Glycerius or Gundobad. The latter was apparently distracted by the involvement of the Burgundians in fighting in Gaul, in which his father died. Gundobad, in fact, soon popped up again as king of the Burgundians; that is, he abandoned Glycerius to his fate in favour of a more comfortable role as Burgundian king. Glycerius' lack of resistance to Nepos permitted him to retire as Bishop of Spalato in Julius Nepos' former province of Dalmatia.

Nepos had travelled to Italy by sea, landing at Portus near Rome. He was proclaimed emperor by Zeno's representative, a man called Domitianus (Leo having died in the meantime). The ceremony, in a different place, was similar to that which emplaced Anthemius, but no local involvement can be seen other than a passive acceptance.[4] Domitianus may have been Zeno's man, but at the time Zeno was only precariously in control in Constantinople, so this did not imply that serious political and military help was available. By this time – June 474 – Leo II and Zeno were in power in Constantinople. It seems unlikely that they, or rather Zeno, bothered to reverse Leo's policy towards the West, even if they had the time, so Nepos would have continued to be acceptable in the East as the Western emperor.

Whatever help and support Nepos hoped for from the East ceased to be possible when Zeno was driven out of Constantinople in January 475. Nepos appointed Ecdicius, the son of the former Emperor Avitus, as *magister militum* for Gaul in order to contest the Visigothic advance in central Gaul, but he was defeated. So Nepos' Eastern and Western policies both failed. In addition he had, as it proved, no real basis of support within Italy. He ordered his *magister militum* in Italy, a man called Orestes, to relieve and succeed Ecdicius in Gaul but instead Orestes turned on his master and Nepos fled back to Dalmatia.[5]

Nepos, as a fifth-century emperor in Italy, was unusual in several aspects: he came at the head of an army to seize the Western throne by force. In this he followed other recent Easterners like Glycerius, but he seems to have done without a military commander as his minister, giving orders to his commanders directly. In these actions he was reminiscent of Majorian and Anthemius, and perhaps of Valentinian III at the end. He also made an apparently serious attempt to recover control in Gaul. He had been an active governor in Dalmatia and this background puts him in the tradition of active emperors in the later fifth century – Majorian, Avitus and Anthemius – compared with those who left the military work to their generals: Libius Severus, Valentinian III (for much of his reign), Glycerius and Olybrius. To make any serious progress, however, the Western emperor needed both local support in the West, particularly in Italy, and in the Western army, composed of barbarian mercenaries. He also required assistance from the East, but with Zeno beset and Leo dead, Nepos was alone. He seems to have gained little or no support in Italy, either from Italians or the military.

Orestes' career, if a particular connection is accepted, was strange. He was from a Pannonian family, and had spent time at the court of Attila until the Hun king's death in 453. Pannonia was a dangerous place in his youth, being on the frontier and subject to frequent attack, traversed repeatedly by armies of all sorts and repeatedly temporarily settled by barbarian groups. Orestes vanishes from our sight after Attila's death, only to reappear as the commander in Italy in 475. He was presumably one of Ricimer's officers, and he had been appointed as Ecdicius' successor as *magister militum* in central Gaul, where he had negotiated a peace treaty with the Visigoths. He was also married to the daughter of Romulus, one of Aetius' commanders. However, it seems that the 'Orestes-Romulus clan' was at enmity with the 'Royal Scirian clan', of which another of the commanders, Odoacer, was a part. The two were certainly at odds in 476.

Nepos fled from Italy, though he did not go any further than his old province of Dalmatia, nor did he abdicate; he continued to be recognized as emperor by Zeno. In Italy Orestes kept the position as *magister militum* for himself and put his own son on the throne.[6] This was a teenage boy called

Romulus, named for his grandfather. His appointment was a reversion to the puppet emperor style of Ricimer and Libius Severus. There is no sign in the (admittedly thin) records that there was any ceremony involved, though since Orestes was commander of the army, no doubt a military acclamation was laid on, but Orestes commanded the loyalty of only part of the army and other commanders were unenthusiastic. Their main demand was to be able to settle their barbarian soldiers on Italian lands; Orestes, perhaps because he looked to senatorial support, refused to allow this attempt to deprive senators of some of their property. This provided an opportunity for his enemies within the army, notably Odoacer, to take away Orestes' military support. He was killed and Odoacer seized control of the army, promising a distribution of land. Romulus was retired and lived out the rest of his life at the family villa in Campania.[7]

Zeno regained control of Constantinople in August 476, the same month that Orestes was killed and Romulus deposed. There were now three men in or close to Italy who had been emperors: Glycerius, Julius Nepos and Romulus. Of these, Nepos had retained some sort of recognition from the East, but he had fled from Italy without a fight when Orestes rose to power. He could be said to have abdicated. Certainly Glycerius had abdicated, and since he had for two years been Bishop of Spalato he was now ineligible to return, apart from which he was living in Nepos' territory and would never be allowed to leave to reclaim the throne. Romulus had never been recognized formally by anyone except his father and his father's faction in the army, and he was still a child; he could be ignored.

Zeno was beset by troubles as soon as he regained the Eastern throne, by invasions in the Balkans, by dissension in the royal family and by a serious shortage of money. He had no available or acceptable candidate for the Western throne, his predecessor having used up three in the past ten years. Anthemius had left three sons in the East, including one called Marcian who aspired to the Eastern throne a few years later, but none of them seems to have shown any interest in the West. In truth the history of the Western throne in the past two decades, since Valentinian III's murder of Aetius, would scarcely attract anyone.

Odoacer, no doubt, could have found a candidate in Italy if he had wanted to; there were hundreds of senators, after all. However, he had decided even before he forced the abdication of Romulus that an emperor in the West was no longer needed, for he had the army proclaim him as 'Rex' ('king') in August 476. He sent an embassy to Zeno, ostensibly in the name of the Senate and Romulus, announcing that the West no longer required an emperor. Zeno replied with a cunningly ambiguous letter, referring to Nepos as the West's rightful emperor, and saying that it was Nepos who should give Odoacer the title of *patricius* which he had requested and that he would confirm it if it was given. Then he ended a letter by addressing Odoacer as a 'patrician'. There was no reference to Odoacer's other title of king.[8]

By this time Spain, Africa, Gaul, the Danube lands and Britain had all been removed from the political authority wielded by anyone in power in Italy. Nepos was recognized in a distant way in Italy and coins were minted in his name, but when he asked for help to recover power there he received none; in 480 he was stabbed to death in a plot in which the other ex-emperor, Bishop Glycerius, was said to be involved. Odoacer took the opportunity to seize control of Nepos' Dalmatian territories in the name of revenge.

There had, perhaps, been no need for an emperor in the West for some time, but it is worth noting that as late as 471 Anthemius was able to send a force into Gaul to contest the advances of King Euric of the Visigoths, and in 472 Olybrius had been able to turn away a Gothic invasion of Italy, while Nepos had been able to appoint two commanders in Gaul as well: Ecdicius and Orestes. That is, even if they had only controlled Italy, Western Roman emperors were still relatively powerful, as Odoacer and Theoderic the Ostrogoth were to demonstrate; between them they ruled the same geographical area as the last of the emperors for the next half-century. Yet the emperors required a firm political base inside Italy to enable them to exercise power outside it. It was this that was their basic difficulty, for their forces owed allegiance to their immediate commanders and not to them. Odoacer's solution, settling his men on Italian land, was the best answer, and was followed by Theoderic; had Julius Nepos done so he might have succeeded in maintaining himself, for such men would owe their prosperity and patrimony to him, and if a precedent for settling soldiers on confiscated land was needed one need only go back as far as Augustus.

From one viewpoint the last twenty years had seen a defensive political campaign by these military commanders against the revival of imperial military pretensions. The death of Ricimer had opened the way for the emperors to reclaim more authority, and the desertion of Gundobad allowed Julius Nepos, an experienced commander, to place himself on the throne with the intention of acting as emperor-commander. This combination of military and civil power and authority would have been a solution to the crisis in the West, but imperial power could only expand at the expense of the military men and Nepos forfeited the chance of any accommodation with Odoacer.

Nor could the Eastern emperors always interfere with any success. Odoacer's message to Zeno in 476, sent in the name of the deposed Emperor Romulus and the Senate, that there was no need of an emperor in the West, was undoubtedly true – most of the West was already doing without – and clearly implied a recognition of Zeno as emperor in Italy. However, Odoacer was not about to accept Zeno's orders, so the message behind the letter was actually one of secession, not submission. The Empire in the West had ended, and it was the failure of the emperors to develop or operate a credible system of succession that was at the heart of the problem, for if a credible system had existed the military regents would have been much restricted in their interference.

Of the emperors since Valentinian III, three – Anthemius, Olybrius and Julius Nepos – had been the candidates of the Eastern emperors and had owed their positions to heredity in some way, though always because of a marriage connection and not a direct descent. This may not have been all that impressive, but it did give them a personal and political authority that was independent of the army commanders and so set up a tension that could only be resolved by one or other being removed. Had there been a clear and accepted system of succession – by heredity, by election or by any other means – that tension would probably not have developed. This was a central part of the problem of governing the Empire, one that had lain at the very heart of the imperial system from the beginning. Augustus had struggled his whole reign to develop an hereditary scheme and had failed; the Senate, the other obvious source of imperial authority, had intervened repeatedly in 68, in 96, in 193, in 238 and even in the last years, with senators as emperors and senatorial participation in installing new emperors. This had helped to prevent the development of an hereditary scheme, and yet had never had the authority to put a system of its own in place in its stead. So when the Senate's authority failed because of its divorce from the imperial government from the mid-third century onwards after Gallienus' law debarred senators from commands or governorships, the only authorities with power to impose any sort of system were existing emperors by appointing their own successors, or the army, which was by definition an erratic, inefficient and murderous entity, incapable of acting with any consistency.

If there is to be a monarchy, only heredity makes sense. This became the preferred system in Western Europe, partly under the influence of the Christian Church and partly because it was the preferred method of the barbarian invaders. In the surviving part of the Roman Empire in the East, however, (the 'Byzantine' Empire), the mixture of heredity punctuated by military *coups d'état* that had operated in the Empire as a whole since the death of Tiberius continued until 1453. Even in the face of the last Turkish assault on Constantinople, the position of the emperor remained unstable; the last emperor had seized power only in 1449.

Conclusion

The Roman Empire had a long life: from 30 BC to AD 476 in its 'imperial' phase, a matter of five centuries; several more centuries before as a Republic; and 1,000 years longer as the 'East Roman' or 'Byzantine' Empire centred at Constantinople. It is no surprise that conditions changed during that time, or that the methods of selecting emperors should alter. Change in the Roman Empire was always slow, though it clearly did take place. On the question of the methods of the succession of the emperors, change tended to be irregular and abrupt. It is perhaps more surprising that the basic elements involved in that selection and succession should still be the same at the end of that long period as they had been at the beginning. These were the previous emperor, the Senate and the army, and at times the Guard and the Roman population, though the Guard was essentially negative and the Romans had little influence for much of the time. Nevertheless, within that time, the importance of each of the elements did change and the interplay between them continued throughout the five centuries between Augustus and Ricimer. Each in turn seemed to control the process, but the others had a considerable influence as well.

There was a basic tension, or conflict, built into the process of finding an imperial successor, for the three essential players in the process had different priorities and claims to authority. The army required a commander, preferably one they already knew before he became emperor, and preferably one who was reasonably generous in his handing out of pay. The Senate, on the other hand, required a politician, a man who was familiar with social and political conditions in the city of Rome and one chosen by the senators themselves. This was a reflection of the Senate's original powers, the fact that the emperor was in effect a magistrate and that magistrates in the Republic had been elected. The Senate claimed an indefinite right of election, which shifted rather into one of investiture and acceptance, but remained a senatorial requirement which, throughout the Empire, was one of the marks of 'legitimacy'.

The influence or intention of the previous emperor was probably always the strongest element in the selection of his successor. This brought immediate conflict with the Senate, and less so with the army, for the automatic choice by an emperor of the man to succeed him would always be his son, if he had one. This hereditary impulse was the basic social building-block of Roman (and every other) society. So whereas the Senate claimed a residual right of confirmation (or refusal, presumably), the normal assumption would be that the emperor's successor would be his son or his nearest male relative. In that case, the Senate would have no role in the choice.

Normally the Senate would accept such hereditary succession, though it could at times resurrect its claim to confirmation with awkward results, but the main problem was that from the time of Augustus to the mid-third century (almost three centuries), only three emperors – Vespasian, Marcus Aurelius and Septimius Severus – had sons who could inherit. Whatever the reasons for this – a genetic condition, the unhealthiness of Rome or homosexuality – it is an extraordinary sequence of procreative failure.

Augustus' attempts to establish a dynasty were thus repeated by almost every emperor who came after him. His own failure to beget a son forced him into elaborate expedients for devising a succession system, and these reappeared throughout the history of the Empire in one guise or another. His one child was a daughter, so the pool of possible successors widened to include his marital relations. He resorted repeatedly to the adoption of ever more distant relations as his son or sons to pretend to an hereditary system. His innovation of suggested emperor-regents such as Agrippa and Tiberius was designed to safeguard the actual succession to those within his own family, and it was an expedient that was resorted to repeatedly by his more distant successors. It culminated in the near institutionalization of the office of patrician-cum-*magister militum*, or army commander, in the fifth century. Ricimer was a direct political descendant of Agrippa: both were rulers by virtue of their military prestige and the support of and their support for the actual emperor, and both married into the imperial family; right at the end Orestes was intending to rule for Romulus as regent for the under-age emperor.

The essential drawback of heredity as a succession system was fairly soon apparent. Gaius/Caligula arrived at the throne with virtually no training for rule, and his peculiar genius was to see that his actual powers were limitless; his fate then showed what happened to a man attempting to exercise that unlimited power. He was followed by an emperor who was widely regarded as being physically unfit, and then by a wilful child. Hereditary succession could produce monsters just as easily as competent men, but Gaius' realization of the sheer power at the emperor's disposal meant that the potential for monsters was significantly increased and the only way of dealing with such a phenomenon was by murder.

All these issues were in fact apparent from the start. Julius Caesar's murder came from his ambition and his sidelining of the traditional system of politics in Rome. Augustus finally, largely by luck, chose his stepson as his successor after neglecting him or favouring others for decades; Tiberius nominated his nearest male relative, who turned into the tyrant Gaius.

It was necessary for Augustus to keep the Senate informed of and involved in his plans, for the Senate still had much of the prestige and experience of its Republican predecessor. Yet Augustus treated it brutally, executing and exiling senators, and repeatedly purging it of men with whom he disagreed, thereby demonstrating his imperial power over it. Even so, it retained a central role in the determination of the succession all through the century after his death. In the civil warfare of 68–69 it came through virtually unscathed in authority, if not in personnel, but it over-reached itself in 96–97. By taking on a central role in elevating Nerva, the Senate effectively claimed the ultimate right to decide the imperial succession. The senators were relying on the prestige of their House and on the effectiveness of their emperor, but politics in the Roman Empire was founded less on influence and more on physical force. It was soon revealed that the Senate's authority was in fact very limited and the Senate's emperor could be forced by threat of death to do the generals' will. Then the near-brutal insistence of the army commanders in conclave on the Danube that Nerva must adopt Trajan as his successor showed exactly where the real power in the Empire lay, and effectively reduced both the Guard – which had developed exaggerated ideas of its influence – and the Senate to subordination. For the next century and a half, until 238, the Senate's role was as a ratifying body only: the decision on the succession was always made elsewhere, by the reigning emperor until 192, then by the army and the reigning emperor, either together or in competition.

The dethronement of the Senate was, however, not solely to the advantage of the army but mainly to that of the sitting emperors. From Trajan to Commodus the successor was always a man designated by the emperor before his death. This had also been the case before Nerva, of course, with the Flavians, but they had gone through the old motions, originating with Augustus, of ensuring that the designated successor accumulated many consulships, thereby involving the Senate in the process, but Trajan and Hadrian did not bother to designate their successors till the very end of their lives (or even, in Trajan's case, after his own death). In both cases, the choice was a senator, but neither man had been singled out in the traditional way beforehand; both Trajan and Hadrian were consulars, but with only one consulship each to their names when they became emperor. There was a considerable number of other men who had more consulships at the time of their accession; that is, the prestige of such offices was much less from Trajan's accession onwards. In theory, of course, this allowed the emperors to select the most suitable candidate; in fact, it turned out to be very messy in both cases: Trajan mounted a coup against Nerva, and Hadrian's search for a successor was murderous. Then when an emperor had an heir of his own body and so had an obvious successor in place from birth, it turned out to be Commodus.

Trajan, Hadrian and Marcus all paid more attention to the army than to the Senate in considering the imperial succession, the result of the generals' coup that brought Trajan to power. Septimius and Caracalla took up that emphasis and expanded it, even further reducing the influence of the Senate. This did not remove the Senate's pretensions, however, but attempted revivals of senatorial authority in 193 and under Alexander Severus were only temporary, yet did succeed in 238 and for several decades after that. This was not a revival at the expense of the army so much as one at the expense of the imperial office. The army, like the old Praetorian Guard, whose apparent power was similarly crushed by Septimius with little effort, was always better at knocking down emperors than finding new ones. The trouble with senatorial selection was that the Senate's criteria for suitability – in particular age and senatorial experience – did not impress the army, and were no longer those that were the best for the Empire in the third century. The rapid removal of emperors between 235 and 284 gave plenty of scope for senatorial influence, but when an emperor was required in the midst of a military campaign the choice had to be left to the army in the field, and this prioritized military command skills above all else, though such men were less effective as politicians. So, for that half-century, the balance of influence between army, Senate and ruling emperor oscillated; in the end it came down on the army's side, first under Carus and his family, and then Diocletian, none of whom paid any heed to the Senate.

The Tetrarchy was, in effect, a military dictatorship. Diocletian had total disdain for the Senate, but carefully maintained his grip on the army and his appointed imperial colleagues. His experimental reforms, of which his organization of the imperial succession was one of the strangest, was just the sort of centralizing and controlling measures to be expected of a general indulging in politics. His succession scheme was apparently designed to promote competent generals from within the army and then cement them into a rigid system, enhanced by intermarriage. Yet it failed at its first test, knocked over by Constantine and Maxentius in favour, once again, of the hereditary principle. The aim of Augustus three centuries earlier had been to establish a dynasty and it had repeatedly emerged with later emperors as well; only with Constantine could it be said that a clear case of a dynastic succession had been finally and successfully established, yet Constantine's dynasty only lasted for three generations.

The Senate's interest in becoming involved in the succession never died, despite the triumph of the army and of the hereditary principle. With these being the determining factors, the scope for senatorial influence faded in the fourth century, but in the end in the West in the fifth century, it partly revived. Between 409 and 475 senatorial candidates for the throne repeatedly emerged, as pretenders, as brief rulers or as actual emperors: Priscus Attalus, Petronius Maximus, Libius Severus and perhaps Avitus and Olybrius. Not since the Gordians and Valerian had so many senators been able to reach the top.

This, however, was also one of the problems that overwhelmed the Western part of the Empire at that time. The last two decades of the Empire in the West, from the time of Valentinian's murder of Aetius in 454, saw another period of oscillating influences as each interested group attempted to install its own man as emperor: the Eastern government, the army commander (*magister militum* or patrician) and the Senate. These were the same elements that had been Augustus' concern five centuries earlier. Then they had been the ruling emperor, the army and the Guard, and the Senate; in the fifth century they emerged as the emperor in Constantinople, the army's warlord and the senators. The balance struck by Augustus between these groups and interests had rocked back and forth, with each having its time of predominant influence ever since. Yet the inherent conflict between them was never resolved and was still being played out in the 470s.

It proved in the end to be an unsustainable tension, even though it had by then operated for five centuries. The final victory went to the army, in the person of Odoacer in 476. It is curious that it was the demand for land for the soldiers that was one of the main problems provoking Odoacer's break with the Empire, for this had been one of the main demands of the several generals whose power had brought the Republic to its knees, and solving it for the time being had been one of Augustus' main achievements. In both cases it was the reluctance of the Senate to comply with the army's demands that provoked the generals into action.

However, the army in the fifth century was no longer the army of the Republic, or even of two centuries before, one composed of citizens or aspirant citizens. Now it was a barbarian war band, and one liable to be all too easily defeated by a competing war band. Therefore the establishment of full control by the army commander meant that what the three groups were fighting for – the Empire itself – was brought down in ruins around them. This was not the inevitable result. In the first two decades of the century dynastic and senatorial emperors had survived rather longer than the army's candidates. In the East, where the senatorial and army influences were so much weaker, the dynastic principle, as modified by *coups d'état* at irregular intervals – in effect the normal system since the death of Gaius – remained the norm for the next 1,000 years.

There was no real reason why this could not have been the case in the West as well. Even as late as 470 the Western emperors' authority extended throughout Italy and its borderlands and into much of Gaul and Spain, and the barbarian settlers within the frontiers were federates – part of the imperial system – and in several cases more than willing to work to sustain the Empire. Recovery, as the third-century crisis had shown and as Justinian demonstrated later, remained perfectly possible. It was the constant disputes over the powers and the person of the emperor in the West that were debilitating, far more so than any fighting with the barbarians. The effective secession of much of the Empire outside Italy was due to the absence of an emperor to whom the Romans in those territories could direct their allegiance, and this made it all too easy for the barbarian kings – notably Geiseric and Euric – to seize and expand their lands and to repudiate imperial authority. Allegiance could not be given to a barbarian *magister militum*, especially when he was liable to dethrone or murder his nominal imperial master and then to leave the throne empty for long periods. It was the disabling tension between emperor and warlord in Italy that paralysed the Western Empire. Odoacer's decision to eliminate the emperor was perfectly rational and permitted a revival of power in Italy, but it was too late to revive the whole of the West; a powerful emperor might have eliminated the warlords, as Valentinian III attempted to do, with the same result. On the other hand, the system of a warlord and an ineffective emperor that had existed since Honorius' time had elements of stability in it and could well have lasted indefinitely. Yet the disagreement between Odoacer, Orestes and the Senate persuaded Odoacer that a *roi-fainéant* ('do-nothing king') kind of emperor was a useless appendage. The emperorship in the West was abolished, and along with it the Empire itself, in this casual manner, as a result of a personal-political disagreement.

The continual disputes over who should be emperor were all effort that could have been more profitably directed elsewhere. In the 60s the success of Corbulo in war in the East was felt by the profoundly unmilitary Emperor Nero to be a threat, and his order for the general to commit suicide was one of the factors that drained the last support for him; in AD 96 senators and others conspired to murder the Emperor Domitian just as he was about to set off to the frontier to lead a major trans-frontier offensive aimed at the conquest of at least Bohemia, one that could well have succeeded. This would have been a change to the northern frontier of much greater strategic significance than Trajan's conquest of Dacia a decade later (and that had to be abandoned later); it was prevented by the senatorial plot. In 238 Maximinus' trans-frontier intentions were sabotaged by the Senate's recognition of Gordian I and II and then its elevation of Balbinus and Papienus. Emperors were repeatedly struck down in the midst of attempts to eliminate the problem of the Eastern frontier, sometimes by disease, occasionally by wounds, often by a murderous plot among their own officers: Germanicus, Trajan, Lucius Verus, Caracalla, Gordian III and Julian, to name but a few. This may be a sign of imperial over-extension, but the agent of striking down was all too often the Senate. It is difficult to accept that senators had the welfare of the Empire as a whole at heart.

Incidentally it is noticeable that the beneficiaries of the murders of emperors were rarely those who carried out the killing. The typical case is the first: the killing of Gaius; he was murdered by a soldier, but then his fellows were at a loss as to what to do until Claudius was found in the Palace. Claudius' killing, if it was murder, did benefit Nero and his mother, though Agrippina, the presumed murderess, was herself soon murdered by her son. Galba's murder only benefited its author Otho for a few months. Vitellius' killing scarcely benefited Vespasian, who had won the civil war already. Domitian's murder did benefit Nerva, who was promoted as the next emperor, but he proved a fairly weak ruler and held power for less than a year before the army coup that made Trajan his heir also sidelined Nerva himself. Commodus' murder briefly brought Pertinax and Didius Iulianus to the throne and they were probably involved in the plot to kill him, but the eventual beneficiary was Septimius, who had not been involved in the killing.

So it went on: the killers of Commodus, Elagabalus and Maximinus did not benefit. The killers of Geta, Caracalla, Macrinus and Alexander Severus did, from anything from a year to six years, but this is scarcely a mark of great success. In the third century, murders of emperors became routine, but they were often followed by conclaves of generals to choose a new ruler and the eventual chosen one was normally not involved in the original plot. The beneficiary of Geta's death was his co-ruler Caracalla, and it was Constantius II who benefited from the murders of his brothers but he was not party to the deeds. In the fifth century it could be said that Petronius Maximus benefited by his murder of Valentinian III, but only for a couple of months; the beneficiaries from Petronius Maximus' own killing (by the Romans) were the Vandals (who sacked Rome). Killers of the emperors from Majorian onwards tended to be non-emperors like Ricimer.

This was therefore a most inefficient way of changing rulers. If the murder was a spur-of-the-moment deed like that of Gaius or Commodus it only produced confusion; if it was the result of a plot, the new ruler's regime was irremediably stained from the start and, of course, it only revealed that it was possible to gain power by a plot and murder. To those who feared or were disgusted by a ruling emperor, however, his killing was the only way of changing things. The absence of any less lethal method of replacing a ruling emperor made murder the only option, unless it was a rising in rebellion and instituting a civil war, in which many more people would die than by the assassination of a single man.

The common factor in all the murders and crises was the failure of the Roman governing system to devise an intelligible and workable system of imperial succession. It is, after all, not something that is too difficult to arrange. Hellenistic kingdoms achieved it from an even less convincing constitutional basis than that of Augustus; the barbarian kings camped in the territory of the Empire had done so; mediaeval Christian states succeeded in doing so; modern democracies have managed it; even empires have produced workable systems, though they have often found it much more difficult than more compact states, since by definition a great empire lacks the legitimacy of a traditional kingdom or city and the rewards of seizing power are always greater. It is a mark of the basic incapacity of the Roman political system: at first the monarchy failed, then its successor Republic (eventually doing so repeatedly over a period of a century and more), and then its method of imperial succession also failed. It did not much matter which of the possible schemes of succession could be settled on: dynastic succession, primogeniture, election for life or for a period of time, or military dictatorship. It was the failure to settle on any of these that was one of the major causes of the fall of the Empire.

List of Emperors

(Table VI)

In the following list the titles of Imperator, Caesar and Augustus are generally omitted since virtually all emperors bore them; the names they are usually known by are capitalized. All dates, except the first three, are AD; many, especially for the later emperors, are only approximate.

The column headed 'Date of Death' includes emperors who ceased the rule before their deaths: Macrinus (deposed), Valerian (captured by the Persians), Tetricus (abdicated), Diocletian (abdicated) and Romulus (deposed). These are marked with an asterisk. Omitted are 'emperors' who reigned only briefly as sons of their fathers and not independently.

Name	Accession Date	Date of Death	Position before Accession
C. Julius CAESAR	48 BC	16/3/44 BC	Provincial governor
Imp. Caesar AUGUSTUS	16/1/27 BC	19/8/14	Victor in civil war
TIBERIUS Caesar	17/9/14	16/3/37	Heir; general
GAIUS Caesar Germanicus (CALIGULA)	18/3/37	24/1/41	Heir
Ti. CLAUDIUS Caesar Germanicus	24/1/41	13/10/54	Courtier
NERO Claudius Caesar Germanicus	13/10/54	9/6/68	Heir
Ser. Sulpicius GALBA	8/6/68	15/1/69	Provincial governor
M. Salvius OTHO	15/1/69	16/4/69	Provincial governor
VITELLIUS	2/1/69	20/12/69	Provincial governor
T. Flavius VESPASIANus	1/7/69	23/7/79	General and governor
TITUS Flavius Vespasianus	24/6/79	13/9/81	Heir; general
T. Flavius DOMITIANus	14/9/81	18/9/96	Heir
M. Cocceius NERVA	18/9/96	27/1/98	Senator; courtier

Name	Accession Date	Date of Death	Position before Accession
M. Ulpius Nerva TRAJANus	28/1/98	7/8/117	Provincial governor
T. Aelius Traianus HADRIANUS	11/8/117	10/7/138	Provincial governor
T. Aelius Hadrianus ANTONINUS PIUS	10/7/138	7/3/161	Senator
MARCUS AURELIUS Antoninus	7/3/161	7/3/180	Heir
LUCIUS Aurelius VERUS	7/3/161	–/2/167	Heir
M. Aurelius COMMODUS Antoninus	17/3/180	31/12/192	Heir
P. Helvius PERTINAX	1/1/193	28/3/193	City Prefect
M. DIDIUS Severus JULIANUS	28/3/193	2/6/193	Senator
L. SEPTIMIUS SEVERUS Pertinax	9/4/193	4/2/211	Provincial governor
D. CLODIUS Septimius ALBINUS	9/4/193	19/2/197	Provincial governor
PESCENNIUS NIGER Justus	9/4/193	–/4/194	Provincial governor
M. Aurelius Antoninus (CARACALLA)	4/2/211	8/4/217	Heir
P. Septimius GETA	4/2/211	–/12/212	Heir
M. Opellius MACRINUS	11/4/217	8/6/218*	Palace official
M. Aurelius Antoninus (ELAGABALUS)	16/5/218	11/3/222	Child; priest
M. Aurelius SEVERUS ALEXANDER	13/3/222	–/3/235	Heir presumptive
Julius Verus MAXIMINUS (THRAX)	–/3/235	–/3/238	Soldier
M. Antonius GORDIANus Sempronianus Africanus Senior (I)	–/1/238	20/1/238	Provincial governor
M. Antonius GORDIANus Sempronianus Africanus Junior (II)	–/1/238	20/1/238	Provincial governor's aide
Caelius Calvinus BALBINUS	–/1/238	–/4/238	Senator
M. Clodius PUPIENUS	–/1/238	–/4/238	Senator
M. Antonius GORDIANus (III)	–/2/238	–/2/244	Heir

Name	Accession Date	Date of Death	Position before Accession
M. Julius PHILIPus	–/3/244	–/3/249	Praetorian Prefect
Messius Quintus Traianus DECIUS	–/3/249	–/6/251	Senator
Vibius TREBONIANUS GALLUS	–/6/251	–/8/253	Provincial governor
M. Aemilius AEMILIANUS	–/8/253	–/10/253	Provincial governor
P. Licinius VALERIANus	–/10/253	–/9/260*	Provincial governor
P. Licinius Egnatius GALLIENUS	–/10/253	–/9/268	Heir
M. Cassianus Latinius POSTUMUS	–/7/260	–/4/269	Provincial governor
M. Aurelius CLAUDIUS (II) GOTHICUS	–/9/268	–/9/270	General
M. Piavvonnius VICTORINUS	–/–/269	–/?3/271	Praetorian Prefect
M. Aurelius Claudius QUINTILLUS	–/9/270	–/9/270	General
L. Domitius AURELIANus	–/10/270	–/10/275	General
Pius Esuvius TETRICUS	–/4/271	–/2/274*	Provincial governor
M. Claudius TACITUS	–/11/275	–/7/276	Senator
M. Annius FLORIANus	–/7/276	–/9/276	Senator
M. Aurelius PROBUS	–/7/276	–/9/282	Provincial governor
M. Aurelius CARUS	–/9/282	–/8/283	Praetorian Prefect
M. Aurelius Numerius NUMERIANus	–/9/282	–/11/284	Heir
M. Aurelius CARINUS	–/9/282	–/8/285	Heir
M. Aurelius Valerius DIOCLETIANus	20/11/284	1/5/305*	Guard commander
M. Aurelius Valerius MAXIMIANus	–/10/285 –/11/306	1/5/305* –/7/310	General
M. Aurelius Maus. CARAUSIUS	–/–/286	–/–/293	Fleet commander
ALLECTUS	–/–/293	–/–/296	Financial official
Flavius Valerius CONSTANTIUS I	1/5/305	25/7/306	Praetorian Prefect; sub-emperor
GALERIUS Valerius Maximinianus	1/5/305	–/5/311	Praetorian Prefect; sub-emperor

Flavius Valerius SEVERUS	–/8/306	–/?/307	Praetorian Prefect; sub-emperor
Name	*Accession Date*	*Date of Death*	*Position before Accession*
M. Aurelius Valerius MAXENTIUS	28/10/306	28/10/312	Son of retired emperor
Flavius Valerius CONSTANTINUS	25/7/306	22/5/337	Heir
Valerius Licinianus LICINIUS	11/11/308	19/9/324*	Praetorian Prefect?
Valerius Galerius MAXIMINus DAIA	–/5/311	–//313	Soldier
Flavius Julius CONSTANTINUS II	9/9/337	–/3/340	Heir
Flavius Julius CONSTANS	9/9/337	–/1/350	Heir
Flavius Julius CONSTANTIUS II	9/9/337	3/11/361	Heir
Flavius Magnus MAGNENTIUS	18/1/350	10/8/353	Soldier
Flavius Claudius JULIANus	–/2/360	27/6/363	Provincial governor
Flavius JOVIANus	27/6/363	17/2/364	Soldier
Flavius VALENTINIANus	26/2/364	17/11/375	Soldier
Flavius Iulius VALENS	9/8/364	27/3/378	Soldier
Flavius GRATIANus	17/11/375	25/8/383	Heir
Flavius VALENTINIANus II	22/11/375	15/8/392	Heir
Flavius THEODOSIUS I	19/1/379	17/1/395	Provincial governor
Flavius MAGNUS MAXIMUS	383	28/8/388	Provincial governor
Flavius EUGENIUS	22/8/392	6/9/394	Palace official
Flavius ARCADIUS	17/1/395	1/5/408	Heir
Flavius HONORIUS	23/1/395	27/8/423	Heir
Flavius CONSTANTINE III	407	18/9/411	Soldier
Flavius THEODOSIUS Iunior II	10/1/408	28/7/450	Heir
Flavius CONSTANTIUS III	21/8/421	2/9/421	*Magister militum*
JOHN (Johannes)	423	–/6/425	Palace official

306 The Roman Imperial Succession

Flavius Placidus VALENTINIAN III	23/10/425	16/3/455	Heir
Flavius MARCIANus	25/8/450	26/1/457	Courtier
Name	*Accession Date*	*Date of Death*	*Position before Accession*
Flavius Anicius PETRONIUS MAXIMUS	17/3/455	2/6/455	Senator
M. Maecilius Flavius Eparchius AVITAS	10/7/455	17/10/456	Praetorian Prefect
Flavius Valerius LEO I	7/2/457	18/1/474	Courtier
Flavius Iulius Valerius MAJORIANus	1/4/457	2/8/461	Soldier
Flavius LIBIUS SEVERUS Serpentinus	19/11/461	–/9/465	Senator
Procopius ANTHEMIUS	12/4/467	11/7/472	Soldier; courtier
Anicius OLYBRIUS	–/4/472	2/11/472	Courtier
Flavius GLYCERIUS	5/3/473	–/6/473*	Courtier
Flavius JULIUS NEPOS	–/6/473	–/6/480	Provincial governor
Flavius LEO II	8/1/474	17/11/474	Heir
Flavius ZENO	9/2/474	9/4/491	Courtier
Flavius BASILISCUS	–/1/475	–/8/476	Imperial relative
Flavius ROMULUS AUGUST[UL]US	31/10/475	31/8/476	Child

Notes

Introduction

1. The only study I have been able to discover that considers the issue is by Blanche Parsi, *Désignation et Investiture de l'Empereur Romain*, Paris 1963, though, as the title shows, it is much more restricted in scope than succession as a whole; M. Hammond, 'The Tribunician Day During the Early Empire', *Memoirs of the American Academy at Rome*, 15, 1938, is also relevant. For the powers and duties of the emperor treated thematically, see Fergus Miller, *The Emperor in the Roman World*, London 1977, and on a smaller scale Barry Baldwin, *The Roman Emperors*, Québec 1980, though neither considers the issue of accession, despite their thematic approaches. From the very opposite angle to this study, there is also F. Meijer, *Emperors Don't Die in Bed*, trans. S.J. Leinach, London 2001. Adrastos Omissi, *Emperors and Usurpers in the Later Roman Empire*, Oxford 2018, takes the idea of a usurper seriously.

Chapter 1

1. By modern convention he is called Octavian until he was awarded the special title of Augustus by the Senate in 27 BC.
2. Biographies of Augustus always examine the 'restoration of the Republic': R. Holland, *Augustus: Godfather of Europe*, Stroud 2004, W. Eck, *The Age of Augustus*, trans. D.L. Schneider, Oxford 2003, are recent works; note also A.H.M. Jones, *Augustus*, London 1970, and the essay by G. Bowersock in F. Millar and E. Segal, *Caesar Augustus: Seven Aspects*, Oxford 1984.
3. The early attempts by Augustus to find and train successors (Marcellus, Agrippa, Gaius and Lucius) are briefly referred to by Tacitus, *Annals* 1.2–4, Suetonius, *Augustus* 63, 65, and Cassius Dio, book 56.
4. Tiberius' selection is discussed by Suetonius, *Augustus* 97–101, and *Tiberius* 7–26, Tacitus, *Annals* 1.3–8, Velleius Paterculus II.123–125, and Cassius Dio 56.31–47.
5. Tacitus, *Annals* 1.3; Cassius Dio 56.30.
6. The most accessible modern study of Tiberius is B. Levick, *Tiberius the Politician*, London 1976.
7. Tacitus, *Annals* 1.4; Cassius Dio 56; see also the account in Meijer, *Emperors*, 19–20.
8. Tacitus, *Annals* 1.5–15.
9. Tacitus, *Annals* 1.4–5; Suetonius, *Tiberius* 22.
10. Tacitus, *Annals* 1.18–29.
11. Tacitus, *Annals* 1.30–48.

Chapter 2
1. Tacitus, *Annals* 1.11–15; Suetonius, *Tiberius* 23–25; B. Levick, *Tiberius the Politician*, London 1976, 71–81.
2. Suetonius, *Tiberius* 25.
3. Tacitus, *Annals* 3.56.
4. Suetonius, *Tiberius* 54–55.
5. Levick, *Tiberius*, ch. 10.
6. Agrippina: Tacitus, *Annals* 4.75; Drusilla and Julia Livilla: Tacitus, *Annals* 6.15.1; Julia: Tacitus, *Annals* 6.27.1.
7. Tacitus, *Annals* 6.46.
8. Tacitus, *Annals*, 6.50; Suetonius, *Tiberius* 73.
9. *PIR* A 32.
10. Tacitus, *Annals* 6.50.6.
11. Josephus, *AJ* 18.124; *ILS* 19.
12. Suetonius, *Caligula* 14.1; Cassius Dio 59.3.1–2.
13. Suetonius, 58.2–3; Josephos *AJ* 19.105–113; Cassius Dio 59.29.7.
14. The conspiracy is discussed in A. Barratt, *Caligula: The Corruption of Power*, London 1989.
15. Josephus *AJ* 19.180; Suetonius, *Claudius* 10.
16. Josephus *AJ* 19.188–284, and *BJ* 2.205–214; Suetonius, *Caligula* 60 and *Claudius* 10; Cassius Dio 60.1.1–4.
17. Suetonius, *Caligula* 15.2 (adoption); and 23.3 (death); Cassius Dio 59.8.1–2.
18. Suetonius, *Caligula* 24.1; Barrett, *Caligula*, ch. 6.
19. A clear account is in B. Levick, *Claudius*, London 1990, ch. 4.
20. Suetonius, *Claudius* 13.2; Cassius Dio 60.15.1–16.8.
21. Tacitus, *Annals* 12.69; Suetonius, *Claudius* 45: M.T. Griffin, *Nero: The End of a Dynasty*, London 1985, 32–33.

Chapter 3
1. The conspiracy of Piso is in Tacitus, *Annals*, 15.46–74.
2. Suetonius, *Nero* 36.1.
3. Suetonius, *Galba* 6–12; Plutarch, *Galba* 6.3.23; Tacitus, *Histories* 1.13.4 and 1.53.
4. Suetonius, *Galba* 11; Plutarch, *Galba* 6.4–7.3.
5. Suetonius, *Nero* 47–49; Plutarch, *Galba* 2; Tacitus, *Histories* 1.3: Cassius Dio 63.29.1.
6. Plutarch, *Galba* 19–21 and 23; Tacitus, *Histories* 1.12–19.
7. Tacitus, *Histories*, Plutarch, *Galba*, *Otho*; Suetonius, *Galba*, *Otho*, *Vitellius*, *Vespasian*; modern accounts include M. Griffin, *Nero: The End of a Dynasty*, London 1984, K. Wellesley, *The Long Year, A.D. 69*, 2nd ed., London 1988, P.A.L. Greenhalgh, *The Year of the Four Emperors*, London 1975, Gwyn Morgan, *69 A.D.: The Year of the Four Emperors*, Oxford 2006.
8. Plutarch, *Galba* 22–27; Suetonius, *Galba* 19–20; Tacitus *Histories* 1.27–46.
9. Tacitus, *Histories* 1.47; Suetonius, *Otho* 6–7; Plutarch, *Galba* 27–28.
10. Suetonius, *Vitellius* 8; he took the title Augustus later.
11. Tacitus, *Histories* 4.3.3.

Chapter 4

1. Tacitus, *Histories* 4.3.3.
2. Commemorated on a coin of c.70: M. McCrum and A.G. Woodhead, *Select Documents of the Principates of the Flavian Emperors, AD 69–96*, Cambridge 1961, no. 85.
3. Cassius Dio 65.12.1; Suetonius, *Vespasian* 25.
4. B. Levick, *Vespasian*, London 1999, 88–89 for the discussion and authorities.
5. Suetonius, *Titus* 9.3.
6. Suetonius, *Titus* 11.
7. Suetonius, *Domitian* 12.3: for discussion see B.W. Jones, *The Emperor Domitian*, London 1992, 44–47.
8. Suetonius, *Domitian*, 15.1; Jones, *Domitian* 47–48.

Chapter 5

1. Suetonius, *Domitian* 17; Cassius Dio 57.15.1–5.
2. The ancient evidence for Nerva is collected by A. Birley in *Lives of the Later Caesars*, Harmondsworth 1976, 29–37; Syme, *Tacitus*, 1–9 and 627–629; also J.D. Grainger, *Nerva and the Roman Succession Crisis of AD 96–99*, London 2003, for details of the plot and the murder.
3. Sir Ronald Syme, *Tacitus*, vol. 1, Oxford 1958, 1.
4. Cassius Dio 68.3.2; *Epitome de Caesaribus* 12.6.
5. Birley, *Lives* 38–39.
6. Birley, *Lives* 35–36.
7. Grainger, *Nerva* 92–94; this is speculative, based on only fragments of evidence.
8. Cassius Dio 68.3.4.
9. Cassius Dio 68.4.2; *Epitome de Caesaribus* 12.10–11.

Chapter 6

1. A.R. Birley, *Hadrian: The Restless Emperor*, London 1997.
2. Cassius Dio 69.1.1–2.1.
3. Cassius Dio 69.2.2.
4. *HA, Hadrian* 5.2.
5. *HA Hadrian* 6.8; Cassius Dio 69.2.5–6.
6. *HA Hadrian* 23.10; Birley, *Hadrian* 289–291.
7. Cassius Dio 69.12.1; *HA Hadrian* 15.8, 23.2, 23.8 and 25.8; Birley, *Hadrian* 291–292.
8. *HA Hadrian* 23.15–16 and *Aelius* 6.6–7; Cassius Dio 69.20.1.
9. *HA Hadrian* 26.6 and *Antoninus* 4.4–7; Cassius Dio 69.20.1–21.2.
10. This has provoked some legalistic theories: J. Carcopino, 'l'Hérédité dynastique chez les Antonins', *Revue des Études Anciennes* 51, 1949, 262–321, P. Grenade, 'Le Règlement successoral d'Hadrien', *Revue des Études Anciennes* 52, 1950, 258–277, and H.G. Pflaum, 'Le Règlement Successoral d'Hadrien', *Historia Augustae Colloquium, Bonn 1963*, Bonn 196, 95–122.
11. *HA Marcus* 7.3–5.
12. Cassius Dio 71.1–3.
13. *HA Commodus* 1.10–13.

14. *HA* Avidius; R. Syme, 'Avidius Cassius: His Rank, Age and Quality', *Bonner Historia Augusta Colloquium 1984/1985*, Bonn 1986, 207–222; Maria Laura Astarita, *Avidio Cassio*, Rome 1983.

Chapter 7

1. *HA Commodus* 16; *Pertinax* 4.4–6; Cassius Dio 72.19.1–22.6; Herodian 1.15–17.
2. *HA Pertinax* 4.5–7; Cassius Dio 73.1.1–3.
3. *HA Pertinax* 5.1–6.2; Cassius Dio 73.1.5–2.3; A. Birley, *Septimius Severus: The African Emperor*, London 1988, 87–91.
4. *HA Pertinax* 10.8–11.13; Cassius Dio 73.9.1–10.
5. Cassius Dio 73.11.2–4; *HA Didius Iulianus* 2.6–7; Herodian 2.6.8–14.
6. *HA Severus* 5.1–5; Herodian 2.10.1–9; *Epitome de Caesaribus* 19.2; Birley, *Septimius* 97–98.
7. *HA Didius Iulianus* 8.2–8; Cassius Dio 74.17.1–5.
8. *HA Severus* 5.1–10.
9. *HA Severus* 6.11; Cassius Dio 75.1.1–2; Herodian 2.13.1.
10. Herodian 2.14.3–4: *HA Severus* 7.4–7; Cassius Dio 74.2.1–2.

Chapter 8

1. *HA Pescennius Niger*, 1.1; the greater part of this biography is either fiction or plagiarized from other biographies.
2. A.R. Birley, *Septimius Severus: The African Emperor*, London 117; the sources for this are coins (*British Museum Catalogue* V, p.136) and a rather confused passage in *HA Severus* 10.3–6; Commodus' deification was proclaimed later.
3. *HA Severus* 10.7–11.8.
4. *HA Severus* 16.8; Birley, *Septimius* 139–140.
5. Cassius Dio 76.15.2–3.
6. *HA Caracalla* 2.4–6; Cassius Dio 77.2.1–6.
7. *HA Caracalla* 2.7–8; Cassius Dio 77.3.1–2.
8. *HA Caracalla* 2.9–11; Cassius Dio 77.3.3.
9. *HA Caracalla* 6.6; Cassius Dio 78.5.4–5; Herodian 4.13.1–7.2.
10. *HA Macrinus* 2.5; Cassius Dio 78.11.4–12.7.
11. Cassius Dio 78.33.1–40.1.
12. For the various women involved see Barbara Levick, *Julia Domna: Syrian Empress*, London 2007, and Geoffrey Turton, *The Syrian Princesses: The Women who Ruled Rome AD 193–235*, London 1974.
13. Cassius Dio 79.17.2–3; Elagabalus is an irresistible subject for biography, see Martijn Icks, *The Crimes of Elagabalus: The Life and Legacy of Rome's Decadent Boy Emperor*, London 2013.
14. *PIR* G 123.
15. *HA Elagabalus* 16.5–17.3; *HA Severus Alexander* 1.1–3; Cassius Dio 79.19.4–20.2.
16. *HA Severus Alexander* 49.3; G. Barbieri, *L'Albo Senatorio da Settimio Severo a Carino (193–285)*, Rome 1952, no 463; R. Syme, *Emperors and Biography*, Oxford 1971, 157; much here is vague and speculative.
17. *Sybilline Oracles* 13.147–153; H.R. Baldus, *Uranius Antoninus*, Bonn 1971.

18. *HA Severus Alexander* 15.6–16.3; Herodian 6.1.2.
19. Herodian 6.9.4–5.
20. A recent biography is Paul N. Pearson, *Maximinus Thrax: From Common Soldier to Emperor of Rome*, Barnsley 2016.
21. Herodian 7.1.9: *HA Thirty Tyrants* 32.1; *HA Maximin* 11.1–6.
22. *HA Maximin* 10.1–6, and *Thirty Tyrants* 32.1.

Chapter 9

1. 'Revolution' was a term used by Prescott W. Townend, 'The Revolution of AD 238: The Leaders and Their Aims', *Yale Classical Studies 14*, 1955, 49–105; it is, perhaps, going a little too far.
2. Herodian 7.3.5.
3. Herodian 7.4.2–5.7; *HA Gordians* 7.2–9.5.
4. Herodian 7.6.3–4; *HA Gordians* 9.6–8.
5. Karen Haegemans, 'The Representation and Perception of Imperial Power in AD 238: The Numismatic Evidence', in L. de Blois (ed.), *The Representation and Perception of Roman Imperial Power: Proceedings of the Third Workshop of the International Network, Impact of Empire, Rome 2002*, Amsterdam 2003.
6. Discussed with a listing of the extensive discussions, by Christian Settipani, *Continuite Gentilice et Continuite Familiale dans les Familles Senatoriales Romaines a l'Epoque Imperiale*, Oxford 2000, 135–138; three possible lines of descent are noted.
7. *HA Gordians* 7.2.
8. Herodian 7.7.2; *HA Gordians* 11.1–10 (including clearly invented speeches).
9. *HA Maximinus* 17.1–18.4 (ignoring the clearly fictional account of Maximinus' reaction); Herodian 7.8.1–2 (more convincing).
10. *HA Gordians* 10.1–2; Zosimus 1.14.2; *HA Maximinus* 32.8.
11. Townend, 'Revolution of 238'; X. Loriot, 'Les prèmiers années de la grande crise du IIIe siècle: De l'avenement de Maximin le Thrace a la Mort de Gordien III', in *Aufsteig und Niedergang das Romische Welt*, II, 2, Berlin 1975, 699–700.
12. *HA Maximinus* 19.1–3; *HA Gordians* 15.1–16.4; Herodian 7.9.1–11.
13. *HA Maximus and Balbinus* 1.1–3.1; *HA Maximinus* 20.1–2; Herodian 7.10.2–5.
14. *HA Maximinus* 20.7–22.7; *HA Maximus and Balbinus* 10.1 and 11.1–3; Herodian 7.12.8 and 8.2.3–5.7.
15. *HA Maximus and Balbinus* 9.1–5 and 10.4–8; Herodian 7.11.1–12.7.
16. Herodian 8.8–9; *HA Maximinus* 23.1–7.
17. *HA Gordians* 32.1–3; Herodian 7.10.6–10; *HA Maximus and Balbinus* 3.3–5.
18. *HA Maximus and Balbinus* 14.2–8; Herodian 8.8.2–7.

Chapter 10

1. Zosimus 1.19.1; Zonaras 12.18; Eutropius 9.2.3.
2. Zosimus 1.20.2–21; Zonaras 12.19.
3. *Epitome de Caesaribus* 28.2; Eutropius 9.3.
4. Aurelius Victor 29; *HA Thirty Tyrants* 20 (but implying that Valens operated in Illyricum).

5. Aurelius Victor 30: Zosimus 1.25.2–3.
6. Zosimus 1.2 8.1–3; Aurelius Victor 31.1; Eutropius 9.5.1.
7. Aurelius Victor 33.34; L. de Blois, *The Policy of the Emperor Gallienus*, London 1976, 57–83.
8. Zosimus 1.14; *HA Gallienus* 14; Aurelius Victor 33.
9. *HA Thirty Tyrants* 3–8 and 24–25: J.E. Drinkwater, *The Gallic Empire, Historia Einszelschriften* 52, Stuttgart 1987.
10. *HA Thirty Tyrants* 11.
11. Aurelius Victor 34; Zosimus 1.40.2; *HA Claudius* 4.2.
12. Eutropius 9.12; Zosimus 1.47; *HA Claudius* 12.3–6.
13. *HA Aurelian* 40.2–4 and *Tacitus* 2.5–6: Zonaras 12.28; Aurelius Victor 35.10–12.
14. *HA Tacitus* 14.1 and *Probus* 10.1.8; Aurelius Victor 6.2; Zonaras 12.29; Zosimus 1.64.1.
15. Zosimus 1.64.1.
16. *HA Probus* 10.9; this is not necessarily convincing in itself, but progress has a good reputation among the historians, which generally means he was in good odour with the Senate.
17. Eutropius 9.17; Aurelius Victor 37; *HA Probus* 20.
18. Aurelius Victor 38; *HA Carus* 5.1–2 and 7.1.
19. Aurelius Victor 39; *HA Carus* 13.1–5; Eutropius 9.20.1.
20. Aurelius Victor 39; *HA Carus* 13.1–5; Eutropius 9.20.1.

Chapter 11
1. *HA Thirty Tyrants* 24.
2. *Sybilline Oracles* 13.119–129; he is also called 'Syriades'.
3. *HA Aurelian* 38.2–3.
4. *HA Thirty Tyrants* 29–33; David S. Potter, *The Roman Empire at Bay*, London 2004, 248–252.
5. *HA Gordians* 23.4; Zosimus 1.17.1; Barbieri, *Albo*, no 1717.
6. Zosimus 1.20.2; Aurelius Victor 29.2; Barbieri, *Albo*, App 1, 17.
7. Zosimus 1.20.2; Zonaras 12.19; Barbieri, *Albo*, no 1522.
8. Aurelius Victor 29.2; Barbieri, *Albo*, no. 1706 (and see 1610).
9. Aurelius Victor 29.3; Barbieri, *Albo*, App 1, no 19; *HA Thirty Tyrants* 20, locates him in Illyricum.
10. *Oracula Sibyllina* 13.147–154; John Malalas 296; H.R. Baldus, *Uranius Antoninus*, Bonn 1971.
11. Potter, *Roman Empire at Bay*, 250.
12. *HA Thirty Tyrants* 9.1; Aurelius Victor 33.2.
13. Zonaras 12.24; Eusebius, *Historia Ecclesia* I 7.10.8; *HA Thirty Tyrants* 12.1.10–12 and 13.1; *HA Gallienus* 1.2–5.
14. *HA Thirty Tyrants* 10.1–2; Aurelius Victor 30.2.
15. Eutropius 9.9.1; *HA Thirty Tyrants* 5.8; Aurelius Victor 33.8.
16. *HA Thirty Tyrants* 22 and *Gallienus* 4.1, 5.6 and 9.1; Barbieri *Albo*, App 1, 22. All
17. *HA Thirty Tyrants* 19 (Valens), 21 (Piso) and 20 (the other Valens); Ammianus Marcellinus 21.16.10: Barbieri, *Albo* 1735.

18. *HA Thirty Tyrants* 5 ('Lolianus' = Laelianus); others are named in 4 (Victorinus); Zosimus 1.49.2 (Domitianus).
19. *HA Thirty Tyrants* 11 and *Gallienus* 14.6–7; Barbieri, *Albo*, App 1, 7.
20. *HA Thirty Tyrants* 15 (Odaenathus), 16 (Herodes), 17 (Maeonius), 30 (Zenobia); this regime, thanks to Zenobia's involvement, has been the subject of plenty of studies.
21. *HA Aurelian* 32.2.3; Zosimus 1.61.1 (Firmus); 31.2–3 (Achilleus and Antiochus).
22. Zosimus 1.49.2.
23. Zosimus 1.66.1; Barbieri, *Albo* 1613.
24. Zosimus 1.66.2 and 1.68.3; Zonaras 12.29; A.R. Birley, *The Fasti of Roman Britain*, Oxford 1981, 180–181.
25. *HA Firmus, etc.* 12–13 (Proculus); 14–15 (Bonosus).
26. Aurelius Victor 39.10; Zosimus 1.73.

Chapter 12

1. *HA Numerian* 12.1–2; Eutropius 9.18; Aurelius Victor 38–39.
2. *HA Numerian* 13.2–4; Eutropius 9.20.1; Aurelius Victor 39.1.
3. *HA Carinus* 17.2 (claiming 'many battles'); Eutropius 9.20.1–2; Aurelius Victor 39.3.
4. Aurelius Victor 39.17–19; Eutropius 20.
5. P.J. Casey, *Carausius and Allectus: The British Usurpers*, London 1994.
6. T.D. Barnes, *The New Empire of Diocletian and Constantine*, Cambridge MA 1982, 4, note 6.
7. Barnes, *New Empire*, 37–38.
8. Casey, *Carausius*, ch. 10.
9. Eutropius 9.22–23; Aurelius Victor 39; Barnes, *New Empire*, 12.
10. Eusebius, *Ecclesiastical History* 6.8.

Chapter 13

1. Barnes, *New Empire*, 69; Zosimus 2.9.1; Lactantius 25.3–5.
2. Zosimus 2.9.2.
3. Lactantius 26.7; Zosimus 2.10.2.
4. Lactantius 7.1; Zosimus 2.10.6–7.
5. Lactantius 28; Eutropius 10.3.
6. Zosimus 2.10.4–5; Lactantius 32.1.
7. Lactantius 35.3; Eusebius, *Ecclesiastical History* 8.17.
8. Zosimus 2.14–17; *Prolegomena Latina* 12.5.1; 16.2; 19.1; Lactantius 44; Eusebius, *Ecclesiastical History* 9.9.

Chapter 14

1. For Constantine's progress, see the biographies by J. Holland Smith, *Constantine the Great*, New York 1971, chs 6 and 7; Ramsay MacMullen, *Constantine*, Beckenham Kent, 1969, chs 4, 5 and 7; T.D. Barnes, *Constantine and Eusebius*, Cambridge MA 1981.
2. *Panegyricus Latinus* 6.2.1–3; R. Syme, 'The Ancestry of Constantine', *Bonner Historia Augusta Colloquium 1971*, Bonn 1974, 237–253.

3. Ammianus 14.11.20.
4. Aurelius Victor 41.11–12; Jerome, *Chronicle* 233; Theophanes, ann. 5825, p.29.
5. Zosimus 2.40; Eutropius 10.9.
6. Eutropius 10.9; Zosimus 11.42–44.
7. Zosimus 2.42.2–4.
8. *Chronicon Paschale*, p. 529.
9. Aurelius Victor, *de Caesaribus* 42.6–9; Eutropius 10.11; Zosimus 2.43.3–4.
10. Mursa: Zosimus 13.8; death of Magnentius: Eutropius 10.11.
11. Ammianus 15.5.2–11.
12. Ammianus 15.5.31.
13. Ammianus 14.7.9–11.
14. Ammianus 23.3.6 and 6.6.
15. Ammianus 25.5.2–4.
16. Ammianus 25.10.12–13; 26.26; 4.3; Zosimus 3.36.1 and 3.
17. Ammianus 26.6.1–10; cf also N.J.E. Austin, 'A Usurper's Claim to Legitimacy: Procopius in AD 365/6', *Rivista storia dell'Antiquita* 2, 1972, 187–194.
18. Ammianus 29.5.
19. A.E. Wardman, 'Usurpers and Internal Conflicts in the 4th Century AD', *Historia* 33, 1984, 220–237.

Chapter 15
1. Ammianus 30.10.4.
2. Ammianus 30.10.4; Zosimus 4.19.1; Philologus, *Ecclesiastical History* 9.16.
3. Ammianus 30.10.4.
4. A. Demandt, 'Der Tod des alteren Theodosius', *Historia* 18, 1969, 598–626.
5. Ammianus 29.6.15 and 31.11.1; R.M. Errington, 'The accession of Theodosius', *Klio*, 78, 1976, 438–453, and H. Sivan, 'Was Theodosius a Usurper?', *Klio* 78, 1996, 198–211.
6. J.F. Matthews, *Western Aristocracies and the Imperial Court, AD 364–425*, Oxford 1975, 91–92; also S. Williams and G. Friel, *Theodosius: The Empire at Bay*, London 1994.

Chapter 16
1. J. Matthews, *Western Aristocracies and the Imperial Court, AD 364–425*, Oxford 1975, ch. 7, is a good account of Maximus, with full references.
2. Matthews, *Western Aristocracies*, 95–96.
3. Ibid.
4. Zosimus 4.47.1.
5. Zosimus 4.54; Philostorgus 11.1; Socrates 5.11; B. Croke, 'Arbogast and the death of Valentinian II', *Historia* 25, 1976, 235–244.
6. Matthews, *Western Aristocracies*, ch. 9, part 2.
7. *De Orbitu Theodosium* 5.
8. The British emperor/usurpers are noted in A.R. Birley, *The Fasti of Roman Britain*, Oxford 1981, and discussed by C.E. Stevens, 'Marcus, Gratian, Constantine', *Athenaeum* 35, 1957, 316–347, which is further discussed by E.A. Thompson, 'Britain AD 406–410', *Britannia* 8, 1977, 303–318.

9. Zosimus 6.7.2; Sozomen 9.8.2.
10. Orosius 7.42.1–5.
11. Olympiordorus frags 17, 19; Orosius 7.42.6.
12. Olympiodorus, frag 24.
13. Paulinus, *Eucharistion* 293–294; Olympiodorus, frag 26; Philostorgus 12.5.
14. Gallic Chronicle of 452, 89; Marcellus, ann 422, 2.
15. Gallic Chronicle, *anno* 423; Philostorgus 12.14.
16. Olympiodorus frag 46; Philostorgus 12.13; Socrates 7.32.1–10.
17. Olympiodorus, frag 46; Socrates 7.24.4–5; Philostorgus 12.13–13a; Marcellinus *anno* 425, 2; *Chronicon Paschale* 1.580; Stewart Irvin Oost, *Galla Placidia Augusta: A Biographical Essay*, Chicago 1968.
18. Fergus Millar, *A Greek Roman Empire: Power and Belief under Theodosius II, 408–450*, Berkeley and Los Angeles, 2006.
19. *Chronicon Paschale ann* 450 and 457; Procopius, *Vandal War* 1.4.7; Theophanes s.a. 5943; Evagrius 2.1; K.G. Holum, *Theodosian Empresses: Women and Imperial Dominion in Late Antiquity*, Berkeley and Los Angeles 1982, 208–209.

Chapter 17
1. John of Antioch 201.
2. John of Antioch 202, Sidonius Apollinaris, 2.13: Evagrius 2.7.
3. John of Antioch 203; Prosper of Aquitaine s.a. 455.
4. Sidonius Apollinaris, *Epistles* 11.13.5.
5. Priscus, Frag 24; Procopius, *Vandal War* 1.5.
6. Sidonius Apollinarius, *Epistles* 7.517.
7. T.S. Mommaerts and D.H. Kelley, 'The Anicii of Gaul and Rome', in John Drinkwater and Hugh Elton (eds), *Fifth Century Gaul: A Crisis of Identity?*, Cambridge 1992, 111–121.
8. John of Antioch 202; see P. MacGeorge, *Late Roman Warlords*, Oxford 2002, 191–196.
9. Sidonius Apollinaris *Ep.* 1.2.6; R.W. Mathiesen, 'Resistance and Reconstruction, Majorian and the Gallic Aristocracy after the Fall of Avitus', *Francia* 7, 1979, 697–627, and 'Avitus, Italy and the East in AD 455–456', *Byzantium* 51, 1981, 232–247; G.E. Max, 'Political Intrigue during the Reigns of the Western Roman Emperors Avitus and Majorian', *Historia* 28, 1979, 225–237.
10. *Fasti Vindobonenis Prior* s.a. 457; Sidonius Apollinaris *Panegyricus* 5.387–388.
11. Hommaerts and Kelley (note 7) suggest that Olybrius was another son of Petronius Maximus.
12. Constantine Porphyrogenitus, *de Caeremonios* 1, ch. 91.

Chapter 18
1. *Fasti Vindobonensis* Prior s.a. 466; *Gallic Chronicle of 511*, 635; Jordanes, *Getica*, 236; John of Antioch 203; Hydatius 205, s.a. 461.
2. *Fasti Vindobonensis* Prior s.a. 46i; *Gallic Chronicle of 511*, 636; Marcellinus s.s. 461; Theophanes 5955.
3. Hydatius 206.

4. Cassiodorus, *Chronicle* 1283, s.a. 467.
5. Hydatius 231, s.a. 467; *Fasti Vindobonensis* Prior s.a. 467; and others.
6. *Gallic Chronicle of 511*, 649; Jordanes, *Getica* 237.
7. John of Antioch 209; Paul the Deacon, *History of Rome*, 15.3.
8. John of Antioch 209; John Malalas 373–375; F.M. Clover, 'The Family and Career of Anicius Olybrius', *Historia* 27, 1978, 169–196.
9. *Paschale Chronicon* 306; John of Antioch 209; *Fasti Vindobonensis* Prior s.a. 473.
10. Theophanes 5964; Marcellinus s.a. 471.
11. John of Antioch 209; Cassiodorus, *Chronicon* 1295, s.a. 473; *Fasti Vindobonensis Prior* s.a. 473; Marcellinus s.a. 473.

Chapter 19
1. Candidus 136; John Malalas 14, 376: Theophanes 5966–5967.
2. Candidus 136; John of Antioch 207.
3. Evagrius 3.24.
4. John of Antioch 209.
5. Jordanes, *Getica* 240–241; Prosper of Aquitaine s.a. 475; J.P.C. Kent, 'Julius Nepos and the Fall of the Western Empire', in *Corolla Memoriae Erich Svoboda Dedicata*, Graz and Cologne, 1966, 146–150.
6. Prosper of Aquitaine s.a. 475; Jordanes, *Getica* 241; *Fasti Vindobonensis* Prior s.a. 475.
7. Marcellinus s.a. 476; Jordanes, *Getica* 247.
8. King: *Fasti Vindobonensis* Prior s.a. 476; *Paschale Chronicon* 476; Patrician: Marcellinus, frag 14; cf MacGeorge, *Late Roman Warlords*, 291–292 and A.H.M. Jones, 'The Constitutional Position of Odoacer and Theoderic', *Journal of Roman Studies* 52, 1962, 126–131.

Bibliography

Abbreviations: most sources are easily identified and the following abbreviations have been used:

HA: *Historia Augusta*
Josephus *AJ*: Josephus, *Jewish War*
PIR: *Prosopographia Imperii Romani*

There are few modern works dealing precisely with the succession of Roman emperors, and a full bibliography would necessarily include virtually every book ever written about the Empire. The following is a selection of books that have been particularly useful in this study:

Astarita, Maria Laura, *Avidio Cassio* (Rome, 1983).
Austin, N.J.E., 'A Usurper's Claim to Legitimacy, Procopius in AD 365/6', in *Rivista Storia dell'Antiquita* 2, 1972, pp.187–94.
Baldwin, B., *The Roman Emperors* (Québec, 1980).
Barbieri, G., *L'Albo Senatorio da Settimio Severo a Carino (193–285)* (Rome, 1952).
Barnes, T.D., *The New Empire of Diocletian and Constantine* (Cambridge MA, 1982).
Barnes, T.D., 'Emperors, Panegyrics, Prefects, Provinces, and Palaces (284–317)', in *Journal of Roman Archaeology* 9, 1997, pp.531–52.
Barnes, T.D., *Constantine and Eusebius* (Cambridge MA, 1981).
Barnish, S.J., 'Transformation and Survival in the Western Senatorial Aristocracy, c.AD 400–700', in *Papers of the British School at Rome* 56, 1988, pp.128–55.
Barrett, A.A., *Caligula: The Corruption of Power* (London, 1989).
Bennett, J., *Trajan Optimus Princeps* (London, 1997).
Birley, A.R., *Hadrian: The Restless Emperor* (London, 1997).
Birley, A.R., *Marcus Aurelius* (London, 1966).
Birley, A.R., *Septimius Severus: The African Emperor* (London, 1988).
Birley, A.R., *Lives of the Later Caesars* (= *Historia Augusta*) (Harmondsworth, 1976).
Birley, A.R., 'The Coups d'État of the Year 193', in *Bonner Jahrbücher* 169, 1969, pp.247–79.

Birley, A.R., *The Fasti of Roman Britain* (Oxford, 1981).

de Blois, L., *The Policy of the Emperor Gallienus* (London, 1976).

Brauer, G.C., *The Decadent Emperors: Power and Depravity in Third-Century Rome* (New York, 1974).

Brauer, G.C., *The Age of the Soldier Emperors* (Park Ridge NJ, 1975).

Bruun, T., 'Portrait of a Conspirator: Constantine's break with the Tetrarchy' in *Arctos* 10, 1976, pp.5–23.

Cambridge Ancient History, vols X and XI.

Carcopino, J., 'L'Hérédité dynastique chez les Antonins', *Revue des Études Anciennes* 51, 1949, pp.262–321.

Casey, P.J., *Carausius and Allectus: The British Usurpers* (London, 1994).

Champlin, F., 'The Heirs of Commodus', *American Journal of Philology* 100, 1979, pp.288–309.

Cizek, E., *Aurelien et son Temps* (Paris, 1994).

Clover, F.M., 'The Family and Career of Anicius Olybrius', *Historia* 27 (1978).

Croke, B., 'Arbogast and the death of Valentinian II', *Historia* 25 (1976).

Demandt, A., 'Der Tod des alteren Theodosius', *Historia* 18 (1969).

Drinkwater, J.E., *The Gallic Empire*, Historia Einszelschriften 52 (Stuttgart, 1987).

Drinkwater, J.E. and Elton, G.E. (eds), *Fifth-Century Gaul: A Crisis of Identity?* (Cambridge, 1992).

Eck, W., *The Age of Augustus*, trans. D.L. Schneider (Oxford, 2003).

Errington, R.M., 'The Accession of Theodosius', *Klio*, 78 (1996), pp.438–53.

Gibson, A.G.G., (ed.), *The Julio-Claudian Succession: Reality and Perception of the 'Augustan Model'* (Leiden, 2013).

Grainger, J.D., *Nerva and the Roman Succession Crisis of AD 96–99* (London, 2003).

Grant, Michael, *The Severans* (London, 1996).

Grant, Michael, *The Climax of Rome* (London, 1968).

Greenhalgh, P.A.L., *The Year of the Four Emperors* (London, 1975).

Grenade, P., 'Le Règlement Successoral d'Hadrien', *Revue des Études Anciennes* 52 (1950), pp.258–77.

Griffin, M.T., *Nero: The End of the Dynasty* (London, 1984).

Hammond, M., 'The Tribunician Day during the Early Empire', *Memoirs of the American Academy at Rome* 15 (1938).

Heckster, O., *Commodus: An Emperor at the Crossroads* (Amsterdam, 2002).

Heckster, O., 'All in the Family: The Appointment of Emperors Designate in the Second Century A.D.', in *Administration, Prosopography, and Appointment Practice in the Roman Empire: Proceedings of the First Workshop of the International Network, Impact of Empire, Leiden 2000* (Amsterdam, 2001), pp.35–49.

Holland, R., *Augustus: Godfather of Europe* (Stroud, 2004).

Holum, K.G., *Theodosian Empresses: Women and Imperial Dominion in Late Antiquity* (Berkeley and Los Angeles, 1982).

Jones, A.H.M., *Augustus* (London, 1970).

Jones, A.H.M., *The Later Roman Empire, 284–602* (Oxford, 1964).

Jones, A.H.M., 'The Constitutional Position of Odoacer and Theoderic', *Journal of Roman Studies* (1962), pp.126–31.

Jones, B.W., *The Emperor Titus* (London, 1984).

Jones, B.W., *The Emperor Domitian* (London, 1992).

Kent, J.P.C., 'Julius Nepos and the Fall of the Western Empire', *Corolla Memoriae Erich Swoboda Dedicata* (Graz and Cologne, 1996), pp.146–50.

Levick, B., *Tiberius the Politician* (London, 1976).

Levick, B., *Claudius* (London, 1990).

Levick, B., *Vespasian* (London, 1984).

Loriot, X., 'Les prèmiers années de la grande crise du IIIe siècle: De l'avenement de Maximin le Thrace a la Mort de Gordien III', in *Aufsteig und Niedergang das Romische Welt*, II, 2 (Berlin, 1975).

MacCormack, S., *Art and Ceremony in Late Antiquity* (Berkeley and Los Angeles, 1981).

MacGeorge, P., *Late Roman Warlords* (Oxford, 2002).

MacMullen, R., *Constantine* (New York, 1969).

Marsh, F.B., *The Reign of Tiberius* (Oxford, 1931).

Mathieson, R.W., 'Resistance and Reconstruction: Majorian and the Gallic Aristocracy after the Fall of Avitus', *Francia* 7 (1979), pp.597–627.

Mathieson, R.W., 'Avitus, Italy and the East in AD455–456', *Byzantion* 51 (1981), pp.232–47.

Matthews, J., *The Roman Empire of Ammianus* (London, 1989).

Matthews, J., *Western Aristocracies and the Imperial Court, AD364–425* (Oxford, 1975).

Max, G.E., 'Political Intrigue during the Reigns of the Western Roman Emperors of Avitus and Majorian', *Historia* 28 (1979), pp.225–37.

McCrum, M. and Woodhead, A.G., *Select Documents of the Principates of the Flavian Emperors, AD69–96* (Cambridge, 1961).

Meijer, F., *Emperors Don't Die in Bed*, trans. S.J. Leinach (London, 2001).

Millar, F., *The Emperor in the Roman World* (London, 1977).

Miller, F. and Segal, E. (eds), *Caesar Augustus: Seven Aspects* (Oxford, 1984).

Morgan, Gwyn, *69AD: The Year of the Four Emperors* (Oxford, 2006).

O'Flynn, J.M., *Generalissimos of the Western Roman Empire* (Edmonton, Canada, 1983).

Omissi, Adrastos, *Emperors and Usurpers in the Later Roman Empire: Civil War, Panegyric and the Construction of Legitimacy* (Oxford, 2018).

Oost, S.I., *Galla Placidia: A Biographical Essay* (Chicago, 1968).

Oost, S.I., 'Aetius and Majorian', *Classical Philology* 59 (1964), pp.23–39.

Oost, S.I., 'D.N. Libius Severus, P. F. Aug', *Classical Philology* 65 (1990), pp.228–40.

Osgood, Josiah, *Rome and the Making of a World State, 150 BCE–20 CE* (Cambridge, 2018).

Parsi, Blanche, *Désignation et Investiture de l'Empereur Romain* (Paris, 1963).

Peachin, M., 'Once More AD 238', *Athenaeum* 67 (1989), pp.594–604.

Potter, David, *Emperors of Rome: The Story of Imperial Rome from Julius Caesar to the Last Emperor* (London, n.d.).

Potter, D.S., *The Roman Empire at Bay, 180–395* (London, 2004).

Raaflaub, K.A. and Toher, M. (eds), *Between Republic and Empire: Interpretations of Augustus and his Principate* (Berkeley CA, 1990).

Rubin, Z., *Civil War, Propaganda and Historiography*, Collection Latomus 173 (Brussels, 1983).

Sivan, H., 'Was Theodosius I a Usurper?', *Klio* 78 (1996), pp.198–211.

Smith, J. Holland, *Constantine the Great* (New York, 1971).

Stevens, C.E., 'Marcus, Gratian, Constantine', *Athenaeum* 35 (1956), pp.316–47.

Syme, R., *Tacitus* (Oxford, 1958).

Syme, R., *Emperors and Biography* (Oxford, 1971).

Syme, R., 'The Ancestry of Constantine', *Bonner Historia-Augusta Colloquium 1971* (Bonn, 1974).

Syme, Ronald, 'Avidius Cassius: His Rank, Age and Qualikty', *Bonner Historia Augusta Colloquium 1984/1985* (Bonn, 1986), pp.2007–222.

Syme, Ronald, *The Augustan Aristocracy* (Oxford, 1986).

Talbert, R.J.A., *The Senate of Imperial Rome* (Princeton NJ, 1984).

Thompson, E.A., 'Britain AD 406–410', *Britannia* 8 (1977), pp.303–18.

Townend, P.W., 'The Revolution of AD 238: The Leaders and their Aims', *Yale Classical Studies* 14 (1955), pp.49–105.

Turton, G., *The Syrian Princesses: The Women who Ruled Rome, AD 193–235* (London, 1994).

Wardman, A.E., 'Usurpers and Internal Conflict in the Fourth Century AD', *Historia* 33 (1984), pp.220–37.

Watson, A., *Aurelian and the Third Century* (London, 1999).

Wellesley, K., *The Long Year: AD 69*, 2nd edition (London, 1988).

Williams, S., *Diocletian and the Roman Recovery* (London, 1985).

Williams, S. and Friel, G., *Theodosius: The Empire at Bay* (London, 1994).

Wozniak, F.E., 'East Rome, Ravenna and Western Illyricum, 454–536 AD', *Historia* 30 (1981), pp.351–82.